A
GRAND STREET
Reader

A
GRAND STREET
Reader

Edited by
BEN SONNENBERG

With an Introduction by
Murray Kempton

SUMMIT BOOKS
New York

1   3   5   7   9   10   8   6   4   2

1   3   5   7   9   10   8   6   4   2 **Pbk.**

Library of Congress Cataloging in Publication Data
A Grand Street reader.

1. Literature, Modern—20th century.   I. Sonnenberg,
Ben.   II. Grand Street.
PN6014.G67   1986   808.8′004   86–5687
ISBN 0–671–60623–9
ISBN 0–671–62969–7 Pbk.

MEMOIRS

POEMS

ARTICLES

INTRODUCTION

The properest introduction to *A Grand Street Reader* is "Lost Property," Ben Sonnenberg's memory of growing up, which can be found on page 261. Nothing could as well serve to suggest the origins of his enterprise or to illuminate the singularity of a magazine whose entire appreciation may well be reserved for those who have come to recognize it as a continuing experiment with its editor's autobiography. What is appended here is only annotation.

Here, then, is *A Grand Street Reader* and there are the readers of *Grand Street*, a small fanatical sect, but not quite so fanatical as not to rejoice at this promise of larger company. All the same, some of us may be excused for thinking that we are more intensely aware of *Grand Street*'s riches than anyone could be who makes their acquaintance in this distillation, because, after awhile, each quarterly issue has taken its place in our consciousness as another installment in a sort of novel; and no abridgement, however sensitive, however indeed its author's chosen own, can ever be the novel entire.

Our joy in what survives is darkened by a degree of sorrow for the casualties ordained by editorial economy; I, for one, especially miss the cumulative effect of all those examinations of the failed fathers who are the epitomes of our age.

They have, to be sure, a powerful incarnation in Ben Sonnenberg's portrait of his own father in the bleak post-luncheon *tristesse* when, having clutched for and missed one of those contrivances of intimacy we depend upon for manipulating the young, he could only fall back upon that ritual formula of failed fathers: "Now, children, I've got to work." "Bitter and baffled," his son reflects.

Perhaps it is only for me that this particular father seems to beat his wings at some great height over *Grand Street*. We met just once, forty-five years ago; and my memory of our encounter is at once vivid and opaque and scarcely qualifies me to define him since it was an experience too much distracting me with the severest definitions of myself.

Until that hour, I had been employed in the straitened household of the Norman Thomas Socialists. The American left was in one of its transition phases, downward as usual; and the never overstuffed larder that fed the servants' quarters was all but bare by now; and I found myself blessed with the liberty to starve that we had so insistently described as capitalism's only lasting benefaction to the working classes.

A comrade who knew more of the great world than I commended me to Benjamin Sonnenberg as a candidate for the patronage his son remembers as a "very large part of my parents' lives." Beyond the universal report that the executives of *Time, Life* and *Fortune* esteemed him as a judge of youthful promise, I knew nothing of Benjamin Sonnenberg; but that was quite enough for me in an era with a number of illusions of which by no means the oddest was the concept of working for the late Henry Luce as a desirable prospect.

I made the pilgrimage, mumbled, and departed, without even earning the compliment of my host's ceremonial "My man will show you out," which I now know would have been the signal that I had not entirely botched my audition. I had, of course. The house had not appeared to me as forbidding as Ben Sonnenberg remembers it; I found it not so much baronial as patroonal. All the same, it was awesome enough to bring out an excess of the virtue of turning tongue-tied in the presence of my betters that I have had the carelessness since to lose.

The cut of my figure must then have been deplorable; and I never heard from Benjamin Sonnenberg, a dismissal leaving no scar of resentment, because the great could not have trusted his references unless they relied on the acuity of his taste in choosing the objects of his patronage; the man you have to see before seeing the man you want to see needs to be especially careful in his assessments of who is worth the bother of seeing.

And yet why had Benjamin Sonnenberg troubled to see me at all, and what surviving sentiment sustained him in these labors, tragic as they had to be, at rescuing the beached minnows of a dried-up revolution? Had there been a revolutionary impulse back in Brest-Litovsk and the Lower East Side; and did a comrade's heart still beat faintly in the Edwardian livery of this valued Master of Hounds for the propertied in their hunt after more property? If his son had not inferred that pulse buried beneath the heavy fabrics of acquisition, then why isn't *Grand Street* called *Gramercy Park*?

We could not, I surmise, feel the intimacy that so uniquely touches us in *Grand Street* if its editor had not dispensed with every barrier between himself and us and signed us on with him in a voyage whose goal is the discovery of his own and perhaps his father's self.

One or two of Ben Sonnenberg's coarser admirers have commended his veneration for the past. And yet it is by no means a long-vanished past; it runs, in fact, mainly within the borders of his own life span; he evokes not what time has entombed but what everyone else has too soon forgotten.

Pretty much every dimmed presence he brings back to our notice was working while he was growing up—working, stopping and being summarily tossed into discard in a surprising number of instances. When *Grand Street* turns to the political, its eye has the habit of falling upon the strayed but never quite lost, on those who came in the end to the sense that they were, as Silone finally had to say he was, socialists without a party and Catholics without a church. That identity surrounds Claud Cockburn and even the Vittorio Vidali-Enea Sormenti-Carlos Contreras who had a dozen names, most of them infamous, and whose itinerations as a Comintern road agent Dorothy Gallagher traces in these pages. In justice she must refuse a eulogy; but she is too merciful and too sensitive to deny his elegy to anyone who had so fiercely ridden his wild horses on their course heedless of regret until it was almost run.

Elegiac recollection, you come at last to feel, is *Grand Street*'s most distinguished and involving tone. It sounds in the poems of Ben Sonnenberg's choice, in his preference for the story of the kind that seeks to restore to permanence the fragile, transient adolescence we all share and think to cover in its grace, in his concern to raise from oblivion so many personages whose time was not long ago but who might otherwise be one with Nineveh and with Tyre.

It is not immodesty that inspires an editor to dare go his own way in heroic confidence that his personal taste is quite enough to satisfy a fair number of the rest of us; it is rather the artist's instinct that the point is not to be current but to make of oneself *a* current and that only those indifferent to fashion are equipped for the truly intense and necessary commitment to style.

Most fathers fail us and most of us fail our fathers. They failed because they could not anticipate us; and we fail because we cannot remember them. But Ben Sonnenberg has not failed, because he has understood and done what his father would rather have done, which is to have lived by the premise that the one good thing is to be one's own master and not one's client's. *Grand Street* is something else and altogether more than 19 Gramercy Park; and the elder Benjamin Sonnenberg would not, you decide, have been the last to know it.

—Murray Kempton

A
GRAND STREET
Reader

HOUSE OPPOSITE

R. K. Narayan

The hermit invariably shuddered when he looked out of his window. The house across the street was occupied by a shameless woman. Late in the evening, men kept coming and knocking on her door—afternoons too if there was a festival or holiday. Sometimes they lounged on the *pyol* of her house, smoking, chewing tobacco and spitting into the gutter—committing all the sins of the world according to the hermit, who was striving to pursue a life of austerity, forswearing family, possessions, and all the comforts of life. He found this single-room tenement with a couple of coconut trees and a well at the backyard adequate, and the narrow street swarmed with children: sometimes he called in the children, seated them around and taught them simple moral lessons and sacred verse. On the walls he had nailed a few pictures of gods cut out of old calendars, and he made the children prostrate in front of them before sending them away with a piece of sugar candy each.

His daily life followed an unvarying pattern. Birdlike, he retired at dusk, lying on the bare floor with a wooden block under his head for a pillow. He woke up at four ahead of the rooster at the street corner, bathed at the well and sat down on a piece of deerskin to meditate. Later he lit the charcoal stove and baked a few *chappathis* for breakfast and lunch and cooked certain restricted vegetables and greens, avoiding potato, onion, okra and such as might stimulate the baser impulses.

Even in the deepest state of meditation, he could not help hearing the creaking of the door across the street when a client left after a night of debauchery. He rigorously suppressed all cravings of the palate and punished his body in a dozen ways. If you asked him why, he would have been at a loss to explain. He was the antithesis of the athlete who flexed his muscles and watched his expanding chest before a mirror. Our hermit, on the contrary, kept a minute check on his emaciation and felt a peculiar thrill out of such an achievement. He was only following without question his ancient guru's instructions and hoped thus to attain spiritual liberation.

One afternoon, opening the window to sweep the dust on the sill, he noticed her standing on her doorstep, watching the street. His temples throbbed with the rush of blood. He studied her person—chiseled features but sunk in fatty folds. She possessed, however, a seductive outline; her forearms were cushionlike and perhaps the feel of those encircling arms attracted men. His gaze, once it had begun to hover about her body, would not return to its anchor—which should normally be the tip of one's nose as enjoined by his guru and the yoga shastras.

Her hips were large, thighs stout like banana stalks, on the whole a mattresslike creature on which a patron could loll all night without a scrap of covering—"Awful monster! Personification of evil." He felt suddenly angry; why on earth should that creature stand there and ruin his *tapas*: all the merit he had so laboriously acquired was draining away like water through a sieve. Difficult to say whether it was those monstrous arms and breasts or thighs that tempted and ruined men . . . he hissed under his breath, "Get in, you devil, don't stand there!" She abruptly turned round and went in, shutting the door behind her. He felt triumphant although his command and her compliance were coincidental. He bolted the window tight and retreated to the farthest corner of the room, settled down on the deerskin and kept repeating, "Om, Om, Rama, Jayarama": the sound "Rama" had a potency all its own— and was reputed to check wandering thoughts and distractions. He had a profound knowledge of mantras and their efficacy. "Sri Rama . . ." he repeated, but it was like a dilute and weak medicine for high fever. It didn't work. "Sri Rama, Jayarama . . ." he repeated with a desperate fervor; but the effect lasted not even a second; unnoticed his thoughts strayed, questioning: "Who was that fellow in a check shirt and silk upper cloth over his shoulder descending the steps last evening when I went out to the market? Seen him somewhere . . . Where? When? . . . Ah, he was the big tailor on Market Road . . . with fashionable men and women clustering round him! Master-cutter who was a member of two or three clubs . . . Hobnobbed with officers and businessmen—and this was how he spent

[*14*]

his evening, lounging on the human mattress! And yet fashionable persons allowed him to touch them with his measuring tape! Contamination, nothing but contamination; sinful life. He cried out in the lonely room, "Rama! Rama!" as if hailing someone hard of hearing. Presently he realized it was a futile exercise. Rama was a perfect incarnation, of course, but he was mild and gentle until provoked beyond limit, when he would storm and annihilate without a trace the evildoer, even if he were a monster like Ravana. Normally, however, he had forbearance, hence the repetition of his name resulted only in calmness and peace; but the present occasion demanded stern measures. God Siva's mantra should help. Did he not open his Third Eye and reduce the God of Love to ashes, when the latter slyly aimed his arrow at him while he was meditating? Our hermit pictured the God of matted locks and fiery eyes and recited aloud: "Om Namasivaya," that lonely hall resounding with his hoarse voice. His rambling, unwholesome thoughts were halted for a while, but presently regained their vigor and raced after the woman. She opened her door at least six times on an evening— Did she sleep with them all together at the same time? He paused to laugh at this notion, and also realized that his meditation on the austere God was gone. He banged his fist on his temples; it pained, but improved his concentration. "Om Namasivaya" . . . Part of his mind noted the creaking of the door of the opposite house. She was a serpent in whose coils everyone was caught and destroyed—old and young and the middle-aged, tailors and students (he had noticed a couple of days ago a young B.Sc. student from Albert Mission Hostel at her door), lawyers and magistrates (Why not?). . . . No wonder the world was getting overpopulated—with such pressure of the elemental urge within every individual! Oh God Siva, this woman must be eliminated. He would confront her some day and tell her to get out. He would tell her, "Oh, sinful wretch, who is spreading disease and filth like an open sewer: think of the contamination you have spread around—from middle-aged tailor to B.Sc. student. You are out to destroy mankind. Repent your sins, shave your head, cover your ample loins with sackcloth, sit at the temple gate and beg

or drown yourself in Sarayu after praying for a cleaner
life at least in the next birth. . . ." Thus went his dialogue
all night, the thought of the woman never leaving his
mind. . . . It turned out to be a wretched, ill-spent night;
he lay tossing on the bare floor. He was up before dawn—
his mind made up. He would clear out immediately, cross
Nallappa's Grove and reach the other side of the river,
he did not need a permanent roof, he would drift and rest
in any temple or *mantap* or the shade of a banyan tree:
he recollected an ancient tale he had heard from his guru
long ago. A harlot was sent to heaven when she died,
while her detractor, a self-righteous reformer, found himself in hell—his guru explained that while the harlot
sinned only with her body, physically, her detractor was
corrupt mentally, obsessed with the harlot and her activities, and could meditate on nothing else.

Our hermit packed his wicker box with his sparse possessions—a god's image in copper, a rosary, the deerskin
and a little brass bowl. Carrying his box in one hand, he
stepped out of the house, closing the door gently behind
him. In the dim hour of the dusk, shadowy figures were
moving—a milkman driving his cow ahead, laborers bearing crowbars and spades, women with baskets on their
way to the market. While he paused to take a final look at
the shelter he was abandoning, he heard a plaintive cry,
"Swamiji," from the opposite house, and saw the woman
approach him with a tray, heaped with fruits and flowers;
she placed it at his feet and said in a low reverential
whisper: "Please accept my offering. This is a day of remembrance of my mother. On this day I pray and seek a
saint's blessing. . . . Forgive me. . . ." All the lines he had
rehearsed for a confrontation deserted him at this moment; looking at her flabby figure, the dark rings under
her eyes, he felt a pity. As she bent down to prostrate he
noticed that her hair was indifferently dyed and that the
parting in the middle widened into a bald patch over
which a string of jasmine dangled loosely. . . . He touched
her tray with the tip of his finger as a token of acceptance
and went down the street without a word.

WORKING FOR A LIVING

Alice Munro

I n the first years of this century there was a notable
difference between people who lived on farms and
people who lived in country towns and villages. Out-
siders—city people—did not understand these differences but the town people and farmers were very sure
of them. In general, people in the towns saw people who
lived on farms as more apt to be slow-witted, tongue-
tied, uncivilized, than themselves, and somewhat more
docile in spite of their strength. Farmers saw people who
lived in towns as having an easy life and being unlikely
to survive in situations calling for fortitude, self-reliance,
lifelong hard work. They believed this in spite of the fact
that the hours men worked at factories or stores or at
any job in town, were long, and the wages low, and
that many houses in town had no running water or flush
toilets or electricity. And to a certain extent they were
right, for the people in town had Sundays and Wednesday or Saturday afternoons off, and the farmers didn't.
The townspeople too were not altogether mistaken, for
the country people when they came into town to church
were often very stiff and shy and the women were never
so pushy and confident as town women in the stores,
and the country children who came in to go to High
School or Continuation School, though they might get
good marks and go on to successful careers later, were
hardly ever elected President of the Literary Society,
or Class Representative, or given the award as Most Outstanding Student. Even money did not make much
difference; farmers maintained a certain proud and wary
reserve that might be seen as diffidence, in the presence
of citizens they could buy and sell.

When my father had gone as far as he could go at
the country school he wrote a set of exams called col-
lectively, the Entrance. He was only twelve years old.
The Entrance meant, literally, the Entrance to High

School, and it also meant the Entrance to the world, if professions such as medicine or law or engineering, which country boys passed into at that time more easily than later. This was just before the First World War, a time of prosperity in Huron County and expansion in the country, a country not yet fifty years old.

He passed the Entrance and went to the Continuation School in Blyth. Continuation Schools were small high schools, without the final fifth Form, now Grade Thirteen; you would have to go to a larger town for that.

At Continuation School my father learned a poem:

> Liza Grayman Ollie Minus
> We must make Eliza Blind.
> Andy Parting, Lee Behinus
> Foo Prince on the Sansa Time.

He used to recite this to us, for a joke, but the fact was, he did not learn it as a joke. This was the poem he heard and accepted. About the same time he went into the stationery store and asked for Sign's Snow Paper. Another joke he told us. But of course he had not done it as a joke. That was what he heard the teacher say.

> Sign's Snow Paper.
> Science Note-paper.

He did not hope for such reasonable clarification, would not dream of asking for it. Later he was surprised to see the poem on the blackboard.

> Lives of Great Men all remind us
> We must make our lives sublime
> And departing, leave behind us
> Footprints on the sands of time.

He had been willing to give the people at the school, and in the little town, the right to have a strange language, or logic; he did not ask that they make sense on his terms. He had a streak of pride posing as humility, making him scared and touchy, ready to bow out, never ask questions. I know it very well. He made a mystery there, a hostile structure of rules and secrets, far beyond anything that really existed. He felt a danger too,

of competition, of ridicule. The family wisdom came to
him then. Stay out of it. He said later that he was too
young, he would have stayed in school, made something
out of himself, if only he had been a couple of years
older. He said he made the wrong choice. But at that
time, he said, he did what many boys wanted to do. He
began to spend more and more days in the bush. He
kept going to school, but not very seriously, so that his
parents realized there was not much point in sending
him somewhere to take Fifth Form, and write the Senior Matriculation exams, and no hope of university, or
the professions. His mother would have liked that for
him but it did not matter so much as it would to city
people, that he turned his back on education and ad-
vancement. They had the farm; he was the only son, the
only child.

There was no more wild country in Huron County
then than there is now. Perhaps there was less. The
farms had been cleared in the period between 1830 and
1860, when the Huron Tract was being opened up, and
they were cleared thoroughly. Many creeks had been
dredged and the progressive thing to do was to straighten
them out, make them run through the flat fields like tame
canals. The early farmers had no liking for trees around
the buildings or along the fences. They must have loved
the look of open land. And the masculine approach to
the land was managerial, firm, suspicious. Only women
were allowed to care about the landscape, not to think
always of its subjugation, productivity. My grandmother
was famous for having saved a line of silver maples
along the lane. These trees grew beside a crop field,
and they were getting big and old, their roots interfered
with plowing and they shaded too much of the crop.
My grandfather and my father went out in the morning
(for my father had to take the manly view of things like
this) and made ready to cut the first tree down. But my
grandmother saw them from the kitchen window and
she flew out in her apron and upbraided and defied them,
so that they finally had to take up the axes and the
cross-cut saw and go away, and the tree stayed and

spoiled the crop at the edge of the field until the terrible winter of 1935 finished them off.

But at the back of the farms the pioneers had to leave a woodlot, a bush, where they cut trees in the early winter before the deep snow. Both for their own use and to sell. Wood of course was the first crop of the country. Rock elm went for ship timbers and white pine for ships' masts, until there were no rock elm or white pine left. Poplar and ash and maple and birch and beech and cedar and hemlock remain; fine trees.

Through the woodlot or bush at the back of my grandfather's farm ran the Blyth Creek, dredged a long time ago, when the farm was first cleared, so that the earth dredged up now made a high, humpy bank with little cedars growing on it. This was where my father started trapping. He eased himself out of school into the life of trapping. He could follow the Blyth Creek for many miles in either direction, to its rising in Grey Township or to the place where it flowed into the Maitland River. In some places, most particularly in the village of Blyth, the creek became public for a mile or so, but for most of its length it ran through the backs of farms, with the bush on either side, so that it was possible to follow it without being aware of the farms, the cleared land, the straight roads and fences; it was possible to imagine you were in the forest, in the Huron Tract just a hundred years ago.

My father had read a lot of books by this time, both at home, and from the Blyth Library, and the Sunday-school library, and he would certainly have read Fenimore Cooper. So he would have absorbed the myths and half-myths about the wilderness that most country boys did not know. Most boys whose imaginations absorbed these myths would live in cities. If they were rich enough they would travel north every summer, with their families, they would learn camping, canoeing; later they would go on hunting trips; if their families were truly rich they would go up the rivers of the far north with Indian guides. That is, if they liked that sort of thing. Many did. There was a whole experience of wilder-

ness which belonged to rich people from cities, a belief
in the wisdom of Indian guides, in the value of solitude
and danger, in the pure manly joys of hunting and fish-
ing (not then corrupted by ease and convenience),
which must have kept some men sane. People who had
this experience of the wilderness would travel right
through our part of the country without noticing there
was any wilderness there. But farm boys from Huron
County, not knowing anything about this huge mythical
wilderness, the deep romantic north (as it was known
for instance by Ernest Hemingway the doctor's son
from Oak Park), nevertheless were drawn, some of them
were, for a time, to the strips of bush along the creeks
and rivers, where they fished and hunted and built rafts
and set traps. They made their forays into this world
but soon gave it up, to enter on the real, heavy work
of their lives, as farmers. And one of the differences
between farmers then and now was that in those days
they did not expect either holidays or recreation to be
part of that life.

My father being a Huron County farm boy with the
extra, Fenimore-Cooper perception, a cultivated hunger,
did not turn aside from these boyish interests at the
age of eighteen, nineteen, twenty. Instead of giving up
the bush he took to it more steadily and seriously. He
began to be talked about and thought about more as a
trapper than as a young farmer, and as an odd and
lonely character, though not somebody that anyone
feared or disliked. He was edging away from the life of
a farmer, just as he had edged away earlier from the
idea of getting an education and becoming a professional
man. He was edging towards a life he probably could
not clearly visualize, since he would know what he didn't
want so much better than what he wanted. The life in
the bush, on the edge of the farms, away from the towns;
how could it be managed? Even here, some men managed it. Even in this tamed country there were a few
hermits, bush-dwellers, men who inherited farms and
didn't keep them up, or were just squatters, who fished
and trapped and hunted and led nomadic lives; not like

the farmers who whenever they left their own areas, traveled by buggy or, more often now, by car, on definite errands to certain destinations.

He was making money now from his trapline. So at home they could not complain. He paid board and he still helped his father when it was necessary. He and his father never talked. They would work all morning cutting wood in the bush and never talk, except when they had to, about the work. His father was not interested in the bush except as a woodlot. It was to him like a field of oats, the crop being wood instead of oats.

My father's mother walked back to the bush on Sunday afternoons. She was a tall woman with a dignified figure, but she still had a tomboy's stride. She would bunch up her skirts and climb a fence; put one foot up on the wire and her hand on the fence post and swing her leg over. He showed her the snares where he was catching fish. She was uneasy, because he was catching fish on Sunday. She was very strict, and this strictness had a peculiar history. She had been brought up in the Anglican church, called locally the Church-of-England; Anglicanism was thought of, in that country, as being next door to Popery but also next door to free-thinking. It was hardly religion at all, just a business of bows and responses, short sermons, easy interpretations, pomp and frivolity. Her father had been a drinker, a storyteller, a convivial Irishman. When she married she wrapped herself up in her husband's Presbyterianism, getting fiercer in it than most; she took on the propriety-competition like the housework competition, with her whole heart. But not for love; not for love. For pride's sake she did it, so that nobody could say she regretted anything, or wanted what she couldn't have.

But she stayed friends with her son in spite of the Sunday fish, which she wouldn't cook. She would look at the skins he had got and hear how much he got for them and she washed his smelly clothes. The smell was from the fish-bait he carried as much as from the animal pelts. She could be pleased and exasperated with him as if he were a much younger son; maybe he seemed younger to her, with his traps, his treks along the creek. He never went after girls; he grew less and less sociable. His mother did not mind. Perhaps it helped her bear the disappointment that he had not gone on to school to be a lawyer or a minister; she could imagine that he would still do that, the plans were not forgotten but merely postponed. At least he was not just turning into a farmer, a copy of his father.

As for the father he passed no opinion, did not say whether he approved or disapproved. He lived a life of discipline, silence, privacy. His grandfather had come from Scotland, from the Vale of Ettrick, on a sailing-ship in 1818, to Quebec and then to the Scotch Block settlement in Halton County. The family grew there and some of the sons came on to Morris Township, in Huron County, in the early eighteen-fifties. They were Grits, Presbyterians; they were against the English Church and the Family Compact, Bishop Strachan, and saloons; they were for universal suffrage (but not for women), free schools, responsible government, the Lord's Day Alliance. Of the young men who came to Huron County, one was killed by a falling tree while they were clearing the bush. The other two lived to be old, and founded families, and kept the family notions going. Family photographs commemorated them: the seated father, bearded, vigorous, with his luxuriant beard and commanding eyes; the drained, flattened, bleak and staring wife, the scared or faintly sullen or ominously dutiful children. For that was what it came to; the powerful fathers died out and the children had learned obedience so thoroughly there was not much room for anything else. They knew how to work till they dropped, but not how to take any risk or manage any change, they lived by hard routines, and by refusals. Not every one of them, of course. Some went away, to California, Iowa, dropped from sight. My grandfather diverged a little, learned to play the violin, married the tall, temperamental Irish girl with eyes of two colors. That done, he reverted; for the rest of his life he was diligent, orderly, silent. They prospered. But prosperity was not pursued

in the same way as it is now. I remember my grandmother saying, "When we needed something done, if it
was time to paint the house or when your father went
into Blyth to school and needed new clothes and so on, I
would say to your grandfather, 'Well, we better raise
another calf and get some extra.'" Now, if they could
get "some extra" when they needed it, by raising a calf
or whatever, it seems they could have got that extra all
along. That is, in their ordinary life they were not always making as much money as they could have, not
stretching themselves to the limit. They did not see life
in those terms. Nor did they see it in terms of saving at
least part of their energies for good times, as some of
their Irish neighbors did. How, then? I believe they
saw it mostly as ritual, seasonal and inflexible, work done
for its own sake. This must have been what my father's
father had in mind for him without mentioning it. And
what my grandmother in spite of her own submission
to it was not altogether sorry to see him avoid.

The animals he trapped were muskrats, marten, mink,
now and then a bobcat, otter, foxes. Most foxes in the
wild are red. Occasionally a black fox will occur there
as a spontaneous mutation. But he had never caught one.
Some of these animals had been caught elsewhere, and
bred selectively to increase the show of white hairs
along the back and tail. They were called silver foxes,
and in the early 1920's silver-fox farming was just starting in Canada. In 1925 my father bought a pair, a silver-
fox male and female, and put them in pens on his father's
farm. At first they must have seemed just another kind
of animal being raised on the farm, rather more bizarre
than the chickens or the pigs, something interesting to
show visitors. When my father bought them and built
pens for them, it might even have been taken as a sign
that he meant to stay, to be a slightly different farmer
than most, but a farmer. The first litter was born, he built
more pens. He took a snapshot of his mother holding
three little pups. He sent off his first pelts. The prices
were very good. The trapline was becoming less important than these animals he raised in captivity.

A young woman came to visit them, a cousin on the Irish side, from Eastern Ontario. She was a school-teacher, lively, importunate, good-looking, and a couple of years older than he. She was interested in the foxes, and not, as his mother thought, pretending to be interested in order to entice him. (Between his mother and the visitor there was an almost instant antipathy, though they were cousins.) The visitor came from a much poorer home, a poorer farm, than this. She had become a school-teacher by her own desperate efforts, and the only reason she had stopped there was that school-teaching was the best thing for women that she had run across so far. She was a popular hard-working teacher but some gifts she knew she had were not being used. These gifts had something to do with taking chances, making money. They were as out-of-place in my father's house as they had been in her own though they were the very gifts (less often mentioned than the hard work, the perseverance) that had built the country. She looked at the foxes and did not see their connection with the wilderness; she saw a new industry, the possibility of riches. She had a little money saved, to help buy a place where all this could get started. She became my mother.

When I think of my parents in the time before they became my parents, after they had made their decision but before their marriage had made it (in those days) irrevocable, they seem not only touching and helpless, marvelously deceived, but more attractive than at any later time, as if nothing was nipped or thwarted then, and life still bloomed with possibilities, as if they enjoyed all sorts of power until they bent themselves to each other. It can't be true, they must have been anxious already (my mother must have been anxious that she was not married), they must have known failures already, they may have turned to each other with reservations, as much as that luxuriant optimism I imagine. But I do imagine it, maybe we all do, so we won't think we were born out of affection that was always stingy, or

[25]

an undertaking that was always half-hearted. I think that when they came and picked out the place where they would live for the rest of their lives, on the banks of the Maitland River just west of Wingham, still in Huron County but in Turnberry Township, they were driving in a car that ran well, on a bright spring day with the roads dry, and they themselves were kind and handsome and healthy and trusting their luck.

Not very long ago I was driving with my husband on the back roads of Bruce County, which is just north of Huron. We passed a country store with long, old-fashioned window-panes, and a stand for gas-pumps which were not there any more. I felt that I had seen the store before and I connected it with a disappointment. I knew I had never driven this way before during my adult life and it did not seem likely I had come past here as a child, because most of our drives out of town were to my grandparents' house in Blyth, where they had retired after they sold the farm, and once a summer to the lake at Goderich. But even as I was saying this to my husband I knew that I connected the store with ice cream, with disappointing ice cream, splinters of ice in the ice cream; and then I knew that we must have stopped here on the trip my father and I made to Muskoka, in the summer of 1941. My mother was already there; she was selling furs at the Pine Tree Hotel north of Orillia.

"But if he was going to Muskoka," my husband said, "wouldn't he go along number nine, then up number eleven? He wouldn't go this way."

That was true, I thought that I must have been mistaken, it must have been another store that looked like this one, where we stopped for gas and he bought me an ice-cream cone. As my husband and I drove west, heading for Highway 21, up and down the long hills, after sunset and before dark, I thought and talked about what long car trips used to be like, how arduous and uncertain. I described to my husband—whose family, more realistic than ours, considered themselves in those days too poor to own a car—how the car's noises and movements, the jolting and rattling, the straining of the engine, the painful groan of the gears, made the crowning of hills, the covering of miles, an effort everybody in the car had to share. Would a tire go flat, would the radiator boil over, would there be a breakdown? The use of the word *breakdown*, made the car seem frail and skittish, with a mysterious almost human vulnerability.

"Of course people who could afford newer cars, or could afford to keep them in good repair, wouldn't have trips like that," I said. "Their trips would be more or less like today's, only slower and shorter."

Then it came to me why we could have been driving to Muskoka through this part of Bruce County. I was not mistaken after all. My father didn't dare take the car through any town or on a main highway; there were too many things wrong with it. It shouldn't have been on the road at all. It was a time when my father could not afford repairs. He did what he could to fix it himself, to keep it running. Sometimes a neighbor helped him. I remember my father saying of this neighbor, "The man's a mechanical genius," which makes me suspect he was no mechanical genius himself. Now I knew why I could remember such a feeling of risk and trepidation, as we found our way over the unpaved sometimes ungraveled roads, with their one-lane bridges. As things came back to me I could even remember my father saying that he had had only enough money for gas to get up to the hotel where my mother was, and that if she didn't have any money he didn't know what they were going to do. He didn't say this to me at the time, of course; he bought me the ice-cream cone, he told me to push on the dashboard when we were going up the hills, he seemed to be enjoying himself. He said it, long after my mother was dead, remembering some times they had gone through together.

The furs my mother was selling to American tourists at the summer hotel (we always spoke of American tourists, perhaps acknowledging that they were the only kind who were of any use to us) were tanned and dressed. Some skins were cut and sewn together in short capes, others were left whole and made into what was called scarfs. A fox scarf was one fox skin, a mink scarf was two or three skins. The head of the animal was left on and was given golden-brown glass eyes and artificial jaws. Fasteners were sewn on the paws. Many of the capes had a fox head sewn on, in the middle of the back.

Thirty years later these furs would have found their way into second-hand clothing stores, and would be bought and worn as a joke. Of all the mouldering and grotesque fashions of the past this wearing of animal skins would seem the most amusing and barbaric.

My mother sold the fox scarfs for twenty-five, thirty-five, forty, fifty dollars, depending on the quality of the fur and the number of white guard hairs, the "silver," it had. Capes cost fifty, seventy-five, perhaps a hundred dollars. My father had started raising mink as well during the late nineteen-thirties, but my mother was selling only fox, because the number of mink we raised was small and we had been able to dispose of them without taking a loss.

At home the colony of fox pens stretched from behind the barn to the high bank overlooking the river flats. The first pens were built of fine wire on a framework of cedar poles, and they had earth floors. Those built later had raised wire floors. All the pens were set side by side like the houses of a town inside the high guard fence, and because the building had been done at different times and not all planned out in the beginning, there were all the differences there are in a real town: some wide streets and some narrow streets, some spacious earth-floored old original pens and some smaller wire-floored modern pens which seemed less well-proportioned even if more sanitary. There were even two long apartment buildings, called The Sheds. The New Sheds had a covered walk between two facing rows of pens with slanting wooden roofs and high wire floors. The Old Sheds had just one short row of pens and was rather primitively patched together. The New Sheds was a hellishly noisy place full of adolescent foxes, due to be pelted, most of them, before they were a year old. The Old Sheds was indeed a slum and contained disappointing breeders who would not be kept another year, a fox who had been crippled, even for a time one red fox. I don't know where it came from; it may have been a sport in a litter.

When the hay was cut in our field some of it was spread on top of the pens, to keep the foxes from suffering too much from the heat, and to protect their fur which otherwise would turn quite brown. They looked very scruffy and shabby anyway, in the summertime, with their old fur falling out and the new fur just starting. By November they were resplendent, the tips of their tails snowy and the back fur deep and black with its silver overlay. Then they were ready to be killed, skinned, the skins stretched, cleaned, sent off to be tanned, sent to the auctions.

Up to this time everything was in my father's control, barring illness and the chanciness of breeding. Everything was of his making: the pens, the wooden kennels inside them where the foxes could hide and have their young, the metal water-dishes that tipped from the outside and were filled twice a day with fresh water, the tank that brought the water from the pump, the feed-trough in the barn where the feed of meal and water and ground horse-meat was mixed, the killing-box with the chloroform. Then when the pelts were shipped away nothing was in his control any more. There was nothing to do but wait; wait to see what the pelts were sold for, far away in Montreal, in great auction sheds he had never seen. The whole year's income, the money to pay the feed bill, the money to pay the bank, as well as the loan he had from his mother, had to come from that. Some years the price was fairly good, some years not too bad, some years terrible. The truth was, though nobody could see it at the time, that he had got into the business just a little too late, and without enough capital to get going in a big way in the first years when the profits were good. Before he was fairly started the Depression came. The effect of the Depression on the market was erratic, not steadily bad as you might think, but in ten years there was more bad than good. Things did not pick up much with the beginning of the war; in fact the price in 1940 was one of the worst ever. During the Depression bad prices were not so hard to take; my father could look around and see that he was still doing better than many other people; but now, with the war jobs opening up, and the country getting prosperous again, it was very hard to have worked as he had, and come up with next to nothing.

He said to my mother that he was thinking of pelting and selling all his stock, by Christmas of 1940. He meant to get out, change his life. He said he could go into the army as a tradesman, he was not too old for that. He could be a carpenter, a butcher.

My mother had another idea. She suggested that they keep out all the best skins, not send them to the auctions, send them instead to be dressed—that is, made into scarfs and capes, provided with eyes and claws—and then take them out and sell them. People were getting some money now. And though we were off the beaten track for tourists, she knew about them. She knew they were up in the hotels and shops of Muskoka, they had come from Detroit and Chicago with money to spend on bone china, Shetland sweaters, Hudson Bay blankets. Why not silver foxes?

There are two kinds of people, when it comes to changes, invasions, upheavals. If a highway is built through their front yard, some people will be affronted, mourning the loss of privacy, peony bushes, lilacs, and a dimension of themselves; the other sort will see their opportunity and build a hot-dog stand, get a fast-food franchise, open a motel. My mother was the second sort of person. The very idea of the tourists and their money flocking to the northern woods filled her with vitality.

In the summer, then, the summer of 1941, she went

off to Muskoka with a trunk-load of furs. My grandmother, my father's mother, arrived, magnificent with
foreboding to take over the house. She hated what my
mother was doing. She said that when she thought of
American tourists all she could hope was that none of
them ever came near her. She was a widow, now. She
disliked my mother and my mother's outlook on life so
much that when we were all together she withdrew
into a harsh and timid version of herself, but after my
mother had been gone a day she thawed out, forgave
my father his marriage and the predictable failure of
his exotic venture, and he forgave her the humiliation
of owing her money. She baked bread and pies and
cooked good meals (though we had no money we were
not in want; the garden flourished, the hens laid, we had
a Jersey cow) and cleaned and mended and served up
more comfort than we were used to. In the evenings she
carried pails of water to the flower border and to the
tomato-plants. Then we all sat out in the yard and
looked at the view. Our nine-acre farm, no farm at all
by my grandmother's standards, had an unusual location.
To the east was the town, the church towers and the
Town Hall visible when the leaves were off the trees,
and on the mile or so of road between us and the main
street there was a gradual thickening of houses, a
turning of dirt paths into sidewalks, an appearance of
street lights that got closer together, so that you could
say that we were at the town's very furthest edge, though
half a mile beyond its municipal boundaries. But to
the west there was only one farm-house to be seen, and
that one far away, at the top of a hill almost at the
mid-point of the western horizon. We called it Roly
Grain's house, but who Roly Grain might be, or what
road led to his house, I never asked or imagined; it was
too far away. The rest of the view was a wide field and
river-flats sloping down to the great hidden curve of the
river, a pattern of over-lapping bare and wooded hills
beyond. It was very seldom that you got a stretch of
country as empty as this, in our thickly populated county.
It is changed now, there is more to watch; the field in

our side of the river has become the town's airport.

When we sat there after supper my father smoked and he and my grandmother talked about the old days on the farm, their old neighbors, and my younger brother and sister pestered my grandmother to let them look in her window. My grandmother's eyes were hazel, but in one of them she had a large spot, taking up about a third of the iris, and this spot was blue. People said her eyes were of different colors; that was not quite true. We called the blue spot her window She would pretend to be cross at being asked to show it, she would duck her head and beat off whoever was trying to see, or she would screw her eyes shut, opening the good one a crack to see if she was still being watched. She was always caught out in the end and had to sit with her eyes wide open, being looked into. The blue was pale and clear without a speck of other colors in it, pure as the sky.

My father and I turned into the hotel driveway in the early evening. We drove between the stone gateposts and there ahead of us was the hotel, a long stone building with gables and a white verandah and hanging pots overflowing with flowers. The semi-circular drive took us closer to the verandah sooner than we might have expected. People were sitting there, in lawn chairs and rocking chairs, with nothing to do but look at us.

We parked in a gravel lot beside the tennis court, and got out of the car. The hot wind we made as we drove along had been blowing in my hair all day. My father saw that something was wrong about me, and asked me if I had a comb. I found one down behind the car seat. It was dirty and some teeth were missing. I tried, he tried, but we had to give it up. Then he combed his own hair, frowning and bending to look in the car mirror. We walked across the lot and my father wondered out loud whether we should try the back or the front door. He seemed to think I might know what to do, something he had never thought in any circumstances before. I said we should try the front, because

I wanted to get another look at the lily-pond in the
semi-circle of lawn bounded by the drive. There was an
elegant toy bridge over it, and an artificial frog as
big as a cat, at the edge.

"Run the gauntlet," said my father softly, and we
went up the steps and entered the lobby. It was very
dark after outside, the walls and ceiling paneled in dark
oiled wood. To one side was the dining-room, with the
glass doors shut and the little tables covered with white
cloth, each one with a bouquet of flowers; to the other
side a long room with a huge stone fireplace at the end,
and the skin of a bear on the wall.

"Look," said my father. "She's here somewhere."

In a corner of the lobby was a waist-high display case,
and behind the glass was a fox cape, beautifully spread
out on white velvet. A sign on top of the case said *Silver
Fox, the Canadian Luxury,* in a flowing script done with
white and silvery paint on a black board.

"Here somewhere," my father said. We looked into
the room with the fireplace. A woman with bobbed hair,
writing at a desk, looked up and said, "I think if you ring
the bell somebody'll come." It sounded strange to me to
hear someone you had never seen before speak to you
so easily. I even wondered if she were somebody my
father knew.

We backed out and crossed to the glass doors of the
dining-room. Across an acre of white tables with their
silver and turned-down glasses and bunches of flowers
and napkins peaked like wigwams we saw two figures,
ladies, seated at a table by the kitchen door, finishing a
late supper or drinking evening tea. My father turned
the door knob, and they looked up. One of them rose
and came toward us between the tables. The moment
in which I did not realize this was my mother was not
long, but there was a moment. I saw not my mother but
a woman in an unfamiliar dress, a cream-colored dress
with a pattern of little red flowers, a pleated skirt, a
belt. The material was crisp and glowing. The woman
who wore it looked brisk and elegant, her dark hair
parted in the middle and pinned up in a neat coronet

of braids. Even when I knew it was my mother and when she put her arms around me and kissed me, spilling an unaccustomed fragrance, I felt that she was still a stranger. She had crossed effortlessly into the world of the hotel; indeed it seemed as if she had always been living there. I felt at first amazed and betrayed, then excited and hopeful, my thoughts running on to what could be got out of this situation for my own enjoyment.

The woman my mother had been sitting with was the dining-room hostess, a fair-haired, tanned, tired-looking woman with heavy red lipstick, who was subsequently revealed to have many troubles, which she had talked about to my mother. She was immediately friendly—there seemed to be no normal warming-up period with people in the hotel—and she brought fresh tea from the kitchen and a very large dish of ice cream for me, because I had told my mother at once about the ice-splinters. Then she went away and left us alone, the three of us, in that splendid dining-room. My parents talked but I took in little of the conversation. I interrupted from time to time. They never told me not to and answered me with such cheerfulness and patience it seemed as if they, too, had taken on the hotel demeanor. My mother said we would sleep tonight in her cabin. She had a little cabin, with a fireplace. She said we would eat breakfast here in the morning. They said that when I was finished I could go and look at the frog.

That must have been a happy conversation; relieved, on my father's side; triumphant, on my mother's. She had done well, she had sold just about everything she had brought, the venture was a success. Vindication; salvation. He must have been thinking of what had to be done at once: what bills to pay; whether to get the car fixed here or chance it again on the back roads and take it to the garage in Wingham, to somebody he trusted. She would have been thinking of the future, of how they could try this in other hotels, of how many furs they should get made up, of whether it could be made into a year-round business. She couldn't have foreseen how soon the Americans were going to get into the war, and how that was going to keep them at home.

She would talk afterwards about how she had done it, how she had known the right way to go about it, never pushing anybody, showing the furs with as much pleasure to those who could not think of buying as to those who could. A sale would seem to be the last thing in her head. She had to show the people who ran the hotel that she would not cheapen the impression they gave; she had to show them that she was a lady, no huckster; she had to become a friend. That was no chore for her. She had the true instinct for mixing friendship and business considerations, that all good salespeople have. She never had to calculate her advantage, and coldly act upon it; she did everything naturally and felt a true warmth where her interests lay. She who had such difficulty with my father's relatives, who was thought stuck-up by our neighbors and somewhat pushy by the women at the church, had found a world of strangers in which she was at once at home.

When she was recalling this summer, and insisting on the gifts she had, later on, I was not sympathetic. I soon came to dislike the whole idea of putting your whole self to use in that way, making yourself dependent on the response of others, employing flattery however subtle, and all for money. I thought it shameful, and took it for granted that my father, and of course my grandmother, must feel the same way. I would not grant that those gifts were anything to be proud of. When I thought of the fox-farm, after it was gone, I thought of the layout of the pens, all the details of that small self-contained kingdom. I thought of the foxes themselves, and their angry golden eyes, their beautiful tails, and as I grew away from childhood and country ways I began for the first time to question their captivity, their killing, their conversion into money, which had all seemed so natural and necessary. (I never got so far as regretting this for the mink, who seemed to me mean-spirited, rat-like, deserving of no better fate.) I mentioned this lightly to my father, in later years, and he said there was some religion in India that believed all the animals went to Heaven too; think, he said, if that were true, he would be met when he got there by packs of snarling foxes and the other fur-bearers he had trapped, and the mink, and a herd of thundering horses he had killed and butchered for their food.

Then he said, not so lightly, "You get into things, you know, you don't realize what you're getting into."

It was in those later years that he would speak of my mother's salesmanship, and how she had saved the day, and say that he didn't know what he was going to do, that time, if she hadn't had the money when he got there.

"But she had it," he said, and the tone in which he said this made me wonder about the reservations I had assumed he shared. Such shame now seemed shameful. It would be a relief to me to think he hadn't shared it.

On a spring evening in 1949, the last spring, in fact the last whole season, I lived at home, I was riding my old bicycle, now mostly ridden by my brother and sister, to the Foundry, to give a message to my father.

My father had started working at the Foundry in 1947. It had become apparent the year before that not just our fox-farm but a whole industry, was going downhill very fast. Perhaps the mink could have tided us over, if we had not owed so much money already, to the feed company, to my grandmother, to the bank. Mink prices were not good enough to save us. My father had made the mistake many fox-farmers had made, in the mid-forties. He had invested borrowed money in new breeders, a Norwegian platinum and a Pearl Platinum male. It was thought that as the popularity of silver foxes declined, that of the new platinums must spectacularly rise. But the fashion went against long-haired furs altogether.

When my father went looking for a job he had to find a night job, because he had to work all day at going out of business. He had to pelt all the stock and sell the skins for what he could get, he had to tear down the pens. I suppose he did not have to tear them down, immediately, but he must have wanted them gone. He got a job as a night-watchman at the Foundry, covering the hours from five in the afternoon till ten in the evening. There was not much money in that but he was able to do piece-work as well. He did something called "shaking down floors." He did some of this after his regular shift was over, and often he would not get home until after midnight or one o'clock.

The message I was taking to my father was important in the family's life, but not serious. It was simply that he must not forget to call in at my grandmother's house on his way home from work, no matter how late it was. My grandmother lived in Wingham now. She tried to be useful to us, she baked pies and bran muffins and mended my father's and brother's socks. My father was supposed to call and pick up these things but often he forgot. She would sit up knitting, dozing under the light, listening to the radio, until the Canadian stations signed off at midnight and she would find herself picking up distant news reports, American jazz. She would wait and wait and my father wouldn't come. She had done this last night and tonight she had phoned at supper-time and said, "Was it tonight or last night your father was planning to come?"

"I don't know," I said. I always felt that something had been done wrong, or not done at all, when I heard my grandmother's voice. I felt that our whole family had failed her. She lived alone, and was still strong enough to carry armchairs up and down stairs, but she needed more company, more gratitude, than she ever got.

"I sat up last night but he didn't come."

"He must be coming tonight, then."

I told my mother what the call was about and she said, "You better ride up and remind your father, or there'll be trouble."

When she had to deal with a problem like this—my grandmother's touchiness—my mother seemed to brighten up, as if for a moment she had got back her compe-

tence. She had Parkinson's disease. It had been over-
taking her for years, with evasive symptoms, but had
only lately been diagnosed, so that she knew it was
hopeless. Its progress took up more and more of her
attention. She could no longer walk or eat or talk normally, she was stiffening out of control. She had a long
time yet to live. When she said something that showed
a concern for other people or even for the housekeeping,
and did not follow it with a reference to herself (*and
that will upset me*) I felt my heart soften towards her.
Most of the time I was angry at her, for her abdication,
and self-absorption. We argued. She would rally her
strength and struggle with me, long after she had given
up on ordinary work and appearances.

I had never been to the Foundry before in the two
years my father had worked there and I did not know
where to find him. Girls of my age did not hang around
men's workplaces. I did not have much interest either. I
mourned the passing of the fox-farm, as my mother did.
I had never thought it might make us rich but I saw
now that it had made us unique and independent. It
made me unhappy to think of my father working in the
Foundry. I felt as if he had suffered a great defeat. But
when my mother said, "He's too *fine* for that," meaning
more or less the same thing, I had to argue, and say she
was a snob. The first Christmas he worked there we received a large basket of fruit, nuts and candy. All the
employees got one. My mother could not bear to think
of herself being on the receiving and not the distributing
end of things, when it came to Christmas baskets, and
so we were not allowed to break the cellophane to eat
one grape. We had to put the basket in the car and drive
down the road to a family she had picked out as suitable recipients. By the next Christmas her authority had
waned. I broke the cellophane and said it was despica-
ble to be proud, and she wept. I pretended to be greedy.
The chocolate was brittle and going grey.

I could not see any light in the Foundry buildings.
The windows were painted blue on the inside. I almost
missed the office, which was an old house at the end of

the long main building. I saw a light there, behind the Venetian blinds, and I thought someone must be working late. I thought that I could knock and ask where to find my father. But when I looked through the little window in the door I saw that it was my father in there. He was alone, and he was scrubbing the floor.

I had not known that scrubbing the floor every night was one of the watchman's duties. This does not mean that my father had made a point of keeping quiet about it. I was surprised, for I had never seen him do any of this sort at home. Now that my mother was sick, I did it, or let it go. He would never have had time. Besides, there was men's work and women's work. I believed that, and so did everybody else I knew.

My father's scrubbing apparatus was unlike anything anybody had at home. He had two buckets on a stand, on rollers, with attachments on the side to hold various mops and brushes. His scrubbing was vigorous and efficient; it had no resigned, feminine, ritualistic rhythm. He seemed to be in a good humor.

He had to come and let me in.

"I thought it was Tom," he said. Tom was the Foundry manager; all the men called him by his first name. "Well. You come up to see if I'm doing this right?"

I gave him the message, and sat on the desk. He said he was almost finished here, and if I waited he could show me around the Foundry.

I said I would wait.

When I say that he was in a good humor here, I don't mean that his humor at home was bad, or sullen or irritable. But it did seem as if his cheerfulness was submerged, there, as if he thought it inappropriate. Here there was a weight off him.

When he had finished the floor to his satisfaction he stuck the mop on the side, and rolled the apparatus down a slanting passage-way into the main building. He opened a door that said *Caretaker*.

"My domain."

He dumped the buckets into an iron tub and the water gurgled away. There on a shelf among piles of unfamiliar things—tools, rubber hose, fuses, window-panes—was his familiar lunch-bucket, that I packed every afternoon when I got home from school. I filled the thermos with strong black tea and put in buttered bran muffins and pie if we had any, and three thick sandwiches of fried meat and ketchup. The meat was cottage rolls ends, the cheapest thing you could buy and the only meat I remember us having in the house over a period of two or three years.

He led the way into the main building. The lights burning there were like street-lights; that is, they cast a little light at the intersections of the passage-ways, but didn't light up the whole inside of the Foundry, which was so large and high that I had the sense of being in a forest with thick dark trees, or in a town with tall, even buildings. My father switched some more lights on and things shrank a bit, as they do; you could now see the brick walls blackened on the inside and the windows not only painted over but covered with black wire mesh. What lined the passage-ways were bins, stacked one on top of the other, and elaborate, uniform, metal trays. My father pointed out a pile of castings disfigured by lumps like warts or barnacles.

"Those aren't cleaned yet. They put them in a contraption that's called a wheelabrator and it blasts shot at them, takes all that off."

There was a heap of black dust, or fine black sand.

"That looks like coal dust but you know what it is? It's green sand."

"*Green* sand?"

"They use it for moulding. It's sand with a bonding agent, like clay, or sometimes they use linseed oil. Are you anyway interested in this?"

I said yes, for pride's sake, and courtesy's. And it was true, I was interested, but my interest kept flying away from the particular explanations my father began to provide me with, to general effects: the gloom, the fine dust in the air; the idea of there being places like this all over the country, with their windows painted over. You went past and never thought about what was going on inside; the never-ending time-consuming life-con-suming process.

"Like a tomb in here," my father said, as if he had an inkling of my thoughts. But he meant something different.

"Compared to the daytime. The racket then, you wouldn't believe it. They try to get them to wear ear-plugs but nobody does."

"Why not?"

"I don't know. Too independent. They won't wear the fire-aprons either. See. Here's the cupola."

This was a huge black pipe which did have a cupola on top. He showed me where they made the fire, in the bottom of it, how the metal passed through, in a pipe, the pipe going through a hole in the brick which was now plugged up with clay. He showed me the ladles they used to carry the molten metal and pour it into the moulds. He showed me chunks of metal that were like grotesque stubby limbs. He said those were the cores, the solid shapes of the hollows in the castings. He told me all these things with satisfaction in his voice, as if he were revealing something that gave him a serious pleasure.

We turned a corner and came on two men working, wearing work pants and undershirts.

"Here's a couple of good hard-working fellows," my father said. "You know Ferg? You know George?" I did know them, or at least I knew who they were. George had a daytime job on the bread-wagon but worked in the Foundry to make extra money, because he had ten children. Ferg had been in the war and had not settled down to any regular daytime job.

"She's seeing how the other half lives," said my father, making a delicate apology. Then, still aware of them, he said in a louder and more humorous voice than necessary, "Now. You see what shaking down floors is all about."

Working carefully together, using long, strong hooks, the two men lifted a heavy casting out of a box of sand.

"That's still plenty hot, it was cast today," he said.

"Now they have to work the sand around and get it ready for the next casting." We moved away.

"Those two fellas always work together. I work on my own."

"It must be heavy."

"It is. It's considered the heaviest job there is here. It took me a while to get used to. But it doesn't bother me now."

Much that I saw was soon to disappear: the cupola, the hand-lifted ladles, the killing dust. Many particular skills and dangers were soon to go. With them went the everyday risks, the foolhardy pride, the random ingenuity and improvisation. The processes I saw were probably closer to those of the Middle Ages than to those of today. And with this I imagine the special character of men who work in the Foundry will have changed; they will not be so different now from men who work in the factories or at other jobs. In those days the men who worked in the Foundry were rougher and stronger and had more pride, were perhaps more given to self-dramatization, than the men whose jobs were not so dirty and hazardous. They were too proud, in fact, to demand any protection, or to use what was provided. They belonged to no union. Instead, they stole from the Foundry.

"Tell you a story about George," my father said, as we walked along. (He was "doing a round" now, and had to punch clocks in different parts of the building.) "You know he likes to take a bit of stuff home with him. The odd bit of whatever he thinks might come in useful. So the other night he had a sack of such stuff, and he went out before dark and hid it under the office steps, where it'd be handy for him to pick up when he got off. And he didn't know, but Tom was in the office watching him. Tom didn't have the car parked outside, he'd walked. His wife had the car. Well, he saw what George was up to and after George went back inside, Tom came out and got the sack and he put it in the back of George's car. Then he waited, he stayed late and turned out the lights and finally George came back and was poking around under the steps, and Tom just watched him, never let on, then just as George was going off he came out and said, would you mind giving me a ride home? George nearly dropped. They got in the car and still Tom never gave a sign, but George had seen the sack right off and apparently he could hardly get the key in the ignition. He's still in the dark."

It would be easy to make too much of this story and to suppose that between the management and the workmen there was an easy familiarity, tolerance, even an appreciation of each other's dilemmas. There was that, but it didn't mean there wasn't also plenty of rancor, and stunning callousness, and deceit. But jokes were always important. The men who worked in the evenings, shaking floors, would gather in my father's room, the Caretaker's room, to smoke and talk—on Friday nights they might have a bottle—and there they talked about jokes that had been played years ago and recently. They talked about jokes played by and on people long dead. They talked seriously, too. They discussed whether there were such things as ghosts, and who had seen them. And money, they talked about that; who had it, in town, what they did with it, where they kept it. My father told me about these talks years later. One night somebody asked: what is the best time in a man's life?

When is a person the happiest?

Someone said, when you're a kid and can fool around all the time and go down to the river and go skating in the winter and that's all you think about, having a good time.

When you're a young fellow and haven't got any responsibilities.

When you're first married if you're fond of your wife, and a little later too when the children are small and running around and don't show any bad characteristics yet.

Then my father said, "I don't know, I think maybe right now."

They asked him why.

He said because you weren't old yet, but you could see ahead to when you would be, and you could see that a lot of the things you used to think you wanted out of life you would never get. It was hard to see how you could be happy in such a situation, but sometimes he thought you were.

When he told this to me, he said, "Those were some of the best fellows I ever met. We used to have some great old discussions. It was a whole new revelation to me because up to then I was always on my own, and I never knew you could enjoy it so much, working with other people."

He also told me that one night not long after he started work at the Foundry he came out at twelve o'clock or so and found a great snowstorm in progress. The roads were full, the snowplows would not be out till dawn. He had to leave the car where it was. He started to walk home. This was a distance of about two miles. The walking was heavy, in the freshly drifted snow, and he was walking in a south-westerly direction, with the west wind coming against him. He had done several floors that night and he was just getting used to the work. He wore a heavy overcoat, an army greatcoat, which one of our neighbors who had fought in the war had given him. Usually he wore a windbreaker. He must have put the coat on because the wind was so cold, and there was no heater in the car.

He felt dragged down, pushing against the storm, and about a quarter of a mile from home he found he wasn't moving. He was standing in the middle of a drift, and he could not move his legs. He could hardly stand against the wind. He was worn out. He thought perhaps his heart was giving out. He thought of his death. He would die leaving a sick crippled wife who could not even take care of herself, an old mother full of disappointment, a younger daughter whose health had always been delicate, an older girl who was often self-centered and mysteriously incompetent, a son who seemed to be bright and reliable but who was still only a little boy. He would die in debt, and before he had even finished pulling down the pens; they would be there to show the ruin of his enterprise.

"Was that all you thought about?" I said when he told me this.

"Wasn't that enough?" he said, and went on to tell how he pulled one leg out of the soft snow, and then the other, he got out of that drift, and there were no others quite so deep, and in a while he was in the shelter of the windbreak of pine trees he himself had planted. He had got home.

But I had meant, didn't he think of himself; of the boy who had trapped along the Blyth Creek, and asked for Sign's Snow Paper; the young man about to be married who had cut cedar poles in the swamp to build the first fox-pens; the forty-year-old man who had thought of joining the army? I meant, was his life now something that only other people had a use for?

My father always said that he didn't really grow up until he went to work in the Foundry. He never wanted to talk much about the fox-farm, until he was old and could talk easily about anything that had happened. But my mother, as she was being walled in by increasing paralysis, often wanted to talk about her three weeks at the Pine Tree Hotel, the friends and money she had made there.

A HOUSE DIVIDED

David Walton

In 1862, when I was a cipher operator in the War Department, Mr. Lincoln often visited the office and was always affable and courteous, sometimes even familiar, in his intercourse with the attachés of the office. He did not recognize me as the young telegraph operator he had met in the West. On one occasion, when he was telling a story to a member of the Cabinet and some prominent army officers, he tried to recall the name of a certain man in Illinois. It seemed to annoy him very much that he could not remember the name. With some trepidation I ventured to say: "Mr. President, permit me to suggest; was it not Judge Puterbough?" He turned upon me with a look of surprise, and shouted: "Why, yes! Did you know him?" "Yes, sir." "Where did you know him?" "Down in Perkin, Illinois, where I had the honor of explaining to the present President of the United States the working of the telegraph, in the little office in the Tazewell House." He turned to his surprised audience, and exclaimed: "Well, isn't it funny that we should have met here?" and confirmed to them how he had first witnessed the working of the telegraph in the Tazewell House.

This is Charles A. Tinker, later Attorney General for the State of Illinois, in *Lincoln Talks* (The Viking Press, 1939), Collected, Collated, and Edited by Emanual Hertz. This is a story I like to carry in my mind going into a job interview.

She spotted me as soon as I stepped inside the corral of desks—huge, years-darkened desks the size of double beds, each with a salmon-pink blotter, a metal lampshade like a coolie's hat, a black dialless telephone. This was in the main downtown branch, a vast, white-granite chamber with bronze entries, that could not have postdated my illustrious progenitor by many more than a score of years.

She sat at the third or fourth desk down the row nearer the colonnade, and I saw her, when she realized I was a person coming to see her, glance around to see the other reactions I was getting—not exactly the most encouraging of signs.

"Claudia Blumer? Hi, I'm Kent Darby."

I observed from her desk plate that her name was -umer, not -oomer, as I'd imagined. She had very long, very fine brown hair, fixed close to her head in an unfussy and well-anchored style. Seated, I could see her attention was caught by the resemblance, and decided to address that at the offset, which is something I usually try to do in any case.

"I ought to mention," I say, "I have a small sideline doing Lincoln impersonations," or, in this case, "subsidiary income offering commemorative portrayals of President Lincoln. It isn't acting, and I don't usually do commercial work. I mention this in case you've noticed a certain resemblance," establishing if I can a casual irony about the matter.

I mention that the resemblance is in fact fairly recent: after I turned forty my face narrowed out, and I went through a period when I lost a certain amount of weight. And a lot of it derives from just a few distinctive features, like the mole in the left crease of the face, and the bushiness of the eyebrows, which is also fairly recent—though now that I go back and look at early photographs of Lincoln, I can see a likeness to ways that I looked when I was younger.

Actually, I say, I'm a bit short for the part, at only six feet two—Lincoln having been six four.

Sometimes I add something like, "Though it has its good side, too—now I can finally say I've grown into my ears."

On this occasion, too, I think I suggested I might be willing to part with the beard, if that were an issue, and ended by saying, "Naturally none of this will interfere with my working hours."

Claudia Blumer twinkled and said, "Well, I'm sure if you give me a minute, I'll start to get used to it. Now, if you could fill out one of these—"

She handed me a standard application form, though I'd mailed her a copy of my résumé and it was setting on the desk beside her. I went over to an unoccupied desk next to one of the columns, giving her a full profile, where the resemblance is least pronounced. Each time somebody going by me gave a reaction, I looked up and smiled. The front of the form was all personal data, which I filled in, but on the back were blocks for schools and prior employment, all of which she had in detail on my résumé. I signed and dated it and took it back, saying, "You probably don't need all of this."

She twinkled apologetically, "—keep our records complete—you can sit here and finish," indicating the chair alongside her desk. It probably would have been wiser not to have brought the resemblance back for closer inspection right at that moment, and this lag now inevitably created an awkwardness.

When I handed back the completed form, she scanned down the front side. She'd decided she was going to handle this, wasn't going to let the Lincoln thing throw her, and was only checking now for traces of lunacy. "Widowed?" It was probably too the first time she'd found that particular space marked.

"Widowered, of course," I said, "is such an ungainly word, and there's no reason, I don't suppose, there can't be the one word for describing the state, the same as 'married.' My wife and our younger son were killed in a car crash fourteen months ago, on Route Twenty-eight along the river, on the part where there's no divider. I was driving. A drunk man, whose wife had been going from bar to bar with him threatening to leave him if he didn't quit his drinking, drove over from the other lanes, saying he was going to kill both of them. He hit us, and the two boys in the lane next to us who were coming back from the rehearsal for the one's wedding the next day, you probably read something about it at the time, it got a good deal of news coverage at the time. I don't entirely regret the amount of coverage that it got."

I took this slowly, giving her time to absorb this new information and make the connection to whatever she might have read or seen on TV.

I said, "I—attacked him outside the courtroom. I am not an angry man, or given to impulsive acts. I never felt any anger toward that man. He was nothing to me except pitiable. He was the most pitiable creature I could ever imagine. In a way, you might say, I was doing him a favor. Up until then it was all set to be a hanging trial. What I did was probably a relief to everyone, I'm certain that it was for him. I know it was, I could see it from his face."

When it seemed she was starting to feel she was hearing really more of this than she needed to know, I stopped myself, curbing the impulse to go on and on; also I've discovered that whenever you tell people more than they want to hear about one part of a thing, they go away feeling they've heard about all of it.

I said, "I made a decision to leave work for a year. There was some money, not as much as if I'd been the one—you never imagine of course you'll be the one who survives. Then for a while our older son, Ross, who's eleven now, was going through I suppose what you would call a period of denial. He lives with his grandparents now, my parents, in Monessen, I see him at least one time every week. I've had corrective surgery on my knees, which appears to have been successful. I continue having some trouble with my ears, and will probably be using a hearing aid in another two or three years. But I'm learning signing—which you may decide could make me useful in additional ways."

Claudia Blumer nodded, and nodded, and nodded, and when I finished speaking, stopped and twinkled. All the female prerogatives had been banished from this conversation except for this twinkle, a matter basically of the corners of her eyes and sides of her mouth, which she employed as a kind of operating tool, and a certain feminine ambiguity—or rather: she offered back the most desired response at every point, so that it was impossible at any given point to know for certain just how she was reacting. I saw her deciding that none of this was really relevant to the matter at hand, and then a minute or two later, when she thought back on the resemblance again, deciding that it was all really too much—there was just too much here. There was no way she could bring me in here without it seeming some sort of personal statement, and there was nothing she could see to gain from that.

"That's why," I said, "I think it would be better, at least at the offset, though of course I don't mean to shun any responsibility, if I started out at a window. As a way of making sure for myself how firmly planted I am, and for you, too, to have a chance for looking me over."

I'd gone on a few lines too long, though, or she heard a note of pleading in my voice. Or she'd decided already several minutes back, and it was only now catching up with her face. Just then, too, one of her associates, an older woman, went by the desk and gave such a look of malicious delight at the sight of me sitting there, I could see it only confirmed whatever reservations Claudia Blumer had still been harboring.

She twinkled again and said, "I'm going to want to call you once we've had a chance to talk to these other candidates—but I know I can tell you one thing. I know I won't encounter a more engrossing story," and rising to her feet, she reached me a firm and conclusive handshake.

Once outside the door I stepped into a brisk and purposeful stride, the body confessing to the failure the mind had yet to admit. I've possibly failed to mention that I live in Pittsburgh, I persist in Pittsburgh, where even in a three-piece suit I've become a familiar oddity, like the men who carry signboards up and down this same street, Smithfield Street, all day—the man who can't get his mail delivered, the man with unredressed grievances against one hundred twenty-seven local law firms, the United States Congress and United Steelworkers of America, and the Republican and Democratic national parties.

You may be wondering why Pittsburgh, not a major stop on the Lincoln itinerary—why not Gettysburg, or Springfield, or Chicago even? As to the former, I can say that Gettysburg already has its resident Lincoln, a Mr. James Getty, about whom I know nothing save that he is highly regarded and firmly rooted in his spot.

Just prior to this I had returned from a commingling—I would not, even in this age of constitutionalized factionalism, title us a convention—of *facsies*, to use the argot of the trade, or, in the language of contractual niceties, of *personages*, in Squaw Valley, home of the 1960 Winter Olympics, where I was testing out the career possibilities of a Lincoln resemblance.

Our headliners for these four days were the stars from

three of last year's Kennedy docudramas, with their
agents, and a pair of "First Ladies": a young actress who
had just scored two consecutive successes playing Marie
Antoinette, first in a rather muddied film version of the
The Queen's Necklace story, where she displayed a truly
regal disdain for the commonplaces of the acting craft,
and in a thirteen-part PBS *Days of the French Revolution,*
in which she had mostly to look appalled in the face of
mounting atrocities, both of them allowing her to display
to good advantage the one quality she most nearly shared
with that unfortunate lady, namely, an ample and un-
confinable bustage; and the actress who won the Emmy
for her Eleanor Roosevelt in the ABC *Sunrise at Campo-
bello.*

Interestingly, in reference to this last, though, was the
real limelight-grabber of the occasion, a woman who had
just come off playing Alice Roosevelt Longworth in an
upcoming NBC investigative theater production of the
behind-the-scenes of the Washington DC establishment
during the breakup of the Watergate scandal—which she
had also reportedly gone a long way toward walking
away with.

She could as much have resembled the legendary Princess Alice as she did the legendary Eleonora Duse, but
she had picked up the essential features of the smartass old
lady in a big-brimmed hat, dangling a lorgnette, and had
obviously done her homework, even to mastering such
esoteric "Mrs. L" freaks as standing on her head and being
able to bring her foot up alongside her chin without bending forward.

"Now *there* was a cheap creature," you'd hear her caus-
tic tones traveling the corridors of the lodge, penetrating
the oaken doors of the session rooms, "I remember him
once coming up to me at a party, putting his arm around
my shoulder, and saying with a kind of yokel jocularity,
'Ah, here is my blind date. I'm going to call you Alice,'
and I said, 'No, Senator McCarthy, you are *not* going to
call me Alice. The truckman, the trashman, and the policeman on the block may call me Alice but you may not.'"

I quickly caught her eye, but managed to fend her off
with a few famous perorations, and my overall dreariness.
Not unsurprisingly, she was most fascinated by the Elea-

nor Roosevelt, whom she found "not tall enough. Not nearly tall enough. Not enough neck, you don't have the neck.
You don't have the *hands*. Oh, we were so ungainly and
shy, we didn't know what to do with these big flippers of
ours," baring big ivory teeth, her strident Eleanor Roosevelt voice carrying up the graveled and, for the first two of
the days, rainsoaked trails: "I call on all Democrats and
all right-thinking Republicans—"

We also had our full contingent of Woodys and Lizas,
a young and an old Cary Grant, but only two Elvises and
no Michaels at all—though these last I understand hold
comminglings of their own. The locals, tanned holistic
relationship units who we passed going to and from their
tennis schedules, were unfazed by any of it. The International Helicopter Association had been there the week
before and been far more popular.

I had come to take part in a mock Douglas-Lincoln
debate, which was not a success. I am not an actor. While
I have a reliable memory, and can convey one and sometimes several elements of a Lincoln persona, I can't
organize these into a characterization. The height of
humiliation for me was watching even the blacks in the
audience applaud Mr. Van Patten's, as Douglas, ringing
extenuation of slavery.

This was late in the afternoon of the second day, and
after it was over I walked over to the skating-rink lounge,
which had a wet bar open after four o'clock. This would
be as good a time as any to mention that an esteem for the
temperance ideal is not a quality I share with The Great
Emancipator. Upon entering the room, I was hailed from
one of the window tables by a portly, big-headed man,
of no particular costume, but from whose fringe of
shoulder-length hair surrounding a bald crown I took to be
a Dr. Franklin, who was in attendance on the beguiling
Miss Antoinette. She was being visited at the table by two
men in fawn flight jackets and turtleneck jerseys, one
oxblood and one Aegean blue, who had flown up that
morning from Los Angeles and been going around all day
with the noncommittal conviviality of strollers in a mall.

In alternation, in what for a long time seemed to me
whispers of amoristic enticement, they were describing
to her the heroism of Dolly Madison—whose story some-

how seemed to have gotten wound up in the tale of the slanderization of President Jackson's wife.

"I don't want to get captured," she was telling them, "I don't want to get captured doing these costume parts, and if I do one more of them, I'm going to get captured doing them forever," and she glanced over for confirmation from Old Ben, as he styled himself and will hereafter be referred to, who apparently had coached her in this line of strategy beforehand—I having been brought to the table, I perceived, partly as a way of masking this covert agenting.

The two West Coast men smiled and nodded, smiled and nodded.

Over her back Old Ben said to me, "Now, you're good. You know your books, and you deliver all right. But you need to give it more personality. Hey, Lincoln was something of a joker, wasn't he? You need to lighten up."

Old Ben's great attribute was a voice that spoke reliability. He told me this as he might have said, as he various times and in various places had said, "Put your money in a place you can trust."

I thanked him, and told him I knew I had a good memory, and could retain a good deal of material and deliver it convincingly, but I couldn't move with it. I couldn't talk dialogue or move through sets; I wasn't an actor. It is, as I say, not a new story.

Old Ben put on a big, jaunty grin—an F.D.R. grin, in fact—and said, "Well, as I think I was the earliest to remark, Those who remember the lessons of history will be condemned to repeat them."

Antoinette, who had now spent longer than two hours in his company, merely sighed at such statements. She had been making her appearances in flouncy shepherdess skirts with laced, or rather, unlaced bodices, very à la Le Petit Trianon. At the start of yesterday's thunderstorm she'd come rushing into the lodge all shivering and exhilarated, to report how lightning had struck a tree trunk not ten feet from the car as she was riding up the hill.

But today she was all languor and ennui—all struck attitudes and fading sighs.

"But I know," she announced, spreading her fingertips across the swells of her bosoms, a gesture indicative of sincerity, "I know, whatever I do'll be purely on impulse, everything I've ever done has been on pure and impetuous impulse," and she fluttered her eyes at Old Ben, who only shrugged and said, "Well, just make sure you don't lose your head."

He exchanged with me, though, a glance of dubious speculation—at whether there might not be yet another level of impersonation operating beneath this queenly guise, and as she dropped her hands sank one of his own inside her *corsage*, probing studiously about for some seconds while she shrieked and flailed her arms in every direction except in that of the intruder, finally, shrugging again, withdrawing it saying, "Still, they could be implants."

The two West Coast men watched all this, smiling and nodding, smiling and nodding. Occasionally their eyes would wander over in my direction, with only cursory interest, for I'd lost a good deal of standing since my showing at the debate that afternoon, though with a certain undeniable fascination, too.

Addressed as Abe or as Mr. President, I generally respond with one of the tales of memorable meetings with Lincoln, who I always refer to as Mr. Lincoln, or as The President. This device, possibly because it so clearly is a device, seems to operate as a naturalism.

I like to do the bit of calling tall men out of the crowd and comparing heights, or reciting some of the Lincoln dimensions, left heel across instep: fourteen and a half inches. Same, right: fourteen and five-eighths. His hat size, an eight and a half.

Or I tell some of the ugly man stories, about the man who was given a knife to keep until he found a man uglier than himself, who tells Lincoln, "Excuse me, sir, but I have an article that belongs to you," or the woman who says, "No, you can't help it, but you might stay at home."

But it is in stillness, I've learned, in repose, that my impact is the greatest. Several summers ago, Karen, my former wife, my deceased wife, and I took the boys to see the Disneyland Lincoln, a spectacle I deplore on the grounds of general atmospherics—the chrome railings leading into specific rows of seats, and out the other side to specific sets of exit doors, the glintzy tape of The Battle

Hymn in the background, the backdrop of the Capitol dome against a dawning, then a bright noontide, and finally a somber twilit sky—but which has taught me an important lesson in the power of basic imagery. As first the mechanism begins to stir, a lift of a finger, then another, a jerky turn of the head, as if the creature were coming to life, the effect is briefly interesting; but when it stands and steps and starts to talk, one's attention is drawn too closely to the fluidity, or lack of it, the accuracy, or lack of it, of the movements. It is in stillness, in the power of the fundamental image, in repose, that the most profound statements are to be made.

The window where we were sitting looked out on the disused ski jump and judging tower—onto the roof of which, at the height of the day before's thunderstorm, the young man who is playing the young Olivier in the *The Making of Wuthering Heights* docudrama climbed in his cloak to shake his fists at the lightning flashes. The rain had at last stopped about an hour before, and now tiny, compactly formed clouds, no larger than basketballs and stoves, went floating by just a few yards from the glass, like souls of the departed sailing into the netherlands.

At dusk, sans the two West Coast men, who Antoinette, perhaps unintendingly, had finally convinced she didn't want to do a costume part, we—she, Old Ben, and myself—drove to Truckee in search of a fabled Mexican restaurant, a veritible El Dorado of Mexican restaurants, the legend of which has lured many a carload of hapless gringos up endless mountain winds. It wasn't far from here that the Donner Party, stranded by early snow in the bad winter of 1846–47, resorted to feeding on their dead to keep alive. Roaring around the curves in Old Ben's Fairlane in the direction of the Nevada line, passing a bottle of Jack Daniel's and a roach the size of a boutonniere, I, who was still young then to the process whereby the living are devoured by the dead, was seized by the spirit of the immortal Otis Redding singing "Loving You Too Long to Stop Now," and rolling down my window wailed to the immutable stars.

At four o'clock that morning we strolled hand in hand out to the end of the Tahoe City pier, Antoinette and Old Ben, who addressed her now exclusively in whispers, per-

petually a step or half a step behind. At several points in
the evening I'd attempted to part from them, but each
time Old Ben had adamantly opposed the idea, my presence there belying any notion of a carnal intent on his part,
so that now, Antoinette's defenses having been lulled, he
was at a point of acting on that intent. As we neared the
end of the pier, her fingers slipped out of mine, and I
walked on to the end alone. Above me burned those same
immutable stars, in such profusion they seemed to nullify
the very principle of gravity, so that with a single leap I
might have sprung up among them. Out on the lake, over
the lap of the water against the pilings, over the cries of
protest, now from back inside the picnic pavilion, of
Antoinette, whose credentials were apparently proving
to be in order, over the cackle of a car radio from somewhere on the other side of the parking strip, I could pick
out the beat of the solitary oarsman, and above the dark
line of the water distinguish the stern angle of his strokes,
drawing steadily nearer, steadily nearer the dock.

The next morning over coffee in the lodge Old Ben said
to me, "I'm thinking it's about time to be clearing out. The
first day at affairs like this, you know, the first couple of
days, you can spot your deals and make them, but after
that, even when you have made them, you know, there's
a kind of staleness sets in—"

"Fish and visitors smell after three days," I suggested,
but he only shrugged and went on with his travel plans.
Verbal pungentry, as I've tried to suggest, was not a cor-
nerstone of Old Ben's concept of Franklin. He thought the
aphorisms were commonplaces, and every time he wanted
to use a Franklinism came up with something like "Sly as a
fox" or "Fastern greased lightnin'." His concept of Franklin was the generic one—thrifty and wise, a great man for
the ladies—less the Dr. Franklin feted by the *philosophes*
in The Lodge of the Nine Sisters and embracing and embraced by the venerable Voltaire, and more the one who,
reading of Sir Hans Sloane's interest in asbestos, wrote
offering to show that virtuoso purses made of the novel
stuff. "Now, I'm a plain-speaking guy—" was his favorite
introductory.

"I wonder," I asked him, "if you could possibly drop my
coat off at the airport on your way by?"

"Well, I suppose so," he answered dubiously, "but how would you get it then?"

"Oh, very readily," I replied, "as I intend to remain inside it," a line that I find travels well, and travels me very well.

As we were walking through the airport in Reno, me now in a pair of Railsplitter jeans and a yellow banlon jersey, I noticed a woman standing at the edge of the magazines alcove, a blond woman in her forties or early fifties, nicely dressed, and not at all effusive-looking, catch sight of me. Pushing the card or paperback novel she'd been browsing back into the rack, her eyes fastened upon me, she began slowly to cross the floor. This is a kind of incident I've encountered several times before, always with older black women of a certain poise-in-rapture, but this woman was crimped, if anything reticent in her advance, and I think had I at any point made a startled or offended motion, would instantly have turned and fled the spot. But instead I smiled and turned up these big hands and spread them wide, as, with a cry that only in intention was a sounding of relief, her hands out in front of her as if she meant to repel me away, she drew herself to my shoulder and began to cry. I can't tell what losses she confided there, the son blindly struck down, the husband ruined. Old Ben had gone off a few paces to stand, and over her shoulder I watched a progression of reactions play upon his face—astonishment, amusement, then impatience mingled with contempt, and then amusement again, laced with a grudging appreciation, as I lifted these big hands up, and set them back, lifted them up, and set them back upon her shoulders again.

"Now then, Mother," I said, as I could feel her beginning to regain control, the first stiffenings of doubt starting to travel up her arms, "when you get home you can truthfully say you have rested in Abraham's bosom."

Colonel Burt was present with others, one of whom, a major, perhaps under the influence of wine, perceived not the fact that Lincoln's face "in every line told the story of anxiety and weariness." After the business which caused them to call upon Lincoln was concluded and they rose to go, he slapped the President on the knee, and said: "Mr. President, tell us one of your good stories." Says Colonel Burt: "If the floor had opened and dropped me out of sight, I should have been happy."

The President drew himself up, and turning his back as far as possible upon the major, with great dignity addressed the rest of us, saying: "I believe I have the popular reputation of being a storyteller, but I do not deserve the name in its general sense, for it is not the story itself, but its purpose, or effect, that interests me. I often avoid a long and useless discussion by others or a laborious explanation on my own part by a short story that illustrates my point of view. So, too, the sharpness of a refusal or the edge of a rebuke may be blunted by an appropriate story. No, I am not simply a storyteller, but storytelling as an emollient saves me much friction and distress."

Following my return from Squaw Valley, and my failure to secure another bank job, I went into a period of withdrawal, likened you might say to the well-known Lincoln melancholia. The start of it was a series of incompletions, I will not term them failures, of communication with my older son, Ross, who's eleven now—I've mentioned that already. After a period of not wanting to know anything at all about the accident, he now wanted to learn all that he could about it, began questioning me on particulars, even made trips to the library to read microfilms of the press accounts. It wouldn't have made a difference if we had been driving on the inside lane, the two boys in the other car had both been killed. It didn't help either to wish that Karen instead of me had been driving, she never drove, hated to drive, everywhere we went I did the driving. I knew what it was he needed to hear, but wasn't able to work out a formulation that accounted for both of them dead and the two of us here alive. For a while I tried having him live with me again, but that quickly proved as impractical as it had in the months that first followed the accident.

Then for a while the dulling of my hearing, which up until then had been gradual and progressive, suddenly became an acute, often piercing sensitivity to sound that left me for days locked up like Roderick Usher in the back storage room with strips of flannel blanket wrapped around my head.

One afternoon as I was coming out of a produce shop in Shadyside, a tall, elderly man, with a handsome head of white hair, took note of me. "Abraham Lincoln," he said.

I put out my hand—but he drew immediately back.

"No—it is red with blood; I can't touch it. When I knew it, it was an honest hand. It has cut the throats of thousands of my people, and their blood, which now lies soaked in the ground, cries aloud to heaven for vengeance. You have come here, protected by your army and navy, to gloat over the desolation you have caused. You are a second Nero!"

I have long since grown accustomed to clown cries of *Sic semper tyrannis!*—although I am always careful to determine their source—but this incident left me strangely shaken. Right about this same time a series of discussions with a neighbor over a wind chime on his rear porch were beginning to turn acrimonious and nearly resulted in a fistfight. It seemed any little disturbance was enough to leave me totally unstrung.

It was right about this time that Old Ben reappeared, heralded first by a letter telling me he would be coming through sometime in the next week on his way to Cincinnati to make a set of TV commercials and might stop in Pittsburgh if he had the chance, followed that same afternoon by a call to tell me his schedule had been moved up and he was already on the road and might give me a call later that evening if he had the time, followed less than two hours later, and well within time for dinner, by his arrival at the door. He was very affable, very hale. I'd started tidying up the rooms, and in the dining room a Supremes Anthology was playing "The Love Bug Done Bit Me" on the stereo, and scattered around the room were a number of library books on Lincoln that I had been mining for useful nuggets. I'd been contracted by a national clipping service to furnish videotapes of local news broadcasts, and in the corner were two decks of Panasonics hooked to cables, their red timer digits all glowing. Next to these was the row of empty 200ml Southern Comfort bottles I was building breast to back across the radiator hat. Old Ben took this all in, nodding to himself in a confirmed and satisfied way. He invited me to come out to a restaurant with him, but allowed himself to be persuaded to stay and share whatever I was having with me, and then proceeded to clear the shelves for travel. While we were having our predinner drinks, he got out, as illustration of a point he had been making, a set of indemnification papers for a holding company for producing television commercials, and just hypothetically filled them in with my name—as vice-president. He put these aside to help me carry out the dishes, but later, while we were sitting over our after-dinner cocktails, brought them out again and spent forty-five minutes explaining why he wasn't trying to suggest that I ought to sign them. I signed them. The next morning I rode to Cincinnati with him, where I made two commercials for a lumberyard, and the next week to Buffalo, where I made one for a Mazda dealership and two more with Old Ben for a Franklin Savings & Loan. For the next four months we traveled together, mostly through Indiana and Ohio and parts of the Northeast. We soon fell into a routine. Old Ben favored Savings & Loans. Around midway through the first morning of shooting, which Old Ben arranged to have outside the main branch building, some complication would be discovered. There would be some lapse found in the safety stipulations, usually in the setup for the kite-flying sequence, some affront to Old Ben's professional dignity would occur, and in the end the only way of appeasing him and preventing him from picketing the front of the building became to grant improved accommodations, a car and driver, a revised schedule of residual guarantees. He was a goader, our Old Ben, and I'm afraid a bit of a pirate. At nighttime we'd go around to the city bars, and he had a genius for spotting the assembled animosities in a place, and drawing these to a head. What larks! By day we robbed Savings & Loans and by night set off barroom brawls. At the beginning of each set of shootings, Old Ben presented me with a stack of waivers, allotments, codicils, and asked me to sign. I signed them all.

In Albany, in an incident you may already have heard of, Old Ben and I sued each other, for breach of contract, an episode that received a lot of what is known as media attention and ended in a hallway scuffle outside the courtroom.

Ah, what larks. You would probably as soon have just the rollicking adventures of these two all-too-recognizable con artists, working their way through The Original Thirteen—around the northern tier of The Original Thirteen.

The day on which Grant's army began the final advance, the President sat in a small telegraph office at City Point, receiving telegrams and examining a pocket chart. Three little kittens were running about the hut, in which was the office. The President of the nation whose fate was in the scale picked up the kittens, placed them on the table, and said: "You poor, little miserable creatures; what brought you into this camp of warriors? Where is your mother?"

"The mother is dead," answered the colonel in charge.

"Then she can't grieve for them," said the President with a sigh. "Many a poor mother is grieving for a son who has fallen in battles. Ah, kittens, thank God you are cats, and can't understand this terrible strife. There, now, go, my little friends," wiping the dirt from their eyes with a handkerchief, "that is all I can do for you. Colonel, get them good milk, and don't let them starve; there is too much starving going on in this land, anyhow; let us mitigate it when we can."

It is wise to keep in mind that Lincoln operates on a broader scale of feeling than most of us would subscribe to today. Also, and this may be the principal defect in the preceding example, and notwithstanding the renown of some of his terser addresses, he tends to the wordy, a feature no doubt enhanced by the understandable desire on the part of chroniclers of a Lincoln anecdote to aggrandize their encounter with the great man. He did say that how long a man's legs should be was long enough to reach the ground, but what he actually said was:

"This question has been a source of controversy for untold ages. It has led to bloodshed in the past and there is no reason to doubt that it will in the future. After much thought and consideration, not to say worry and mental effort, it is my opinion, all side issues being swept away, that a man's lower limbs, in order to preserve harmony of proportion, should be at least long enough to reach from his body to the ground."

He was addicted to puns, early and late. In the days when Mr. Lincoln was practicing law he was not over-careful of his dress. This was partly due to a scarcity of funds. A friend encountered him leaving a clothing store with a new coat on.

"Got a new coat, Abe?" he asked after the greetings.

"Yes," said Mr. Lincoln, "it appears so."

"But it's a little short, isn't it?" asked the friend.

"Yes, perhaps it is," said Lincoln, "but it will be long enough before I get another one."

Mr. Lincoln was walking up Pennsylvania Avenue, relating "a little story" to Secretary Seward, when the latter called his attention to a new sign bearing the name of T.R. Strong. "Ha!" says Old Abe, his countenance lighting up, "T.R. Strong, but coffee are stronger."

You may be curious, speaking of Renowned Addresses, how well I can do a Gettysburg. You will not be surprised if I tell you it's a characteristic of these remarkable memories that they retain certain tiny, unbridgeable gaps, when I say that I'm unable to remember a full sentence of The Gettysburg Address. And that my solution has been to write the words out on the back of an envelope, which I carry with me everywhere I go. I've even had to write along the side, "Grasp lapel." This sheepishness, which is what it comes out to be, returns some measure of freshness and spontaneity to words too familiar and too often rote recited. One can recall that the speech was not thought impressive at the time. The crowd was disappointed, and only the Chicago newspapers gave the President good marks.

I lift my eyes, searching the faces for the sentiment that underlies the written words. I recall that in his final eight months in the White House, Lincoln's most frequent form of correspondence was the letter of pardon.

> Washington, 15 February, 1865
> Suspend execution in case of Luther T. Palmer 5th N.Y. Artillery for fourteen (14) days and send record to me for examination.

Washington, Feb'y 16, 1865
Suspend execution of death sentence of George W.
Brown, Company A Fifteenth New York Engineers, now
at City Point, until further orders, and forward record for
examination.

Washington, Feb'y 16, 1865
Suspend execution of death sentence of Charles Love,
Seventh New Hampshire Vols. at City Point until further
orders, and forward record for examination.

And I recall this:

My wife's family came from Donora, Pennsylvania, almost directly across the river from the town where I grew
up, but when the U.S. Steel plant there closed down,
Karen's father transferred to the mill in Joliet, Illinois,
and the next year brought the family out there to live.
Karen and I hadn't met at that time, but when we were
sixteen she came back for a summer to visit with some
cousins who I knew, and after she returned we corre-
sponded.

Following the accident, it turned out that both our sets
of parents had reserved spaces for us and the boys in their
family plots. We'd known this, of course, but it's a kind of
decision you imagine yourself never having to make. I
decided early enough that I would take the bodies out
there, to Illinois, but through the day that followed the
accident there were a number of telephone calls back and
forth, with the result, though for lesser reasons as well,
that my parents decided not to make the trip with me.

When the time came for closing the casket—we had
decided, again at his grandparents' urging, on a single
casket, although the boy was almost three then—I wasn't
able to release my son's arms. Karen and I had paid our
farewells to a thousand shared moments, and there was no
need to take leave of these now; but this boy had not even
been three years old. His name was Jonah, Jonah who
would have been twenty-one in the year 2000. That particular bit of fancy had never much appealed to me one
way or another, but now it became the focus of all my
grief. He used to talk about chocked liver and having
grandsisters. He hadn't gotten things straightened out yet.
I couldn't have borne the idea of trading my sons, but my

other boy, Ross, was nine then, and at least had seen a little of the world.

Some sense of this, of my horror at the thought of thinking like this, must have transferred itself to Ross, standing up so stiff and solemn at my side, already my little soldier of recrimination. I should have turned and embraced him and held him hard, but I couldn't do that, I couldn't release my hands. Already, with awful foresight, I could see the separations stretching out before us, but still I couldn't release my hold, and after these complications of earlier, there wasn't anyone there who felt able to come and guide me.

Finally an old man who I hadn't seen before, a tall, somewhat wild-eyed fellow with raging white hair, who I understood from later comments to be something of a neighborhood character, but to me at that moment looked like the father of a thousand sons, came over and tapped my wrist, saying, "Let loose, lad. Let loose now, it's time to return them to the task," and I did; and so I have; oh my brothers, and oh my sisters, so I have ever since.

THIEVING

Norman Rush

As from 1978, God chose me for a thief. Could I, a boy,
withstand Him? If God marks you, you must fall,
always.

Why must God choose out one Mokgalagadi who is poor
and who in all times past loved all things of God and
BVM? I was very much in churches. I was foremost in
singing of hymns, praising God most highly. My name
of Paul is found in scripture. To me, God hates all thieves.
And if Lord Jesus may forgive a thief at times, always it
is just because this thief is vowing he shall steal no more.
What book is my greatest treasure, if not *St. Joseph Daily
Missal?*

As well, I am Mokgalagadi, of a tribe that in all ages of
time is misfortunate and despised in Botswana and always made to be enslaved and mocked, and having any
treasures taken from it, never taking them from others.
Only Basarwa are less than we to the prideful Bamang-
wato and Bakwena, our masters. At Tsane I never took
items from my mother as children do. Always I was truthful. I only sought to prosper with good English-speaking.
My tutor was Sister Honoria at St. Boniface Mission, God-
sent to me. But she was taken out from Tsane to aid others.

I came to my fate by an egg, at Lobatse, at Boiteko
School. A cooked egg came to be found in my bed. At
Boiteko, we few Bakgalagadi were ill-treated by Bama-
lete and Colored boys at times, myself the most. It was
because I am tall, and fast in my English. I was first in
Geography by far. To this day I state Headmaster Sebina
and the bursar Chibaya made a crime-ring, with hiding of
sports fees and claiming of a cash-box stolen, with, then,
Sebina found as owner of a new van for hire. They feared
inspectors coming. So that if some boys could be shown
out as thieves for taking food and cooked eggs from the
kitchen, those boys could be given all blame, and so forward with more crimes! They said Here is Paul Ojang
who is late on fees and with no relations to aid him in the
Board of Trust, and he is a boarder from far-distant Tsane,

from where he cannot be heard again. So a miracle passed and an egg was found to walk. Still today I can cry at this wrong done to me.

The cur Sebina said I was only telling falsehoods—he, the master liar. When that cash-box was taken, keen boys were sleeping two hands from the office, yet they heard no sounds when doors were broken through. Miracles were all about. I said to him If at all I am a thief, why am I known to say to some chaps who are stealing in shops in Lobatse it is wrong? But he said I must pack and go. He said I was known to name him as Headmonster. He knew it only from spies. Who set that egg into my bed? It was boys or the crime-ring, or God's hand.

At any time, Sebina stopped our food, as when there was a turmoil at film night. Always he would punish us a day when there must be meat provided. He sold our meat, I know it. Always the head-boy for our form was in fear, because I said he must report to the inspectors on all manner of wrongdoing. I said he must report as to food, as to cabbages crushing us day upon day. But he was afraid.

Why was I not given strokes only, if I took that egg? It was because I had no protector. My father is unknown. My form-mates were silent. Sebina forced me to sit one night through at Central Transport yard, with my goods, to wait for the Bedford sent to carry me in shame back to Tsane. I was chopped from my Junior Certificate by that cur with yellow eyes.

You are put to shame. You must go atop a Bedford to your mother, who shall thrash you. You must hold fast to ropes. Your goods are pushed under ropes. Much wind scrapes off tears from your cheeks. When you need some water, there is just but one hosepipe siphon, used the same for petrol and for taking water, so you must fall ill with swallowed petrol. You shall be sent to herding by your mother. After Kanye, you come to bush, with no houses. At Jwaneng Mine, you pass far-distant houses behind fences caused by diamonds buried there. After Jwaneng, it is bush evermore. Those drivers were fast.

What! at Sekgoma Pan those drivers turned from the road to go straight for the bush. They shall make me a mother too soon, was said by Monusi Maome, a pregnant girl who was a passenger with me. They were shaking us every way. At last they halted at a tree. They jumped down with rifles to go for duiker, whilst sparing no words to us of returning back.

What must I find at Tsane? Thrashings, a mother ever seeking beer, harsh words and all such things until I am forced away to Ghanzi to work for Boers. Of all white-men, you cannot love them, even if as brother citizens we should do. You cannot love these white Batswana, in no way. Because they will not teach you. In the freehold farms you are paid by food and with some pinches of coins at times. You toil endless days.

I determined I must go before those men returned back, go to the capital even if I must go every click by foot. Then I took down my goods and took from them what I could carry, and all the rest put under heaped-up stones, laughing because it was a beacon for thieves to come, I knew it. I took clothes, provisions, water, my best books: *St. Joseph Missal* and my set-book of *Shane*. I took fare-well of Monusi, who was saying I must stay with her. She said I must post a letter to my mother, from Gaborone, at the soonest. She said to guard as to snakes. I went away, marching, trusting to God to help a boy.

I fled fast from Sekgoma Pan, lest those men come searching. As well, the closer you become to Jwaneng, you are the safer as to lions, which do not venture nearby Jwaneng unless at drought-times. I was bold, striving with all things such as hunger and hot sun. I made two lifts, always by Europeans. One night I lay in a tree. I lay all day in the gum-tree forest at Lobatse, too weak. I was quenched out.

I came to our capital. I saw rich housing, tarred streets, vehicles crowding up. Yet every day my schemes were blasted. In all shops a sign says *Ga Gona Tiro*: No work in Here. With no sponsor, no testimonial, no relations, I saw I must become as animals. By night I lay in the bush nearby the university, changing my place at times. I must wash up in Bontleng at some standpipes. By day I asked jobs or sought to carry parcels at the Hyper Store amongst the *tsotsi* boys, forcing myself foremost among them. All about Gaborone you discern many boys with no home. My funds were drained. I dreamed of milk.

A cobbler sits amidst a multitude of shoes, at Dove Close. I said I can be apprentice to you. He felt my hands and saw I was a student. He said no. I said But I can carry shoes to homes roundabouts for payment, because now you wait endless days for payment. But he asked if at all I would give gold coins for polishing to a vagabond. I went away. They no more take novices for the mines in South Africa. I went for labor at the Industrial Site, for building-work, but was thrust back by ruffians. Biting sores came in the sides of my mouth. I feared always as to lice.

Ever slowly I was sinking down, until God moved his hand to give me aid, a savior, the true thief Elias Odireng.

He was called Alias. He found me in a ruin, lying ill. That ruin was to be a bottle-store one day. But in those times it was mere walls. Work was stopped, it seems. No watchman came. Bush was springing back from whence it had been chopped. He was three years my senior. Already he had been at prison. He knew this place where I was found. He knew many sites. At once he took pity. He said if I am well I can aid him many ways. If he would bring some girls there, I could stand lookout. He prophesied I would soon be healed by him.

So at once he was gone to steal food. He made true feasts, with pilchards, sour milk, scones, polonies, tinned sea fish, Pine Nut soda and others, Fray Bentos tinned beef, *naartjies*, some cooked foods still warmed, peaches, mince, sweets. All thanks to him I was made well.

I said Where can you unearth such food? He said he would gladly tell me just because he would soon be gone to South Africa, to Diepkloof, to join in thieving cars with guys he knew from prison, soon to be free. He was await-ing one master-thief only. He said on Notwane Road I should find two houses wherein Peace Corps guys were passing through. He said that if at all they hide door-keys it is in one place only. He said they were carefree, most times not locking that place whatever. I must take plastic sakkies in my pocket and go to the kitchen, but I must take only sums of food, never the whole of any food. But I must never take beers, because then Peace Corps guys

would go raging all about, with lights switched on, eager
for fighting. He said You can rob there every day, with
ease. Too many guys are holding food in just one fridge,
he said. I said Why do they not complain to the police?
He said Because they are themselves thieves, and you
shall see very many plates and tumblers marked from
Rhodesian Railways in those hostels.

Always sometimes now I say what! was this thief a Holy
Guardian Angel and not a true man, not born out of a
woman, in fact? Because it says in *St. Joseph* at page 1078
that everyone of the faithful has a Guardian Angel from
God, even unto some pagans as well. I know this page
until today. On it the Lord God says *I am sending my
Angel to guard you and bring you to the place I have
prepared.* Alias was very quick in coming and going, like
a ghost. He was ever advising against evils such as cigarettes and beer-drinking. And as well he healed me in so
short a time and prophesied when I should be made well
and going about. What was he? He ate in small amounts.
The house-dogs thereabouts were silent when he was
there. He was very becoming, he was smooth-faced, with
no initiation scars. At every hour he advised me. He said
I must never borrow someone any money. He said You
must not hide stolen things at your mother's house, for the
police always go first to her. He warned against long-
holding of stolen goods, saying you must sell them, even
for a little, to escape danger. He showed me to make tea
in a jar of water set in sunlight, with no fire. Amounts of
good things fell from this known thief, to confuse me.

Soon one morning he was gone. Withinside my shoe
was twenty pula, left by him. I was cast down. Never shall
I see his face again.

I was once more at Hyper Store, amongst those boys.
They said Chumza, hello, where is your boyfriend Alias,
tell us for we must see him, where is that guy just now?
I said to them he was gone. Now they said What! he has
taken so much cash and some items from us, promising
studies with a mastermind thief from Diepkloof. I said
On this I know nothing. They told to me all that he was
promising; means against watch-dogs, means for temptation of servants, means to divine if someone is abroad
within a dark house, much about keys, much about thiev-

ing through window-bars with wire hooks. They pushed me, and after many kind of threats said they shall watch me day unto night. They said to beware them.

Those were cruel days, I may say. Always I wished only to slip down from God's eye. I ceased from prayers. I ceased from reading of St. Joseph. At the library I could not be granted pockets, as I had no postal bag, so I must study books there what hours I could steal from bearing parcels, weary and too weak. I feared as to my English, with no studies and conversing.

At last one night I saw great throngs passing in at Town Council Hall, rejoicing. It was when after long struggle Zimbabwe was free in victory. Some way I could not be glad in this, because in this free nation of Botswana I was not progressing. Soon those bush fighters would be as kings in Zimbabwe, and it was said many brave fighters were in fact mere boys, not school-trained even up to Standard Three.

In no way could I gain a seat within. Thick as bees, some guys made noises chatting even whilst ministers were giving off statements of great importance. Therefore I lingered on the outside, regarding many posters of the war that were stating as to all kind of tasks and vowing *chimurenga* many times over.

So at once a fat whiteman saw me there. He was rushing, with a camera. He said to come aside to the shadows. With no greetings whatsoever he asked me if I speak English and if I can greatly help him. If I can swiftly pull down some posters, he shall give me at his house three pula each, which he said as "puler." He said he must go forward to the stage, else he should pull down these mementos for himself. He stayed in Seepapitso Crescent, plot number three-zed-twenty. He said I am a friend to these comrades, never fear. Those posters are mounted up with mere spots of chewing-gum, he said. Others shall take them, he said, unless we are fast.

All whilst he spoke, I said to beware, for this was thieving. But yet if this guy was well-pleased, I could venture with asking any kind of job from him. So I saw I must do it.

In all I saved six posters, very fast. Then at once some guys saw me, hailing out cries that said I was a traitor.

So I ran fast, going all about amongst vehicles until I could turn up these things tight into a stick and thus escape.

All the night to come I was fearful. As children we are made always to beseech God. But I was blocked from prayer, fearing even as to prayers to Sister Honoria, a mortal, because clergy are at all times watched on by God. But at last I saw my hope. I said if you hand up these things freely for no payments whatsoever, you are no thief, and this guy will be the more pleased about it. If at all there was to be a thief, he would be the thief, as I would take nothing. So at that I slept on.

I found his place with ease, as there was a sign naming Jarvis and the plot number as I had it. My heart played fast, for all this plot within the fence was in ruins and un-tidy. Dog-holes stood throughout the street fence. I said what! a Type One house with no-one raking, arms of trees scraping on the roof, gum-tree bark fallen-down, dry gardens. It was evening-time.

There was no dog about, yet signs stated to beware a dog. I walked slowly there. I saw dark ghostly quarters at the rear, thus there were no servants with them, I was sure of it. His Land-Rover was brown with dust all over. I was at the back way. A white woman was before me in the kitchen, in her lips a Santos Dumont burned whilst she cooked up meat, stirring. I knocked the window-pane. She too was fat. She shook her head, sharp, as if to send me straight away, and thus some ashes of her smoking fell down into that food. She took no notice, I may say. I have no job, she said. *Ga ke na tiro*, she said, over again.

So I went at the front to find this man. He was there. I knocked. He rejoiced at once, with those posters in his hands. He said I must come in. He said we must see them, both together. That floor was in disorder. We pushed ar-ticles aside. That place was heaped on every hand with books, journals, all kind of papers and photographs wide-spread, tumblers, photographs in boxes. He praised those posters endlessly. He must have his wife to see. That place was in great disorder.

Soon enough it came up to payments. I refused. Then he said he cannot believe me. At once I spoke of work. I said I can do yard work. I said I was homeless. Still always I refused money. He said they must forever have no servants, because of some very great beliefs. I told him of my straits. He said I must take more money than three pula for each one. But always still I refused. Then he said I must take tea.

He went aside to his wife to discuss. He said they can hire me. It was against her will, I could hear it, and worst as it came up to accommodation. She was in fear lest she always overtake me on the inside of her house. He said there was primus and WC in quarters, so I can stay out. As well, he said if I should go there they can cease their shame as to many Batswana homeless and no-one in that empty place. But she said she was afraid lest I arouse her every day from sleep as I set about working. He said But sometimes if I am away a gecko can drop down upon you, as we know, and this lad can chase it out. But she said Why must you forever force this thing when our food is hot?; that is the only reason you are succeeding. So at the end it was all right, but I must swear to many rules. I must never use such words as master or mistress, and many other rules as well.

So at last I was a bit safe. I could lock my goods. Mma Jarvis gave to me all such things as chairs, wardrobe, table, pots, cloths, tub, primus cooker, bed, paraffin lamp, as well as mealie, thousand cabbages, and wash-powder. Can you borrow me some books at times? I said to Rra Jarvis. You may choose every book, he said. With all pleasure he would do it. Very great-sized atlas, he borrowed me at once, and more books thereafter. Really, those people were by far too carefree, with payments time and again beyond my terms. He said I must become more fat. He explained me *chimurenga* as "great storm of people," very freely, so I said there can be many countless questions solved at last.

Endless days I worked to clean that plot and all the verge as well. I healed some trees, I know it. I scalded ants within their holes. I pulled down mistletoe from trees. Where termites pushed their nest-mud high on treesides, I scraped them to hell. I was a savior many fold. Guys passing in the road saw me watchful there and stepped onwards. Because you can go for asking jobs and just take some things. You can open cars. You can take shirts found hanging.

That man was strong for Africans, I may say. Without fail at morning he would shower curses on the news reader of Springbok station from Johannesburg, as You are murderers, or cretins, at times. Refugee guys came there rather much for drinks and meals. He was helping them.

By my terms of work, I must be always without the house. Mma Jarvis was ever painting scenes of life and must be in silence thus. So it was okay. I liked it best. I was progressing. Soon I would post a letter to my mother, I knew.

But all too soon, what! I must be made to have a house-key. They must go some days to Tuli Block on holiday. I said I rathermore have no key, yet they said I must. They praised me. I must only switch on lights at night, and water in some pots of plants. My heart was choked. If at all some goods or cameras could go missing, they would name one thief: Paul Ojang. Thrice I spoke against this. But I was forced to hold a key, in fact. Before I took that house-key, Mma Jarvis gave me oftentimes the key for post, that I must bring. All such signs of trust were scaring to me.

At my tasks withinside, I ran, to finish off and be spared. I said I must cope up. That house was pushed full. You discerned such things heaped, as, fish-traps, beer-sieves, thousand baskets, thumb harps, Basarwa aprons and pouches, some spears, stools, cameras, wood serpents and *tokoloshi*, books just tossed. I looked straight to my task.

So but when they returned back from Tuli Block and all was well, they said I must hold that key for all time. But when thrice I refused, he agreed to say okay. He said he likes me. He wished greatly he could one day arising find all government officers gone at one blow and fine boys in their place, rather. He said You shall be perm sec one day, I know it.

I was prospering, if I may say. Because he said I can make a market garden if it pleases me. So every day I was selling freely amongst cookmaids such things as marrows, tamaties, radish and lettuces. As well, he vowed he will never surcharge me as to water. I was rich, a bit. He gave me seeds he had from others.

Soon one day he said I must aid in *omnium gatherum*, great function for honoring some heroes. These too were refugees, but heroes set free from prison in South Africa. I must stand close and listen to such guys passing through Botswana. He praised those guys the most by far. First I must dig a *braai*-pit and clean about the plot as if Jesus will be at tea, he said. He must hire lights in all colors.

But at that function I served out goat-meat and *wors* countless hours, longing to be freed. At last I could go. But then I must make errands for the woman, to find some costly steel-made platters demanded by the caterers and lost. When I came to eat, it was at best bread-rolls and beet-root salad, and some guava seeds left in fluids. Turmoil! Over-drinking on beer and Autumn Harvest! That place was thronged full. I saw many guys from university, two perm secs, Europeans, refugees, Angolans, two Chinese men, Swazis. I went to hear at last.

It was hot, with motor fans switched on. It was too full in that parlor. On the outside, guys pressed to our flyscreens, in time commanding anyone to switch off some fans to help them hear Sinuka well enough. It was half-twelve.

All those South Africans stood as one, nearby the hero Sinuka, guarding and watchful always. Great unceasing arguments! Those guys were sharp, finding out very many falsehoods spoken there. I liked them.

Now at once Sinuka was repeating on one theme. He said In Azania, when the Boers are overthrown, we the Africans shall take all power over shops and mines of all kind, as to banks, as to farms, no matter if some Europeans or UK have put their money in keeping of the Boers at one time. At this, some Europeans hopped up. One said All that is mere thieving, then, and you shall forge enemies out of once-true friends, if you do so. Sinuka cried out some way.

Then I was blasted once again, because Sinuka said Yes, we shall be thieves, because you Europeans have taken Africa and all that is upon it from us over many years time, and we have studied you well and shall become as you, who are the greatest thieves under God's eyes! He said Yes, you must call us thieves, for we are graduands of long years' teaching and must be proud! He said If you steal from a thief who has tutored you, are you then a thief at all, for if you say yes, then very well! Thieves forward!

Here was danger calling me. I said I shall never follow thieves. So I went away, rather trembling.

I passed some days in fear. I said to be brave.

Soon enough God slashed me twice. I make it three days from that function. A cookmaid of the Vice Mayor came, stating I must tell you from the radio that your mother is late! What! I said, you cannot tell me so! She said It is from that program of messages of such things, they are searching out Paul Ojang. Your mother was taken by sickness, at Tsane, she said. I was crying, then, for my late mother and for being left alone as such.

Mothers, never be rash! Because one day we must recall you. And ever be watchful as to funds! I journeyed by costly transport to Tsane. At Tsane I met charges on every hand. Our herd was long sold-up, I knew, yet some men told me of two beasts taken as strays, yet she always failed to claim them at the chief's *kraal*, so they fell to him in time. She was a defaulter at the health post. I was left with medicines and rubbish. From on the hill, I saw beasts going every way upon Tsane Pan to find out water, like ants. The pan was cracked. Sand wind came over day by day. Many houses there stand empty.

I feared about my saved money at Tsane and my fear was proved. I wished only to return back from there. A pastor asked money more and more, as to burial charges. Even if a mother is a scourge to you, you must regret when she is late, it seems. I was too sad there. I must soon return to my smooth-walled housing at Seepapitso Road or become mad. I feared as to my lettuces.

It was at Kanye I said may that egg be my clue to riches. I said Jarvis must let me rear up chickens to be sold. They take little water, as they bathe in dust. I saw I could gain back some funds quite fast.

Then, I was returned back. No matter if it was on Sunday, I set to work. But in days, what! God moved his waiting blow.

Jarvis called me to come to them for sweets. Then it was told to me. I must leave them, as they must quit our nation to stay untold years in Mozambique. I fell sick at heart. I cried. It was to make a film about Frelimo and how that struggle could win out. He must go for duty. He was summoned to it. Once more I was chopped from hope, just crying, as God pleased.

Where could I turn? At night I was even retching. By one fortnight I must aid Stuttafords to pack up their goods completely and be left alone. Was I not like Shane, who only wished to be a farmer yet was forced once again to fire upon his fellowmen? Or was I not as some saints, because many saints were forced, as to marrying of pagans, or beheading, like Felicitas, by God the ruler over all this world?

Rra Jarvis came to raise my cheer some way. He said Letty is striving, ringing up some women every day to unearth a post with accommodation. For farewell, he gave me a dictionary of words.

At last a job was found out. They said I may go as yard boy for some people differing to Jarvises but yet nice. Mma said All what you do for us is just all right to us if it is your true best, but these Wrens are rich to an extent. Thus you must work to perfection, she said. I should have coveralls provided and accommodation up to a sleeping-room, but no showerplace or toilet to myself, of course. She said This Rra Wren is high director of your nation's bank and shall stay this side some five years until returning back to London, so you can be full-grown. She said As well, he can sponsor you for Capital Continuation night studies if he likes you well enough, but I am not too sure.

She advised me all kind of things, over again. Never must I purge my nostrils in my fingers. Always I must guard on bearing tales. One thing above others she said many times: I must befriend that woman, because she was very strained with bad fortune. If at all Batswana might tease or so, they were only misled. She was nice, Mma Jarvis said. She was American. Mma Jarvis bought me varied new clothing, with shoes. She said I was bonny.

Every day she gave me presents such as half-remaining foods as chutney, sunflower oil, *tamatie sous*, maizena, bread-crumbs in packets, some tins of lichees, jelly, dry soup.

Rra Jarvis brought me there. That place was risen from the dreaming brains of a thief. All about was wealth. You must enter by two gates in order. You must give in your name and reasons. You can see one man with no duties beyond tending on dogs. Another is hunting over and forth along the walks to pinch out any spear of grass to come amongst the pavements. You pass hedges made as balls and boxes throughout, many lawns, many bowers growing. You see Waygards always two and two, so that if one should chance to sleep his comrade shall report on him. Everything in that place, you must crave for. The air itself must be made sweet, by women with spray-canisters, at times.

At once Bastiaan brought me to sit withinside. He commanded tea. Bastiaan was headservant there, or captain, a Xhosa, very fierce, to me. He was like Ken Gampu. His head was shaved. He wore fine suits. He took away my letter of reference, leaving me. Those carpets were soft, to make you wish to spring about. My plate was gold-ringed. My serviette was in a bracelet.

I saw this master was one for fish and the sea. All on the walls were caught fish, as thick-through as dogs, made hard and shining. Save for pilchards, we Batswana do not trust in fish. Far in the north, the Mmbkushu are fish-eating, but we do not know them well and they are from Angola, really.

At once I was brought farther, to Mma Wren. It was by day, yet she wore dark glasses. She was white-haired and white-dressed. She discussed with Bastiaan about my letter, a time, discerning me through those dark glasses. She said Are you quiet? Because here we are quiet. It was true, because that staff was quiet-spoken, differing to the shouting and ragging staffs of houses roundabout Jarvises. She said she regretted as to my mother. She pressed my hands. She wore finger-rings and gold hair-clips. She was little. Then it was fixed. I may come and toil amongst all those treasures.

Those maids were as cruel as nurses. I alone of all Batswana in that place refused to laugh against Mma Wren
in secret. They would speak insults of her in Setswana at
any time, if only Bastiaan was not nearby, of course. They
said I must think what fanciful meaning I can say for my
surname when she shall ask me. They said she was well-
pleased when Bibiana Mathlapeng told that her name
meant "There are too many rocks in this place," and as
well when Kebonyetsala Gaolekwe told that her surname
says "You cannot do anything to God." But I said those
were true meanings. They said You are just argumental.
They said You must be fanciful and please her, she is like
a child. They said Others have done so. They said She
is ever saying we Batswana are too mean at times with
naming our children, as when Bibiana named her son
Molebi, "He who is ever staring at you." They said She
says it is not fair on children and she bothers us on this,
extremely. As well, they said Mma Wren is ever asking
why certain kinds of English first names are given, as,
Extra, or Fabric. They said She must not tell Tswana people how to put names, yet she does so. They said But we
name our children as we please, and we give names as
Beauty or Idol, if we please, so this white woman must
just cease. They said she torments them. They said You
shall see, she shall carry you *Daily News* asking why is
this man named as Icks, or Slow, or Lucifer.

In those days Mma Wren must no longer drive freely
on her own, but only go about with Bastiaan or Rra Wren.
It was because when once she was driving, she stopped in
North Ring Road but not pulling to one side, those women
said, because she wished to chase up an albino boy. They
said Mma Wren stated that this boy was over-red from
sunlight and that albinos could die thus, they must all
wear broad hats in summertime. Those women said She
is mental, that is all, she is mental. They said Now she is
held from driving, as she made commotions in North
Ring. She is bewitched, they said, she has transgressed
something, so she has become mental, and it is we alone
who must suffer. And they said The master bought that
Peugeot for a present for her alone, at one time. She fears
fires, they said.

At Wrens we were Tswana in our food: mealie and

sorghum. We must join to stamp mealie. Those women would beg and tease to make me join. Food from the table was sent for the dogs, and these women saw it, bemoaning. But worse by far was about the fruits, because Mma Wren must have filled-full baskets in every room, of apples, and bananas growing spots, and these fruits were just lost. But I said this rule was good, in fact, because those women would scheme about who is to get this or so, as to who would be favored. We were too many. As to stamping, in secret I liked it because at each stroke I fancied I am stamping down God and his snares, to become safe. When the drought came, you could not buy costly fruit, so these women raged the more. But they watched against Bastiaan, who can hear as far as birds.

Rra Wren's many books were fit for a thief, with gold letters and all such things. You cannot ask to loan such books, I knew. So I was silent. For speaking English, those maids refused me every way. They said I was tormenting them. Some Batswana tell you everything of English is just torment and that some day it shall be thrown down. At school, if you should speak Setswana in the hearing of teachers, it was told to you it would bring strokes. But that was false. Many Batswana teachers spoke Setswana in classes, with no shame. The cur Sebina told that headboys must report on Setswana-speaking at play-times or revision, but never did they. I was brave many times to say back words in English for Setswana said by older boys, but they came to hate me and said I was a traitor and scheming Mokgalagadi.

I was caring for that rose-bower above all. After midday it was allowed for staff to sleep, but I alone would not sleep on many days, but would at times be found reading in *St. Joseph*. Now, Mma Wren could as well be found in that bower, under the net-shade, with some drinks. Those maids ragged me for not sleeping as they did. Ever slowly, Mma Wren grew kind to me. She asked my name over again. She said I must sit in a chair, not upon the ground, for reading. Those maids said Why must you go that side to read?; you can read here, we have chairs if you greatly love to sit in a chair, you can do so among us. Of course, Batswana must ever love best to lie or sit at ease upon the earth, as we know. They said I was seeking favor. That was their way, always, yet all were strong Christians. Mma Wren saw I was one for books. So she said can I be most careful if she finds some precious books for me to read? She said I must never harm or mislay them, only. I said yes. Always she repeated how precious were these books to come. She would give me one at one time and I must return it back to her perfect as she gave it to me. She said these were the most precious books to a boy, she knew it. Over again I said I would be glad.

She came forth with one book. It was *Erik Noble and the Forty-Niners the Big Little Book.* It was old, from 1934, with pages breaking. It was one picture-page, one writing-page, all repeating up to the end. Many pages were spoiled with hand-writing of a name, Brian. I read that book, sweating strings lest I break some page of it. It is about the orphan boy Erik Noble. After many countless adventures and missteps, he becomes a partner of a kind man. They make a café in San Francisco, California, at the end. I must always remember those last words, *With a young Yankee watching the cash, their enterprise had to succeed.* I handed back that book unharmed. She said I must relate how I liked that book. I said In America there is very much helping of lone boys if only they are bold and glad to work their hardest, but if it is so today I am not sure. She said she knew all boys loved these *Big Littles* and she must search to find yet more, for she had another at present-time lost.

Bastiaan came to me. He said Your duties are altered, we shall say you are to work inside for training to become a steward, but it is untrue because you are too young. But Mma Wren wished me at her orders, it seems. He said she was greatly favoring me in this. Above all else, I must never put my hand to cleaning, for there would be cries unending from the house staff, but I must always say I am steward-in-training, full stop. He said Perhaps there shall be some assisting Mma Wren in cutting out of pictures from journals. But there was one room, called the sewing-room, where I must pitch up every day and see what was to be. At other times she would see to my English, with lessons. Bastiaan was crossed, I saw. He said I was to be under him alone, and the mistress and master, and never under the kitchen maids, despite them. At some times I must take meals with Mma Wren, if she commanded it. He brought me to Rra Wren and left me.

It was at night. In his private room was more to do with fish, by far, with many fishing-poles and chests of items. He came there to smoke. You must wish to drink down such sweet kind of smoke. He said the same to me as Bastiaan. I must help Mma Wren with filling of empty books. If she shall vanish at times to find out some thing, I must remain waiting with patience. He said one day I shall see her store-room, which was disgracing, with many papers and mementos confused together. I must never laugh, as she was striving to bring this room to order, but too slowly. He said You can make her prosper. He said She is collecting too many damned little items from our travels world-over. As well, he said If you can, by little, question as to if she may play a bit upon the piano that is standing silent, do so. I told him my liking as to singing and indeed all kind of music. He said I was fine. Then, I must pledge to come to him, if at all I am strained or unhappy in this. Bastiaan must always stand ready to bring me straightaway to see him soonest he was at home. He said that above all things I must pitch nothing out from our endeavors, lest at some time she discern a need of it and be cast down if it was gone. Then he praised my English-speaking as a pleasure.

Those maids said I was no more than a toy of late. I made no reply. They said she must keep her eyeglasses enchained about her neck and fix her watch to her breast with pins and as well with a chain for safety, and now she must have a follower at every step. In part, it was true. Mma Wren was forever searching up mislaid things with my help. Nothing was safe from her mislayings. Soon she stated I may search up items in her store-room and bedroom, at her order. I was uneasy and in straits, because it seemed God was trying me anew, as I could freely take some thing and only say that it was lost, full stop. At that, I am a thief, full-made. She said Your young eyes can find out every thing.

Most slowly we made four books full with many senseless pictures of small boys, all kind of mothers and fathers together with children. By little, I said Can we now and again bring in some pictures of musicians? She said it would be pleasing, and said Do you love music? I said What! I am great as to singing and all such things. I told how I wished to know music and instruments but was forced from school. I said You can see my voice. I sang two hymns.

Because at times I was idling there, I fell to more reasoning as to God's ways. When I set myself against thieving, always God punished me. And if I go near to thieving, as with Alias and Rra Jarvis for his posters, always I am saved. I saw God's doing in these endless mislayings, as a sign to me. I saw I must block this. I said perhaps if once you obey Him, He could be pleased and ask no more of you. I said if only one time God can see me a thief full-made, and see me then in straits, lamenting, He shall know His error. I said I must be as grieving mothers, or some wronged people, crying.

In those days Rra Wren said I was fine, praising me. He said I was a jewel found. I said many thinks. In fact, it was strange to me. If you discuss some theme, she could rise up flat and go from the room before you answer. Where did she go? To any place, to unknown rooms, about the drive, oftentimes to the garage, those maids told me. And I must just idle, or set to reading what is at hand. Still it was my best time. I drew her to the piano, by steps. Now she even played me tunes. She said You have fine hands for music. She said You shall study. I should one day read music freely, with her, she said. I saw she was my savior.

So it was then I knew I must be bold, and steal, or again be punished.

What must I take? To deceive God, it must be such as a schoolboy must covet, though I was not at school. It must be of worth and not a mere toy only. Because of danger, it must not be some prized possession of Mma Wren, lest they look straight and foremost to me as one who is at her side by far the most. It must be such as to be missed, yet not so greatly as to call forth police to oppress you. Slowly, I came to it.

It was a case out of leather. I saw it twice or so, in the garage. It was in behind some boards, pushed from view save for its handles at times. You must mount upon a box to feel it. This case was for a rich kind of student. It was old. Withinside, it held only some papers as letters and some crayon pictures from a child. It was not locked.

I took away that school case with ease, leaving no sign. I hid it for safekeeping in a hole prepared far off. I was unseen, I know it.

So I went to Bastiaan to say I must depart for two days, Saturday and Sunday, for a funeral at Mochudi. He was unkind, saying it was bad, as Rra Wren was gone to Maun for some days. But I said I am strained and I must. So he said he would allow it only for this, that he knew I would in all cases lead Mma Wren to say go. He said I must not stay off above two nights.

I went to Molepolole, not Mochudi as I told Bastiaan. Because I am too tall I can be in hotels. I stayed three nights at Slayer of Hunger Hotel—Mafenya Tlala Hotel. They said I must pay beforehand. I did. My saved money was fast going.

As to meals, I ate little, for proving to God I am oppressed even up to my hunger, even when on every hand they are eating chicken peri-peri and such things. One day I ate nothing. Over Sunday I ate mere soup and some ground-nuts, at most. I was just lingering in sorrow, waiting long hours in my chalet. I read *St. Joseph*. My scheme was to go at the last to visit Livingstone Tree that is in Manyana. It is where Livingstone brought God and Christ upon the Batswana by his preaching. I schemed to stand nearby that tree, all sorrowing, because such a place must be at all times under God's view. When I saw that tree, what! I saw names carved freely in its side. But I saw these were names of Europeans. I said what! they have set their names down to be cursed hereafter, why? It was surprising to me. I lingered about. I said, loud, I can hang myself from this suffering, I can hang myself to this tree, even. Slowly I went away.

Yet one day farther I stayed at Molepolole, lamenting. I broke my pledge to Bastiaan. I said God must see me faced with sacking rathermore than going freely back to that place where I am now a thief. I hid from God my scheme to put that case back, in fact, as soon as I may.

Tuesday I returned back. It was late. At once I was

trembling an amount, for I saw police about, and many vehicles. I was afraid. Many lights were switched on.

I said to the women What has happened? All within the house was coming and going, but no staff could be there, only Bastiaan. Bibiana said They say we are unworthy, yet at most we obeyed our mistress and now we shall be punished. Time and again I asked them to tell me what has happened.

They told me that days past Mma Wren came searching all about for some mislaid thing, but not as when a thing was mislaid in times past, because she would not say what was this thing, but only said over again to staff that they already know and must surrender it to her. Over again she refused to name this thing and thus aid them any way. She said it was precious. She accused them the more, if they said she was misled. She accused Bastiaan, in time, as well. In fact, she sacked him, commanding him to go away in his clothes. He was trying long hours to ring up Maun to find Rra Wren, with no success because those lines were down as always. She banished him off. She was gone mad with searching. Those women saw him go with pleasure, I know it. They hated him. They said Let him return back to white-rule South Africa, where he was reared amidst snakes.

Sunday Mma Wren came forth at sunrise to awaken them. She was quiet, no longer raging and hard. She said they must not go to church, but rather aid her in some task of importance. She said We must not store up possessions in our life, as you can find in scripture. She said you must give your goods out. She said I am punished, now I must do it.

So at once she carried out countless things to set before those women, saying to take them from the face of the earth. At times she would bear many items to them, as towels and cushions. At times she would carry them one item, down to a spoon. Those maids say they warned against it many times, but failed, but yet why did they summon friends to come from nearby? Food was carried out. Goods flew like sand across the fence: shoes, knives, a clock. At every turn, the women said Is it your order that we take this thing away? and always she agreed.

They are clever. Some guys who came said to Mma Wren
Can you carry me some tools, Mma? But those maids
crushed them to silence. They said No-one shall ask any
goods beforehand. They said She is serving God in this
way.

Those women are of differing churches. Sunday one
pastor came, and then another, seeking gifts for God. One
came with men for bearing loads. There are many tales
of men swiftly bearing off chairs and tables with no-one
hailing them to say, What! It is because they are clever
and went by the back-paths and not where cars could
mark them. And much was taken as from Monday, very
early, before Europeans rise and see from their windows.
A pastor came to thank Mma Wren for helping Africans
with enriching of their churches so as to gain level some
day with Europeans, because without such aid they must
always remain poor.

The end of taking goods came about. Some women of
one church saw too many prizes falling to another church,
and grew jealous. Always if you ring up the police they
can say you must come for us, for our transport is gone
out. So then one woman went to them by foot to force
them to return back with her. And so it was all ended.

Bastiaan was returned back with Rra Wren. He was
shamed. He became cruel. Soon Mma Wren was taken
off. They said she must stay at a house of rest at Bloem-
fontein. Bastiaan said we may not see her face, we are
unworthy, we must be driven out from that place. All
power was with Bastiaan, as Rra Wren must go to join
Mma Wren on leave for a time. When he could return
back, we could not know, we are too lowly, and culprits.

At last Bastiaan summoned me. I said What have I done
that is wrong? But Bastiaan said that only because I was
absent I was no better than the others. He said there was
no more a place for me there. He said I was hired-on to
cater for Mma Wren, in fact, because she favored me. I
saw my crime of thieving was unknown. He cursed all
staff and even fell to naming tribes for shortcomings. I
was crying. Those women begged mercy of Bastiaan, yet
still lashed him with words in secret when he said they
must depart. The officer from Labor came and said Clear
off as this man tells you, and be glad of his Christian heart

to prevent you from jail. Then those women were raging as to reference-letter they must be provided. And Bastiaan said Go to your *moruti*, your thief-pastor, and let him write for you and all others in your thief-churches, but never come to me with this matter. They said it was revenge. Many said they would complain to heaven at the Labor Office and the Office of the President as well, but if they did this I am not sure. All were sacked.

It was at night. I was pushed out. Again I must carry my goods about, lost, like ants searching. It was at Churchill Roundabout, where four roads go out and you see Holy Cross Cathedral of the Anglicans rising up before you.

I stood with burning eyes. Many people passed-in there. Cars blocked up the verges nearby. Choirs sang hymns I knew already. I saw lights beaming on some bright things. The Anglicans are rich. You can see their priests in costly robes. Always their church is built-up the highest. Over countless years these European churches saved their funds well, whilst Africans prayed in the bush, never scheming as to collections. Those Anglicans have strong-rooms.

At once I saw my onward path. I said what! I can get treasure from God's many churches. They bid you to come inside. There is always money found there. I said I can be nice, I can sing, they shall help me, even, as an orphan. I can join in choirs, I said. I can be in their bosom and then rob them freely. I can rob from collections, I said, I can rob at fetes. At pastors' houses there is endless passing in or out of women bearing tales, and I could thus find chances there. I said I shall be God's enemy and servant both in one, and nothing shall escape my hand. I said I can go farther, to great churches beyond Botswana, where you can find crosses made from gold, and shawls and clothing all with gold. I said I can pull out every thread of gold, until God shall at last cry out He wishes me to cease.

At once my heart was light.

CATHAY

Steven Millhauser

SINGING BIRDS

The twelve singing birds in the throne room of the Imperial Palace are made of beaten gold, except for the throats, which are of silver, and the eyes, which are of transparent emerald-green jade. The leaves of the great tree in which they sit are of copper, and the trunk and branches of opaque jade, the whole painted to imitate the natural colors of leaf, stem, and bark. When they sit on the branches, among the thick foliage, the birds are visible as only a glint of gold or flash of jade, although their sublime song is readily heard from every quarter of the throne room, and even in the outer hall. The birds do not always remain in the leaves, but now and then rise from their branches and fly about the tree. Sometimes one settles on the shoulder of the Emperor and pours into his ear the notes of its melodious and melancholy song. It is known that the tones are produced by an inner mechanism containing a minute crystalline pin, but the secret of its construction remains well guarded. The series of motions performed by the mechanical birds is of necessity repetitive, but the art is so skillful that one is never aware of recurrence, and indeed only by concentrating one's attention ruthlessly upon the motions of a single bird is one able, after a time, to discover at what point the series begins again, for the motions of all twelve birds are different and have been cleverly devised to draw attention away from any one of them. The shape and motions of the birds are so lifelike that they might easily be mistaken for real birds were it not for their golden forms, and many believe that it was to avoid such a mistake, and to increase our wonder, that the birds were permitted in this manner alone to retain the appearance of artifice.

[*87*]

CLOUDS

The clouds of Cathay are of an unusual purity of whiteness, and distinguish themselves clearly against the rich
lapis lazuli of our skies. Perhaps for this reason we have
been able to classify our cloud-shapes with a precision
and thoroughness unknown to other lands. It may safely
be said that no cloud in our heavens can assume a shape
which has not already been named. The name is always
of an object, natural or artificial, that exists in our empire,
which is so vast that it is said to contain all things. Thus
a cloud may be Wave Number One, or Wave Number
Six Hundred Sixty-Two, or Dragon's Tail Number Seven,
or Wind in Wheat Number Forty-Five, or Imperial Sad-
dle Number Twenty-Three. The result of our complete-
ness is that our clouds lack the vagueness and indecision
that sadden other skies, and are forbidden randomness
except in the order of appearance of images. It is as if
they are a fluid form of sculpture, arranging themselves
at will into a succession of imitations. The artistry of our
skies, for one well trained in the catalogues of shape,
does not cause monotony by banishing the unknown;
rather, it fills us with joyful surprise, as if, tossing into
the air a handful of sand, one should see it assume, in
quick succession, the shape of dragon, hourglass, stirrup,
palace, swan.

THE CORRIDORS OF INSOMNIA

When the Emperor cannot sleep, he leaves his chamber
and walks in either of two private corridors, which have
been designed for this purpose and have become known
as the Corridors of Insomnia. The corridors are so long
that a man galloping on horseback would fail to reach
the end of either in the space of a night. One corridor
has walls of jade polished to the brightness of mirrors.
The floor is covered with a scarlet carpet and the corridor
is brightly lit by the fires of many chandeliers. In the
jade mirrors, divided by vertical bands of gold, the Emperor can see himself endlessly reflected in depth after
depth of dark green, while in the distance the perfectly

straight walls appear to come to a point. The second corridor is dark, rough, and winding. The walls have been fashioned to resemble the walls of a cave, and the distance between them is highly irregular; sometimes they come so close together that the Emperor can barely force his way through, while at other times they are twice the distance apart of the jade walls of the straight corridor. This corridor is lit by sputtering torches that leave long spaces of blackness. The floor is earthen and littered with stones; an occasional dark puddle reflects a torch.

HOURGLASSES

The art of the hourglass is highly developed in Cathay. White sand and red sand are most common, but sands of all colors are widely used, although many prefer snow-water or quicksilver. The glass containers assume a lavish variety of forms; the monkey hourglasses of our Northeast provinces are justly renowned. Exquisite erotic hourglasses, often draped in translucent silks, are seen in the home of every nobleman. Our Emperor has a passion for hourglasses; aside from his private collection there are innumerable hourglasses throughout the vast reaches of the Imperial Palace, including the gardens and parks, so that the Turner of Hourglasses and his many assistants are continually busy. It is said that the Emperor carries with him, sewn into his robe, a tiny golden hourglass, fashioned by one of the court miniaturists. It is said that if you stand in any of the myriad halls, chambers, and corridors of the Imperial Palace, and listen intently in the silence of the night, you can hear the faint and never-ending sound of sand sifting through hourglasses.

CONCUBINES

The Emperor's concubines live in secluded but splendid apartments in the Northwest Wing, where the mechanicians and miniaturists are also lodged. The proximity

is not fanciful, for the concubines are honored as arti-
ficers. The walk of a concubine is a masterpiece of
lubricity in comparison to which the tumultuous motions
of an ordinary woman carried to rapture by the act of
love are a formal expression of polite interest in a boring
conversation. For an ordinary mortal to witness the walk
of a concubine, even accidentally and through a distant
lattice-window, is for him to experience a destructive
ecstasy far in excess of the intensest pleasures he has
known. These unfortunate courtiers, broken by a glance,
pass the remainder of their lives in a feverish torment
of unsatisfied longing. The concubines, some of whom
are as young as fourteen, are said to wear four transparent silk robes, of scarlet, rose-yellow, white, and plum,
respectively. What we know of their art comes to us by
way of the eunuchs, who enjoy their privileged position
and are not always to be trusted. That art appears to
depend in large part upon the erotic paradoxes of transparent concealment and opaque revelation. Mirrors, silks,
the dark velvet of rugs and coverlets, transparent blue
pools in the concealed courtyard, scarves and sashes,
veils, scarlet and jade light through colored glass, shadows, implications, illusions, duplicities of disclosure, a
profound understanding of monotony and surprise—such
are the tools of the concubines' art. Although they live
in the palace, they have about them an insubstantiality,
an air of legend, for they are never seen except by the
Emperor, who is divine, by the attendant eunuchs, who
are not real men, and by such courtiers as are half mad
with tormented longing and cannot explain what they
have seen. It has been said that the concubines do not
exist; the jest contains a deep truth, for like all artists
they live so profoundly in illusion that gradually their
lives grow illusory. It is not too much to say that these
high representatives of the flesh, these lavish expressions
of desire, live entirely in spirit; they are abstract as
scholars; they are our only virgins.

BOREDOM

Our boredom, like our zest, can only be as great as our lives. How much greater and more terrible, then, must be the boredom of our Emperor, which flows into every corridor of the palace, spills into the parks and gardens, stretches to the utmost edges of our unimaginably vast empire, and, still not exhausted, but perhaps even strengthened by such exercise, rises to the height of heaven itself.

DWARFS

The Emperor has two dwarfs, both of whom are disliked by the court, although for different reasons. One dwarf is dark, humpbacked, and coarse-featured, with long unruly hair. This dwarf mocks the Emperor, imitates his gestures in a disrespectful way, contradicts his opinions, and in general plays the buffoon. Sometimes he runs among the Court ladies, brushing against them as he passes, and even, to the horror of everyone, lifting their robes and concealing himself beneath them. Nothing is more disturbing than to see a beautiful Court lady standing with this impudent lump beneath her robe. The ladies are nevertheless forced to endure such indignities, for the Emperor has given his dwarf freedoms which no one else receives. The other dwarf is neat, aloof, and severe in feature and dress. The Emperor often discusses with him questions of philosophy, art, and warfare. This dwarf detests the dark dwarf, whom he once wounded gravely in a duel; so far as possible they avoid each other. Far from approving of the dark dwarf's rival, we are intensely jealous of his intimacy with the Emperor. If one were to ask us which dwarf is more pleasing, our unhesitating answer would be: we want them both dead.

EYELIDS

The art of illuminating the eyelid is old and honorable, and no Court lady is without her miniaturist. These delicate and precise paintings, in black, white, red, green, and blue ink, are highly prized by our courtiers, and especially by lovers, who read in them profound and ambiguous messages. One can never be certain, when one sees a handsome courtier gazing passionately into the eyes of a beautiful lady, whether he is searching for the soul behind her eyes or whether he is striving to attain a glimpse of her elegant and dangerous eyelids. These paintings are never the same, and indeed are different for each eyelid, and one cannot know, gazing across the room at a beautiful lady with whom one has not yet become intimate, whether her lowered eyelids will reveal a tall willow with dripping branches; an arched bridge in snow; a pear blossom and humming-bird; a crane among cocks; rice leaves bending in the wind; a wall with open gate, through which can be seen a distant village on a hillside. When speaking, a Court lady will lower her eyelids many times, offering tan-talizing glimpses of little scenes that seem to express the elusive mystery of her soul. The lover well knows that these eyelid miniatures, at once public and intimate, half-exposed and always hiding, allude to the secret miniatures of the hidden eyes, or the eyes of the breast. These miniature masterpieces are inked upon the rosy areola surrounding the nipple and sometimes upon the sides and tip of the nipple itself. A lover disrobing his mistress in the first ecstasy of her consent is so eager for his sight of those secret miniatures that sometimes he lingers too long in rapturous contemplation and thereby incurs severe displeasure. Some Court ladies delight in erotic miniatures of the most startling kind, and it is impossible to express the troubled excitement with which a lover, stirred to exaltation by the elegant turn of a cheekbone and the shy purity of a glance, discovers upon the breast of his beloved an exquisitely inked scene of riot and debauchery.

DRAGONS

The dragons of Cathay dwell in caves in the mountains of the North and in the depths of the Eastern sea. The dragons rarely show themselves, but we are always aware of them, for their motions are responsible for storms at sea, great waves, hurricanes, tornadoes, and earthquakes. A sea dragon rising from the waves can sink an entire fleet with one lash of its terrible tail. Sometimes a northern dragon will leave its cave and fly through the air, covering whole cities with its immense shadow. Those who have stood in the shadow of the dragon say it is accompanied by an icy wind. The tail of a dragon, glittering in the light of the sun, is said to be covered with blue and yellow scales. The head of a dragon is emerald and gold, its tongue scarlet, its eyes pits of fire. It is said that the venom which drips from its terrible jaws is hotter than boiling pitch. It is said that to see a dragon is to be changed forever. Some do not believe in dragons, because they have not seen them; it is like not believing in one's own death, because one has not yet died.

MINIATURES

Our passion for the miniature is by no means exhausted by the painting of eyelids; the art of carving in miniature is one of the oldest and most esteemed of our arts. Well known is the Emperor's miniature palace, which sits upon a jade cabinet beside the tree with the twelve singing birds, and which is said to reproduce with absolute fidelity the vast Imperial Palace, with its thousands of chambers and corridors, as well as its innumerable courtyards, parks, and gardens. Within the miniature palace, which is no larger than a small table, one can see, by means of a magnifying lens, myriad pieces of precise furniture, as well as entire sets of cups, bowls, and dishes, and even a pair of scissors so tiny that even when extended they can be concealed behind the leg of a fly. In the miniature throne room one can see a minute jade table with a miniature palace, and it is said that within this second

[93]

palace, which can scarcely be seen by the naked eye, the artist has again reproduced the entire Imperial Palace.

SUMMER NIGHTS

On a summer night, when the moon is a white blossom in a blue garden, it is good to go out of the palace and walk in the Garden of Islands. The arched wooden bridges over their perfect reflections, the hanging willows, the white swans over the swans in the dark water, the yellow and blue lights in the palace, the smell of plum blossoms, all these speak of peace and harmony, and quell the rebellious restlessness of the soul. If, on such a night, one happens to see a dark-green frog leap into the water, sending out a rainbow of ripples that make the moon waver, one's happiness is complete.

UGLY WOMEN

It is well known that the Court ladies are the loveliest in the empire, but among them one always sees several who can only be called ugly. We are not speaking of ladies who are grotesque, monstrous, or unclean, but merely of ladies who are strikingly unpleasing to our eyes. Instead of thin, arched eyebrows they have thick, straight eyebrows, which sometimes grow together; one or more of their teeth may be noticeably crooked; their noses and mouths are too large, their eyes too wide apart or close together. Since no one can remain at the palace without the consent of the Emperor, it is clear that he considers their presence inoffensive, and perhaps even desirable. Indeed, to the embarrassment of the court, he has sometimes chosen an ugly lady for his mistress. It is a mystery that teases the understanding, for to say that the Emperor is an admirer of beauty is to speak with misleading coolness. Our Emperor reveres beauty, lives and breathes in a world of beautiful objects, lavishes wealth and honor on the creators of beauty, is, despite his terrible omnipotence, entirely submissive to the beauty of a teacup, a plum blossom, a white cheek. The Empress is renowned for her delicate loveliness. How is it, then, that our Emperor can bear to have ugly women in his court, and appears even to encourage their presence? It is easy of course to imagine that he sometimes grows weary of the exquisitely beautiful women who meet his gaze wherever he turns. In the same way our court poets are advised to introduce occasional small dullnesses and imperfections into their verses, in order to relieve the hearer from the monotony of perfection. One can even go further, and grant that the beauty of our ladies has about it a high, noble, and spiritual quality that lifts it above the realm of the merely physical. But ugliness, by its very nature, draws attention to the physical. One might imagine, then, that the Emperor longs to escape from the spiritual beauty of our Court ladies and to abandon himself to the physical pleasures which seem to be promised by the ugly ladies—as if the coarseness and impropriety of their faces were an intimation or revelation of dark, coarse, improper pleasures hidden beneath their elegant silks. Yet it is difficult to see how this can be the true explanation, since the Emperor's longing for sensual pleasure may always be satisfied by his incomparable concubines. Another explanation remains. It is known that the Emperor is an admirer of beauty; there is no reason to assume that in this instance he has changed. Is it not possible that the Emperor sees in these ugly women a beauty to which we, with our smaller understanding, are hopelessly blind? Our poets have said that there can be no beauty without strangeness. One imagines our Emperor returning to his chamber from the stimulation of his concubines. From those unimaginably desirable women, those masterpieces of the art of appearance, who express in every feature of face and body the physical loveliness he has craved, he is returning to a world of Court ladies, themselves flowers of beauty who in some turn of the lip, some glance, some look of sweet pensiveness may even surpass the wholly sensual beauty of his concubines. As he passes through the corridors leading to the East Wing, he comes upon a lady and her maids. The lady has thick, straight eyebrows that nearly grow together; her nose is broad; she gives a clumsy curtsey. The ugly eyebrows, the broad nose, the clumsy gestures irritate his dulled senses into attention, and many days later, when he has passed long hours among his concubines and lovely ladies, he will suddenly recall, with a burst of excitement, those thick eyebrows, that broad nose, that clumsy curtsey, for like a beautiful woman suddenly glimpsed behind a lattice-window she will lead his soul away from the torpor of the familiar into a dark realm of strangeness and wonder.

ISLANDS

The floating islands of Cathay are most commonly found in our lakes, especially the great southern lakes, but they occur in our rivers as well. Nothing is more delightful, for a group of Court ladies walking by a pleasant riverside, than to see one of these islands floating by. The younger ladies, little more than girls, laugh and cry out, and even older and more sober women can scarcely suppress their joy. It is quite different when these same ladies are in a boat on the water, for then the island, whose motions are entirely unpredictable, is an object of great terror. Except for their motion, these islands are like ordinary islands, and the question of their origin has never been answered. Our ancient historians classified floating islands with water-animals, but we are less certain. Some believe that floating islands are a special race of islands, which reproduce and which have no relation whatever to common islands. Others believe that floating islands are common islands that have broken away; animated by boredom, melancholy, and restlessness, they follow no certain path, bringing with them the joy of surprise and the pain of the unknown.

MIRRORS

The ladies of Cathay, and above all the Court ladies, have for their mirrors a passion so intense that a lover feels he can never inspire such ardors of uninterrupted attention. The mirror of a lady holds her with its powerful and irresistible gaze, desires her to be wholly his, and in the privacy of the night encourages disrobings. What torture for the yearning and neglected lover to imagine his lady at night in her chamber, alone with her amorous mirror. He imagines the mirror's passionate and hungry gaze, which holds her spellbound; the long, searching look, deep into her treacherous eyes; her slow surrender to the act of reflection. The mirror, having drawn the lady into his silver depths, begins to yearn for still greater intimacies. Once in the glass, she begins to feel an inner tickling; she feels about to swoon; her eyes, half-closed, have a veiled and drowsy look; and all at once, yielding to her mirror's imperious need, she slips from her robe, and boldly gives her nakedness to the glass. And perhaps, when she turns her back to her mirror, in preparation for peering slyly over her shoulder, for a moment she hesitates, permitting herself to be seen and savored by the insatiable glass, feeling her skin tingle in that stern, lecherous, unsparing gaze. Is it surprising that her lover, meeting her the next morning, sees that she is pale and somewhat tired, not yet recovered from the excesses of the night?

YEARNING

There are fifty-four Steps of Love, of which the fifth is Yearning. There are seventeen degrees of yearning, through all of which the lover must pass before reaching the Sixth Step, which is Restlessness.

THE PALACE

The palace of the Emperor is so vast that a man cannot pass through all its chambers in a lifetime. Whole portions of the palace are neglected and abandoned, and begin to lead a strange, independent existence. It is told how the Emperor, riding alone one day in one of the

southeastern gardens, dismounted and entered a wing of
the palace through an open window. He had never seen
the chambers of this wing before; their decorations had
for him an inexpressible and faintly troubling charm.
Coming upon an old man, dressed in old-fashioned ceremonial robes, he asked a question; the man replied in an
accent which the Emperor had never heard. In time the
Emperor discovered that the inhabitants of this wing were
descendants of the Emperor's great-grandfather; living
for four generations in this unfrequented part of the
palace, they had kept to the old ways, and the old pro-
nunciation. Shaken, the Emperor rode away, and in the
ensuing nights paid many visits to his concubines.

BLUE HORSES

The Emperor's blue horses in a field of white snow.

SORROW

The Twelve Images of Sorrow are: the autumn moon
behind three black branches, a mirror when it does not
reflect a face, a single white plum-petal hanging from
a bough, the eyes of a beautiful lady at dusk, a garden
in summer rain, frosty breath on an autumn night, an
old man gazing at a river, a faded fan, a dead sparrow
in the snow, a lover leaving his mistress at dawn, an old
abandoned hourglass, the black form of the wild duck
against the red setting sun. These are the sorrows known
to all men, but there is a sorrow that is only of Cathay.
Our sorrow is the sorrow hidden in the depths of rich,
deep-blue summer afternoons, the sorrow of sunshine
on the blossoming plum tree, the sorrow that lies like a
faint purple shadow in the iris of a beautiful, laughing
girl.

THE MAN IN A MAZE

It sometimes happens that a child's toy, newly invented by one of the sublime toymakers of Cathay, enchants our Emperor. The toy is at once taken up by his courtiers, and for days or weeks or even months at a time the entire court is in a fever over that toy, which suddenly drops into disfavor and soon passes out of existence altogether. One such toy that took the fancy of the Emperor was a small closed ivory box, of a size easily held in the hand. The inside of the box was composed of many partitions, forming a maze. The partitions were invisible but were shown by black lines on the outside of the box. The tiny, invisible ball, which was of gold, was called The Man in a Maze. One would often see the Emperor standing alone by a window, his head bowed gravely over the little toy that he held in the palm of his hand.

BARBARIANS

Often there is talk of the barbarians who press upon us at the outermost limits of the empire. Although our armies are invincible, our fortifications impregnable, our mountains impassable, and our forests impenetrable, our women shudder and look about with uneasy eyes. Sometimes a forbidden thought comes: to be a barbarian, to sit upon a black horse with flaming nostrils and hooves of thunder, to ride swifter than fire with one's long hair streaming in the wind.

THE CONTEST OF MAGICIANS

In the shimmering and legendary past of Cathay, when history and fable were often confounded, an Emperor is said to have held a contest of magicians. From all four quarters of the empire the magicians flocked to the Imperial Palace, to perform in the throne room and seek to be chosen as Court Magician. In those days the art of magic was taken far more seriously than it is today, and scarcely a boy in the empire but could turn a peach blossom into

[99]

a dove. The Emperor, seated high on his throne in the presence of his most powerful courtiers and his most beautiful Court ladies, permitted each magician only a single trick, after which the magician was informed, by means of a folded note brought to him on a silver tray outside the doors of the throne room, whether he was to depart or stay. Those chosen to remain were lodged in elegant chambers, and later were asked to perform a second time before the Emperor, although on this occasion the performance took place in the presence of two rival magicians. Since two of the three magicians were destined to be dismissed, there was a strong air of drama about this stage of the contest, and it is said that the magicians continually sought to bribe the courtiers and Court ladies, all of whom, however, remained incorruptible. Some magicians wished to be the first of the three to perform, others longed to be second, and still others believed that the advantage lay with him who was third, and many arguments raged on all three sides of the question—quite in vain, since the order was decided by lot, the rice-leaves being drawn by the Empress herself. The one hundred twenty-eight magicians remaining after this stage of the battle were now requested to perform in pairs; and in this manner the magicians were gradually reduced to sixty-four, and to thirty-two, and to sixteen, and to eight, and to four, and at last to only two. When there were only two magicians left, one of whom was a vigorous man of ripe years, and the other an old man with a white beard, there was a pause for one week, during which the court prepared for the final match, while the magicians were permitted to rest or practice, as they pleased. At last the great day came, the lots were drawn, and the younger man was chosen to perform first. He had astonished everyone with the daring and elegance of his earlier performances, and a hush came over the court as he climbed the carpeted steps of the handsome ebony and ivory platform constructed for the magicians by the Emperor's own carpenter. The magician bowed, and announced that he had a request. He asked a member of the court to bring to him, there on his platform, the statue of a beautiful woman. He himself would gladly bring a jade or marble statue out of the ends of his fingers; but he asked for a statue to be brought to him so that there could be no question concerning the true nature of the statue. This unusual request produced murmurs of uncertainty, but at last it was decided to humor his whim; and six strong courtiers were dispatched to fetch from the Emperor's collection the statue of a beautiful woman. It was promptly done; and the beautiful jade statue stood upon the ebony and ivory platform. The magician moved his hands before the stone woman, and as the court watched in awe, the statue slowly began to wake. The jade body turned to flesh, the jade lips to red lips, the jade hair to shiny black hair; and a beautiful living girl stood on the platform, looking about in bewilderment. The magician at once robed her, and led her forth among the astonished court; she spoke, and laughed, and in every way was a real, live girl. So awestruck were the courtiers, who had never seen any trick like it before, that they almost forgot the second magician, who sat to one side and waited. After a while the attention of the court returned to the neglected magician, about whom they were now curious, for no one could imagine a more brilliant trick than the godlike deed of breathing life into inanimate matter. The old magician, who was by no means feeble, took his place on the platform, and to the surprise of all present he praised his rival, saying that in all his years of devotion to the noble art of magic he had seen nothing to equal such a deed. For certainly it was wonderful to bring life out of stone, just as in the ancient fables. He hoped, too, that a woman of such high beauty would not frown upon the praises of an old magician. At this the newly created woman smiled, and looked all the more beautiful. The old magician then bowed, and said that he too had a request: he would like the six courtiers to bring him the statue of a beautiful woman. The court was surprised at the old magician's request, for even if he had mastered the art of bringing forth a live woman from the stone, his deed could only equal that of his rival, without surpassing it; and by virtue of being second, he would seem only an imitator, without daring or originality. Meanwhile the six courtiers fetched a second jade statue, and placed it upon the ebony and ivory platform. In beauty the second statue rivaled the first, and young courtiers crowded close to the platform, eagerly awaiting her transformation. The old magician waved his hands before the stone, and slowly it began to wake. The jade arms moved, the jade lips parted, the jade eyes blinked and looked about; and a beautiful jade girl stood on the platform, smiling and crossing her smooth jade arms. The magician led her forth among the marveling courtiers, who reached out to touch her green arms and her green hair; and some said her arms were jade, yet warm, and some said her arms were flesh, but stony cold. All crowded around her, staring and wondering; and the old magician led her up to the Emperor. His Imperial Majesty said that although there were many beautiful women in his court, there was but one breathing statue; and without hesitation he awarded the prize to the old magician. It is said that the first woman grew ill-tempered at the attention showered upon her rival, and that the first task of the new Court Magician was to change her back into a beautiful statue.

LOST SONS

James Salter

A ll afternoon the cars, many with out-of-state plates,
had been coming along the road. The long row of
lofty brick quarters appeared above. The grey walls began. By the corner of the library a military policeman, his
arm moving with fierce precision, directed traffic past
a sign for the reunion of 1960, a class on which Viet
Nam had fallen as stars fell on 1915 and 1931.

West Point was majestic in the early evening. Its dignified foliage lay still. June with its heat was at hand. Beneath, the river was silent, mysterious islands floating
in the dusk. Darkened generals stood posed about the
Plain. Far out on Trophy Point a few couples strolled
past the rows of ancient guns.

In the reception area a welcoming party was going
on. There were faces that hadn't changed and others less
familiar, like Reemstma's whose name tag was read
more than once. Someone with a camera and flash at-
tachment was running around in a cadet bathrobe. Over
in barracks a number of those who had come without
their wives were staying. Doors were open. Voices
spilled loudly out.

"Hooknose will be here," Dunning insisted. There was
a bottle of Jack Daniel's on the desk near his feet. "He'll
show, don't worry. I had a letter from him."

"A letter? He's never written a letter."

"His secretary wrote it," Dunning said. He looked like
a judge, large and well fed. His glasses lent a dainty
touch. "He's teaching her to write," he said.

"Where's he living now?"

"Florida."

"Remember the time we were sneaking back to Buck-
ner at two in the morning and all of a sudden a car
came down the road?"

Dunning was trying to arrange a serious expression.

"We dove in the bushes. It turned out it was a taxi.
It slammed on the brakes and backed up. The door

opens and there's Klingbeil in the back seat, drunk as a lord. Get in, boys, he says."

Dunning roared. His blouse with its rows of colored ribbons was unbuttoned, gluteal power hinted by the width of his lap.

"Remember," he said, "when we threw Devereaux's Spanish book with all his notes in it out the window? Into the snow. He never found it. He went bananas. You bastards, I'll kill you!"

"He'd have been a star man if he wasn't living with you."

"We tried to broaden him," Dunning explained.

They used to do the sinking of the *Bismarck* while he was studying. Klingbeil was the captain. They would jump on the desks. *Der Schiff ist kaputt!* they shouted. They were firing the guns. The rudder was jammed, they were turning in circles. Devereaux sat head down with his hands pressed over his ears. Will you bastards shut up, he screamed.

Bush, Buford, Jap Andrus, Doane, and George Hilmo were sitting on the beds and windowsill. An uncertain face in the doorway looked in.

"Who's that?"

It was Reemstma whom no one had seen for years. His hair had turned grey and was thin. He smiled awkwardly.

"What's going on?"

They looked at him.

"Come in and have a drink," someone finally said.

He found himself next to Hilmo, who reached across to shake hands with an iron grip. "How are you?" he said. The others went on talking. "You look great."

"You do, too."

Hilmo seemed not to hear. "Where are you living?" he said.

"Rosemont. Rosemont, New Jersey. It's where my wife's family's from," Reemstma said. He spoke with a strange intensity. He had always been odd. Everyone wondered how he had ever made it through. He did all right in class but the image that persisted was of someone bewildered by close order drill which he seemed to master only after two full years and then with the stiffness of a cat trying to swim. He had red lips which were the source of one unpleasant nickname. He was also known as To The Rear March because of the disasters he caused at the command.

He'd been given a used paper cup. "Whose bottle is this?" he asked.

"I don't know," Hilmo said. "Here."

"Are a lot of people coming?"

"Boy, you're full of questions," Hilmo said.

Reemstma fell silent. For half an hour they told stories. He sat by the window, sometimes looking in his cup. Outside, the clock with its black numerals began to brighten. From the distance came the faint sound of a train. Lighted coaches were strung along the river. There were cries of occasional greeting from below, people talking, voices. Feet were leisurely descending the stairs.

"Hey," someone said abruptly, "what the hell is that thing you're wearing?"

Reemstma looked down. It was a necktie of red, flowered cloth. His wife had made it. He changed it before going to dinner.

"Hello, there."

Walking calmly alone was a white-haired figure with an armband that read, 1930.

"What class are you?"

"Nineteen-sixty," Reemstma said.

"I was just thinking as I walked along, I was wondering what finally happened to everybody. It's hard to believe but when I was here we had men who simply packed up after a few weeks and went home without a word to anyone. Ever hear of anything like that? Nineteen-sixty, you say?"

"Yes, sir."

"You ever hear of Frank Kissner? I was his chief of staff. He was a tough guy. Regimental commander in Italy. One day Mark Clark showed up and said, Frank, come here a minute, I want to talk to you. Haven't got time, I'm too busy, Frank said."

"Really?"

"Mark Clark said, Frank, I want to make you a B.G.

I've got time, Frank said."

The mess hall, in which the alumni dinner was being held, loomed before them, its doors open. Its scale had always been heroic. It seemed to have doubled in size. It was filled with the white of tablecloths as far as one could see. The bars were crowded, there were lines fifteen and twenty deep of men waiting patiently. Many of the women were in dinner dresses. Above it all was the echoing clamor of conversation.

There were those with the definite look of success, like Hilmo who wore a grey summer suit with a metallic sheen and to whom everyone liked to talk although he was given to abrupt silences, and there were also the unfading heroes, those who had been cadet officers, come to life again. Early form had not always held. Among those now of high rank were men who in their schooldays had been relatively undistinguished. Reemstma, who had been out of touch, was somewhat surprised by this. For him the hierarchy had never been altered.

A terrifying face blotched with red suddenly appeared. It was Cranmer, who had lived down the hall.

"Hey, Eddie, how's it going?"

He was holding two drinks. He had just retired a year ago, Cranmer said. He was working for a law firm in Reading.

"Are you a lawyer?"

"I run the office," Cranmer said. "You married? Is your wife here?"

"No."

"Why not?"

"She couldn't come," Reemstma said.

His wife had met him when he was thirty. Why would she want to go, she had asked? In a way he was glad she hadn't. She knew no one and given the chance she would often turn the conversation to religion. There would be two weird people instead of one. Of course, he did not really think of himself as weird, it was only in their eyes. Perhaps not even. He was being greeted, talked to. The women, especially, unaware of established judgments, were friendly. He found himself talking to the lively wife of a man he vaguely remembered, R. C. Walker, a lean man with a somewhat sardonic smile.

"You're a what?" she said in astonishment. "A painter? You mean an artist?" She had thick, naturally curly blond hair and a pleasant softness to her cheeks. Her chin had a slight double fold. "I think that's fabulous!" She called to a friend, "Nita, you have to meet someone. It's Ed, isn't it?"

"Ed Reemstma."

"He's a painter," Kit Walker said exuberantly.

Reemstma was dazed by the attention. When they learned that he actually sold things they were even more interested.

"Do you make a living at it?"

"Well, I have a waiting list for paintings."

"You do!"

He began to describe the color and light—he painted landscapes—of the countryside near the Delaware, the shape of the earth, its furrows, hedges, how things changed slightly from year to year, little things, how hard it was to do the sky. He described the beautiful, glinting green of a hummingbird his wife had brought to him. She had found it in the garage; it was dead, of course.

"Dead?" Nita said.

"The eyes were closed. Except for that, you wouldn't have known."

He had a soft, almost wistful smile. Nita nodded warily.

Later there was dancing. Reemstma would have liked to go on talking but he had gotten sleepy and the tables had broken up after dinner into groups of friends.

"Bye for now," Kit Walker had said.

He saw her talking to Hilmo, who gave him a brief wave. He wandered about for a while. They were playing *Army Blue*. A wave of sadness went through him, memories of parades, the end of dances, Christmas leave. Four years of it, the classes ahead leaving in pride and excitement, unknown faces filling in behind. It was finished, but no one turns his back on it completely. The life he might have led came back to him, almost whole.

Outside barracks, late at night, five or six figures were

sitting on the steps, drinking and talking. Reemstma sat near them, not speaking, not wanting to break the spell. He was one of them, as he had been on frantic evenings when they cleaned rifles and polished their shoes to a mirror-like gleam. The haze of June lay over the great expanse that separated him from those endless tasks of years before. How deeply he had immersed himself in them. How ardently he had believed in the image of a soldier. He had known it as a faith. He had clung to it dumbly, as a cripple clings to God.

In the morning Hilmo trotted down the stairs, tennis shorts tight over his muscled legs, and disappeared through one of the salley-ports for an early match. His insouciance was unchanged. They said that before the Penn State game when he had been first-string the coach had told them they were not only going to beat Penn State, they were going to beat them by two touchdowns. Turning to Hilmo, he said,

"And who's going to be the greatest back in the East?"

"I don't know. Who?" Hilmo said.

Empty morning. As usual, except for sports there was little to do. Shortly after ten they formed up to march to a memorial ceremony at the corner of the Plain. Before a statue of Sylvanus Thayer they stood at attention, one tall maverick head in a cowboy hat, while the choir sang *The Corps*. The thrilling voices, the solemn, staggered parts rose through the air. Behind Reemstma someone said quietly, "You know, the best friends I ever had or ever will have are the ones I had here."

Afterward they walked out to take their places on the parade ground. The superintendent, a trim lieutenant general, stood not far off with his staff and the oldest living graduate, who was in a wheelchair.

"Look at him. That's what's wrong with this place," Dunning said. He was referring to the superintendent.

"That's what's wrong with the whole army."

Faint waves of band music beat toward them. It was warm. There were bees in the grass. The first miniature formations of cadets, bayonets glinting, began to move into view. Above, against the sky, a lone distinguished building and that a replica, the chapel, stood. Many Sundays there with their manly sermons on virtue and the glittering choir marching toward the door with graceful, halting tread, gold stripes shining on the sleeves of the leaders. Down below, partly hidden, the gymnasium. The ominous, dark patina on everything within, the floor, the walls, the heavy boxing gloves. There were champions enshrined there who would never be unseated, maxims that would never be erased.

At the picnic the class secretary announced that of the 550 original members, 529 were living and 176 present so far.

"Not counting Klingbeil!"

"One seventy-six plus a possible Klingbeil."

"An *im*possible Klingbeil," someone called out.

There was a cheer.

The tables were in a large, screened pavilion on the edge of the lake. Reemstma looked for Kit Walker. He'd caught sight of her earlier, in the food line, but now he could not find her. The speeches were continuing.

"We got a card from Joe Waltsak. Joe retired this year. He wanted to come but his daughter's graduating from high school. I don't know if you know this story. Joe lives in Palo Alto and there was a bill before the California legislature to change the name of any street an All-American lived on and name it after him. Joe lives on Parkwood Drive. They were going to call it Waltsak Drive, but the bill didn't pass, so instead they're calling him Joe Parkwood."

The elections were next. The class treasurer and the vice-president were not running again. There would have to be nominations for these.

"Let's have somebody different for a change," someone commented in a low voice.

"Somebody we know," Dunning muttered.

"You want to run, Mike?"

"Yeah, sure, that would be great," Dunning said.

"How about Reemstma?" someone asked. It was Cranmer, the blossoms of alcoholism ablaze in his face. The edges of his teeth were uneven as he smiled, as if eaten away.

"Good idea."

"Who, me?" Reemstma said. He was flustered. He looked around in surprise.

"How about it, Eddie?"

He could not tell if they were serious. It was all off-handed—the way Grant had been picked from obscurity one evening when he was sitting on a bench in St. Louis. He murmured something in protest. His face had become red.

Other names were being proposed. Reemstma felt his heart pounding. He had stopped saying, no, no, and sat there, full lips open a bit in bewilderment. He dared not look around him. He shook his head slightly, no. A hand went up.

"I move that the nominations be closed."

Reemstma felt foolish. They had tricked him again. He felt as if he had been betrayed. No one was paying any attention to him. They were counting raised hands.

"Come on, you can't vote," someone told his wife.

"I can't?" she said.

Wandering around as the afternoon ended Reemstma finally caught sight of Kit Walker. She acted a little strange. She didn't seem to recognize him at first. There was a soiled spot on her skirt.

"Oh, hello," she said.

"I was looking for you."

"Would you do me a favor?" she said. "Would you mind getting me a drink? My husband seems to be ignoring me."

Though Reemstma did not notice, someone else was ignoring her, too. It was Hilmo, standing some way off. They had come back to the pavilion separately. The absence of the two of them during much of the afternoon had not been put together yet. Friends who would soon be parting were talking in small groups, their faces shadowy against the water that leapt in light behind them. Reemstma returned with some wine in a plastic glass.

"Here you are. Is anything wrong?"

"Thank you. No, why? You know, you're very nice,"

she said. She had noticed something over his shoulder. "Oh, dear."

"What?"

"Nothing. It looks like we're going."

"Do you have to?" he managed to say.

"Rick's over by the door. You know him, he hates to be kept waiting."

"I was hoping we could talk."

He turned. Walker was standing outside in the sunlight. He was wearing an aloha shirt and tan slacks. He seemed somewhat aloof. Reemstma was envious of him.

"We have to drive back to Belvoir tonight," she said.

"I guess it's a long way."

"It was very nice meeting you," she said.

She left the drink untouched on the corner of the table. Reemstma watched her white skirt make its way across the floor. She was not like the others, he thought. He saw them walking to their car. Did she have children, he found himself wondering? Did she really find him interesting?

In the hour before twilight, at six in the evening, he heard the shouting and looked out. Crossing the area toward them was the unconquerable schoolboy, longlegged as a crane, the ex-infantry officer now with a small, well-rounded paunch, waving an arm.

Dunning was leaning from a window.

"Hooknose!"

"Look who I've got!" Klingbeil called back.

It was Devereaux, the tormented scholar. Their arms were around each other's shoulders. They were crossing together, grinning, friends since cadet days, friends for life. They started up the stairs.

"Hooknose!" Dunning shouted.

Klingbeil threw open his arms in mocking joy.

He was the son of an army officer. As a boy he had sailed on the Matson Line and gone back and forth across the country. He was irredeemable, he had the common touch, his men adored him. Promoted slowly, he had gotten out and become a land developer. He drove a green Cadillac famous in Tampa. He was a king of poker games, drinking, late nights.

She had probably not meant it, Reemstma was thinking. His experience had taught him that. He was not susceptible to lies.

"Oh," wives would say, "of course. I think I've heard my husband talk about you."

" I don't know your husband," Reemstma would say.

A moment of alarm.

"Of course, you do. Aren't you in the same class?"

He could hear them downstairs.

"Der Schiff ist kaputt!" they were shouting. *"Der Schiff ist kaputt!"*

THE OLD LEFT

Daniel Menaker

Uncle Will is supposed to leave for Mexico next Sunday, escorted by the Blooms, a couple of retired-schoolteacher friends who are younger than he is but still of the Very Old Left. They own a house in San Miguel. They have been in my uncle's thrall ever since they did volunteer work for the settlement house he ran in Brooklyn until he retired, fifteen years ago. But today, which is *this* Sunday, Uncle Will is having his doubts. He is eighty-six now, which is old, no getting around it. He still puts in some unpaid time writing captions for the *Daily World,* and he still calls me "boy," but he doesn't make any more jokes about being middle-aged, and he has stopped saying things like, "I'd like to visit Russia when I grow up." All his doctors have been warning him that to stay in the Northeast for the rest of January and February and March would be dangerous for him. There are a lot of them—a heart specialist for his heart failure, a joint man for the arthritis in his neck and back, an ear-nose-and-throat man for his chronically inflamed sinuses, and an eye man for his aged, tearless eyes. And there are a lot of other people who from a safe distance (usually over the telephone) give advice to Uncle Will—a few old pals in the city from the Spanish Civil War, ancient progressives and their children and grandchildren, and locals and summer people up in the Berkshires, where Uncle Will lives from May through September in his big, red farmhouse. Everyone has been urging him to get out for the winter.

Still, when he called me earlier this morning, an hour or so ago, to maneuver me into offering him a ride to the dentist tomorrow, to have a bad tooth looked at, he seemed to be taking a strange pleasure in describing the swelling of his face and the pain he'd been suffering for the last couple of days. The affliction sounded like an unexpected but welcome guest whom Uncle Will would have to entertain for some time. "I don't know, Nicky," he said feebly on the phone. "If this keeps up, I'll have wings of my own by the end of the week. I won't need to take a plane anywhere."

He didn't ask me to drive him to the dentist. (He never asks me directly to do any of the small favors I do for him when he's in the city, like picking up a prescription for him on a nasty day, helping him balance his checkbook, or spending a couple of hours at his place on a Saturday afternoon while he inveighs against the evils of our system and the lies of the press—this last he pokes at me like a prospector looking for pay dirt, since I was once a re-porter at City Hall for the *Times* and now teach at Colum-bia Journalism School.) He simply asked me to remind him which number bus would take him from Chelsea, where he has an apartment in a city housing project, to Central Park West, where his dentist's office is. When I first said I'd take him, he said, "Don't be ridiculous." But I kept at it until, finally, he found the generousness of spirit to accommodate my stubborn and foolish insistence.

When I hung up, I found my wife, Patricia—not Pat, mind you, or Patty or Patsy or Trish, but Patricia—stand-ing behind me. She's got to know what's going on.

"Why can't he get someone who lives nearer to help?" Patricia said. She walked back into the bedroom, where she collapsed on the bed. "I guess nobody else has a car."

"Oh, it's O.K.," I said. "I've got a whole week of semes-ter break left with no papers to grade."

"But you were going to start on course plans for the fall tomorrow," Patricia said. She shivered and pulled her brown bathrobe—which is actually *my* brown bathrobe—around her. It turned lethally cold in New York New Year's Day—the worst cold of the century, the papers and television have been calling it, as if it were a circus at-traction—and only the bedroom in our apartment has been halfway habitable, because the living room, study, and kitchen all face the Hudson River and the keen, cold winds that rush across it and detonate on Morningside Heights.

"All that can wait," I said. "Listen, if he doesn't get

[*114*]

away now, I'm going to have to be running down to his place for the next two or three months. Besides, the Blooms think he's the cat's pajamas, and they have a separate little suite for him down there, and a doctor lives next door. And it's warm. I'd rather take him to the dentist than—"

"The cat's pajamas?" Patricia said.

Patricia is eight years younger than I am—thirty-two. We got married two years ago, when I was thirty-eight. Late. She had come to New York to be assistant curator of the Museum of Natural History's Hall of Marsupials after working at the Endicott Museum in Boston for four years, and after six years of a bad marriage to a fellow-biology graduate student, who to this day is working on his thesis at Boston University. Actually, the last I heard, he hadn't even finished the outline. Patricia introduced herself to me at the museum, in front of a sort of variety-pack diorama of extinct pouched creatures, and got me to take her out to lunch. Patricia's mother and father, who still live in Sharon, Connecticut, where she was born, are in their mid-fifties. *My* parents are in their mid-seventies, having had me, their only child, in their mid-thirties. Late again, especially for that day and age. Soon I'll have to be running up to Palisades to attend to them, just as I go downtown now for Uncle Will. And when that sadness is over, Patricia's parents will need looking after. And then it will be my turn. And then Patricia's. Before all that happens, we want to have a child or two, to balance the future with a little youth and hope.

Anyway, I have a repertoire of antique expressions, like "spooning" and "bub" and "the cat's pajamas" that I learned from Uncle Will or my parents, and that Patricia finds quite hilarious. When I use one of them, or idly sing some vintage popular tune, like "The Band Played On," or "Sleepy Time Gal," Patricia raises her eyebrows and looks at me as though one of her fossils had suddenly come to life and turned up in her apartment. It's all very funny, but often at those moments I get the feeling that Patricia doesn't really know me and never will—the kind

[*115*]

of feeling that until she came along and put me in her pocket had been strong enough to give me a secret excuse for not settling down with anyone. You don't stay unmarried until you're thirty-eight unless you think you've got secrets.

It's Sunday night, and Patricia and I are eating dinner in front of the television set in the bedroom, wishing we could join the little English girl who with her family is trying to make a go of it in Kenya. It looks very warm in Kenya. The temperature in New York today never got above ten, and now it's five, and the windows in all the other rooms are covered with ice, especially the kitchen, where the water that boiled off while I made spaghetti, under Patricia's watchful eye, reappeared quickly as a thick rime on the frigid glass. While the spaghetti was cooking, I went into the living room and with a table knife scraped out a peephole on one of the windows there. On the river, five freighters had dropped anchor during the day; we assumed it was because the ice farther north was impassable. When I peered out, the freighters all had their deck lights on, and they looked like a line of stores in a shopping mall. It must be frustrating for the men on board, who most likely became sailors because they wanted to stay on the move, to sit paralyzed in the middle of what they probably thought was nowhere. Each ship was surrounded by a flange of ice, like a ballerina's tutu, and just before sunset they all pivoted in a cumbersome half pirouette as the tide turned.

Now the little girl is going to get an old Dutch trekker to help her family and their neighbors kill a leopard that has been skulking around their homesteads. "I think it's rather important," she says to the grizzled hunter as she gives him the note from her father. She is handling him as if he were the child and she the adult.

The phone rings in the hall. I go out and answer it and reclose the door, to keep the warmth in.

"Well, where are you, boy?" Uncle Will says, in a weak voice.

"I'm here at home—what do you mean?" I say.

"Well, it's nine-thirty. Aren't you supposed to pick me up for the dentist now?"

"But that's tomorrow morning, Uncle Will." The door opens behind me. Patricia, *semper vigilis*.

"Is it morning or night?" Uncle Will asks.

"Night."

"Oh, God, I'm all balled up. I took a sleeping pill. I think I did. But that was at night. It's crazy."

"It's nighttime now, Uncle Will. You probably took the pill and woke up, and now you're confused."

"Well, this is a fine fettle of kish. O.K., boy, see you tomorrow. If you'd just quit calling me at all hours, maybe I could get some rest."

"Didn't take enough to finish the job, huh?" Patricia says after I hang up. "I didn't mean it, I didn't mean it."

"Why aren't you in there keeping an eye on the leopard?" I say.

"I brought you this blanket in case you had to stand out here for a long time," she says.

Uncle Will and I are waiting for the elevator outside his apartment, on the twenty-third floor. His black overcoat hangs on his small frame like a hand-me-down, and his big bald head looks too heavy for the rest of him. He's wearing his jaunty brown beret. Only artists and Communists wear brown berets. His jaw is badly swollen, I must admit, and he seems weak and still confused, and I can understand a little better how he might fear the prospect of a long trip. He took forever to get ready to leave for the dentist, as I expected he would. In his apartment, he picked up a set of keys, looked at it as though it were a Martian artifact, put it down again, and picked up another. He put on and then took off two pairs of gloves before settling on a third. He gave me a letter he wanted to mail and a little later spent five minutes looking for it, before I figured out what was going on. He's forgetful, of course, but I'd never before seen him so baffled by ordinary tasks. And his place seemed unutterably lonely, with its north view of the tall slabs of Midtown skyscrapers, the desolate West Side, and, farther to the west, the river.

[*117*]

It is clear and stunningly cold outside, and far up the river I could make out my five freighters, motionless amid the rubble of ice washing down from somewhere north of the Tappan Zee Bridge, north of my parents' house. And inside, every object—the small upright piano, the television set, the pots and pans in the kitchen, the furniture, the desk top with its windfall of little reminder notes—seemed brushed with the dust of a lonely old age.

The elevator arrives, but instead of getting on, Uncle Will turns around and walks back to his door.

"Where are you going now?" I say.

"Timbuktoo—where do you think?" he says.

He lets himself in and reappears almost immediately with a small black leather bag.

"You look like you're about to make a house call," I say. "What have you got in there?"

"Wait-and-see pudding," he says.

Finally we get down to the street. Just before we reach the car, a terrific gust of wind comes along and nearly sends Uncle Will sprawling into a dirty, icy snowbank. I reach out to steady him, and am surprised at the raptor-like strength with which he grasps my arm. "Aren't you ashamed of yourself—pushing an old man," he says, shading his eyes against the sun. I open the door for him, and he eases himself into the front seat as if he were danger-ous cargo, I go around to the driver's side, and we're off at last.

Traffic is slow. Pedestrians, bundled up as round as onions, are crossing against the lights because they can't bear to stand still in the raw, blustery weather. For no particular reason that I can see, Uncle Will starts a story about my mother and father's wedding. We stop at a red light, and I look over at him and see that he is nearly enveloped by the bucket seat. His eyes are far away. I think I know this story—these twelve stories, I should say. "Well, your father did get nervous after all," Uncle Will says. "He couldn't seem to forget that Emily's father didn't approve of the marriage. I'd gotten to know the old man—we had become good friends—and I can assure you it wasn't because our family was Jewish or radical or anything like that. No, it was because your father was so handsome and charming that he was kinda spoiled, and the old boy wasn't sure how responsible he would be as a husband." I was right. I do know this complicated tale, almost by heart. It used to be that Uncle Will's stories enchanted me, even after I learned that they involved considerable embroidery. He had a way of making me and himself and the rest of my family seem colorful and funny and sometimes heroic, of endowing our lives with a kind of shape and meaning. That bright gift has become tarnished by the garrulousness of age, and I often find myself daydreaming like this instead of listening. "Oh, Emily was a knockout herself," Uncle Will says. "But she was bright and serious besides—a most remarkable gal, as she still is. So, as I was saying, your father was so nervous that he took a flask with him when I drove him to the church, and"

My mother's parents will watch in shock as my father takes a swig from a flask while Uncle Will drives him past the church. Later, Uncle Will's role as peacemaker will loom larger and larger, until he has become the principal figure in the marriage. It is as if he had married the marriage. The enchantment has given way to a kind of desperate self-reassurance. Maybe it was that all along, only better disguised.

We stop for another light at Fifty-seventh Street. Uncle Will has come to the end of a chapter, and, in case I think he has finished, he utters a drawn-out "So," as if he were beginning a new verse of the kind of old-time ballad that would cause Patricia's eyebrows to rise.

"There's no reason why this should keep you from going away," the dentist tells Uncle Will as we're about to leave his office. "Barring complications, of course," he adds, peering over his eyeglasses for admonitory effect. The catch is that Uncle Will will have to have three more appointments during the week.

We are standing at the elevator, when Uncle Will turns to me and says, "Are you in a hurry?" I say no. "Of course you are," he says. "But you're just going to have to hold your horses. I have some private business to attend to. Wait here." He takes from me the little black bag that he had almost forgotten to bring along this morning and totters back down the hall toward the dentist's receptionist. I follow him. He puts the bag down on the receptionist's desk, opens it, and takes out a clear plastic bag containing four or five potatoes. "Something for you from the country," he says to the receptionist, a West Indian woman with an extremely reserved manner. She breaks into a delighted smile, as if she'd just been named Queen of the Bahamas and were being presented with the crown jewels, and thanks Uncle Will profusely. What is private about this? Is it that he has no potatoes for me? Or did he trick me into following him? When he turns around and sees me standing there, he says, "Well, if it isn't Mr. Nosy Parker."

I returned from Uncle Will's after four. I did some shopping, went home, and in the face of three more such dental odysseys fell asleep. When Patricia came home from work, she woke me from a dream in which I was trying to drive a Galapagos tortoise to Mexico in a truck that wouldn't start moving because vines and tendrils, anchored to huge rocks under the surface of the soil, were growing out of its sides and tires. I got up, and Patricia and I huddled together in the kitchen for warmth while I made some salad and some saffron rice and cleaned and sautéed the shrimp I'd bought on the way back from putting the car in the garage. Patricia coached me on the rice and the shrimp.

Once again, we are eating in the bedroom. The outdoor-indoor thermometer in the living room says four and fifty-two, and the blanket that Patricia hung over the door to the living room is stirring in the draft like a ghost's robe. The freighters are still moored there, in the middle of the river, pointing upstream after another imperceptibly slow tidal sweep.

"Nosy Parker?" Patricia says quizzically, after I describe the potato episode for her. "Is that some kind of Australian slang?"

"And on the way back to his place," I go on, like a witness warming to his own testimony, "he took a half an hour to explain to me how he had managed to persuade someone to participate in the sixties antiwar demonstrations."

"It's going to be a rough week," Patricia says.

"He told me how he had made this person read the *Daily World* and practically dragged him to the Moratorium marches."

"How extremely annoying that must have been for the person," Patricia says.

"The trouble is, this whole conversion story was a complete fabrication, because it was me he was talking about."

"Oh, no!"

"He just sat there and bald-facedly said, 'And then, Nicky, don't you remember, I made the train reservations for both of us, because I knew you'd end up doing the right thing.'"

"And did you correct him?"

"I said, 'Look, Uncle Will, oddly enough I happened to be inhabiting my own body at the time, and I can tell you that I didn't read the *Daily World* and I took a bus to Washington all by myself."

"And what did he say?"

"He said, 'I'm surprised at you, boy. I didn't know you had such a bad temper. To say nothing of your memory.'"

"Yes, it's a wonder he can put up with you," Patricia says.

Patricia was right. It has been a rough week. A rough six days, I should say, since today is Sunday. Uncle Will takes off for Mexico in a few hours. I mean, he's supposed to. Every day he has told me that he doesn't think he's going to make it, even though the swelling in his jaw has gone way down and he has complained about his pain only when he remembered to. I'm lying here in bed trying to figure out why he's dragging his heels up to the last minute like this, especially since many past winters have seen him depart, with no louder complaint than "I

don't really want to go but they're begging me," for a stay
with one of his old Progressive friends who long ago gave
up New York's ideological and climatic extremes for
Arizona, California, and Mexico. The only thing I can
come up with is that for the first time in his life, he really
believes that he's not too far away from death, and that
he wants to die at home. I think of New York as his Krem-
lin, and that if he dies somewhere outside its walls he
will have been caught out in some kind of geographical
revisionism.

He has also been warning his escorts for the trip, the
patient Blooms, that he might decide to stay behind.
Every night he has called them and every night they have
called me, to ask me what I think the chances are. My
father has been calling me, too, to ask the same question
and to apologize for being too old to be his brother's
keeper, and so have some of Uncle Will's other friends.
I've been urging the trip on him—quietly and subtly, I
thought, until Friday, after his last dentist appointment.
When I dropped him off and promised to go back down
this morning and help him pack if he decided to go, he
said, with an edge of bitterness, "You can't wait to see the
last of me, can you?"

That was merely the most direct evidence that Uncle
Will had put me on trial. During the week I've been told
that the CIA is solely responsible for the unrest in Poland,
that my interest in food is probably a sign of moral de-
generacy, that members of the Moral Majority shouldn't
even be allowed to speak, and that it's a crime to let
people have private cars in the city—this last just after
we'd driven past a subway station with a token line that
for some subterranean reason extended up the stairs and
halfway down the block.

We were on our way to pick up some Percodan that the
dentist had prescribed for Uncle Will. I'd bet it was that
Percodan, in combination with a Seconal, or one of the
other narcotics that Uncle Will has on hand and on occasion dips into at the wrong time of day, that caused
Thursday's frightening Unscheduled Appearance. It was
the coldest day so far, and the only one that held any

promise of being uncle-free. Even the bedroom was cold, and to be able to sit still and read I'd not only put on many layers of clothing but wrapped myself in Patricia's voluminous Icelandic-wool shawl. At about four-thirty, having stuffed myself into an armchair and feeling like somebody's granny, I got a call from Uncle Will's dentist. He said that Uncle Will had just shown up, looking woozy and pale, for a nonexistent appointment. Had he left again? Yes.

Oh, terrific! Uncle Will, who shunned taxis as if they were as retrograde as royal litters, was out there somewhere, stunned by drugs, staggering through the frozen twilight to catch a bus that would probably land him in front of a gutted tenement in the South Bronx. Even if he got the right one, he had a tough two-block crosstown walk at the other end against the cutting Arctic winds to get to his place.

Patricia got home a little after five, her nose and ears as red as stoplights. When I told her what was going on, she looked utterly stricken. "That poor old man," she said.

"Poor old man my ass," I said. "He's doing it so that he'll get sick and won't be able to leave. He's doing it to make us worry about him. God forbid I should go one day without him at the center of my attention." But in my mind I saw him fighting his way through the deepening gloom of Chelsea, going slower and slower, as if in a dream, and finally freezing in his tracks in the midst of his abstractly beloved poor, his hand up to hold his thin and pitifully rakish brown beret against the wind. I only hoped that his eyes were filled with euphoric visions of a world without taxis or tuxedos, that his ears were ringing with the "Internationale," and his soul was brimming with joy as Marx and Engels, their beards even more magnificent than they had been in life, gathered him from the dark streets and into the bosom of a stateless, profitless, Godless paradise.

Together, Patricia and I, fat with clothes, paced the bedroom waiting till it made sense to start calling him at home. Then I dialed him every five minutes for half an hour, and just before I was going to hang up and call in the police to start looking for a petrified Communist with the *World* folded into the pocket of his overcoat, he picked up the phone. He was all right.

I get to Uncle Will's place at about nine. The limousine that the Blooms have hired to pick him up and then them for the trip out to LaGuardia is due at ten. I knock on Uncle Will's door and let myself in with the set of keys he gave me a long time ago, "so that the undertaker won't have to break the door down," as he put it. He is sitting in his living room reading the Sunday *Times,* which his neighbor, a Puerto Rican woman he has been trying to indoctrinate for ten years, bought for him on her way back from early Mass. He hasn't done any packing.

"What are you doing here, bub?" he says to me, looking over his glasses. "You were supposed to call first."

"I decided to take matters into my own hands," I say.

"You're just going to ship me off, huh? Well, I'm sorry, Nicky, but I think I may not be up to it. I was just about to call the Blooms."

"Where's your suitcase?"

"Listen to him," Uncle Will says.

"You're going; I've decided for you," I say. I find a large leather suitcase in a closet off the hall between the living room and the bedroom. I take it into the bedroom and open it on the bed, which is made, and neat as a pin. "I'm starting with your delicate underthings," I call to Uncle Will. "If there's anything you think you're going to have particular need of in Siberia, you better let me know."

I hear Uncle Will shuffling in the hall. He stands in the doorway to his bedroom and watches me as I open one of the drawers in his dresser, a handsome old thing, mahogany, and almost as tall as its proprietor.

"So the Cossacks have finally arrived," Uncle Will says. "Look on the top of the dresser. I found it in my desk the other day."

I do, and there is a silver-framed picture of me from my college graduation, looking as though I had nothing more to learn.

"Too bad you've regressed so badly since then," Uncle Will says.

"I'm not the only one," I say, beginning to pack.

"O.K., this has gone far enough," he says.

I straighten up and face him. "Listen, if you can take four hours in no degrees traipsing all over the city and waiting for buses and giving your relatives heart attacks, you can sit on a plane for five hours to Mexico."

"You know what's best for me, do you?" he says.

"That's right."

"You don't."

"Oh, all right, I give up," I say. I start to unpack the few things I've put in the suitcase.

"Don't sulk," Uncle Will says.

"Well, it's ridiculous."

"Everyone is just trying to get rid of me," Uncle Will says, with not quite enough irony.

"I'm not," I say, and slam the drawer closed. "I'm trying to keep you."

Uncle Will scrutinizes me as if he were trying to read some complicated meteorological instrument. "Well, then," he says, "the least you could do is use the right suitcase. It's in the closet behind you."

"Someday you will drive me as crazy as you already are," I say, wheeling around and snatching the other suitcase from the closet.

"When you're finished in here," Uncle Will says, "you can go into the kitchen and pack the potatoes."

It's Sunday night, and Patricia and I are having dinner in front of the TV again, watching the apparently endless series about the masterful little English girl. We turned it on a bit late, and I'm having trouble distinguishing one young frontiersman with a mustache from another. Actually, there is a dark one with a mustache, a blond one with a mustache, and a blond one without a mustache. Patricia flattered me into watching the show by telling me that the dark one looked like me. Anyway, the wife of one of these men is having an affair with another of them, probably because she can't tell them apart, either. It's all too much for me, and to keep from eating too fast in the presence of narrative confusion and the absence of conversation, I get up and walk out to the living room. It became habitable again this afternoon, with the day's rising temperatures and falling winds. In fact, when I got home from Uncle Will's, at about one, after Uncle Will was picked up by the Tel Aviv limousine service (which he grumbled about, because of the Zionism implicit in its name), I found Patricia in the process of reclaiming the front part of our apartment. Sun was streaming in the living-room windows, and Patricia, having dusted and swept and watered all the plants, which seem to have flourished in the chilliness, was playing hymns on the piano.

"Did he get away all right?" she asked.

"Yes—barely," I said.

"What a relief. Well, he's probably over Missouri right now, making them earn their wings."

"I had to convince him that I wasn't just trying to get him out of my hair. I told him it was only because I cared about him. The thing is, I'm not sure it's true."

"Of course it's true," Patricia said. She turned back to the piano and started picking out "After the Ball."

"When did you learn that?" I said.

"I heard you humming it when you were making the marinade last night," she said. "It's pretty. What's it called?"

Now I'm standing in the dark at the window. Patricia comes and stands beside me. She kisses me on the cheek. "It's nothing but shots of water buffalo right now," she says. "Look—there's another freighter way down at the end of the line. Can you see it?"

"So there is," I say.

"If this thaw keeps up, they'll probably leave soon."

"I hope so," I say. "They're beginning to get on my nerves."

SAKS FIFTH AVENUE

Leon Rooke

A woman called me up on the telephone. She was going to give me twenty thousand dollars, she said. I said come right over, I'm not doing anything this evening. Then I went back into the living room where my wife was, seated on the sofa with her nail files and paint, painting her nails. I wanted to keep it to myself for a bit. I strolled around, pawing the knickknacks, glancing now and then at myself in the mirror. I was feeling pretty breezy.

Twenty thousand, I thought. Holy Christ!

Those knickknacks were really dusty; I had to go in and wash my hands. While I was in there, in the bathroom, I splashed on a little cologne and smiled at myself. There are going to be some changes around here, is what I told myself. These old mirror tiles got to go.

The old lady looked up. She'd finished her left hand, which she always does first, God knows why. Her nails were the vilest color I ever saw—dried blood. What they call Songbird Red in the ads. Songbird Red: how about that? It's her favorite color for nails. Also, she says it protects them, and keeps her from chewing.

So she looked up. "You're smirking," she said. "God, I hate it when you smirk. Why don't you go get us a beer?"

I went into the kitchen and got the beer.

"Thanks," she said. "You look like you swallowed a monkey. It's disgusting. You disgust me, Cecil." She folded her fingers over and blew on the songbirds. Then she fluttered her fingers. I watched her do it. That's a pretty sexy act, that nail-blowing act. It's about as sexy as anything I can imagine. Seeing old Coolie blow on her nails is enough to make me forgive her for all of her sins, including how she talks to me.

Coolie, I forgive you.

Coolie, you set my heart a'racing.

Coolie, let's go to bed.

Silly, but that's how it is. I was really feeling mellowed out.

"Well?" she said. "Why the honey-licking grin? Why don't you take a walk? Polish your shoes, do something! You're full of yourself this evening. God knows why, after the way you behaved last night."

She said a lot of stuff like that. Once she gets going you never know when she's going to wind down. I figure she doesn't even hear herself. She talks to her mother—to her mother and her girl friends—that same way. They never slow down. They don't even hear each other.

"Stop pacing, Cecil," she said.

I got out my shoes and the polish box. We keep the polish—the white and the neutral, blacks and red and tans, and a tin of Arctic Dubbin that must have been in there fifteen years—in a thick white cardboard box that says Saks Fifth Avenue. I always look at that box. I try to figure out what must have come in that box. How we came to have it. It's one of the mysteries of my life, that box. I look at it and sometimes wonder if old Coolie hasn't had a life I don't know about.

That's deep, deep business, but I get that way sometimes. I can be watching TV for instance, the old prime time, and right out of the blue that thought will come to me: how'd we get that box? Where did it come from? What was in it? Sometimes I'll look up and find the show ending, and I've been thinking about that box the whole hour.

"Can you believe it!" Coolie will say. "Why do they show trash like that? Wasn't that the most impossible crap you ever saw?"

"I don't know, Coolie," I say. "That car chase was pretty good. You got to admit that car chase was pretty good."

She gives me this level gaze. "You are totally without taste," she says. "They make this crap for imbeciles like you."

I mention this box business as an example of the kind

of secret life that some of us have. How you can pass old
Joe Blow on the street, have a conversation with him, even
a real interesting one, and then you walk away wondering what the heck either of you said.

I mean we don't even hear each other.

So I got out the box. I couldn't decide which pair
needed doing, the loafers or the old cowboy boots. None
of them really needed it. What the loafers needed was
new heels.

"These heels are worn down," I told Coolie. "Look at
these heels."

She didn't look.

"How long have I had these shoes?" I asked her. "I bet
I had these shoes a good ten years. Did I ever ask you
where this Saks box came from? That one's going to drive
me crazy if I don't figure it out."

"Would you shut up?" said Coolie. "Would you please
hush your mouth?"

She'd gone back to painting her other fingers. She had
her tongue between her lips and sat all bunched over,
scrunched up tight, with her right hand spread out over
her knees and this look of utter concentration on her face.
I'd noticed that tongue before. Usually she's biting down
on it with her teeth, the upper lip curled back, but tonight she just had it hanging there. Squinting, because
she had her contacts out. She was wearing this pink gown
I got for her one Christmas Eve at K-Mart, and she had
it flung back away from her knees so no paint would get
on it. None of that Songbird Red.

It had already got pretty grimy, that gown. I don't
think she's washed it once. I find this odd, and maybe a
little bit out of character, her always wearing that filthy
gown, because she's got this idea she's the sharpest dresser
in town. "And on my budget!"—is what she's always
saying.

"Would you stop looking at me!" she says now. "Would
you stop it! Would you put a lid on it!"

What I figure is it's just like Coolie is. It's how she
talks. Say when she's with her girlfriends or with her

mother, she doesn't hear herself or them. They don't either. I've never understood a word, not a word, any of them have said. You come into the room and they are all eating cake and clattering cups and all going at once. Not even a pause for breath. It beats me. I'm really fascinated by it.

"What did they say?" I'll ask her once everyone has gone. "What were you talking about?"

She'll give me her withering look. "Oh you're such a dope," she'll say. "Oh, Cecil, you are the world's prize dope. Don't concern yourself. Go on with your life. Go out and rake the yard."

Maybe I am a dope. Maybe they do hear each other. But I got my doubts. I'm going to hold on to my doubts. I figure it's like that gown. She doesn't *know* how grimy that gown is. To her, all that dirt is invisible. She'd be mortally offended if I took a notion to drop hints. "*Are you calling me dirty, Cecil! Are you saying I am unclean!*" No, she grabs that gown off the hook every evening, she whips it on and comes running downstairs, and that's the end of it.

"Dammit, Cecil!" she says now. "Stop staring! Haven't I told you? I'm going to throw this bottle at you!"

That bottle. That little bottle of nail polish. What I really wanted was for that bottle to spill over, dribble over her knees and down her leg and spot the carpet. Spot it real nice. Then when people ask me what color that carpet is I could say, well, some of it is Songbird Red. Some of it is.

Coolie would kill me, but I'd say it anyhow.

A little drama, you see, is what I wanted. A bit of cold, hard action. For if old Coolie accidentally knocked over that polish she'd leap up screeching, turning over tables and slamming the knickknacks about, and go on flapping her arms for a full ten minutes.

That's how Coolie is. Pretty high-strung. I love it when old Coolie goes into her screeching routine.

Those little bottles are insane. That's what I think. Big white cap built like a finger, with a nail two inches long.

Painted Songbird Red. Dried blood. Quite a knickknack
itself, that bottle. I sat there watching her dab the color
on her nails, wondering how many of those little bottles
it would take to paint the house. How *long* it would take,
using that stupid brush. What the house would look like
done up in a dynamite Dried Blood. Songbird Red.

About fifty million, I thought.

Take about twenty-seven years.

Coolie flipped the gown up over her knees. Groaned.
She figured I had been staring at her naked knees. Getting
an eyeful of the famous Coolie legs. Getting ideas.

"Last night," she said. "Last night. We just won't speak
of last night."

She gave me this long look. Long, *mean*, and intense.
"No," that look said. "Last night is not to be spoken of.
We'd best, both of us, forget last night."

She was right, too. Last night we'd had a bit of erotica
around here. A dab of it. Pretty high-powered stuff, too,
for a while. Kissing and fondling—hell, *rapture*, if you
want to know the truth.

"Kiss me, Cecil! Kiss me till my mouth bursts into
flames!"

A *hot* time, I'm saying, and straight out of right field.
She came in at five, said, "Cecil, mix us a drink!" At ten
after, she said, "Lead the way." A minute later there's that
"mouth into flames" line. And no doubt about it, either.
Sparks all over the place. Erotic *art*, for God's sake. Then
the phone rings. Coolie snatches it up. "Not now!' she
says. She starts to slam it back down and is already rolling
into me, but the voice is chattering on. "What?" says
Coolie. "What?" And she's got that phone back at her ear.
"Six glasses for fourteen ninety-five? Long-stemmed! Gold-
rimmed! That's unheard of! You're sure?"

But not only glassware, it seems.

"Fur coats at half price! *Shoes*! Did you say *shoes*!"

I roll away. Reach for something to read. There's *Redbook*. Well, by God, I'll read *Redbook*—that's what I say
to myself. It's a jam-packed issue, too. I could spend a
month just turning the pages.

"Blues and greens!" Coolie says. "They've got them in blues and greens! At twelve eighty-*eight!* Jesus, Mother!"

So I get up. I have a long shower. I go downstairs and make myself a roast beef. I have four or five hard drinks. I sponge the counter. Get the garbage taken out. Read the paper.

"I've got to go, Mother," I hear Coolie saying. "Cecil's sulking."

Half an hour later they are still going strong. Not even hearing each other.

Well, it's getting dark. It's way *past* dark. Heck, in another minute or two it will be morning. But they are still going at it.

So I get dressed. I get on the old cowboy boots and go for a walk. All over the neighborhood. Maybe ten or twelve miles. When I get back old Coolie is standing in the open doorway. She's got on her grimy robe. She's patting her foot.

"You sonofabitch!" she says. And she whirls and strides away.

No. We best not speak of last night. We best let that sleeping dog stay where he is.

What I say is: Thank God for the nail polish. That little act, for the moment, has taken care of both our emotional needs.

I checked my watch. The woman on the phone had said she'd be over about eight. Give or take a few minutes. She'd be bringing the money with her. Every last dollar.

I was thinking I might mention this to Coolie. I was thinking she might want to run a comb through her hair. Maybe step into that hotshot pantsuit she got at Zellers. Got for practically nothing, I might add. What they did was they had this big flashing green light went off every hour, and if you were one of the first five thousand to rush over in the next five minutes then you could get this great pantsuit for practically nothing. The Green Light Special, they called it. Coolie got two of them, one black and the other a kind of orange. I hadn't seen her wearing that black one yet. I figured it either didn't fit—too tight in the hips is what it usually was—or she was saving it for something special. Tonight it might be just what the doctor ordered. She'd want to look snazzy for that woman coming over with the money.

I was going to say something along these lines, but Coolie beat me to the punch. She got in her two bits first.

"Supper tonight was terrible," she said. "You can't do casseroles. I wish you wouldn't even try. Your cooking has sure gone downhill. I've been sitting here thinking of what you cook and what I let go into my stomach, and the whole thing makes me sick. I can't bear to think of it. Christ, for once can't you follow a recipe?"

My face went a little hard at this. I'm touchy about my cooking. There was nothing wrong with my casserole.

Anyway, she ate it. Had seconds, too.

"I mean it," she said. "If I eat another casserole in this house I will puke. I will. I think I will die."

She started that nail-blowing act again. She'd put on a second coat.

Bless you, Coolie, I thought. You are such a wizard.

She straightened her two hands up in front of her face, flipped them over, flipped them back, then shot out her arms and bent her wrists and squinted long-range at those fingers. Then she shook them.

She kept on doing that.

I shaded my face and watched. It was better than TV. It had prime time beat by a mile. I was thinking of bones. Thinking of a woman's bones and how old Coolie could fold her hands down until they practically lay alongside her wrists. Fold them back the same. Supple as a shoe rag.

Well, they are contortionists, that's what they are.

Wizards, from head to toe.

"God, you make me sick," Coolie said. "I don't know what I am to do with you. My mother's right, you know. You know what she said? Only the other day she said to me, 'Coolie, what your husband needs is a pacemaker. A good pacemaker, secondhand.' Seriously, that's what she said. 'Otherwise,' she said, 'otherwise, someone is going

[*133*]

to mistake him for dead. You're going to come home one day from work and find men in white coats rolling him out of there.' It's true, too, Cecil. You're going to be mistaken for the dead."

She said that, but she wasn't looking at me. First she was looking at the bottle, then at her feet, then at the nail polish again. She was trying to figure out whether she wanted to paint her toes. She couldn't decide. Should I or should I not? She has this little argument with herself about once a week. Sometimes the toenails win and sometimes they lose.

"What do you think?" she said. "Should I?"

If I say "Don't," then she will paint them. If I say "Do," she will look at me as if I've lost my mind. If I hem and haw over the question, then she's liable to storm out. Or sulk. She's liable to say I'm the most offensive, scatter-brained, illogical, indecisive and demented person who ever drew a human breath. She'll wonder aloud why she bothers to talk to me.

What I say is: Talk away. I'm not listening. I'm not hearing a word you're saying.

What *are* you saying, Coolie? Lay it on me, sweetheart.

Tonight I really wasn't listening. Coolie's toenails, painted or not, lovely as they are, wasn't something I felt like dwelling on. I was looking out our front window. We had the curtains back and I was looking out there. It was dark, but I still thought I could see him. I could see the boy out there plain as day, just as I'd seen him earlier. This little kid. Maybe three years old. Certainly no older than that. I had been going about the room, straightening up things, getting rid of what Coolie calls the clutter, and there he was. This little kid walking by. He had on this blue sunsuit and this white shirt with a funny collar, and these little sandals—thongs, I guess they are. They were flip-flopping up and down and once or twice he'd lift his feet and they'd fall off. He had on this kind of hat, but even so you could see he had a nice head of golden hair. And this fine fair skin. The sun was shining on him and I swear he seemed to be glowing. He was about the pret-

tiest kid I ever saw. But that's not why I kept looking. He
had these two adults with him, what I would say were
his parents. Nice-looking pair, young, maybe thirty. Both
had on white slacks and the man wore one of those soft-
knit shirts with an alligator over the pocket. The woman
had on this wide-brimmed hat, white, very stylish. I wondered what they were doing strolling the sidewalk in our
neighborhood. They didn't seem to fit in. We don't get
many parents with young children out here. We don't
have any nearby schools, or day-care centers, and no play-
grounds. We got one park but the benches are all broken.
No, young parents come out here looking over the real
estate, and right away they know they want no part of it.
You can't blame them. But I was talking about that kid.
The reason I was watching that kid was because of the
golf bag. It was a real one, I mean, slung over his shoulder, about the size of a loaf of French bread. And it was
a good one, I could see that. That kid's parents were not
fooling around. This golf bag was made of finest leather,
and it had about eight to ten putts—irons, whatever they're
called—stuck in it. Protruding from the bag, you know,
like a dozen gleaming metal heads. Expensive, I could
see that. Two hundred smackers, minimum, I'd say. And
heavy, too, because that little kid could hardly carry it.
He kept trying to drag it along the sidewalk, but the parents wouldn't have it. First you'd hear the father, then the
mother, then the father again.

Carry the bag, the father would say.

Then the mother: *Carry the bag, Buster. Keep it up high
on your shoulder.*

It took them ten minutes just to pass my house.

Don't drag the bag, Buster.

They were pretty angry. They were trying to stay calm
but you could see they wanted to swat him.

Pick up the bag, Buster.

Finally, the kid stopped. Just stopped. You could see
he didn't mean to take another step. He threw down the
bag. He sailed off his hat about ten feet up the street. He
gave his parents this dark look.

What are you doing, Buster? they said. *Come on, Buster.*
I'm golfing, he said. *Me and him are golfing.* And he
gave me this lidded, dark look. He'd seen me all right. He
had my number. He then sorted through his clubs and
took out the one he liked best. A big iron. He swung it
around a time or two, getting the feel of it. His legs looked
rubbery. He looked like a good breeze would send him
flying. But he was cute. He was the cutest kid I ever saw.
Then he got out this yellow golf ball and got out a tee
and put the ball on it. The ball kept rolling off, but finally
he managed. He stood up straight, on his tippy-toes, and
got the club swung way back over his shoulder.

Stand back! he said. *Watch out!*

I had the side of my face pressed up against the window. Christ, I was barely breathing. He was really going
to hit that sonofabitch. He was going to hit it hard. He
was going to maul that bastard. He had his tongue between his teeth and this look of terrible wrath on his face
and he was going to knock holy shit out of that stupid ball.

His father rushed up and grabbed him from behind just
as he was swinging. *Wait,* he said. *That's not how you do
it. Let me show you.* And the kid was trapped. He had to
do it the way his father said. *Back up. Widen your stance.
Don't hold it like a baseball bat. This club isn't an axe.
And your swing? Haven't I told you how to swing?*

Listen to your father, Buster, the mother kept saying.
Listen to your father.

The kid crumpled. He just folded up. He squatted down
on the sidewalk and the father had to keep yanking
him up.

Damn you, Buster!

The kid wailed. He wailed and wailed. He squirmed
and wriggled. He grabbed the ball and flung it into my
hedge. He kicked at the golfing bag. He clamped his teeth
into the father's arm.

The father yanked up the kid and tucked him under his
arm. The kid yelled. Oh boy, how he squalled. The mother
scooped up the clubs. The three of them went on out of

sight. But I heard that wailing a long time. I still could.

So that's what was going through my mind as I stared out our black window. That kid. Old Buster.

Stand back! Watch out!

Coolie, I noticed, was giving me the once-over. She wasn't saying anything just yet, though she was looking hard. I had these two shoes I'd been shining, up in my hands. One on each hand and I figured, from the way Coolie was staring, that I must have been waving these shoes about. Slapping golf balls. Kicking at the father. I didn't know for sure, but that's what I figured.

"I worry about you," she said. "I really do. There are times, Cecil, when I know you don't have a brain in your head. You're just not all here. You're off God-knows-where."

She meant it, too. There was a different sound in the air. A different note struck. She'd made a new turn in the way she regarded me. What she said came from some more distant, more objective place. I even figured I knew what she was thinking: *Maybe one day we had something, this crackpot and me. Now God help us.*

That's what I figured.

So I decided I wouldn't mention just yet the lady with the money. When she came, I'd spread it out on the floor. Every dollar. Coolie could do with it whatever she wanted.

So I sat there smiling, pondering things. Considering that Saks bag. Old Buster. Talking about shoes. "See these loafers," I said. "Look at these heels. It isn't healthy walking around in heels like this. What I think I'll do is go down to the shoe repair tomorrow and get me a new set put on. Maybe even throw these out, buy a new pair. What do you think?"

Coolie was eyeing me hard. Her jaw was set and she had her squint locked in; her mouth twitched; I could see her sucking in her breath. She looked old. I swear to hell she looked older than me. Yet I never felt so old as what I knew she felt, looking at me.

She wouldn't have called it age. She would have called it something that happened to us a long time ago. A decision we made.

I put the shoes down. I went over and closed the drapes.

Coolie whipped the cap over the polish bottle. No toe-painting tonight.

"You are the most boring creature who ever lived," she said. "I sometimes wonder what it would be like to be you and to have your mind and to have to go through life with the mind-boggling triviality of thought that you have. How do you do it? I know these are extraordinary times and that there is no end to the bizarre, low creatures that exist on this planet, but how in God's name do you do it? In your shoes I would jump off the first cliff I came to. I would go over headfirst. As Christ is my witness, I certainly would. Now would you put away your stupid shoe stuff? Would you stop fondling that stupid Saks box? Don't leave it for me to pick up. You can go to the repair shop or go to the moon or take a flying leap, I don't care. Cecil, I really don't. First your casseroles and now your shoes. Did you think you were conducting an orchestra? You're going to drive me out of my mind, Cecil. You really are."

Old Coolie is a killer. She knows how to get you right between the eyes, when being got is the last thing you want. If you blink, there it comes again.

I threw up my hands. "I surrender," I said. "You got me cornered, officer. Just read me my rights."

She covered her face. She sat a moment on the sofa's edge, shaking her head. Moaning a little.

But she came out of it smiling. Still shaking her head, but smiling now. Old Coolie's smile knocks me out.

She padded over on her naked feet and for a second clung to me, patting my head. She worked her warm face up under my neck. "A child," she said, in a low, husky voice. "You're like a little child."

I knew that voice: Veronica Lake.

Old Coolie the sorcerer.

I gave her a tight hug. Her body stiffened and she

pulled away. "Get me another beer," she said. "Another pound or two, why the Christ not!"

She flung herself down on the sofa and her fingers went *snap snap.*

"And bring it in a glass this time," she said. "I'm not an animal yet."

Ah, Coolie, you're a demon.

Coolie, sweetheart, you're a dream.

In the kitchen, opening the bottle, pouring the beer into a fake crystal glass with a golden rim, I have these thoughts. I am thinking of that Saks box and trying to set a date for when it first showed up in the house. Five years or ten—the time flows together. It isn't my box, it isn't Coolie's, it belongs to neither of us. Maybe it was just here; maybe it goes with the house. It's just a box, god-dammit, anyway. I am looking at the leftover casserole on the table and trying to figure whether I should put it away or throw it out. I give it a sniff. It smells okay. All the right stuff has gone into it. I get out the book and flip it open to the recipe. I run a finger down what's printed there. The page is greasy and stained and it has an aroma, too. I've found a lot of goodness in that page. With minor variations, I've made this casserole a hundred times.

Maybe, I think, that's where the trouble is.

I can hear Coolie at the dining table. I can hear what Coolie is saying. What she'll say tomorrow, if I can't mend my ways. "This dish tastes like manure. This dish is hor-rible. But spoon me another teensy helping. I've got to eat. A person has to live."

We don't hear each other any more. I wonder why it is I am hearing that.

Habit: me with my dishes, Coolie with her words.

What I am mostly wondering about, as I stand there, is what we'd do if we had us a kid. What we would have done, way back when.

I wonder whether that kid would be like me, God help him . . . or like Coolie, God help her.

I wonder what that kid would look like.

And how old that kid would be now.

If we had us a kid I'd get that kid alone when Coolie was out of the house and I'd sit that kid down and we'd figure out a few things. We'd figure out where that Saks box came from and what came in it. We'd figure out a thousand things like that. I'd have the kid with me in the kitchen and I'd say, "Flip to page two forty-eight, kid, and let's see what goes into the old casserole tonight." And the kid would do it because me and that kid were tight as twins. The kid would slice up the onions and sauté them over a slow fire. "What next, kid?" I'd say. And the kid would dice the tomatoes and slice up the green peppers and mince a few dozen cloves of garlic. We'd pour in the olive oil. "Is that enough, kid?" I'd say, and the kid would say, "No, Dad, I think that dish needs another cup or so." And I'd watch the kid pour it in. We'd stir the bastard around. I'd say, "Get me that bottle of white wine, kid," and the kid would get it and we'd smile and have us a little swig. Then before we got skunked we'd cube the shoulder of veal, forgotten until now, and we'd throw that into the skillet and brown the sonofabitch just right. We'd salt it and pepper it and butter it and I'd say, "How's that, kid?" "Just right, Dad," my kid would say. "Mmmm-mmmm, I can't wait!" We'd join everything together in a big clay pot and then cover it and drop the heat to low and we'd let that bastard cook for a good two hours and fifteen minutes.

We'd stand over it, drooling.

"What's that, kid?" I'd ask. "What fine dish do we have here?"

"We have Spezzatino di Vitèllo," the kid would say. "We've got the best Spezzatino di Vitèllo any Dad and his kid ever cooked up on the face of this earth."

"Bet your ass, kid," I'd say.

Then we'd light the fourteen candles and call old Coolie in. We'd install her at the table head on plump cushions and spread a lacy serviette over her lap. We'd hum her a few notes from a nice Puccini opera as we ladled up Spezzatino di Vitèllo on her plate. We'd click our heels as we poured her a robust wine in the table's tallest, most glittering glass.

"Eat and be merry," we'd say.

That's what we'd do, me and the kid.

I brought in Coolie her glass of beer, pulling up the side table so she could get at it without disturbing herself. She was stretched out on the sofa with one pillow over her face and another tucked between her legs.

"I would have ordered it from China," she said, "if I had known you were going to take all day. What in the name of God were you doing back there?"

Having me a kid, I thought I'd say. But I stayed quiet. All hell would break loose if I said that. Coolie would fly up screeching. She'd come at me like a bat out to suck blood. To suck it and ladle it on her nails. Songbird Red.

Coolie sipped at her beer. "It's not cold," she said. "It's gone flat."

I turned on a lamp or two.

"But far be it for me to complain," she said. "That's right. Run up the bills."

I tried my loafers out. Tested the shine. They were buffed up to a nice gleam all around. They looked pretty good, although my heels sank down into the floor. It was like walking on eggs, kind of curvy, I mean. I wondered how I'd ever let them get run down like that.

I rolled the TV up, got it going, then settled down into my chair.

"I'm not watching that junk," Coolie said.

I got up and turned the TV off. It made a sizzling sound, like fat in a frying pan. It always does. That TV, I thought, it's got a mind of its own.

Coolie took the pillow off her face and jammed it under her head. I watched her toes go through their ABC's.

"Last night," she said. "Where did you go last night?"

"Bowling," I said.

She snatched herself up, glaring. "You sonofabitch," she said. "You haven't been bowling in twenty years."

Old Coolie: I find nothing in life so buoyant to me as her abuse.

Something else got her attention. She leapt up and stalked over to the wall. She stayed there the longest time, gravely studying the floor, one hand under her chin.

"You missed a spot," she said. "Did the vacuum break down? You missed this whole area."

I don't hear you, I thought. Coolie, I don't hear a word you're saying.

"Come here," she said.

I went over.

She pointed.

"That's dirt," she said. "Now that is what I call genuine dirt. That's *dirt*, Cecil. Were you planning on putting in a field of corn?"

I laughed. Old Coolie and her corn: to hear her tell it I've put in a thousand acres in the living room alone. I started off after the vacuum. Coolie brushed by me, racing fast. "No, no," she said, "don't tax yourself. I know some things are just beyond you."

She wrestled out the vacuum and got the spot cleaned to her satisfaction. But her gown got caught in the suction—she shrieked. It was nearly ripped off her.

"It's trying to tell you something, Coolie," I said. "It's maybe telling you that gown needs a little attention."

This remark went past her. But it gave me this little idea. I figured that tomorrow while she was out at work I'd soak it in the Ivory Snow. I'd soak it for about nine hours.

"You're right about that floor," I said. "Heck, I can see the difference. Heck, a person could eat off it now."

"*You* eat off it, Cecil. Not me."

"Spezzatino di Vitèllo," I said. "A fine floor dish."

She ignored this. She flung herself down on the sofa, groaned, then leapt up again. She got the TV going. "Anything is better than your company," she said. "I'm worn out, just knowing you're here."

I put her nail polish away, up on the mantel where she keeps it, behind the brass deer.

[*142*]

I put the cowboy boots back in the closet.

I gathered up the shoe polish stuff and put it into the Saks box and stored it away.

Saks, it said. *Saks Fifth Avenue.* It said this on the top and on all four sides, in a nice black script. Flaring across, black on white. Pretty sharp. But where did we get it? When? What had come in this box?

Now kid, I said, *this one is for you to figure out. You get no sleep tonight until you figure it out.*

Okay, Dad.

I must have said this aloud, or something like it, for Coolie was calling me. She had her "Yell" button pushed. You'd have thought she'd just busted her kneecap up against a fire hydrant.

"You silly old bastard," she said. "What are you doing? Why are you in there mumbling to yourself? I thought someone was with you. Get in here. There's a movie on."

I came back in smiling, and took my chair.

The old TV music was getting zippy. It was really going.

"Look at that!" Coolie said, bolting up. "Can you believe it? What rubbish!"

It was some guy up in an old two-seater, two-engine plane, in pretty bad weather. In black and white this one was—how I like it best. This guy was out on the wet storm-tossed wing, slipping and sliding. Squirming along. Dana Andrews it was. Dana? I wasn't sure. He looked a bit like Dana. Fog or clouds—this white stuff—kept swirling across his face. But getting blacker all the time. Whoever he was, he meant business. He wasn't out for a Sunday stroll. He was up to something, out on that wing. *Zap! Zap!* Lightning was flashing all across the sky. Jagged, bristling bolts. *Crack!* Another one. There went a propeller. The camera came in on this guy's face—it wasn't Dana, too bad—and you could see he was worried. He was desperate. But squirming along. Then we got another shot. He had this knife sticking out of his back. A delicate—what I would say was definitely a feminine—item. That knife. Pearl handle. Oodles of blood.

When the wings tilted you could see the raging sea, and swollen ice caps beyond.

"Oh God!" cried Coolie, slapping her head. "I can't believe this! Who do they think we are!"

The old music was really waltzing; it was jitterbugging to beat the band.

The man on the wing was shouting at someone as he crawled. You couldn't hear what he was saying. The wind just whistled it away. It doesn't matter. People don't hear you anyway. We heard something though. Yep. There it went. That old prop. It ripped away and plunged whining into the sea.

Coolie was twisting about. Shrieking. She had herself tied up in knots. "Get on with it, man! Shake that load out of your britches."

I kept getting a glimpse of this white hand at the bottom of the screen.

Coolie kicked her foot out at the man. At Dana. Maybe it was Dana. He had Dana's lips. That way of measuring things.

"Will he save her?" Coolie asked. "Christ, this is a new low even for them!"

Save what *her*, I wondered. Save *who*?

Oh. That hand.

My mind was drifting a bit. The *Pick Pix of the Week* was sailing by me. Hold the phone, I was thinking. Hold that phone. Because I was thinking of that kid. My kitchen ace. Of kids, with maybe that Saks box thrown in. What if we had us *two* kids living here, I thought. A boy and a girl. Say we had a girl to match up with my kitchen ace. Brother and sister. Say that girl-kid was named . . . well, what? There is Louise, after my mother. Louise Proffit. Now that's not bad. A girl can get along with a calling card like that. Or Celeste. Suppose we call her Celeste. Or Cynthia. How about Cynthia? Clea? Clea would be all right. That's a thought. Nothing wrong with Clea. Wait a minute though. Hold the phone. Clea Proffit? That's no good. What that is is a joke. Clear profit, get it? Actually, it isn't that bad. It's jokey, but has a certain style. Class.

Clea Proffit, attorney-at-law. Clea Proffit, brain surgeon. Something like that. Secretary-General, United Nations. Heck, she'd be about twelve now, old Clea would. Maybe the oldest. Say she's the oldest. Though she still sucks her thumb. Probably always will. Who cares. Clea, darling, you can suck your thumb.

"*All right, Daddy.*"

Christ yes, I was really getting into it. I could *hear* old Clea.

"*Whatever you say, Daddy.*"

Beautiful voice. Clea Proffit, star of stage and screen.

All right, this is how it is. This is how it would be. While the kid and me are out in the kitchen getting a bead on dinner, sipping the wine, talking about that box, Clea is in here keeping Coolie company. Talking away. Having a fine chat. Neither hearing the other, of course, but . . . well, she'd have nice long hair, Clea would, maybe golden like that boy with the golf clubs. A perky little nose. Beautiful eyes, a lively face. Creamy complexion. Bit of a mess around the lips just now because she's been out in the kitchen checking out our dish. Saying "Ummmmgood!" Now she's in here. Chatting. Smart as a whip. "Too many missiles, Mama. Too many warheads. Stamp out the warheads." Coolie's platting her hair. Yes. Talking shop. "No, no, Mama. Allende was a *good* man. He was a *good* man." Pretty but not too pretty. She'd have my looks and Coolie's character. She'd have Coolie's screech if ever something riled her. "No, no, Mama. The Tomb of the Unknown is a *symbol*; it isn't a Communist plot." Good at her books. No trouble to anyone. A free spirit. She'd have friends, about a hundred. They'd always be over, smushing the cushions, emptying the fridge. Playing records. Whispering, giggling. She'd have this best friend, a wee, waifish, reddish-haired creature named Prissy. No, named Scarlet. She and that Scarlet kid would be always together. Chattering away, not hearing each other. "No, no, Scarlet. Turkey *claims* Cyprus. That's where they are trying to stamp out the Kurds." But they'd hear me and my kitchen ace when we called them in to dinner.

[*145*]

"Soup's on! Come get your Spezzatino di Vitèllo!"

And Coolie would roar: "Not *again!* I *hate* Spezzatino di Vitèllo! I can't *stand* Spezzatino di Vitèllo! Spezzatino makes me *sick!*"

But my daughter and little Scarlet would go to her. They'd bring her around. They'd say, "Yes, you do, Mama. Yes you do. You know you love Spezzatino di Vitèllo. We all do. Our Spezzatino is delicious."

"I know," Coolie would whisper. "I adore it. I just can't admit it to *him.*"

That's what I was thinking as I watched the black and white. These were bad thoughts. Depressing thoughts. I hadn't had thoughts like this in a month of Sundays—which isn't so long, now I think of it.

"Are you listening, Cecil!" Coolie cried. "Are you *alert* to this! Can you believe it!"

The music thundered.

The plane was burning.

One wing had fallen off.

A girl was dangling in the sky. The man was holding her by one arm. His grip slipping inch by inch. The poor girl was weeping. Weeping and screeching. She reminded me of Coolie. Coolie, too, was accustomed to seeing life from this woman's point of view. You could see sharks circling in the water below. Lightning flashing. The careening plane a black line of smoke. The girl in the sky, wriggling. She was terrified. The wind throwing her about. She had on this flimsy dress that looked a bit like Coolie's gown. Flapping about. Shredding. Now and then the music would drop so you could hear their speech. Their gasps. Their hard breath. The lick of flames fast approaching. Hold on, the man kept saying. Hold tight. The girl was getting more naked by the minute. Pretty soon we were going to have us an X-rated movie. She was trying to tell him something, though you couldn't make it out. The music boomed in each time we went to her. But she seemed to be saying something about that knife. Yes, the knife, for the camera kept swaying to the knife

in old Dana's back. Forgive me, she was saying. Forgive
me, my lover, my pet. My lamb.

Coolie, I forgive you.

Coolie, you set my heart a'racing.

Coolie, let's climb into bed.

"Hush up," said Coolie. "Be quiet. I'm listening to this."

The other wing fell off.

The fuselage cracked in half.

The music crashed in. The scene faded to black.

"Jesus help us," said Coolie in a moan. She was wrench-
ing about on the sofa, her eyes closed, a pillow clenched
under her chin. Old Coolie loves her movies. "What's the
point!" she yelled to the TV. "Jesus, I hate these miserable
endings. Do they live or die? Are you morons? Do you
think *we* are!"

Just then I heard the doorbell ring. Coolie didn't notice.
She had her hands up over her ears now, watching the
quivering screen.

Bing-pong!—there went the bell again. I took the time
to check myself in the mirror. I smoothed back my hair.
Put on my polished shoes.

I walked on out to the front door and swung it open.

She was dressed in a belted coat so immaculate it
seemed to shimmer, and sheer white stockings the same
color, and I never got to notice her shoes because she was
speaking to me, her hair swept back on both sides and her
face so pale, white, and clean she looked the twin of her
pristine garments.

"It's all here," she said, "every last penny. I'm glad you
let me bring it out this evening. I tell you, it will be a load
off my mind, getting rid of this money. We don't usually
handle so much."

She had a nice voice, on the soft side. Silver earrings
gleamed from her lobes and there was a silk scarf, not
exactly white, circling her throat. She was about my height
and her hair had a reddish tinge. She had this fine leather
satchel strapped to one arm.

She was younger than I had figured.

She had a sweet shape.

An easy, comfortable way of looking you in the eye.

"No trouble, I hope," I said. "I wouldn't want you to go to any extra trouble on my account."

"No trouble at all," she said.

I asked if she wanted to come inside. Maybe take off that coat, meet the wife, have a quiet chat. She said no. No, she had to run. She had plans, she said. The evening was still young.

I peeked around her. There was a small shiny car by the curb, with someone sitting in it.

"Do you want to count it?" she said.

I told her no, no point in that.

I took the satchel.

"Do I have to sign for it?" I asked. "The old John Henry? Are there any strings attached? Is there anything I ought to know about this money?"

"No," she said. "It's yours. It's yours and that's all there is to it."

She was a nice girl with a nice sweet voice and she had these remarkable eyes, clear as rainwater.

I had no trouble hearing her.

"We were wondering," she said—hesitating, not wanting to pry—"we were wondering what you intend doing with it."

"Do with it?" I said. "I don't know."

"Well . . . good night then."

"There's this kid," I said. "Down in Nigeria."

"Oh yes?"

"He's been getting fifty cents a week. I've been sending him that much. Now I might raise it to a dollar."

"We hoped you'd do something like that," she said.

She was turning to go. She had this handbag strapped over her shoulder, not white exactly but more the color of that scarf, and she was digging into it. She brought out a pair of high heels.

"Do you figure a dollar is enough?" I asked.

She slowed her steps. I could see her mulling this over. Fifty cents or a dollar—it was an important question.

"I *suppose* so," she said. "You have to keep these things in proportion."

I could see that little kid with his hand out, stretching all across the continent. Those big eyes. The scabs. The spindly legs. Named Lopé, I think. Lopé something-or-other. Something like that.

Lopé Proffit. It killed me everytime I thought of that kid.

"Hell," I said, "I might make it *two* dollars! What the hell."

She leaned up against the porch post, taking off her low business heels and sliding the new ones on. Then she pitched the lows into her handbag and snapped it shut.

"Wait a minute," I said. "There's another one down in Peru. Peru, of all places. Can you beat that? A little girl this one is. Pathetic-looking, but the energy she has! These stick legs, sores all over her body—pus!—and her feet turned in so you know she'll never be much of a runner. Never a golfer. Millet and rice, that's what she eats. Not much of that, either. The flies! She's got a thousand flies buzzing all over. On her mouth too, feeding on those sores. Giving itch to the scabs. Lice in her hair. But what stamina! Christ, my heart bleeds. Marjula her name is. Marjula, what kind of name is that? But I like it. Christ, Marjula is plenty good enough for me. Hard H, you get it? Hula, a real hula girl. Take ten of our kids over here just to hold her down, and I'm including that kid with the golf clubs and the golden hair. *Watch out! Stand back! Don't get in my way!* That what old Marjula is always saying. It's the message I get. What do you think? Am I on the right track? I think five dollars a week myself. Five, just until she learns how to count. Maybe hook her up with that Nigeria fella. Get something going. Lopé and Marjula. What do you think? I could call it my Green Light Special, what's coming at them this week from our neck of the woods. Would that knock out her eyes? Shoo away them flies? An orphan, you know. No mama, no daddy. Scabby like him. Big protruding belly. But she's ours now, old Coolie's and mine. Did I say five? Forget five. I say ten, minimum, and that's cheap, my bargain this week. Am I on the right track? Am I talking sense?"

She had got down the steps and out onto the walk. She looked pretty sharp in her high heels. She was a pretty handsome woman, what you'd call a bit of all right.

"It's a question of their *perspective*," she said. "You can't raise false expectations. That would never do."

This baffled me. I wondered how it was she thought any of us lived. How any of us had survived.

"Clear up the drinking water," I said. "Buy *real* milk. Speed that up. Hey, I got it. Another water buffalo!"

She laughed. It was a good, high, hard laugh, lots of enjoyment in it. I forgave her all her sins.

"I hear you," she said. "You're coming in loud and clear. It's your money. All yours. Ta-ta."

She went on down the path, that coat shimmering. It was nicely cut, that coat, beautifully form-fitting. She had wonderful legs, a strong stride.

"Going dancing?" I said.

She swirled. She gave a little rat-tat-tat to the pavement. "You bet!" she said. "All night long!"

The man in the car grinned and waved.

"So long."

I walked into the living room with the satchel of money.

"It isn't over," Coolie said without turning around.

She meant the movie. The man from the airplane and the woman in the tattered dress were up in the Andes somewhere. Snow all over. I wondered how they had survived the crash. But I granted them that. Funny things happen in this world.

"Where've you been?" Coolie said. "You missed the best part."

These two were hugging each other. Trembling. They looked pretty beaten. It was cold up there. The highest peak, old Clea would say, this side of Asia. Snow swirling every which way. They were trying to talk but their teeth were chattering too hard.

"She's his wife," Coolie said.

Now they were trying to get a fire going. They scooped out a deep hole in the snow. They scratched up a few twigs. They crouched down inside the hole. He got out his matches. They studied each other over the flame. They got this dark, serious look in their eyes. You could see it happening: the desire swelling up. The music, too. They were crying. Suddenly they slammed into each other, moaning and twisting, driving at each other's lips and throat, as the snow dropped over them like huge wafers. The matches got kicked over with snow. They got kicked further. Not that this pair noticed or cared. They were going at it. You can't say no to such desire. You can't say no, I guess, whether you're in the Andes, at the Proffit house, or on a bridge in Venice.

Coolie didn't agree. Her face was up at the screen. She was shaking her fists and yelling at them. "Build the fire!" she said. "Oh, you suckers, build the fire! You'll die, damn you!"

Snow blanketed the screen. You could just peer through it to see that human beings were there.

"They won't die, Coolie," I said. "It's only a movie."

I started spreading the money out over the carpet.

I started counting the money.

ARCADIA

Charles Dickinson

Arcadia comes toward Sutton talking, talking, with that lovable grin and that mouthful of dazzling teeth, and Sutton hasn't a clue what is being said.

They work together on a mountain of bricks. One building has come down, another is going up. The old bricks are better than new, sturdy and valuable. Their job is to find whole bricks among the cracked and stack them at the foot of the mountain.

Arcadia is good at this work. He is like a dancer on this brick mountain, finding good bricks, arranging them carefully along his forearm, stepping down to add them to the rest. He works in old leather boots his little toes show through.

Sutton can only guess that Arcadia is proud of his perfect teeth, he displays them so much. Behind these teeth is a pink point of tongue that creates long incoherent stretches of sound. His smiling eyes, curly hair, white teeth, his pure happy countenance, make Arcadia a hit with the ladies at lunch. All the men on the job gather at a restaurant down the street and Arcadia talks, talks. He talks and smiles and the girls just appear. Sutton wonders, Do they understand what he is saying? Does Arcadia speak some code of love?

Sutton has a smile of his own on his face. He guesses it looks pretty false; it feels false. But through the incomprehensibility of Arcadia's words comes a love of life Sutton envies. He suspects this quality alone would bring the girls around. He would hate for Arcadia to think Sutton did not love life so much.

So Sutton listens and smiles. He listens to the cadence of Arcadia's jabbering and produces a frozen laugh when he thinks a punch line has been delivered or a point made. He looks Arcadia straight in the eye and laughs to celebrate their common love of life.

Sutton stops Zeeland where they can talk in private.

Zeeland is always laughing and chattering with Arcadia; he is a fun-loving guy who grabs the seat next to Arcadia every day at lunch. Sutton envies Zeeland because he seems so attuned.

"How long did you know Arcadia before you understood him?" Sutton asks.

"I understood him from Day One."

"You did?"

"Sure. What's not to understand?"

"Everything. Everything that comes out of his mouth is a mystery to me. I couldn't even tell you the language he speaks."

Zeeland says, "You got it all wrong, Sutton. I didn't say I understand what he's saying. I said I understand *him*. I sit next to him because that's where all the girls will be."

"But you talk to him," Sutton says.

"Sure. I'm no stiff. He's got no more idea what I'm saying than I've got what he's saying. We're both after the same thing. Just smile and get your two cents in. That's all any of us try to do."

Arcadia holds a brick in front of him with both hands. He is smiling, his eyes flashing black, his voice musical and baffling. As Sutton watches Arcadia breaks the brick in two by slamming it against his forehead. Sutton is amazed. But it's only a trick. The brick was in two pieces held together to look like one. Arcadia laughs and performs the trick again. Brick dust clings to his forehead. He takes the broken brick to lunch and delights the girls with it.

When the men return to work Sutton hangs back and says to one of the girls, "Nice fella, Arcadia." He wants to turn on his smile like Arcadia, sound the charm gong, but there is nothing there and it shows in the girl's face. He talks to her because she is among the prettiest of them.

"Who?" she asks.

"Arcadia." Sutton points to the man's spot; Arcadia sits in the same seat every day, smiling king of that domain.

"You work with him?" she asks.

"Sure. We're good friends."

"He's always got a smile."

"One for everyone," Sutton agrees. "You ever date him?"

Her eyes flash up at Sutton. He has broken through her disinterest in the wrong way. "None of your business," she snaps, "even if I had."

Arcadia's car reminds Sutton of Arcadia's work boots; there are brick-sized rust holes he expects Arcadia's feet to show through. Arcadia is often the last to leave at the end of the day. He laughs and chatters, trying to get his car to start. Each man sounds his horn as he drives past and Arcadia always looks up and grins and waves good-bye. Arcadia is also often the first man at work in the morning.

Arcadia lives somewhere away from work. Sutton often wonders if he has been told where and didn't realize it. He might have been invited over and accepted the invitation and not shown up.

Zeeland says, "I saw him downtown once. He saw me first and came right up to me. Talking a mile a minute. I talked right back to him. We each bought a round of beers. A great guy. Nothing but women hanging all over him."

"Did they talk to him?"

"Hell, Sutton, everybody talked to him. You're too stiff. Everybody says that about you. Loosen up. Be sociable for once in your life."

Arcadia returns from an errand, talking, talking, and scrambles up the brick mountain to where Sutton works. Sutton smiles into Arcadia's beaming face. The happy words, Arcadia's moist breath, break over Sutton's false face. He's being sociable, he thinks; he wants to be. But he can't loosen up enough to comment or respond to something that baffles him.

Instead, he says, "What?"

Arcadia stops talking. He doesn't stop smiling, only talking. The bricks clink beneath their feet.

Sutton says, "I don't understand you."

Arcadia talks for a moment, smiling hopefully at Sutton.

"I'm sorry," Sutton says. "I've got no idea what you're saying."

Arcadia talks through his smile, talking, talking.

"Stop. Stop," Sutton says. "I don't know how to tell you this but all the time I've worked with you and laughed at what I think were jokes, I haven't had the faintest idea what you were saying. I haven't understood a single word."

Arcadia laughs, scratches his head, taps one of his big front teeth. He talks, talks, and Sutton gives up and goes back to sorting bricks. He looks for Zeeland after work but Zeeland is quick leaving at the end of the day in ways totally unrelated to his pace of work.

The men leave in a hurry, they wave to Arcadia, who smiles and waves back. In minutes Sutton is alone in the lot with Arcadia and his car, which won't start. He grinds the ignition, talking, talking to himself, and the picture so frustrates Sutton he hasn't the courage to offer to help and speeds away without looking back.

It rains hard all night. Sutton and Arcadia are taken off the brick mountain, given buckets and shovels and high boots, and sent inside where neither the roof nor the floor have been completed. The floor is mud, and beneath those sections of the roof that remain uncovered a million little lakes have formed. Their new job is to drain this ground.

Arcadia does not share Sutton's sense of their task's ridiculousness. He works like a civil engineer or a child at the beach cutting canals with his shovel blade so one lake can run into another. From these larger pools he delicately shovels the water into the bucket and when the bucket is full he carries it across the muddy floor, outside to a hill, and flings it down where there is no chance of its ever running back inside. Arcadia has the perfect temperament for this job. He seems to draw pride and bottomless delight from slowly shoveling a shallow keystone of water on the blade of a shovel up and into a bucket while spilling a third to a half of his original cargo. Nothing upsets him.

Sutton can't get the hang of it. His canals are only wet trails in the mud. They don't consolidate any significant amounts of water. And the act of shoveling water is just too ludicrous for words.

At lunch he sits by himself in his muddy clothes listening to Arcadia's happy chatter and the echoing bleats of Zeeland and all the others. Girls appear as if conjured. There is nobody but the men from work and then Arcadia talks, talks, and girls are present. There is camaraderie, low-grade flirting, an exchange of desires.

Arcadia walks with Sutton back to where their buckets and shovels wait. Sutton ignores everything Arcadia says now. He has made his point; he is free to be himself.

Sutton sees no improvement in the ground they have gone over. A million lakes remain. It could rain again that night and set them back to the start. This does not seem to bother Arcadia. Even more than picking through bricks, digging canals and draining tiny lakes hold a real charm for him.

When the whistle blows at five o'clock Arcadia reluctantly turns in his shovel and bucket and high boots. He goes to his car and gets in, but he does not try to start it. As the rest of the men sweep past out of the parking lot, honking, waving, Arcadia doesn't wave, doesn't smile, doesn't look at any of them.

Sutton drives away, too. But after dinner he keeps thinking about Arcadia and his life away from work. It is a short drive back and when he arrives Arcadia's car is still in the lot. Sutton finds him stretched out in the back seat. He has his socks off and rolled into a small pillow. He is reading a newspaper in a nest of fast-food wrappers, he sucks the last of his shake with a straw.

Sutton taps on the window. Arcadia lowers the paper. A big smile breaks across his face. He starts talking, talking, even as he pulls on his socks and boots and gets out of the car.

"You live in your car," Sutton says.

Arcadia laughs, shrugs, talks. He locks his car door and gets into Sutton's car, his arms loaded with dirty clothes, old newspapers, a pair of work gloves.

[156]

They move out onto the highway. Arcadia points toward the city.

"I tell you," Sutton says. "I've got no idea what you're saying or where I'm going."

Arcadia points, laughs. The sun is going down and Sutton wants to be home. Arcadia seems to have a destination. Through his happy jabbering he directs Sutton onto links of highway that stretch toward the city, then through the city, then out the other side. He leads Sutton down streets between bunched buildings that thin like the light until it is dark and nobody, nothing, is around.

Sutton thinks he sees the state line flash past on the edge of his headlights. Arcadia is truly happy now. At a stop sign he points right and two blocks on he points left. He tells Sutton to stop at a tiny house in the middle of the block.

Arcadia is out of the car while it is still rolling. He runs up the driveway with his armload of belongings. An outside light goes on. A pretty little girl with Arcadia's dark, curly hair and jabbering tongue bursts out the door and sprints toward him. She hits the things in Arcadia's arms like they were a cloud meant to catch her. A short, voluptuous woman follows the little girl. This woman is cross, but too happy to sustain it. Her wide hips and bowed legs swing like a gunfighter's as she advances on Arcadia, who faces her squarely and gives her a long kiss and a smack on the rump. They all talk, talk, and Arcadia turns to wave Sutton into their net.

The little girl takes Sutton's arm. He is pulled into the house like a hero. The woman clears laundry from a chair and the little girl pulls him into it. There is barely room for all of them in the kitchen. The girl has been doing arithmetic at the table. Dinner was over long ago but the woman goes to work fixing a meal for Sutton and Arcadia. She talks, talks.

Sutton feels obliged to say, "I've got no idea what you're talking about."

No one listens. The woman and the girl are intent on Arcadia. Sutton looks at the girl's arithmetic. He is afraid it is in the alien tongue the family converses in; he fears he has wandered into another world entirely.

But the girl's work is clearly earthling. Her numbers are carefully put down in pencil on sheets of manila paper perforated to tear free from the workbook. Sutton even sees two problems done incorrectly. He will have to leave them be. How could he ever explain them to her?

A porcelain blue plate full of pork chops, niblet corn and buttered rolls is placed before him. The woman beams down on him, talking, talking. She pours coffee. She's a beautiful woman. Sutton senses springiness in everything about her; her happy manner, the coiled wires of her hair, the swing of her body in her thin housedress. Sutton is envious of Arcadia and sees him in a new light. He wonders why he made no more effort to get home to this woman, dead car or not.

The woman is out of the room for a few minutes and reappears to remove the dirty plates. Arcadia yawns. He has talked all through dinner, fitting his words haphazardly around the food in his mouth. Now he runs his hands down the front of his shirt, unbuttoning as he goes, and Sutton gets the hint. It is a long way home and he has no idea how to get there.

The little girl appears washed and ready for bed. She carries a limp toy rabbit in the crook of her arm. Her mother has bound her hair in two thick sheaves atop her head. Sutton is kissed on the cheek, Arcadia on the lips, and the girl is off to bed.

Sutton is looking for his jacket when the woman takes his arm. She says a few words. He follows her into the next room, where a bed has been made for him on a couch. TV light spills over the turned sheets, blanket, pillow, making them look soiled.

The woman talks, talks, Sutton can't bear to look at her. The house pinches in on him and this woman and Arcadia. Already he hears the gentle rhythm of the little girl's sleep. It passes effortlessly through the house. He does not think he can lie on this narrow bed and listen to Arcadia and his wife reunited after untold nights apart. He hears the water running in the shower, Arcadia singing, singing.

But Sutton has no choice.

He undresses in the dark and slides between the cool bedding. Out the room's only window he sees a red light beating high in the distance, a warning to planes.

He thinks he sleeps, but he can't be sure. He is awake now. The small house is quiet but for three rhythms of sleep. The red light pulses on, the darkness at its back subtly different, a half-shade lighter, or darker, he can't say.

There is nothing for him to do but dress and sit at the window, waiting to take Arcadia back.

HIDING

Susan Minot

O ur father doesn't go to church with us but we're all
downstairs in the hall at the same time, bumbling,
getting ready to go. Mum knuckles the buttons of
Chicky's snowsuit till he's knot-tight, crouching, her
heels lifted out of the backs of her shoes, her nylons
creased at the ankles. She wears a black lace veil that
stays on her hair like magic. Sherman ripples by, coat
flapping, and Mum grabs him by the hood, reeling him
in, and zips him up with a pinch at his chin. Gus stands
there with his bottom lip out, waiting, looking like someone's smacked him except not that hard. Even though
he's nine, he still wants Mum to do him up. Delilah
comes half-hurrying down the stairs, late, looking like a
ragamuffin with her skirt slid down to her hips and her
hair all slept on wrong. Caitlin says, "It's about time."
Delilah sweeps along the curve of the banister, looks at
Caitlin who's all ready to go herself with her pea jacket
on and her loafers and bare legs, and tells her, "You're
going to freeze." Everyone's in a bad mood because we
just woke up.

Dad's outside already on the other side of the French
doors, waiting for us to go. You can tell it's cold out
there by his white breath blowing by his cheek in spurts.
He just stands on the porch, hands shoved in his black
parka, feet pressed together, looking at the crusty snow
on the lawn. He doesn't wear a hat but that's because
he barely feels the cold. Mum's the one who's warm-
blooded. At skiing, she'll take you in when your toes get
numb. You sit there with hot chocolate and a carton of
french fries and the other mothers and she rubs your foot
to get the circulation back. Down on the driveway the
car is warming up and the exhaust goes straight up, dis-
appearing in thin white curls.

"Okay, Monkeys," says Mum filing us out the door.
Chicky starts down the steps one red boot at a time till
Mum whisks him up under a wing. The driveway is

wrinkled over with ice so we take little shuffle steps across it, blinking at how bright it is, still only half-awake. Only the station wagon can fit everybody. Gus and Sherman scamper in across the huge backseat. Caitlin's head is the only one that shows over the front. (Caitlin is the oldest and she's twelve. I'm next, then Delilah, then the boys.) Mum rubs her thumbs on the steering wheel so that her gloves are shiny and round at the knuckles. Dad is doing things like checking the gutters, waiting till we leave. When we finally barrel down the hill, he turns and goes back into the house which is big and empty now and quiet.

We keep our coats on in church. Except for the O'Shaunesseys, we have the most children in one pew. Dad only comes on Christmas and Easter, because he's not Catholic. A lot of times you only see the mothers there. When Dad stays at home, he does things like cuts prickles in the woods or tears up thorns, or rakes leaves for burning, or just stands around on the other side of the house by the lilacs, surveying his garden, wondering what to do next. We usually sit up near the front and there's a lot of kneeling near the end. One time Gus got his finger stuck in the diamond-shaped holes of the heating vent and Mum had to yank it out. When the man comes around for the collection, we each put in a nickel or a dime and the handle goes by like a rake. If Mum drops in a five-dollar bill, she'll pluck out a couple of bills for her change.

The church is huge. Out loud in the dead quiet, a baby blares out *DAH-DEE*. We giggle and Mum goes *Ssshhh* but smiles too. A baby always yells at the quietest part. Only the girls are old enough to go to Communion; you're not allowed to chew it. The priest's neck is peeling and I try not to look. "He leaves me cold," Mum says when we leave, touching her forehead with a fingertip after dipping it into the holy water.

On the way home, we pick up the paper at Cage's and a bag of eight lollipops—one for each of us, plus Mum and Dad, even though Dad never eats his. I choose root beer. Sherman crinkles his wrapper, flicking his eyes around to see if anyone's looking. Gus says, "Sherman, you have to wait till after breakfast." Sherman gives a fierce look and shoves it in his mouth. Up in front, Mum, flicking on the blinker, says, "Take that out," with eyes in the back of her head.

Depending on what time of year it is, we do different things on the weekends. In the fall we might go to Castle Hill and stop by the orchard in Ipswich for cider and apples and red licorice. Castle Hill is closed after the summer so there's nobody else there and it's all covered with leaves. Mum goes up to the windows on the terrace and tries to peer in, cupping her hands around her eyes and seeing curtains. We do things like roll down the hills, making our arms stiff like mummies, or climb around on the marble statues which are really cold, or balance along the edge of the fountains without falling. Mum says *Be careful* even though there's no water in them, just red leaves plastered against the sides. When Dad notices us he yells *Get down*.

One garden has a ghost, according to Mum. A lady used to sneak out and meet her lover in the garden behind the grape trellis. Or she'd hide in the garden somewhere and he'd look for her and find her. But one night she crept out and he didn't come and didn't come and finally when she couldn't stand it any longer, she went crazy and ran off the cliff and killed herself and now her ghost comes back and keeps waiting. We creep into the boxed-in place smelling the yellow berries and the wet bark and Delilah jumps—"What was that?"—trying to scare us. Dad shakes the wood to see if it's rotten. We run ahead and hide in a pile of leaves. Little twigs get in your mouth and your nostrils; we hold still underneath listening to the brittle ticking leaves. When we hear Mum and Dad get close, we burst up to surprise them, all the leaves fluttering down, sputtering from the dust and tiny grits that get all over your face like grey ash, like Ash Wednesday. Mum and Dad just keep walking. She brushes a pine needle from his collar and he jerks his head, thinking of something else, probably that it's a fly. We follow them back to the car in a line all scruffy with leaf scraps.

After church, we have breakfast because you're not

allowed to eat before. Dad comes in for the paper or a
sliver of bacon. One thing about Dad, he has the weird-
est taste. Spam is his favorite thing or this cheese that
no one can stand the smell of. He barely sits down at all,
glancing at the paper with his feet flat down on either
side of him, ready to get up any minute to go back outside and sprinkle white fertilizer on the lawn. After, it
looks like frost.

This Sunday we get to go skating at Ice House Pond.
Dad drives. "Pipe down," he says into the back seat.
Mum faces him with white fur around her hood. She
calls him Uncs, short for Uncle, a kind of joke, I guess,
calling him Uncs while he calls her Mum, same as we
do. We are making a racket.
"Will you quit it?" Caitlin elbows Gus.
"What? I'm not doing anything."
"Just taking up all the room."
Sherman's in the way back. "How come Chicky always
gets the front?"
"Cause he's the baby." Delilah is always explaining
everything.
"I en not a baby," says Chicky without turning around.
Caitlin frowns at me. "Who said you could wear my
scarf?"
I ask into the front seat, "Can we go to the Fairy
Garden?" even though I know we won't.
"Why couldn't Rummy come?"
Delilah says, "Because Dad didn't want him to."
Sherman wants to know how old Dad was when he
learned how to skate.
Dad says, "About your age." He has a deep voice.
"Really?" I think about that for a minute, about Dad
being Sherman's age.
"What about Mum?" says Caitlin.
This isn't his department so he just keeps driving.
Mum shifts her shoulders more toward us but still looks
at Dad.
"When I was a little girl on the Boston Common."
Her teeth are white and she wears fuchsia lipstick. "We
used to have skating parties."

Caitlin leans close to Mum's fur hood, crossing her arms into a pillow. "What? With dates?"

Mum bats her eyelashes. "Oh sure. Lots of beaux." She smiles, acting like a flirt. I look at Dad but he's concentrating on the road.

We saw one at a football game once. He had a huge mustard overcoat and a bow tie and a pink face like a ham. He bent down to shake our tiny hands, half-looking at Mum the whole time. Dad was someplace else getting the tickets. His name was Hank. After he went, Mum put her sunglasses on her head and told us she used to watch him play football at BC. Dad never wears a tie except to work. One time Gus got lost. We waited until the last people had trickled out and the stadium was practically empty. It had started to get dark and the headlights were crisscrossing out of the parking field. Finally Dad came back carrying him, walking fast, Gus's head bobbing around and his face all blotchy. Dad rolled his eyes and made a kidding groan to Mum and we laughed because Gus was always getting lost. When Mum took him, he rammed his head onto her shoulder and hid his face while we walked back to the car, and under Mum's hand you could see his back twitching, trying to hide his crying.

We have Ice House Pond all to ourselves. In certain places the ice is bumpy and if you glide on it going *Aauuuuhhhh* in a low tone, your voice wobbles and vibrates. Every once in a while, a crack shoots across the pond, echoing just beneath the surface, and you feel something drop in the hollow of your back. It sounds like someone's jumped off a steel wire and left it twanging in the air.

I try to teach Delilah how to skate backwards but she's flopping all over the ice, making me laugh, with her hat lopsided and her mittens dangling out of her sleeves. When Gus falls, he just stays there, polishing the ice with his mitten. Dad sees him and says, "I don't care if my son is a violin player," kidding.

Dad played hockey in college and was so good his name is on a plaque that's right as you walk into the Harvard rink. He can go really fast. He takes off—*whooosh*

—whizzing, circling at the edge of the pond, taking long strides, then gliding, chopping his skates, crossing over in little jumps. He goes zipping by and we watch him: his hands behind him in a tight clasp, his face as calm as if he were just walking along, only slightly forward. When he sweeps a corner, he tips in, then rolls into a hunch, and starts the long side-pushing again. After he stops, his face is red and the tears leak from the sides of his eyes and there's a white smudge around his mouth like frostbite. Sherman, copying, goes chopping forward on collapsed ankles and it sounds like someone sharpening knives.

Mum practices her 3s from when she used to figure skate. She pushes forward on one skate, turning in the middle like a petal flipped suddenly in the wind. We always make her do a spin. First she does backwards crossovers, holding her wrists like a tulip in her fluorescent pink parka, then stops straight up on her toes, sucking in her breath and dips, twisted, following her own tight circle, faster and faster, drawing her feet together. Whirring around, she lowers into a crouch, ventures out one balanced leg, a twirling whirlpool, hot pink, rises again, spinning, into a blurred pillar or a tornado, her arms going above her head and her hands like the eye of a needle. Then suddenly: stop. Hiss of ice shavings, stopped. We clap our mittens. Her hood has slipped off and her hair is spread across her shoulders like when she's reading in bed, and she takes white breaths with her teeth showing and her pink mouth smiling. She squints over our heads. Dad is way off at the car, unlacing his skates on the tailgate but he doesn't turn. Mum's face means that it's time to go.

Chicky stands in the front seat leaning against Dad. Our parkas crinkle in the cold car. Sherman has been chewing on his thumb and it's a pointed black witch's hat. A rumble goes through the car like a monster growl and before we back up Dad lifts Chicky and sets him leaning against Mum instead.

The speed bumps are marked with yellow stripes and it's like sea serpents have crawled under the tar. When we bounce, Mum says, "Thank-you-Ma'am" with a lilt in her voice. If it was only Mum, the radio would be on and she'd turn it up on the good ones. Dad snaps it off because there's enough racket already. He used to listen to opera when he got home from work but not anymore. Now we give him hard hugs and he changes upstairs then goes into the TV room to the same place on the couch, propping his book on his crossed knees and reaching for his drink without looking up. At supper, he comes in for a handful of onion-flavored bacon crisps or a dish of miniature corn-on-the-cobs pickled. Mum keeps us in the kitchen longer so he can have a little peace and quiet. Ask him what he wants for Christmas and he'll say *No more arguing.* When Mum clears our plates, she takes a bite of someone's hot dog or a quick spoonful of peas before dumping the rest down the pig.

In the car, we ask Dad if we can stop at Shucker's for candy. When he doesn't answer, it means *No.* Mum's eyes mean *Not today.* She says, "It's treat night anyway." Treats are ginger ale and vanilla ice cream.

On Sunday nights we have treats and BLTs and get to watch Ted Mack and Ed Sullivan. There are circus people on almost every time, doing cartwheels or flips or balancing. We stand up in our socks and try some of it. Delilah does an imitation of Elvis by making jump rope handles into a microphone. Girls come on with silver shoes and their stomachs showing and do clappity tap dances. "That's a cinch," says Mum behind us.

"Let's see you then," we say and she goes over to the brick in front of the fireplace to show us. She bangs the floor with her sneakers, pumping and kicking, thudding her heels in smacks, not like clicking at all, swinging her arms out in front of her like she's wading through the jungle. She speeds up, staring straight at Dad who's reading his book, making us laugh even harder. He's always like that. Sometimes for no reason, he'll snap out of it going, "What? What? What's all this? What's going on?" as if he's emerged from a dark tunnel, looking like he does when we wake him up and he hasn't put on his glasses yet, sort of angry. He sits there before dinner, popping black olives into his mouth one at a time, eyes never leaving his book. His huge glass mug is from college and in the lamplight you can see the liquid separate. One layer is beer, the rest is gin. Even smelling it makes you gag.

Dad would never take us to Shucker's for candy. With him, we do things outside. If there's a storm we go down to the rocks to see the waves—you have to yell—and get sopped. Or if Mum needs a nap, we go to the beach. In the spring it's wild and windy as anything, which I love. The wind presses against you and you kind of choke but in a good way. Sherman and I run, run, run! Couples at the end are so far away you can hardly tell they're moving. Rummy races around with other dogs, flipping his rear like a goldfish, snapping at the air, or careening in big looping circles across the beach. Caitlin jabs a stick into the wet part and draws flowers. Chicky smells the seaweed by smushing it all over his face. Delilah's dark bangs jitter across her forehead like magnets and she yells back to Gus lagging behind. Dad looks at things far away. He points out birds—a great blue heron near the breakers as thin as a safety pin or an osprey in the sky, tilting like a paper cutout. We collect little things. Delilah holds out a razor shell on one sandy palm for Dad to take and he says *Uh-huh* and calls Rummy. When Sherman, grinning, carries a dead seagull to him, Dad says, "Cut that out." Once in Maine, I found a triangle of blue and white china and showed it to Dad. "Ah yes, a bit of crockery," he said.

"Do you think it's from the Indians?" I whispered. They had made the arrowheads we found on the beach.

"I think it's probably debris," he said and handed it back to me. According to Mum, debris is the same thing as litter, as in Don't Be a Litter Bug.

When we get home from skating, it's already started to get dark. Sherman runs up first and beats us to the door but can't open it himself. We are all used to how warm it was in the car so everybody's going *Brrrr*, or *Hurry up*, banging our feet on the porch so it thunders. The sky is dark blue glass and the railing seems whiter and the fur on Mum's hood glows. From the driveway Dad yells, "I'm going downtown. Be right back," slamming the door and starting the car again.

Delilah yells, "Can I come?" and Gus goes, "Me too!" as we watch the car back up.

"Right back," says his deep voice through the crack in the window and he rounds the side of the house.

"How come he didn't stop on the way home?" asks Caitlin, sticking out her chin.

"Yah," says Delilah. "How come?" We look at Mum. She kicks the door with her boot. "In we go, Totsies," she says instead of answering and drops someone's skate on the porch because she's carrying so much stuff.

Gus gets in a bad mood, standing by the door with his coat on, not moving a muscle. His hat has flaps over the ears. Delilah flops onto the hall sofa, her neck bent, ramming her chin into her chest. "Why don't you take off your coat and stay awhile?" she says, drumming her fingers as slow as a spider on her stomach.

"I don't have to."

"Yah," Sherman butts in. "Who says you're the boss?" He's lying on the marble tile with Rummy, scissor-kicking his legs like windshield wipers.

"No one," says Delilah, her fingers rippling along.

On the piano bench, Caitlin is picking at her split ends. We can hear Mum in the kitchen putting the dishes away.

Banging on the piano fast because she knows it by heart, Caitlin plays "Walking in a Winter Wonderland." Delilah sits up and imitates her behind her back, shifting her hips from side to side, making us all laugh. Caitlin whips around, "What?"

"Nothing." But we can't help laughing.

"Nothing what?" says Mum coming around the corner, picking up mittens and socks from the floor, snapping on the lights.

Delilah stiffens her legs. "We weren't doing anything," she says.

We make room for Mum on the couch and huddle. Gus perches at the edge, sideways.

"When's Dad coming back?" he says.

"You know your father," says Mum vaguely, smoothing Delilah's hair on her lap, daydreaming at the floor but thinking about something. When Dad goes to the store,

[*168*]

he only gets one thing, like a can of black bean soup or watermelon rind.

"What shall we play?" says Sherman, strangling Rummy in a hug.

"Yah. Yah. Let's do something," we say and turn to Mum.

She narrows her eyes into spying slits. "All rightee. I might have a little idea."

"What?" we all shout, excited. "What?" Mum hardly ever plays with us because she has to do everything else.

She rises, slowly, lifting her eyebrows, hinting. "You'll see."

"What?" says Gus and his bottom lip loosens nervously.

Delilah's dark eyes flash like jumping beans. "Yah, Mum. What?"

"Just come with me," says Mum in a singsong and we scamper after her. At the bottom of the stairs, she crouches in the middle of us. Upstairs behind her, it's dark.

"Where are we going?" asks Caitlin and everybody watches Mum's face, thinking of the darkness up there.

"Hee hee hee," she says in her witch voice. "We're going to surprise your father, play a little trick."

"What?" asks Caitlin again, getting ready to worry but Mum's already creeping up the stairs so we follow, going one mile per hour like her, not making a peep even though there's no one in the house to hear us.

Suddenly she wheels around. "We're going to hide," she cackles.

"Where?" we all want to know, sneaking along like burglars.

Her voice is hushed. "Just come with me."

At the top of the stairs it is dark and we whisper.

"How about your room?" says Delilah. "Maybe under the bed."

"No," says Sherman breathlessly. "In the fireplace." We all laugh because we could never fit in there.

Standing in the hall, Mum opens the door to the linen closet and pulls the light string. "How about right here?" The light falls across our faces. On the shelves are stacks

of bed covers and rolled puffs, red and white striped
sheets and pink towels, everything clean and folded and
smelling of soap.

All of a sudden Caitlin gasps, "Wait— I hear the car!"

Quickly we all jumble and scramble around, bumbling
and knocking and trying to cram ourselves inside. Sherman makes whimpering noises like an excited dog.
Sshhhh, we say or *Hurry Hurry,* or *Wait.* I knee up to a
top shelf and Sherman gets a boost after me and then
Delilah comes grunting up. We play in here sometimes.
Gus and Chicky crawl into the shelf underneath, wedg-
ing themselves in sideways. Caitlin half-sits on molding
with her legs dangling and one hand braced against the
door frame. When the rushing settles, Mum pulls out the
light and hikes herself up on the other ledge. Everyone
is off the ground then, and quiet.

Delilah giggles. Caitlin says *Ssshhhh* and I say *Come
on* in a whisper. Only when Mum says *Hush* do we all
stop and listen. Everyone is breathing; a shelf creaks.
Chicky knocks a towel off and it hits the ground like a
pillow. Gus says, "I don't hear anything." *Ssshhh,* we
say. Mum touches the door and light widens and we
listen. Nothing.

"False alarm," says Sherman.

Our eyes start to get used to the dark. Next to me
Delilah gurgles her spit.

"What do you think he'll do?" whispers Caitlin. We
all smile, curled up in the darkness with Mum thinking
how fooled he'll be, coming back and not a soul anywhere, standing in the hall with all the lights glaring
not hearing a sound.

"Where will he think we've gone?" We picture him
looking around for a long time, till finally we all pour out
of the closet.

"He'll find out," Mum whispers. Someone laughs at
the back of his throat, like a cricket quietly ticking.

Delilah hisses, "Wait—"

"Forget it," says Caitlin who knows it's a false alarm.

"What will he do?" we ask Mum.

She's in the darkest part of the closet, on the other
side of the light slant. We hear her voice. "We'll see."

"My foot's completely fallen asleep," says Caitlin.

"Kick it," says Mum's voice.

"Ssshhh," lisps Chicky and we laugh at him copying everybody.

Gus's muffled voice comes from under the shelf. "My head's getting squished."

"Move it," says Delilah.

"Quiet!"

And then we really do hear the car.

"Silence, Monkeys," says Mum and we all hush, holding our breaths. The car hums up the hill.

The motor dies and the car shuts off. We hear the door crack, then clip shut. Footsteps bang up the echoing porch, loud, toe-hard and scuffing. The glass panes rattle when the door opens, resounding in the empty hall, and then the door slams in the dead quiet, reverberating through the whole side of the house. Someone in the closet squeaks like a hamster. Downstairs there isn't a sound.

"Anybody home?" he bellows, and we try not to giggle.

Now what will he do? He strides across the deep hall, going by the foot of the stairs, obviously wondering where everybody's gone, stopping at the hooks to hang up his parka.

"What's he doing?" whispers Caitlin to herself.

"He's by the mitten basket," says Sherman. We all have smiles, our teeth like watermelon wedges, grinning in the dark.

He yells toward the kitchen, "Hello?" and we hunch our shoulders to keep from laughing, holding onto something tight like our toes or the shelf, or biting the side of our mouths.

He starts back into the hall.

"He's getting warmer," whispers Mum's voice, far away. We all wait for his footsteps on the stairs.

But he stops by the TV room doorway. We hear him rustling something, a paper bag, taking out what he's bought, the bag crinkling, setting something down on the hall table, then crumpling up the bag and pitching it in the wastebasket. Gus says, "Why doesn't he—?" *Ssshhh,* says Mum like spitting and we all freeze. He

[*171*]

moves again—his footsteps turn and bang on the hollow threshold into the TV room where the rug pads the sound.

Next we hear the TV click on, the sound swelling and the dial switching *tick-ah tikka tikka tick* till it lands on a crowd roar, a football game. We can hear the announcer's voice and the hiss-breath behind it of cheering.

Then it's the only sound in the house.

"What do we do now?" says Delilah only half-whispering. Mum slips down from her shelf and her legs appear in the light, touching down.

Still hushed, Sherman goes, "Let's keep hiding."

The loud thud is from Caitlin jumping down. She uses her regular voice. "Forget it. I'm sick of this anyway." Everyone starts to rustle. Chicky panics, "I can't get down," as if we're about to desert him.

"Stop being such a baby," says Delilah, disgusted.

Mum doesn't say anything, just opens the door all the way. Past the banister in the hall it is yellow and bright. We climb out of the closet, feet-feeling our way down backwards, bumping out one at a time, knocking down blankets and washcloths by mistake. Mum guides our backs and checks our landings. We don't leave the narrow hallway. The light from downstairs shines up through the railing and casts shadows on the wall—bars of light and dark like a fence. Standing in it we have stripes all over us. *Hey look,* we say whispering, with the football drone in the background, even though this isn't anything new—we always see this, holding out your arms and seeing the stripes. Lingering near the linen closet we wait. Mum picks up the tumbled things, restacking the stuff we knocked down, folding things, clinching a towel with her chin, smoothing it over her stomach and then matching the corners left and right, like crossing herself, patting everything into neat piles. The light gets like this every night after we've gone to bed and we creep into the hall to listen to Mum and Dad downstairs. The bands of shadows go across our nightgowns and pajamas and we press our foreheads against the railing trying to hear the mumbling of what Mum and Dad are saying down there. Then we hear the deep boom of Dad clearing his throat and look up at Mum. Though she is turned away, we can still see the wince on her face like when you are waiting to be hit or right after you have been. So we keep standing there, our hearts pounding, waving our hands through the flickered stripes, suddenly interested the way you get when it's time to take a bath and you are mesmerized by something. We're stalling, waiting for Mum to finish folding, waiting to see what she's going to do next because we don't want to go downstairs yet, where Dad is, without her.

CLAIRE'S LOVER'S CHURCH

Teri Ruch

The city fathers did not like the church on the other side of the ditch by the welcome-to-our-city sign. They didn't like the dolls' heads with empty eye sockets in the churchyard dirt. They wondered about the midgets from out of town who appeared and disappeared at the rear of the church with stuffed duffel bags bouncing on their backs. They didn't appreciate the stained-glass windows showing naked women leaping around a handsome shepherd. And the glare of the church's gold front doors blinded people driving in and out of the city. The city fathers moved the welcome sign three feet to keep the church outside the city limits.

As a child Claire crawled down in the ditch, under the highway through the drainage pipe, and up the opposite bank. She pressed an ear to the glowing doors and listened to altos and sopranos hum the same three notes repeatedly. It reminded her of the chant she hummed herself to sleep with. The doors were always locked.

Rumor spread that a minister lived inside, that he kept many women with him. Claire started the rumor.

On Claire's twenty-first birthday, her mother gave her seven gilt-edged Bibles. "For your friends taking Philosophy of Religion 101 with you," she said. Her eyes were set so deep Claire wondered if she saw the edges of her sockets when she glanced left and right. Her straight thin lips reminded Claire of an equal sign.

By the gold doors of the humming church Claire dropped her seven Bibles. Twenty hands pulled her inside, ten naked women hugged her. "Remove your shoes," they said. "Shade your eyes. Overwhelming is the brilliance of our lover, blinding is the radiance of the women he has taught. Close your mouth, ye who would enter, for your gasp echoes. Close your mouth, be silent, our lover may soon utter. Unerring is his wisdom, unending is his grace."

They guided Claire to the organ bench and pressed her shoulders until she lay on her back. They held her hands and feet. "Where is the minister?" Claire asked. They opened their mouths then closed them. No words, just three notes hummed in harmony. They unzipped Claire's skirt, removed her blouse, unbuckled her sandals. Was it unreasonable of her, Claire asked, to demand to see the minister? A woman held her hand on Claire's lips while another, with a sponge, dabbed frankincense on her. Two women touched her nipples, another leaned close to her lips. Three slid their hands along her neck, her arms, her waist. One held Claire's thighs. Then they dressed her in a surplice and said, "You are prepared to meet our lover."

In the east Cry Room, the women sat Claire on the floor. Before them, a gold-skinned man in a large paper bag ate biscuits. When he saw Claire he embraced her and offered her, with the others, biscuits and beer. Claire could not look at him directly, but held the sleeve of her surplice before her eyes. Not even the bag could hide this man's beauty. He addressed the women:

A woman gave birth to a handsome boy at the same moment another woman gave birth to a headless boy. The handsome and the headless boys became best friends. One day the handsome boy's father fell in love with the headless boy's mother and the headless boy's father fell in love with the handsome boy's mother. The parents swapped. Now the handsome and the headless boys had four parents. How happy and confused they were.

The handsome boy grew up bad. He robbed rich families of their grandparents. One day he borrowed a baby. This was too much. One of his fathers sought to whip him. "Where's your mother?" he asked the kid. "Which mother?" "My wife, your mother." "She's with my other mother and my other father," he said. "Where?" cried the father. "In bed," the bad kid said. The father ran off with his whip and the handsome boy was never punished for his crimes.

[*175*]

But the headless boy was not intelligent enough to be bad like his handsome brother. He had no head, poor bastard. His life was sad and uneventful.

All afternoon the minister spoke in parables. At sunset a midget opened a duffel bag for Claire. The minister held her hands. "We enjoy our evenings here," he said. "You're always welcome back." She thanked him. Unwillingly she took her surplice off, dressed again in her clothes and climbed inside the bag.

Wild women fill Claire's lover's church, leaping pew to pew and laughing. "All women will be bad," the lover says. They are. Hymnals show teeth marks from gentle gnawing and indented spines from being thrown against the pews, the altar, hip bones. Singing Glorias, the naked women flip from altar to organ, from organ to altar. They make love to each other, then dress in robes made from the paraments pulled off the altar and the pulpit. They practice scandals with bad boys bagged in from nearby cities. The women grin. They are bad, bad, bad, and love it.

None have seen the minister naked. He appears in the Cry Room fully bagged for morning parables. Near noon he stands behind the pulpit and guides the women in scandal practice. Late afternoons he counsels them, on his knees. They kiss him and each other.

Claire is not satisfied. She wants to see the lover bagless. In the men's room she lies on her back in a stall, peeking up as the minister looks in the mirror. He pulls her up beside him and points in the mirror. "Look how young you are," he says. He shows her his hands, says, "Old," and hits them against the wall. Claire slaps his golden ass and drags him to her mattress. She rips his paper off.

The minister can't get Claire off his back. She clings to his neck as he showers and shaves. While he bakes biscuits, she breathes in his ear and presses her breasts against his shoulder blades. She climbs off only so he can dress in his new paper bag and meet his women for breakfast parables and popovers.

He stares at Claire. He cannot concentrate on his parables. He wants her on his back again.

The minister rearranges his schedule to spend more time with Claire than with the other women. "We can't let them know," he says. "It will disrupt my ministry."

"Why do you teach us bad?" Claire asks. "Bad will be with us always," he explains. "We must be thoughtful so our bad behavior hurts as few as possible. My women will be bad responsibly." Claire requests a sermon on the relationship of bad to sad.

Outside, spitters gather on the premises. It must be winter now, Claire thinks. Standing in their steamy breath, the spitters stare in the Cry Room windows. In packs they glare at their spit as it freezes on a stained-glass shepherd spitting golden biscuits on naked women. The spitters are jealous of the minister. So is Claire. According to the laws he created, Claire should love each woman and the minister equally. But she prefers the minister. She writes a parable:

> A man had eleven wives. One loved the man more than the others and the man loved her more than he loved the others. He threw a party and invited ten men, hoping they would take away ten of his wives. The ten men raped the wife he loved the most and left her behind ten casks of sour wine.

Claire throws the parable away. Outside, the spitters comb their hair. They practice jumping jacks.

On Sunday, the minister repeats a sermon he delivered two months earlier. His congregation regards the large log in his eye.

He writes a parable for Claire:

> A married man sowed pennies in a supermarket parking lot. Some rolled into a drain. Others fell before the front tires of a Mack truck. Wedged in the tire cracks, the pennies were slapped against cement repeatedly before they flew in weedy fields beside the freeways. Still others were swallowed by hungry babies. But one a young woman

[*177*]

found and, considering it good luck, she slipped it into her bra. She fell in love with the married man. But the penny, which the frugal girl hid in her bedroom closet, grew into a young, well-speaking and warmhearted man who was not married. He and the woman fell in love. The married man swore never again to sow his pennies in a supermarket parking lot.

The parable disturbs Claire and the minister. Claire tries to write one:

A young woman kept tickets to Iceland in her freezer. Each morning she defrosted them and read the itinerary. Each afternoon she replaced the tickets underneath the trays of ice. Her lover asked if he could go with her. She bought him tickets, but had to sell the last of her goat milk to do so. Grateful, the lover moved in with her. This made the young woman happier than she'd ever been.

The minister interrupts Claire. "This parable is horrible," he says. "It rambles. What's the point?"

"The point," says Claire, "is that the minister does not stay with his lover and he never goes to Iceland, so the young woman stays on ice forever, fucking young, blond men."

"I don't think the parable as you started it can hang together," he says. "And the relationship between the lovers isn't clear. What is it?"

"The man is interested in the woman's anxiety."

"Is that all? Does he love her?"

"It's not in the parable," says Claire. "That's all I know. It's not in the parable."

Claire writes another:

A greedy man took three fat women to bed. In the night, one stole his wallet. "Who's got it?" he asked at breakfast. None would confess. The women ate and ate—bacon, sausage, popovers—growing ever larger. The greedy man considered kicking them away, but he didn't want to sleep alone. He said, "She who confesses gets a foot-long ice cream sundae." The thief confessed and the greedy man gave her the sundae. She grew. Next morning the greedy man's gun was missing. Naked, he quaked. "Who's got it?" he cried. The women sat at the end of his bed gnawing on his feet. He offered them fried potatoes, shrimp and oysters. The villain pulled the greedy man's gun from behind her back. She ate, she grew.

All four hit the highways. This mobile mountain range struck terror in the hearts of hale pedestrians. The greedy man trembled.

Next morning he couldn't find his clothes. None of my ladies can fit into my clothes, he thought. He knew the evil in their hearts. "Ladies," he cried. "Why do you torture me?"

"What will you feed us?" they asked. He offered them fruit.

"No, no," they said.

"Celery, tomatoes."

"NO."

"Cheese cake?" The clothes fell on his face.

Now each woman measured fifteen feet by fifteen feet. The greedy man moved quickly, but not quick enough. Before the multitude of tow trucks came, the greedy women ate him.

In his room the minister tries to write his sermon on bad and sad. He's thinking of Claire. He wants to be with her, but the women would be upset. Why can't he please himself? Why does he have to be sad? Claire's parables disturb him. She says she has committed the worst bad yet, that she's in love with him. He tries to sleep.

Claire sits in the empty Cry Room. If the minister believes in bad, she thinks, why isn't he with her, now? He has responsibilities to his women. He promised he would train them in decent badness. Claire understands, but she does not feel loved. "Here is my body," she says. "Where is his?"

[*179*]

She looks outside at the spitters smearing each other's spit in their hair. Their primping disgusts her. Why is no handsome man among them, no man with heart and wisdom? Still, they are available. Claire undresses and steps outside. It's lovely weather here, she thinks. It's glorious to be in love, to fall in half-iced puddles, to grin in my sopping slip and bra, to freeze in my sopping slip and bra. I can even get a cold without worrying anyone. "Sick," Mom used to say. "Get ye the hell to bed then. Here's a box of tissues and a throw-up bucket. Best be well tomorrow. I'll have no messes in my house." And the teacher who wore elf-earrings isn't here to give me aspirin from the fat bottle she kept in her top desk drawer. Nor is my lover.

A horde of hungry spitters grabs Claire, wraps her in electrician's tape and rolls her behind a mound of dolls' heads. The spitters take turns raping her. At night they practice spitting by the fireside. Legs taped together, Claire tries to hop away. A spitter lassos her. "Where you going?" he asks. "Back to church," she says. "To praise your lord?" "To sing him hymns." "Sorry, sweetheart," he says. "Can't leave yet. Must pay for stepping out. I won't hurt you *too bad*. One bite here, a bit of blood, a bruise."

Three days Claire has been missing. The minister has not slept. He does not eat. At night he sees a body wrapped in silver, glowing in the light of the spitters' fire. He sends five bad boys out with duffel bags. The spitters toss the boys against the church walls. They run back to the minister. Dare the minister emerge in person? Will the spitters laugh to see he cares so much for Claire? Will they think he is too old? The minister paces the pew ways, looks outside, paces. He leaves the church. He lifts Claire in his arms. Silent, the spitters stare. None try to stop him. The gold man carries his silver lover back to the church. Realizing they cannot penetrate, the spitters slink away in single file.

The minister unwraps his lover and lies beside her on her mattress. He kisses her bruises and anoints her cuts. She wakes ungrateful, with one eye open. "You've been

[*180*]

sleeping with your women," she says. "A different one
each night."

"Ritual," he says.

"Crap," says Claire. "It ain't all pain, this late night
partaking."

"You should leave," he says. "This isn't good for you. I
can't give you what you want."

"Your women need you," she says.

He nods.

The minister is not well. He has begun to disappear
while he is speaking. Several of the women question his
existence. One claims she walked through him twice—
once in the transept, once in the narthex. "He was the
scent of caramel," she says. Another says he disappears
when the choir sings high E. Only Claire can reach the
note and she refuses to repeat it. "He belongs in this
world he created," she says bitterly. "He is the minister."

The women are jealous of the minister's distraction.
They have begun to misbehave their own way instead of
following the minister's instructions. Some have bitten
the bad boys. The boys will not come back. Some women
have stuffed biscuits in the organ pipes. The organ will
not play on key.

Claire is losing patience. Why hasn't the minister addressed his congregation on the relationship of bad to
sad? Why does he say he wants to sleep with her forever,
but sleep with her only once a month? Why does he say
she makes him happy, then tell her he's unhappy?

Claire leaves notes in her lover's Bibles asking him to
meet her. He doesn't. "The other women might . . ." "I
know," says Claire. "They might get jealous." Claire has
lost her patience.

Rumor spreads that those who enter a crack in the north
wall of the men's room will be taken to a land where bad
conscience does not accompany bad action, a land of no
responsibilities. Claire started the rumor. One by one the
women disappear.

The minister is depressed. He wants his women back.
Claire hugs him. "Come to my mattress," she says. "You
told me once you wanted to lie beside me forever, your

left arm under my shoulder, your right arm around me."

The minister retreats behind his pulpit. "I am a minister," he says. "I need my women." He pauses. "And I need you."

"You're a bit too needy then," Claire says. "So am I." She packs her hymnal and her seven Bibles. She removes her surplice, dresses in the blouse and skirt she came in and steps outside in the dark. She hadn't realized it was night. In the church she lost her sense of endings and beginnings.

Beside the welcome-to-our-city sign, Claire watches the gold doors of her lover's church. She will give her lover three hours.

SHOE

Heidi Jon Schmidt

I 've never seen a picture of my grandfather, and in my idea of him, he's not old. I've never seen a photograph, even a poster of a movie star, that can compete with my image of him: very dark in every way, moving powerfully but fluidly, without great thought or care. I believe he's too powerful to be elegant, but that he appears elegant when he wears a suit, that his elegance is assumed with the suit. He's tailored, mustached, composed, a perfect line drawing of a man.

He once designed a famous building, the New York office of the Bank of the Lesser Antilles. He fought in World War Two, was in Paris when the city fell. He grew up in Maine, one of a fatherless family of fourteen, living on potato soup. Somewhere in upstate New York, a town is named for him. These are facts, but they may not pertain to my grandfather. I've heard them or overheard them, but when I repeat them I suspect myself of lying: if I'm talking to an architect, I make my grandfather a criminal lawyer, or a chef. I know that he lives in Sioux City, Iowa, or in Arizona now that he's retired.

I tell people that I'm a dancer, and I usually feel this is the truth. I'm not a ballerina or a chorus girl, but a dancer without the jewels and veils. I study with a well-known master who keeps a studio on the Lower East Side of New York. We lean over, curve our backs, swing our arms loose from our shoulders, jutting one hip upward. We topple and thud to the floor. Taught to consider ourselves substantial, we rarely leap. We move "sinuously—like globs of syrup."

I'm not good at what I do. My muscles are naturally tense. I picture Isadora Duncan wistfully as I flop along with the corps.

We have, as an exercise, to find an attitude for one of our grandparents, to "fit our muscles along their bones." I choose my grandfather. He walks along Gramercy Park, with his pipe. He is wearing a suit. He stops, standing at the wrought-iron gate, holding the pipe just away from his mouth. His other arm is loose at his side. It is evening, and around him everyone is hurrying. They might as well blur. He stands distinct and relaxed, looking away from the street, into the park. Light slants around him, through the tops of the trees.

When I was a child, perhaps six, I found a shoe in my grandmother's closet. She was a schoolteacher, a woman with many small bottles of perfume, and a great number of shoes, all leather, all subdued. Among these was a single shoe, a delightful shoe compared with the others: a high, wedged heel covered in white canvas, stitched all over with glass beads, red and gold and blue. It had no mate that I could find, and it seemed to be a work of art, placed mistakenly, because of its shape, among the shoes.

My mother took it from me before Grandma could see it. Ma's anger has always been cold and terrible. She loses her peripheral vision and sees only the offending act. It is as if she would tear you apart. I stood absolutely silent in front of her, hoping she would overlook me, and she did. She took the shoe straight back to the bedroom, and then she went into the bathroom and took a shower. I climbed up on the back of the couch and pressed my face against my grandmother's window, watching the customers at the deli across the street. When I heard the water stop, I slid down and sat delicately, my feet flat on the floor, a magazine open on my lap.

I am improving the attitude of my grandfather. I think of him in Paris, in uniform. He stands very erect, but easy. My shoulders are loose, one hand rests against the wall in place of Gramercy Park gate, the other is cupped around the space for a pipe. My eyes are absolutely clear, but I don't see the deeply colored leaves that drift in front of me, in the park. He is picturing some scene from the past or the future, not a hazy fantasy, but a sharp-edged vision that would precede action, and in which he is entirely absorbed.

One man in the class is lucky. His grandfather was a hunchback. He stoops and each day the hump is more pronounced. His muscles really work. I am amazed at how close he can come to deformity, and how easily he stands up, stretches out, and returns to his own form.

Some months after my mother turned thirty-five, she got a birthday card from my grandfather. It was a "Happy belated birthday" card for a child, with a pastel circus tent embossed on it, signed "Love, Dad," with his name in parentheses below.

"My father had a wonderful sense of humor," my mother said. Then she looked at the postmark. "Chicago," she said, "I wonder if he lives there." She read the little printed poem on the card out loud, but it didn't seem to mean anything special. She put her arms out to me and held me, and cried.

It was that year, I think, that I found the shoe again. At first I thought it was the mate to the one at my grand-mother's. I had forgotten the shoe, probably forgotten it the same day I first saw it, but now, discovering it in the back of an unused bureau stored in the cellar, I remembered my mother's face, distorted with anger, returned to composure only after she came out of the shower, her hair wrapped in a towel that gave her the height of a statue. I did not mention it to her this time. I reached into the drawer for the shoe and carried it up to my room, where I stuffed it inside one of my own boots. Knowing my mother's response to it, I waited until I was alone with my grandmother.

"Where did you get that?" she said, when she saw the shoe in my hand. I had never heard her speak so sharply.

"It's just like the one at your house," I said.

"There's only one shoe like that," she said. "Give it to me." She took it out of the room, and when she returned, she was kind and befuddled again, asking if I wanted to help her make caramel apples.

That night, I sat on the top stair and listened to her arguing with my mother. Grandma sounded tired, frustrated. Over and over again she said, "I don't know." Ma's voice was bitter, sarcastic, very low. I could hardly hear it, and what I heard, I couldn't understand.

I searched the shoe stores for a pair like the jeweled wedgie I had found, but there were no wedged heels at all that year. When I finally described the shoe to a saleswoman she went behind the counter and said to the cashier, "Marty, this girl wants a pair of hooker shoes."

I'm at work on the hips, in particular. My grandfather is not a man who would place great emphasis on his hips, I don't think. His shoulders are very sharp, his spine is straight, but his hips are casually at rest. His feet are slightly apart, and his body rises comfortably out of this powerful stance, mannered and elegant in his straight neck, his direct gaze.

My classmates regard me with derisive awe.

"What was this guy, a male model?"

"One of the first," I say, "that's how he put himself through architecture school. It was the Depression, you know."

"Well," says this woman, whose grandmother must have been a potato farmer, from the attitude she strikes, "maybe you should think of him later in life, give him some more character."

She means to be helpful, I know. "He died in World War Two," I say. I don't think of this as a real lie.

"Well, you can't just do a pose. Look how stylized this is." I look into the mirror as she runs her finger along the curve of my outstretched arm. Maybe he was just a stylized kind of guy. "You've really got to get in there and give us his heart," she tells me.

I strive. I know he stands at the fence. I know he's attractive, intriguing to the men and women who pass him, carrying baskets of bread, sausages, and cabbage. The air is stingingly cool, the sweetness of the decaying leaves is masked by an odor of coffee and diesel exhaust. Two children squeeze through a break in the fence and my grandfather looks above them, outward, making a plan, I think. He's too stiff, too separate. I sag a little and lose him altogether. I want to be stoop-shouldered and cross-armed, to hang my head. It is his ideas, his emotions, that give him his substance. I don't know how to work backward.

When I was sixteen, my boyfriend went away for the summer and came back engaged to be married. For weeks I was despondent. My mother was despondent for me. We stayed up all night watching late movies and I shuffled to school exhausted, got high in the parking lot at noon, giggled through French class and fell asleep in study hall.

One night, in the middle of *Zombies from Beneath the Swamp,* we were picturing the married life of my boyfriend and his fiancée: grey dish towels figured prominently in the discussion. I would get even with them just by letting them live their drab little wedded life. "And," Ma said, laughing, "as a last resort, you can always send her your shoe."

"What?" I said.

We were terribly punchy; she had a pillow over her face and was laughing uncontrollably. She dropped the pillow slightly, so she could see me. "Of course, I don't think *those* shoes would do it." She pointed to my desert boots, drying beside the fireplace. "It should be something a little risqué, preferably something that reveals some toe." She put the pillow back over her face and laughed.

The zombies had gained entrance to the manor house, and the pretty blond girl sat up in bed suddenly, the silk strap of her nightgown slipping over her shoulder as she screamed.

"That's what your grandfather's lover did," she said, "and it worked like a charm. Just the shoe, no message, but

[*187*]

my mother didn't have much trouble figuring it out. It's not every day that people send single shoes in the overseas mail."

The girl in the silk nightgown was, by now, a zombie. She still looked pretty to us, but she tilted her head and turned toward the camera and we could see it: her eyes were dead.

"Of course," my mother said, "*she* had the shoes for it. Your grandmother had boots. *Out* went philandering Philip."

"Where did he go from there?"

"Well," she said, "he lived on Gramercy Park for a little while, and he didn't go back to France, but otherwise I just don't know."

"Don't you wonder where he is?"

"Why? Do you think he wonders about me?" She was quiet for a few minutes. Then she said, "I'm sorry I brought it up."

The next night I stayed up alone.

When my parents were divorced and we moved out of the house, I found the shoe again. It was very well hidden this time, in a barrel of old stuffed toys that had long since been turned into mouse nests. I was alone when I found it, and I packed it with my few clothes and books, and took it to New York with me.

I can't find an attitude for my grandfather. I know it's an attitude, not a pose, I know I'm supposed to look for his heart. We're not supposed to do research, but I have to resort to it. I find the New York office of the Bank of the Lesser Antilles: it takes up three rooms in a hideous blue and white box of a building downtown.

Finally, I take the shoe out with me, to Little Italy, where I ask people until I find the address of a shoemaker. He lives in an apartment with beaded curtains, beaded radiator covers, and a vat of soup in which whole chickens roll in boiling stock. Yes, he can make another shoe like this. It will cost one hundred dollars. Beadwork is expensive. I talk him down to fifty-five, which still means I have to cancel my dentist appointment. As I leave, he says, "Fifty-five for you only," and pinches my ass quickly twice, once on each cheek. I don't turn when he does this, but the next week, when I return to pick them up, I stand in the doorway to hand him the cash, and back all the way to the stairs.

Now that I have the shoes, I have everything. They very nearly match. The beadwork of the older shoe has a harsh glow; I imagine there's gold in the dye. The new pigments are too basic, too exact. I want to run home, but I walk, taking the stairs two at a time all the way up the six flights to my apartment.

I've never asked again about my grandfather or the shoe. My mother got one more card from him, at Christmas, years after her divorce. Its printed message read:

> To wish you loads of Christmas cheer,
> and love that grows each passing year.

She threw it out in a pile of sale announcements and grocery circulars, and I didn't bother to retrieve it. It was postmarked Sioux City, Iowa. Maybe he's a salesman. Maybe he's been a hog farmer all these years. I suppose he's retired now, but I can't think he would retire to Sioux City, Iowa.

In the center of my room, I stretch my arm out. I'm my grandfather outside one of the Gramercy Park gates, in 1945. It's autumn, and the sky is steel grey, just before dusk. Children play in the park, their coats folded over schoolbooks on the benches. I look out over their heads over the fallen leaves in the park. I wait to feel my muscles drawn into place around some specific emotion. My grandfather looks out over the gate into the network of color and movement that makes up the city, but he sees the horizon of Sioux City, Iowa: uniform and yellowish grey.

I myself see, at this moment, a pair of extravagantly, surpassingly gaudy shoes. I give up on my grandfather and put them on.

They are the highest heels I've ever worn, and the minute I stand in them my body conforms to their dictates: my ankles tilt forward and every other bone leans back to balance them. I stretch my arm out, bring the other to my mouth with the imaginary pipe, and I am indeed a ridiculous figure. I walk confidently in these shoes, taller and more fluid, and I cannot possibly move like my grandfather now. I stand straighter than I ever have, my breasts thrust forward against the cloth of my shirt, my head back, almost thrown back. If I were to laugh right now, it would be a strong but not derisive laugh that I think my grandfather would attend; the laugh of someone who understands what he looks for, and what he sees.

THE NUISANCE

Penelope Gilliatt

A woman on her own, in a knitted hat and navy-blue mackintosh. Thin, no makeup, kind face, wrinkles around pleasant eyes. She stands at a table in a bacon-and-chip shop, apparently waiting for something. She looks at the open door.

"Cold, isn't it?" She speaks to anyone.

A fat woman with her back to the door says: "I don't feel it."

"It's cold, I said. Isn't it?" Pleading.

"I don't feel it."

"You're all right, then?"

"Close it if you like but I don't feel it. I don't mind what you do."

A young girl sitting at a table with her boyfriend shrugs, gets up, closes the door herself.

The thin woman hasn't anything else to talk about for the moment. She sits down with a cup of tea, undoes her shoulder bag, which is pinned together with a safety pin, and puts the pin in her coat like a nappy pin. In the bag there is visible a folded evening paper, a handkerchief, and something wrapped up in a grocer's bag that has been creased and flattened out and reused several times so that it is soft and pliant, like a fabric. She takes out the paper bag, unfolds it, and sets half a buttered roll in front of her on top of the bag. The man behind the counter looks at her, because she hasn't bought anything, but trade is slack at three-thirty in the afternoon and there are empty tables, so he says nothing.

"Makes you sick, doesn't it?" she says, in a loud voice. Her tone is conversational, as though she were passing down a village street full of people whom she saw every day instead of sitting alone in a Blackpool café off-season in the presence of strangers.

"This weather. You can't wait for spring, can you? You get fed up with it."

The fat woman whispers something to her friend and laughs. An old man leaves a single chip on the side of his plate in the way his mother had taught him and props a paper against the sauce bottle. The thin woman looks carefully at each table in turn and then goes up to the counter for a cup of tea.

"No sugar. I can't stand sugar in tea, can you?" The owner of the café turns the steel handle of the urn and pushes a sugar basin at her with the tea. She sits down again with her hands in her lap and looks at the cup for a time.

"What a lovely cup. I do like nice china. I can't seem to fancy tea in a thick cup." The girl sitting with her boy-friend makes a ga-ga face to him and giggles.

"The reason I'm on my own is I enjoy it. I can't stand people who don't know how to be alone, can you? Neighbors, neighbors, neighbors, you can't hear yourself think with the sort of neighbors I've got. Talk! Sometimes I think I should go and find a desert island. How many words do you think they get through in a day? Thousands, I should think. Ten or twenty thousand. Will they leave me alone? I ask you. Their noses are longer than their arms. Chatter chatter chatter. Keeping you gossiping when you're in a hurry. Get me? I've got a lot to do. I haven't got the time."

She falls silent for five or ten minutes. The old man finishes his paper and goes out without looking at her. The young couple play a game with some matches and press their noses together. The fat woman and her friend collect their shopping bags onto their knees and then go on sitting there, muttering low enough to be able to hear her when she speaks again without having to acknowledge that they are listening. A workman in overalls comes in and collects a cup of tea, a ham sandwich and a slice of apple pie at the counter. He looks in her direction when he turns round with the plates. She moves up in her cubicle and shifts her roll and the cup to make room for him, and then watches him sit down at another table. After a moment she goes up to the counter.

"Give me a ham sandwich and a slice of apple pie, will you, love? The pie looks beautiful. Homemade, I expect. I like cooking with materials, don't you, not with a tin opener."

The owner looks irritable and takes his time. She stands there silently for a few minutes and he tells her to go and sit down. He ignores the existing pile of ham sandwiches and makes another one, using margarine out of a packet instead of the mixture of butter and margarine ready in a white pie dish. While she is waiting at the table she opens her shoulder bag again and counts out the right money, putting it neatly into a pile of coins with six coppers at the bottom, then a shilling, then a threepenny bit, and two sixpences at the top.

"I'm lucky. I live in a corner house. I pity people in the middle of the row, don't you? Houses each side, everlasting chat chat chat over the fence, heads hanging over like horses. I've just got them on the one side. They don't wait for me to speak, you know. They break the ice straight off. When I had my baby my husband was away, and my neighbor said I only had to knock on the wall and she'd come. Mind you, she said she weren't forced to hear me, but I took that as a joke. I soon put her at her ease. We laughed—you should have heard it. I'm close, of course. I'm a Cheshire cat. She don't call me by my Christian name. I don't care. You might say I'm the square peg. When I run out of tea I don't go knocking. They come round to me all the time, they drive me mad. That's the beauty of living on your own, isn't it? You don't have to speak to anyone if you don't want to. My mum used to say to me, you shut your mouth or I'll put a sticking plaster on it. She took me out to work with her when she was in service and I'd sit on the potato urn hour after hour just watching her. Only once I got on her wick, shouting I expect like children do, and she learned me a lesson I'll always be grateful for though I didn't appreciate it at the time. She shoved me in the broom cupboard with an Elastoplast on me mouth and after that I knew how to keep out of people's hair. When I got the pains I remembered that. I check the layette, then I go out and telephone the doctor, I bank up the fire with some damp coal dust so it keeps in, then I make myself a cup of tea. I take my time. You got to try not to think about things. There's never anything wrong with me. If you think about it, it gets a hold on you. Then I wind up the clocks because I never like to see a clock run down and I don't know how long it'll be before I'm up and about again. I lie down, then I get up and make a sandwich and put it by the bed in case I fancy it but by then the pains is coming quite fast and I don't want it yet. Then I lie down again and listen to the clocks ticking and think, by the time I have that sandwich there'll be a baby in the house, making such a racket I won't be able to hear myself think; I'll regret it I shouldn't wonder. Of course I know I won't but I make myself laugh. Because I've got used to being on my own, you see. I don't depend on company. The time goes by. I thought, my time's my own, I wouldn't change places with anyone in the world. Then the doctor don't come and I start not to feel too good. Nothing to write about, though. I bang on the wall, more to take my mind off it than anything. I knew she were in because I heard her kettle whistling. She were in the room right next to me. It's only a partition wall and I could hear her moving about. She weren't deaf neither because she used to complain about the kids on the other side of her. You wouldn't think anyone would let a baby die just because it was going to cry, would you? But I'm right. I know I'm right. I've been over it in my mind. The truth is she's a single woman and she's jealous. She's never been married. She don't know how to converse with people. In the case of my husband she was jealous because he was a gentleman, like a doctor. He had a beautiful sunny disposition and he indited the best letters a wife ever had. He were away in the navy in Hong Kong etcetera and I got a letter from everywhere he went, sometimes a picture postcard and sometimes a letter airmail.

When he were home in the old days he used to go fish-
ing at the weekends and he'd sell the fish and put it towards a motor bike. He bought a B.S.A., not secondhand,
it cost two hundred pounds, he used to clean it with Min
cream in the evenings and I'd stand in the door so the
light shone out for him and we'd talk and laugh until gone
midnight and then sometimes go out for a spin with me
on the pillion. I expect that was what got her. Then when
he were off she started getting her knife into me because
she knew I were on my own. But I can stand up for myself. I don't need her. It were just that time. I'm glad she
didn't come when you think about it because she'd have
made a nuisance of herself. I were better off on my own."

HARRY AND SYLVIA AND SYLVIA AND SO ON

Welch D. Everman

Once upon a time, Harry and Sylvia were husband and wife. Now Harry is single and Sylvia is married to Tom. This kind of thing happens all the time nowadays.

Harry sits in his apartment and realizes that he is not satisfied with his new life. And so one Friday night he goes to the 5 & 10 and buys a parakeet. He takes it home in its shiny cage and hangs it in a corner of the living room. The bird is bright green with a pale blue chest and a yellow beak. He calls it Sylvia.

For a week, Harry tries to teach the parakeet to say its own name. Then he spends another week trying to teach it to say his name. The bird says nothing. It does not make a sound. It never sings. It sits on its perch all day, in silent thought.

Harry goes to the local pound and gets a huge overweight gray and white tomcat. They give him a large cardboard box with air holes and a handle so he can carry it home. He puts out a dish of dry cat food, a bowl of water, and a litter box in one corner of the kitchen. The cat pisses in the opposite corner, next to the refrigerator. He calls it Sylvia.

Sylvia the cat seems to like him well enough. It rubs against his legs at mealtime. Of course Harry does not expect the cat to speak, and of course it doesn't. It is as silent as Sylvia the bird. And also like Sylvia the bird, Sylvia the cat does not answer to its name. Harry sits in his chair in the living room and calls the cat again and again, but it never comes. It does not even look at him. Most of the time, it sleeps on the sofa or on top of the TV.

Harry goes back to the pound and gets a huge multicolored dog, part golden retriever and part German shepherd. They don't have a box large enough for the dog, and Harry wouldn't be able to carry it in any case. They give Harry a piece of rope to use as a leash, and the dog pulls him home. He calls it Sylvia.

He takes Sylvia the dog out for a walk twice a day. The dog loves to walk and sniff at things. It also loves Harry. Whenever he calls its name, it runs to him, wagging its tail, and jumps into his lap if he is sitting or knocks him down if he is standing up. Sylvia the dog barks constantly, day and night.

But Sylvia the dog cannot bring him a beer, fix his breakfast, or clean up the apartment. Neither can Sylvia the cat or Sylvia the bird. The apartment really needs cleaning. The dog fur, cat fur, and feathers are everywhere. But Harry understands that housekeeping is too much to ask of his new pets. Half-heartedly, he tries to teach Sylvia the dog how to open the refrigerator door, take a beer in its mouth, and bring it to him in the living room. The dog only barks and wags its tail.

Now Harry's apartment is full of animals and animal smells, but Harry's life is not so very different from what it was. Still, Sylvia the dog, Sylvia the cat, and Sylvia the bird keep him busy. He feeds them, cleans the cage and the litter box, walks the dog. Having the pets there with him gives him something to do. The animals seem to get along well enough. They ignore each other.

Then one day Harry comes home with a bag of bird seed, dry cat food, and dog burgers to find the cage lying on the floor, empty. There are green and blue feathers all over the living room. Sylvia the dog meets him at the door, licks his hand, then romps across the furniture. Sylvia the cat is alseep on top of the TV. Sylvia the bird is nowhere in sight.

Harry looks for the parakeet in the bedroom, the bathroom, and the kitchen, though he doesn't expect to find it. Sylvia the bird is gone.

At last Harry returns to the living room, sits in his chair, and stares at Sylvia the cat until it wakes up and looks at him. There is not a sign of guilt in its hard green eyes.

The next morning Harry opens his apartment door to get his newspaper. As he bends down to pick it up, he hears a terrible screech behind him and turns in time to see Sylvia the cat dash past him and into the hall, its ears back and its fur standing on end. Sylvia the dog follows quickly, barking and wagging its tail, its tongue dangling from the side of its mouth. The dog knocks Harry to the floor, then jumps over him and chases the cat down the hall. Harry gets to his feet and hurries after them.

The front door of the apartment building is propped open. Harry runs out to the sidewalk and looks up and down the street. Sylvia the dog and Sylvia the cat are gone.

That night Harry is watching TV when he hears a scratching and whining at the door. He finds Sylvia the dog standing out in the hall alone, wagging its tail and slobbering on the rug.

Harry puts the bird cage and the litter box in the trash and buys Sylvia the dog a new collar. Now Harry and Sylvia are together almost constantly. They watch TV together and sit together on the sofa; Harry even lets the dog sleep across the foot of his bed. When he goes to the grocery store or the laundromat, he takes the dog with him and ties it to a parking meter outside. Sylvia always waits for him, crying, barking, rocking back and forth impatiently. Of course the dog still cannot bring him a beer or clean the apartment, but it keeps his feet warm at night.

In truth, Sylvia bores him. The dog isn't very bright and has no personality. The fact is that Sylvia is incapable of being anything but a dog. Harry has no right to expect any more. Each morning Sylvia greets him by licking his face like a dog, and at night Sylvia curls up like a dog at his feet and goes to sleep. Again, Harry spends a day or two trying to teach Sylvia to bring him a beer. He soon realizes that this is not something a dog is likely to do.

And then one afternoon Harry comes out of the grocery store and finds Sylvia's empty collar lying on the sidewalk, still attached to the leash he tied to the parking meter. The dog is gone. Somehow, for some reason, it slipped out of the collar and ran away. Harry waits there in front of the store for an hour or more, but Sylvia does not return. In time he walks back to his apartment alone, leaving the collar and the leash behind.

The days pass slowly until one night Harry knows he cannot spend another minute alone in the apartment. He goes out to the street and walks through the city, going nowhere in particular. It is a cool evening, and the sky is clear and full of stars. He walks slowly for an hour or so before he realizes that he is looking for Sylvia. The idea is foolish, of course. He is nowhere near the grocery store where he last saw the dog. And yet, for no good reason, he expects to see it again at any moment, running toward him down the street, barking and wagging and slobbering. He walks quickly now, knowing that Sylvia could be waiting for him around the next corner.

In time, he comes to a street full of bars, movie theaters, and women in short tight skirts. The women stand on the corners or in front of magazine and novelty shops, alone, in couples, or in small groups. They look at Harry as he walks by, and he looks back. Finally one of them, a short dark girl with big breasts and heavy thighs, says:

"Hi, lover."

Her voice is deep and husky.

Harry stops and looks at her closely. He does not remember having seen her before.

"Sylvia?" he asks.

She shakes her head. "Dolores," she says.

At the other end of the block, a tall broad-shouldered young woman in a tight green dress stands alone. Harry walks up to her slowly.

"Got something in mind, baby?" she says.

He shrugs. "Sylvia?"

"If you say so." She smiles.

He says nothing more for the moment. Her smiles fades quickly.

"You got a place?" she asks.

"Sure."

She whistles for a cab.

Back in his apartment, Sylvia pushes the newspapers and magazines off the sofa, sits down, and crosses her long legs. The mess does not seem to bother her. Harry had hoped it might.

"This is a nice neighborhood," she says. "I grew up only a couple of blocks from here."

"My name's Harry," Harry says.

Sylvia nods and stands up. "I ain't got all night," she mutters as she undoes the buttons down the front of her dress. She is naked underneath.

Harry sits in his chair. "Sylvia?" he says.

"Yeah, right, what is it?"

"Will you get me a beer?"

She puts her hands on her broad hips, glares at him, and shakes her head. A long heavy breast pops out of her green dress, but she doesn't seem to notice.

"I ain't your fucking serving girl," she says. Then suddenly she smiles. "Unless that's your thing, huh? Is that it? You're Harry, and I'm Sylvia, the happy housewife, right? I bring you a beer, maybe your pipe and slippers, and then we get down to it. Hey, it's okay with me, as long as nobody gets hurt. That's out. I'll be Sylvia and all that shit, but no pain. I don't dish it out, and I don't take it."

"No pain," Harry mumbles. He still doesn't have his beer.

"Hey," Sylvia says, turning away from him, "did you hear that?"

There is a strange scratching sound at his door. Harry gets up and opens it. Sylvia the dog trots into the apartment, its tail wagging furiously.

Sylvia the woman looks at the dog and frowns. "Cute," she says.

The dog doesn't even glance at Harry. It stops in front of Sylvia the woman and growls ominously. Harry doesn't understand. Sylvia the woman backs away slowly, and the dog follows, snarling.

"What the hell is this?" she screams. "Is the fucking dog part of the act, too? You didn't say anything about no fucking dog. I don't go for that."

Harry looks on as Sylvia the woman and Sylvia the dog move slowly and dramatically around the living room. He has never seen the dog act like this before.

Sylvia the woman backs toward the door cautiously, buttoning her dress with one hand while she covers her mouth with the other as if to keep herself from screaming. She is terrified, and with good reason. The dog bares its teeth and inches toward her, ready to attack, its fur bristling.

"Call it off," Sylvia the woman says in a harsh whisper. "Please!"

"Sylvia?" Harry says. There is nothing he can do. He only looks on as the woman opens the door slowly and steps back into the hall. But before she can get the door closed again, the dog bolts after her. She screams and runs toward the stairs with the dog snapping at her spiked heels. Harry knows that he will not see either of them again.

He closes the door after them and turns the lock. Then Harry goes to the kitchen to get himself a beer.

NARCISSUS EXPLAINS

Richard Howard

Any number of stories are told
   (mostly tedious sermons
   on Vanity. If you ask me,
     where there's an image
   there's hope—without an idol
   in it, what's a heaven for?)
and any number of theories spawned
   from the dawn of time until
   this afternoon—endeavors
     by the inventive
   to decipher the reasons
   I loiter here, perched on my
riverbank, pondering the features
   which incessantly reform
   under my gaze (reforms
     are Nature's *forte,*
   as I have found—if She has
   one weakness, it's that She can't
do Her thing just once. Rivers resume . . .),
   although some sources assert
   it is no more than a pond,
     barely a freshet
   which fastens my attention
   so fast to myself: "the springs
of Narcissism," they say, "are shallow."

And of course there is Freud's myth of me
   which proposes that I act
   (if you can call it acting—
     let's say I *behave*)
   as if I were my mother
   "and thus enjoy being loved"—

this is Freud—"by myself." Note that *thus*!
   Mums, you know, is a minor
   Naiad named Leriope,
     madly *dégagée*
   about the consequences
   of a dip in my father—
you may have heard of him: Cephisus?
   He passes, in Boeotia,
   for a torrent. Anyway,
     according to Freud,
   I love myself-as-a-boy
   because (now get this) I "tend
to identify with the parent
   at whose hands I have suffered
   the more severe frustrations."
     Need I remind you,
   Daddy has *no hands at all,*
   and Leriope is far
too silly to frustrate anyone!

I say, we love not only ourselves
   but what ourselves can become:
   best to keep an eye—keep both!—
     on what we *have* loved
   if we cultivate fond hopes
   of there being any future
in it. That's what I'm doing right now
   where the river serves my turn,
   my academy, my rule . . .
     It is religion,
   this belief that whatever
   happens to me must matter,
and can never, for just that reason,
   altogether disappear
   from the world. Body dearest,
     all I have is you,
   you and the water that knows
   forever the things of once . . .

Have I so much? My darling flesh,
  even the loveliest of
  mortals can make love to no
    more than what you are:
  the shroud or is it the shrine
  dividing us—bodily—
from what we call our divinity?

No, the tale's truth is to be defined
  elsewhere. To be found, in fact,
  by night, when the dark water
    comes into its own;
  after sunset you can hear
  the solar system laughing
in the stream. I think it laughs in Greek.
  Once my pored-over image
  is effaced by the longed-for
    metamorphosis,
  in its place the entire sky
  is rife with stars reflected
by unseen water. I wait for night
  to become such a glory,
  and then I become the night.
    Now you understand
  why there is no Narcissus
  among the stars: I engross
all figures there by my gradual
  consideration! I faint
  beside the river until
    night and the stars fill
  my emptiness. I cite your saint
  who minted *soliloquy*:
"having found amazement, I found peace."

BABEL ABOARD THE HELLAS
INTERNATIONAL EXPRESS

Amy Clampitt

Border halt, an hour out of Saloniki.
Washrooms already filthy. Corridor
a frisson of peaked caps, red-seaweed
postage-stamp outlandishnesses at a
standoff. *Gastarbeiter* bound for Munich

in a second-class couchette: sad Greek
whose wife is sick (he tells us in
sepulchral German), who can't stop smoking—
a brown man, brown-suited, runneled face
a map of nicotine. Slaves of caffeine,

we hop down, throng the last-chance café (none
aboard the train, none in Yugoslavia. No
food either. Warned, we've brought aboard
bread, cheese, wine, olives, peaches), stoke
ourselves with swarthy oversweetened coffee

while brown man lays in his own supply
of what? It's yogurt: five, six, seven
plastic-lidded tublets' curded slime. He
stacks them (and we shudder) on the filthy
floor. We cut cheese. He smokes. He can't

stop smoking. By designation the compartment
is *Nicht Raucher,* Ἀπαγορεύεται τό κάπνισμα.
Useless to complain. We're sorry for him.
And anyhow there's a fourth occupant, a
brown man too, who seems inscrutable (he might

be Greek, might not be) and who, without
apology, murkily, incessantly, *ist auch ein
Raucher*—though mainly in the corridor.
Dusk. We're moving. We've crossed the border.
We halt again. We're sots and thralls

of Babel and demography. New ghouls
have come aboard. We scare each other,
telling of papers gone astray. We're passing
through a gorge. The lockstep trudge brings in
new hues, new snarls of peaked-cap seaweed,

old mores, old anxieties: our pasteboard
vitals handed over, peered into, returned or
not returned, repeatedly. It's dark outside.
Glimpses of halted freight cars. Someone
flourishing a flashlight walks the track, to spy

out what spies? what contraband? It's coffee,
someone says. They opened up somebody's suitcase
back there, found it packed with kilo bagfuls. Took
them all. Detained the passenger. We're pouring
wine. Trudge, trudge. Visa control again:

passports one by one are handed back. Mine
not among them. Why? Where is it? Ghoul
shrugs. Trapdoor opening—fright, indignation,
fury, sputtered futile questions. Gallantry
between us: "I'll stay with you." "No,

no. You go on to Munich. You know you
must." I don't believe a word of this, of
course. I take a Miltown. Reiterated gusts
of asking why, dire glee of strangers. Next,
Skopje. I'm being brave. I'm not being brave, I am

in fact behaving childishly. Washroom
so filthy you can't squat. No drinking
water either. Worse: it now turns out
I'm not a martyr. The latest peaked-cap-
wearer fingers my shoulder bag. I look

and squirm: It's there. Who put it back?
No way of knowing. "I do feel such a fool.
You won't tell anybody? I'll never live it down."
"It might have been some trick of theirs,"
you say, still gallant. Maybe. I doubt it.

The Skopje passengers flood in. "Komplett!
Komplett!" Our brown companions fend them off.
We settle onto our couchettes. Wake in Belgrade.
No coffee. Hawkers of pasty, tasteless pastries.
New hordes crowd aboard. It's Sunday morning.

"Komplett! Komplett!" All Yugoslavia is traveling,
won't be kept out. The kerchiefed proletariat
from Istanbul, who got on back at Nis, may
be deterred, but not the middle class.
A couple and their little boy have joined us—

sad, tight-garbed, stodgy-prosperous.
Their little boy is blind. Their burden,
shared, is our affliction. Salamander-pale,
he sways, croons, laughs convulsively,
is told to hush; whimpers, subsides again

to sea-cave solitudes we can't imagine.
At Zagreb they leave us. The crowds are worse.
"Komplett! Komplett!" No use. Disconsolate
brown man whose wife is sick climbs back
onto top berth to sleep—the one last solace.

His untouched yogurt has begun to spill. A mess.
The washrooms are by now a costive-making,
hopeless *cauchemar.* The Serbs, Slovenes,
Croatians, Bosnians, Albanians, who knows what
else, who swarm the corridors, are civil,

appeal to reason, persist, at last prevail.
Stout ruddy woman; lean, fair-haired, ruddy man;
two small dark nondescripts; one human barrel,
chalk-stripe-tailored, glistening-curly-haired,
Lech Walesa-mustachioed, jovial: with these,

till Munich, we're to share what space there is.
They speak some common dialect, we're not
sure which. A bag of prunes is passed.
We offer olives. The conversation grows
expansive: we listen in on every syllable,

[*207*]

uncomprehending, entranced. A bottle
circulates: I hesitate, see what it is,
and sip. Stupendous. Not to be missed,
this brew. It burns, it blazes. Anecdote
evolves, extends, achieves a high adagio,

grows confidential, ends in guffaws. O
for a muse of slivovitz, that fiery booze,
to celebrate this Babel, this untranslatable
divertimento all the way to Munich,
aboard a filthy train that's four hours late!

EFFET DE NEIGE

Claude Monet
La Route de la Ferme St-Siméon,
Honfleur, about 1867

John Hollander

Saying: Figures of light and dark, these two are walking
The winter road from the St. Simeon farm
Toward something that the world is pointing toward
At the white place of the road's vanishing
Between the vertex that the far-lit gray
Of tree-dividing sky finally comes down to
And the wide arrowhead the road itself
Comes up with as a means to its own end.
Père and Mère Chose could be in conversation
Or else, like us, sunk into some long gaze
Unreadable from behind—they are well down
The road, but not yet far enough ahead
For any part of them we can make out
To have been claimed by what we see of what
They move against, or through, or by, or toward.
Toward . . . that seems to be the whispered question
That images of roads, whether composed
By the design of our own silent eyes
Or by the loud hand of painting, always put.
Where does this all end? What is the vanishing
Point, after all, when finally one reaches
The ordinary, wide scene which begins
To reach out into its own vanishing
From there. Toward . . .

Seeing: :   :   :   :   :

Saying: Yes. You'd want that said, (if you
Want anything said at all, which I still doubt)
—The place the road ends, that patch of white paint
Marked with a dark stroke from the left, encroached
Upon from the right by far trees, that white place
Sits at the limit of a kind of world
That only you and I can know. Les deux

Choses, Mère and Père, undreaming even of fields
Of meaning like these—the world created by
That square—Oh, 56 x 56
Centimeters—that the height of the canvas
Cuts out of its width (81). Unfair
To mark that square, perhaps: were Mère and Père
Chose to walk out of it, they'd have to pass
Out of the picture of life, as it were, out
Through the back of the picture at the patch of white
At the end of the road. Even if they are staring
Down the long course of the gray slush of things
How can they get the point of how a world
Like theirs ends? From what distant point of vision
Would their world not remain comfortably
Coextensive with everything? How could they know?
What can we know of whatever picture-plane
Against which we have been projected? What . . .

Seeing: :   :   :   :   :

Saying: Oh, I know. The snow. The effective snow
Of observation lying on the ground
Given by nature will soak into it.
Wheel tracks entrench themselves in snow, yet painted
Traces of those deep cuts lie thickly upon
The high whites spread over the buried earth.
Shadows keep piling up as surfaces
Are muffled into silence that refuses
To pick up even the quickening of wind
In dense bare branches, or the ubiquitous
Snaps of ice cracking in the hidden air.
Silence. Your way of being. Your way of seeing
Still has to be intoned, as in a lonely
Place of absorbing snow, itself to be
Seen. What you know is only manifest
When I am heard, and what I say is solely
A matter of getting all that right . . .

Seeing: :   :   :   :   :

Saying: I know,
I've drifted somewhat from the distant heart

Of the matter of snow here. Both of us have grasped
That patch of white at the very end of the road
As it sits there like an eventual
Sphinx of questioning substance, or a sort
Of Boyg of Normandy . . .

Seeing: :   :   :   :   :

Saying: Yes. The obvious
Standing in the way of the truth. A white
Close at the end of distance the two Chose
People might see to be the opening
Out of the road into a way across
Wide, whited fields, a way unframed at last
By trees—or might see as the masonry
Of a far barn, just where the road curves sharply
Right, and appears from here to be overcome
By what it seems to have moved toward. In any
Event, the end of the painted road ends up
In white, in paint too representative
Of too much truth to do much more than lie
High on this surface, guarding the edge of Père
And Mère Chose's square of world, even as they
—Now that you notice it—have just moved past
The edge of that other square cut from the right
Side of the painting, the world of that wise, white,
Silent patch of ultimate paint. You are
Grateful, I know, for just such compensations,
That neither the motionless farm couple trudging
Toward the still dab of white that oscillates
From point to point of meaning—open? closed?—
Nor, indeed, the bit of paint itself can know of.

Seeing: :   :   :   :   :

Saying: Mère and Père Chose are walking away from the
Two of us, Docteur and Madame Machin, who stand
Away from their profundity of surface.

Seeing: :   :   :   :   :

Saying: The truth, blocking the path of the obvious.

SALISBURY CATHEDRAL FROM THE BISHOP'S GROUND

Donald Finkel

Constable, 1823

If, by melting or smelting, by roasting
or blasting, solution or dissolution,
they wrought the transmutations of lead,
by precipitation, by flaking or grinding
from greasy slate to chinese scarlet,
from grizzled ash to royal red,

to what might humble lead aspire,
burning yellow, blending green,
that grey stones reach for milky clouds,
that under Salisbury's soaring towers
Constable's cows might safely graze
and meek grass turn to clotted cream?

THE BIOGRAPHIES OF SOLITUDE

Irving Feldman

Blue the hills, red the fields,
where the kisses and blows were dealt . . .
How eager they were, marching away,
enlistees in the horde of love.
Farewell the sweethearts
—they never came back.
Welcome, sisters of solitude.

And who will say these lives have been?

Solitude has no biographers.

Nonetheless, hands move across the pages.
Nonetheless, empty pages go from hand to hand.
Nonetheless, papers blow over the landscape
of magical names, the beautiful promises.

One is in snowy Idaho, raging.
One in California sits before her mirror,
considering death.
One takes hot baths in Tennessee,
to calm herself, calm herself down.
In Kansas one scribbles madly.
One walks in a daze in the crowds
on Forty-second Street, barefoot,
her feet bruised, day after day.
In the hospital of the wind.

What the flood has spared is given
into the keeping of the whirlwind.

Day after day the wind
numbering the losses . . .

"From now on I will love only myself."
"I no longer try to make sense to people."
"It's all a game anyway."
"Back then I still had my ideals.
No sacrifice was too much for me.
I was strong. I felt everything."
"I don't even pity myself anymore."

They bite their lips.
Shrug their shoulders.

"What is there left to protect?"
"Who can you trust?"

How America is immense and filled with solitudes!

TELEMETRY BEFORE IMPACT

George Starbuck

Fact: Large parts of Times Square are
to be demolished and rebuilt in time for
celebration of the Columbiad in 1992.

(the expanse of sidewalk)

A mass of savages. A pair of glasses.
A protozoa population crisis.
Clean slate and a phalanx of kazoos.

A potentate in carnival regalia
Plays pylon and panjandrum to the traffic
Debouching from a towering garage.

They told him this would happen in Columbus.
They told him to get back up off the canvas.
God's avalanche, the Ace of Dames approaches
Wilder than the Godiva of the Luge.

It's like a Steinberg. Only it's enormous.
It's oceanic. Even in the onrush
St. Diatom premeditates the whitewash,
St. Jeroboam bodes the vernissage.
O monument and sacrament and snowjob!

Totaled again. Braille billboard that she was.

(the expense of spearmint)

The dumpster and the dowager. Two stooges
Auditioning for dingbat. Not a chance.

The monumental Macy's-Day masseuses
Have galvanized their straphanger corteges
Into a hangdog shamble through the glitz.

[*215*]

Demimillennial expos in contraption.
Demimillennial lunchbars out for bid.

Averted from the hadj, ensconced askance
Where lapsed therapsids scumble to the loge,
The mailbox mounts unshakable safari
Beneath his hat, in hatchet-faced repose.

He budgeth not to infiltrate the fury
Or ruminate the worm of circumstance.
He grudgeth not the flatness of the badge.

(the explicit statement)

Sensation. In the boîte around the corner
Sacred to the apostles of Le Boxe,
The novelist has punched out the director.
Their film is getting noir and going nowhere.

A cabinet of two-bit Howard Hugheses
And marinated Moho-maharajahs
Negotiates the marginal provisions
Of an escape clause in the tablecloth.

The bankable preadolescent bombshell
Dissolves placebos in her Shirley Temple.
The stunt man knows a goodie. Waxes Roth.

The monkey wrenches, thrown into perspective
As icons in the Nevelson decor,
Do such a job of looking nonobjective
They ought to get an Oscar for it. More
Mousse for the little lady. Waxes Roth.

The stunt man hunches forward and explains it.

He wishes he were talking to a mailbox.
He wishes they had given him a mailbox
To satchel, like De Niro in *Mean Streets*.

[216]

(the exploited starlet)

The emptiness is staggering, but staggers
On, through the stult and dundancy and heat.
The badlands knuckle under. Golden logos
Follow the flag. The product is complete.
The pinball in the basement skips a beat.
The mountains have a message on them. EAT.

The line around infinity approaches
St. nothing for his autograph. They meet.
She poses for some 40-second sketches.
He comes up with a title for them: "St."

She stands, in each, transformed into an object
Transformed into the person of its dreams.
She is the adulation of the lamppost.
She is the Duke of Hydrant, full of hemes.

She christens him St. Monolith der Mahler.
St. einberg of the emptiness. She sighs.
Are we the muse? the medium? the model?
Or nothing but a mailbox in disguise?
It's OK, she's wised up, she gets the message.
He doesn't have to act as if she mattered.
She goes all brave and squinches up her eyes.

He gives her a brassiere. She starts to bawl.
He puts his arm around her. Call me Saul.

(theoretic framework)

He puts a finger on the false horizon.
He puts a sidewalk on the window shade.
He draws her over next to him and shows her
Something in a toque, at a parade.

And how to let a mailbox be a mailbox,
And how to let the landscape have its tantrum

[*217*]

And die there all exhausted in a heap,
And how to set a table in your sleep
And leave it there, to teeter with its platter
Until the waiting radiator utter
The crucial, terse, insinuating "st."

(the exploded notion)

Embarked on his blue-chip itinerary,
His holiness the horizon undergoes
The agonies of absence. Is she true?
He sends a wire. A lot of wires. A slew.

Her mother the Madonna of the Rockers
Had wanted a Rockette, but there it is:
You give them what you can: a set of feathers,
A little verbum sap about the biz.

And she herself? Ecstatic. Like an empress
Exemplifying transport on a barge.
She likes it here. She likes the Egg McMuffin.
She likes it when her friend the sidewalk artist
Transmogrifies the logos on the placemats.
She breaks up into giggles and conniptions
And squiggles and contraptions like a dope.
Oh dearie me. Historical convulsions.
Oh dearie me. Great gales and parking systems
And pyroclastic stratamatic fits.
She holds herself and howls until she splits.

(theodicy of the Abbie of the LEM)

Far from the madding franchise, at a table
Above the fair Potomac sits assembled
The legendary sachem of the tribe.

But it would take an artist to transcribe
The setting. The Colonial appointments.

[218]

The cobwebby display case full of jerseys
Dating to his great days as number one.
The back wall with its classical medallions
Like something from the sub shops of New London
Or half a quadraphonic speaker set-up
Or decorated patriotic hubcaps.
Pillar of smoke by day, and what is this?
Insomnia ensepulchred but serving
As distant-early-warning pyramid
While out the other window the bald eagle
Spreadeagles where he batters at the porthole
To bring to his progenitor's attention
A mighty confluence of telegrams.

(the Endowment enters)

They send an emissary for an artist.
The emissary chortles and absconds.

They send an emissary with an escort
Of samurais in samite. Shall these bronze
Originals get grungy and go green?

They send a squad of missing persons experts
Careering in a tinted limousine.

They send for the Endowment. An engraver
Had better get these likenesses and soon.
The eagle is in desperate condition.
The diagram the Rosenbergs were fried for
Appears above his noggin like a notion
Occurring to a bird in a cartoon.

(the endorsement shortened)

Manhattan. Five blocks south of a McDonalds.
The missing emissary counts his change.

[219]

And bides his time. His counterfeit accomplice
Has passages and passports to arrange.

He saunters up the avenue for breakfast.
The sunlight in the sidestreets is tremendous.
The hilltop where the distant vision grazes
Bobs like a mere meniscus of the henge.

The pavement is in factory condition
And shimmering from sea to shining sea.

So why not. He initials it. "St."

THE THOUGHT THAT COUNTS

Tom Disch

as though a light had gone on

the thought that counts
suddenly was conscious

and thought of the numbers
from one to ten,
each number higher than the one

or two or three before,
a fact the thought that counted
chose to ignore:
for these were not apples or oranges,

they were not even the names
of all the registered atoms
in the universe,
but rather the address
of the registration office itself,

where an endless flux
of elemental mush
waited in long, long, long lines
to get their visas
for existence and the privilege
of being particular,

a privilege we who possess it
are too liable to take for granted,
just as we tend to forget
the enormousness of virtually everything:
the long highways so variously numbered,
the fleets of licensed vans
bearing invoiced boxes of grapefruits

for tomorrow's breakfast, tomorrow being
the eighth and a good morning for
a grapefruit, as indeed what morning is not,
for its proper preparation affords us
the first periodicitous paradigm
of the day, as our knives slip
along its radii and we think,
along with the thought that counts,

not of any individual grapefruit
in our hands but of the grapefruit
single as the sun
that burns its identifying brand
on the mind's eye: one,
and one again, and still one
more—what idea could be
as pure? as sweetly apt
to bear repeating:

one
and one
and then one more
and then another one
and so on for
as long as one can,
in cadence with the count
of the thought that is counting
the numbers from one to ten, and then
onwards: it is as though . . .

as though a light had gone on,
as though the thought that counts
suddenly were conscious
and were to think of the numbers from one
to ten, each number higher than the one
preceding, a fact we may choose
to ignore, for these are not apples or oranges,
not even the names of all that is numerable
in the universe but rather the address
to which one sends each issue of a serial
that always ends: (to be continued)

SOUNDS

Luis Buñuel

MEMORY

During the last ten years of her life, my mother gradually lost her memory. When I went to see her in Zaragoza, where she lived with my brothers, I watched the way she read magazines, turning the pages carefully, one by one, from the first to the last. When she finished, I'd take the magazine from her, then give it back, only to see her leaf through it again, slowly, page by page.

She was in perfect physical health and remarkably agile for her age, but in the end she no longer recognized her children. She didn't know who we were, or who she was. I'd walk into her room, kiss her, sit with her awhile. Sometimes I'd leave, then turn around and walk back in again. She greeted me with the same smile and invited me to sit down—as if she were seeing me for the first time. She didn't remember my name.

When I was a schoolboy in Zaragoza, I knew the names of all the Visigoth kings of Spain by heart, as well as the areas and populations of each country in Europe. In fact, I was a gold mine of useless facts. These mechanical pyrotechnics were the object of countless jokes: students who were particularly good at it were called *memoriones*. Virtuoso *memorión* that I was, I too had nothing but contempt for such pedestrian exercises.

Now, of course, I'm not so scornful. As time goes by, we don't give a second thought to all the memories we so unconsciously accumulate, until suddenly, one day, we can't think of the name of a good friend or a relative. It's simply gone; we've forgotten it. In vain, we struggle furiously to think of a commonplace word. It's on the tip of our tongues but refuses to go any farther.

Once this happens, there are other lapses, and only then do we understand, and acknowledge, the importance of memory. This sort of amnesia came upon me first as

I neared seventy. It started with proper names, and with the immediate past. Where did I put my lighter? (I had it in my hand just five minutes ago!) What did I want to say when I started this sentence? All too soon, the amnesia spreads, covering events that happened a few months or years ago—the name of that hotel I stayed at in Madrid in May 1980, the title of a book I was so excited about six months ago. I search and search, but it's always futile, and I can only wait for the final amnesia, the one that can erase an entire life, as it did my mother's.

So far, I've managed to keep this final darkness at bay. From my distant past, I can still conjure up countless names and faces; and when I forget one, I remain calm. You have to begin to lose your memory, if only in bits and pieces, to realize that memory is what makes our lives. Life without memory is no life at all, just as an intelligence without the possibility of expression is not really an intelligence. Our memory is our coherence, our reason, our feeling, even our action. Without it, we are nothing.

Imagine (as I often have) a scene in a film where a man tries to tell a friend a story but forgets one word out of four, a simple word like "car" or "street" or "policeman." He stammers, hesitates, waves his hands in the air, gropes for synonyms. Finally, his friend gets so annoyed that he slaps him and walks away. Sometimes, too, resorting to humor to ward off panic, I tell the story about the man who goes to see a psychiatrist, complaining of lapses in memory. The psychiatrist asks him a couple of routine questions, and then says:

"So? These lapses?"

"What lapses?" the man replies.

FROM THE MIDDLE AGES

I was thirteen or fourteen years old when I left the province of Aragón for the first time to visit some friends of the family who were spending the summer in Vega de Pas near Santander, in northern Spain. The Basque country was astonishing, a new landscape completely the opposite of my own. There were clouds, rain, forests drip-

ping with fog, damp moss, stones; from then on, I adored
the north—the cold, the snow, the great rushing mountain
rivers. In southern Aragón, the earth is fertile, but dry
and dusty. A year can go by, even two, without so much
as a single cloud in the impassive sky. Whenever an ad-
venturesome cumulus wandered into view just above the
mountain peaks, all the clerks in the grocery next door
would rush to our house and clamber up onto the roof.
There, from the vantage point of a small gable, they'd
spend hours watching the creeping cloud, shaking their
heads and murmuring sadly:

"Wind's from the south. It'll never get here."

And they were always right.

I remember one agonizingly dry year when the population of the neighboring town of Castelceras organized
a procession called a *rogativa*, led by the priests, to beg
the heavens for just one small shower. When the ap-
pointed morning arrived, a mass of clouds appeared suddenly and hung darkly over the village. The procession
seemed irrelevant; but, true to form, the clouds dispersed
before it was over. When the blistering sun reappeared,
a gang of ruffians retaliated. They snatched the statue of
the Virgin from her pedestal at the head of the procession,
and as they ran across the bridge, they threw her into
the Guadalope River.

In my own village of Calanda, where I was born on the
twenty-second of February, 1900, the Middle Ages lasted
until World War One. It was a closed and isolated society,
with clear and unchanging distinctions among the classes.
The respectful subordination of the peasants to the big
landowners was deeply rooted in tradition, and seemed
unshakable. Life unfolded in a linear fashion, the major
moments marked by the daily bells of the Church of
Pilar. They tolled for masses, vespers, and the Angelus,
as well as for certain critical, and more secular, events—
the tocsin that signaled fire, and the glorious chimes
that rang only for major Sunday festivals. There was
also a special *toque de agonía*, a deep, somber bell that
tolled slowly when someone had begun his final combat,

and a lighter bronze bell that rang for a dying child. In the fields, on the roads, in the streets of the town, everyone stopped whatever he was doing to ask who was about to die.

JOTA OLIVARERA

Southern Aragón produced the best olive oil in Spain, perhaps even in the world; and despite the ever-present threat of drought, which could strip the trees of their olives, we had some particularly superb years. The Calanda peasants were renowned for their expertise; some went each year to oversee the harvests in Andalucía, near Jaén and Córdoba. The olive harvest began at the onset of winter; while everyone sang the *jota olivarera,* the men climbed ladders and beat the branches with sticks, and the women gathered the fallen fruit. (In curious contrast to the brutal power of the typical Aragonian song, the *jota olivarera* has a delicate, lilting melody.)

I remember, too, another song from that period, which often comes to me halfway between waking and sleeping. (It's probably vanished by now, since to my knowledge it's never been written down, only transmitted orally from generation to generation.) The "Song of Sunrise" was sung every day during the harvest season by a group of boys running through the streets to rouse the workers at dawn. Perhaps some of these singers are still alive and would remember the words and the melody; it was a magnificent song, half sacred, half profane, a relic from the distant past. I remember waking to it as a child in what seemed to me to be the middle of the night.

During the rest of the year, two night watchmen, armed with oil lamps and small spears, punctuated our sleep.

"God be praised!" one would cry. "*Alabado sea Dios!*"

"May He be praised forever and ever," the other replied. "*Por siempre sea alabado.*"

Or, "Eleven o'clock, fair weather." "*Las once, sereno.*"

Much more rarely—what a joy!—"It's cloudy." And every once in a while—a miracle—"It's raining!"

LOS POBRES

There were eight mills in Calanda for making olive oil; one was operated hydraulically, but the others functioned exactly as they had in Roman times—a massive conical stone turned by horses or mules which ground the olives on another heavy stone. Indeed, it seemed pointless to change anything at all in Calanda. The same gestures and desires were repeated from father to son, mother to daughter. Progress, a word no one seemed to have heard, passed Calanda by, just like the rain clouds.

Every Friday morning would find a dozen old men and women sitting with their backs against the church wall opposite our house; they were the poorest of the poor, *los pobres de solemnidad*. One of our servants would give each of them a piece of bread, which they kissed respectfully, and a ten-centavo coin—generous alms compared to the "penny a head" wealthy people in the village usually gave.

It was in Calanda that I had my first encounters with death, which along with profound religious faith and the awakening of sexuality constituted the dominating forces of my adolescence. I remember walking one day in the olive grove with my father when a sickeningly sweet odor came to us on the breeze. A dead donkey lay about a hundred yards away, swollen and mangled, serving as a banquet for a dozen vultures, not to mention several dogs. The sight of it both attracted and repelled me. Sated, the birds staggered about the cadaver, unable to take to the air. (The peasants never removed dead animals, convinced that their remains were good for the soil.) I stood there hypnotized, sensing that beyond this rotten carcass lay some obscure metaphysical significance. My father finally took hold of my arm and dragged me away.

Another time, one of our shepherds was killed by a knife in the back during a stupid argument. There was an autopsy, performed in the chapel in the middle of the cemetery by the village doctor, assisted by the barber. Four or five of the doctor's friends were also present. I managed to sneak in, and as a bottle of brandy passed from hand to hand, I drank nervously to bolster my courage, which had begun to flag at the sounds of the saw grinding through the skull and the dead man's ribs being broken, one by one. When it was all over, I was blind drunk and had to be carried home, where I was severely punished, not only for drunkenness, but for what my father called "sadism."

In our village, when there was a funeral for one of the peasants, the coffin stood in front of the church door. The priests chanted while a vicar circled the flimsy catafalque sprinkling holy water, then raised the veil and scattered ashes on the chest of the corpse (a gesture reminiscent of the last scene of my *Wuthering Heights*). The heavy bell tolled, and as the pallbearers carried the coffin to the cemetery a few hundred yards from the village, the heart-rending cries of the dead man's mother rang through the streets:

"My son! My son!" she wailed. "Don't leave me! Don't leave me all alone!"

The dead man's sisters, along with other female relatives and friends, joined in the lamentations, forming a chorus of mourners, of *planideras*.

HATPINS

With so heavy a dosage of death and religion, our *joie de vivre* was strong. Pleasures long desired only increased in intensity because we so rarely managed to satisfy them. Despite our sincere religious faith, nothing could assuage our impatient sexual curiosity and our erotic obsessions. At the age of twelve, I still believed that babies came from Paris—brought not by a stork, of course, but simply by train or car. One day an older friend set me straight, and suddenly there I was, initiated at long last into the great mystery and involved in those endless adolescent discussions and suppositions that characterize the tyranny of sex over youth. At the same time, "they" never ceased to remind us that the highest virtue was chastity, without which no life was worthy of praise. In addition, the strict separation between the sexes in village life served only to fuel our fantasies. In the end, we were worn out with our oppressive sense of sin, coupled with the interminable war between instinct and virtue.

When I reached my early teens, I discovered the bathing cabanas in San Sebastián, fertile ground for other educational experiences. These cabanas were divided by partitions, and it was easy to enter one side, make a peephole in the wood, and watch the women undressing on the other side. Unfortunately, long hatpins were in fashion, and once the women realized they were being spied upon, they would thrust their hatpins into the holes, blithely unconcerned about putting out curious eyes. (I used this detail much later, in *El*.)

THE EXPLICADOR

I was about eight when I discovered the cinema, at a theater called the Farrucini. There were two doors, one exclusively for exiting, one for entering, set in a beautiful wooden facade. Outside, a cluster of lemonade sellers equipped with a variety of musical instruments hawked their wares to passersby. In reality, the Farrucini was little more than a shack; it had wooden benches and a tarpaulin for a roof.

I wasn't allowed to go to the movies alone but was always accompanied, as everywhere, by my nurse, even when I only went across the street to play with my friend Pelayo. I remember how enthralled I was by my first cartoon; it was about a pig who wore a tricolor sash around its waist and sang. (The sound came from a record player hidden behind the screen.) I'm quite sure that it was a color film, which at that time meant that each image had been painted by hand.

Movies then were little more than a curiosity, like the sideshow at a county fair. They were simply the primitive products of a newly discovered technique. Apart from trains and streetcars, already habitual parts of our lives, such "modern" techniques were not much in evidence in Zaragoza. In fact, in 1908, there was only one automobile in the entire city, an electric one.

Yet movies did signify a dramatic intrusion into our medieval universe, and soon several permanent movie

[*229*]

theaters appeared, equipped with either armchairs or benches, depending on the price of admission. By 1914, there were actually three good theaters: the Salon Doré, the Coïné (named after the famous photographer), and the Ena Victoria. (There was a fourth, on the calle de los Estebanes, but I've forgotten the name. My cousin lived on that street, and we had a terrific view of the screen from her kitchen window. Her family finally boarded it up, however, and put in a skylight instead; but we managed to dig a small hole in the bricks, where we took turns watching soundless moving pictures.)

When it comes to the movies I saw when I was very young, my memory grows cloudy; I often confuse them with movies I saw later in Madrid. But I do remember a French comedian who kept falling down; we used to call him Toribio. (Could it have been Onésime?) We also saw the films of Max Linder and of Méliès, particularly his *Le Voyage dans la lune*. The first American films— adventure serials and burlesques—arrived later. There were also some terribly romantic Italian melodramas; I can still see Francesca Bertini, the Greta Garbo of Italy, twisting the long curtain at her window and weeping. (It was both wildly sentimental and very boring.) The most popular actors at the time were the Americans Conde Hugo (Count Hugo) and Lucilla Love (pronounced Lové in Spanish). They were famous for their romances and action-packed serials.

In addition to the traditional piano player, each theater in Zaragoza was equipped with its *explicador*, or narrator, who stood next to the screen and "explained" the action to the audience. "Count Hugo sees his wife go by on the arm of another man," he would declaim. "And now, ladies and gentlemen, you will see how he opens the drawer of his desk and takes out a revolver to assassinate his unfaithful wife!"

It's hard to imagine today, but when the cinema was in its infancy, it was such a new and unusual narrative form that most spectators had difficulty understanding what was happening. Now we're so used to film language, to the elements of montage, to both simultaneous and successive action, to flashbacks, that our comprehension is automatic; but in the early years, the public had a hard time deciphering this new pictorial grammar. They needed an *explicador* to guide them from scene to scene.

I'll never forget, for example, everyone's terror when we saw our first zoom. There on the screen was a head coming closer and closer, growing larger and larger. We simply couldn't understand that the camera was moving nearer to the head, or that because of trick photography (as in Méliès's films) the head only appeared to grow larger. All we saw was a head coming toward us, swelling hideously out of all proportion. Like Thomas the Apostle, we believed in the reality of what we saw.

THE DRUMS OF CALANDA

There is a custom, practiced perhaps only in certain Aragonian villages, called the Drums of Good Friday. On that days, drums are beaten from Alcañiz to Híjar; but nowhere are they beaten with such mysterious power as in Calanda. The ritual dates from the end of the eighteenth century and had already died out by 1900, but one of Calanda's priests, Mosen Vicente Allanegui, brought it back to life.

The drums of Calanda beat almost without pause from noon on Good Friday until noon on Saturday, in recognition of the shadows that covered the earth at the moment Christ died, as well as the earthquakes, the falling rocks, and the rending of the temple veil. It's a powerful and strangely moving communal ceremony which I heard for the first time in my cradle. Up until recently, I often beat the drums myself; in fact, I've introduced these famous drums to many friends, who were all as strongly affected as I was. I remember a reunion in 1980 with a few friends in a medieval castle not far from Madrid where we surprised everyone with a drum serenade imported directly from Calanda. Many of my closest friends were among the guests—Julio Alejandro, Fernando Rey, José-Luis Barros—and all of them were profoundly moved, although unable to say exactly why. (Five even confessed to having cried.) I don't really know what evokes this emotion, which resembles the kind of feeling often aroused when one listens to music. It seems to echo some secret rhythm in the outside world, and provokes a real physical shiver that defies the rational mind. My son, Juan-Luis, once made a short film about these drums, and I myself have used their somber rhythms in several movies, especially *L'Age d'or* and *Nazarin.*

Back in my childhood, only a couple hundred drummers were involved in this rite, but nowadays there are over a thousand, including six hundred to seven hundred drums and four hundred *bombos.* Toward noon on Good Friday, the drummers gather in the main square opposite the church and wait there in total silence; if anyone nervously raps out a few beats, the crowd silences him. When the first bell in the church tower begins to toll, a burst of sound, like a terrific thunderclap, electrifies the entire village, for all the drums explode at the same instant. A sort of wild drunkenness surges through the players; they beat for two hours until the procession (called El Pregón, after the official "town crier" drum) forms, then leaves the square and makes a complete tour of the town. The procession is usually so long that the rear is still in the square when the leaders have already reappeared at the opposite side.

When I was young, there were all sorts of wonderful characters in the parade—Roman soldiers with false beards called *putuntunes* (a word that sounds very like the beating of the drums), centurions, a Roman general, and Longinos, a personage dressed in a full suit of medieval armor. Longinos, the man who theoretically defended Christ against his attackers, used to fight a duel with the general. As they locked swords, the host of drummers would form a circle around them, but when the general spun around once, an act that symbolized his death, Longinos sealed the sepulcher and began his watch. Nearby, Christ himself was represented by a statue lying in a glass box.

During the procession, everyone chants the biblical story of the Passion; in fact, the phrase "vile Jews" used to crop up frequently, until it was finally removed by

Pope John XXIII. By five o'clock, the ceremony itself is over and there's a moment of silence, until the drums begin again, to continue until noon on the following day.

Another fascinating aspect of this ritual are the drumrolls, which are composed of five or six different rhythms, all of which I remember vividly. When two groups beating two different tempi meet on one of the village streets, they engage in a veritable duel which may last as long as an hour—or at least until the weaker group relents and takes up the victor's rhythm. By the early hours of Saturday morning, the skin on the drums is stained with blood, even though the beating hands belong to hardworking peasants.

On Saturday morning, many villagers put down their drums and retrace the Calvary, climbing a Way of the Cross on a hillside near the village. The rest continue beating, however, until everyone gathers at seven o'clock for the funeral procession, *el entierro*. As the bell tolls the noon hour, the drums suddenly fall silent, but even after the normal rhythms of daily life have been reestablished, some villagers still speak in an oddly halting manner, an involuntary echo of the beating drums.

Translated from French by Abigail Israel

HEATHERDOWN
A LATE IMPERIAL MEMOIR

Alexander Cockburn

One brave morning in Manhattan, when fall was still holding winter at bay, my daughter Daisy called from London in some excitement. The casting director for a TV movie had been holding some auditions in her school in Hammersmith; she and two schoolmates had been selected for major parts; filming would begin almost at once. Then my former wife came on the phone. She had read the script. Certain scenes could, in the hands of an unscrupulous director, exploit the thirteen-year-old child. Vigilance was necessary. Besides, there was the matter of what Daisy should be paid. . . .

A few days later Daisy called again to report. With the help of a lawyer, proper safeguards had been established and adequate sums guaranteed. It turned out that the director of *Secrets*, one in a series of films generically entitled *First Love,* was to be Gavin Millar. He had been at Oxford at the same time as I had and in my recollection had not seemed then to be an embryonic pornographer.

Daisy added that filming would start in ten days at a recently closed prep school near Ascot. My heart tripped. What was the name of the school? "Hold on while I find the address." The wind outside was stripping golden leaves off the trees in Central Park and I waited, foot poised on the threshold of memory. Daisy picked up the phone again. "Heatherdown. It's called Heatherdown." The past welcomed me in.

In the hard winter of 1947 we moved from London to county Cork, Ireland, and after several months my parents decided that I had better start going to some sort of local school. I would have been happy to go on spending my days playing with Doreen French, the sexton's daughter, and my evenings listening to my father read *Don Quixote*. I was shy and already felt awkward in Ireland, where social divisions were much more transparent

than in London. To walk out of the gates of my grandparents' big house and walk along Main Street where the
unemployed men lounged all day in front of Farrell's was
bad enough. Staring idly at everything, they stared at me
too. School meant ridicule at closer quarters.

But my parents were adamant. I was seven and it was
time to retrieve the education abandoned when we had
left London. They proposed to send me to the Loretto
Convent, a large red building overlooking Youghal Bay.
My grandmother was horrified. The Loretto Convent was
a Roman Catholic institution and we, as members of the
Anglo-Irish class were, however notionally, Protestant.

My parents pointed out there was no Protestant school
in Youghal. My grandmother was scarcely a bigot but in
the late 1940s the gulf between Protestants and Catholics
was still fixed and deep—as it is in our town no
longer. Brought up in the government houses of varying
British colonies from Jamaica to Hong Kong, she took
certain social and religious proprieties absolutely for
granted. She discovered that there was a tiny parochial
school for Protestant children. It was about to close since
attendance had just dropped below the quorum of seven
children which the Church of Ireland reckoned as the
minimum its budget would permit.

There had been, before the achievement of Irish independence, a substantial British garrison in Youghal. St.
Mary's Church, whose ancient bell tower loomed behind
the wall of my grandparents' equally ancient Tudor house,
could hold a congregation of three thousand. Back at the
turn of the century certain tradesmen, eager for the business of this garrison, had thought it opportune to convert
to Protestantism. They changed ships on a falling tide.
The garrison left in 1922 and a quarter of a century later
we could see the descendants of the apostates, beached
on the shoals of history. Their stores were ill favored by
the overwhelmingly Catholic population of Youghal and
they had the added misfortune, as members of the
shrunken congregation of some sixty-odd souls attending
St. Mary's, to have to endure the Reverend Watts's annual
Christmas sermon. Peering down from his pulpit at the
shopkeepers who were making a couple of shillings out
of the Christmas buying spree, Watts would savagely de-

nounce the gross commercialization of a holy festival cele-
brating the birth of the Savior. Then he took to attacking
the atom bomb too and the shopkeepers saw their chance.
They complained to the bishop and Watts was demoted
and became curate of Watergrass Hill, a desolate hamlet
twenty miles inland.

These shopkeepers had children, still officially within
the Protestant fold, and these were the cannon fodder in
my grandmother's campaign. Their parents were told
firmly that attendance at the parochial school was essential. A few weeks later a donkey and trap, purchased by
my grandmother, made its rounds, depositing me and my
new companions at the parochial school, a grey stone
building just down the road from the Loretto Convent. In
the last months of my sojourn at the school workmen
erected a little shrine across the street. There was a statue
of the Virgin and under it some lines, the first of which
read "Dogma of the Ass-." The next line continued with
"umption of the Virgin Mary." The shrine and plaque
celebrated the dogma promulgated by Pope Pius XII in
1950, which asserted that Mary had been bodily assumed
into the bosom of the heavenly father. We used to wonder
what archaeologists of the future would make of the
plaque, if it got broken and only the top line survived.

My grandmother rejoiced that I had been saved from
priestcraft and the donkey groaned as he dragged us
through the town. A few months later my parents bought
a house of their own three miles from Youghal, a distance
beyond the powers of the donkey. A new pony, trap and
gardener's boy took me to school in the morning and then
would return home. In late morning my mother would
drive the trap in again for shopping and to take me home
for lunch. The gardener's boy would drive me in again
to school after lunch and at the end of the afternoon
make the final trip to take me home once more. Blackie
thus trotted or walked twenty-four miles a day. Once the
gardener's boy forgot to fasten Blackie's reins to the bridle
but buckled them to the shoulder collar instead. It made
no difference to Blackie, who started, stopped and swerved
left or right at all the proper points. A photograph of Main
Street in Youghal in 1948 would have shown that eighty
percent of all the transportation was horsedrawn. Fifteen

years later the proportions were reversed. We got our first car in 1958 when I turned seventeen, got a license and was thus able to chauffeur our family into the twentieth century.

Secure from popish influence, my education did not noticeably improve. The problem was that though Rome was held at bay, the Irish state played an important part in our instruction. It was mandatory that we be taught Gaelic and much time was set aside for that purpose every day. Thus after two years I was the regional champion in Scripture knowledge and could say "Shut the door" and some other useful phrases in Irish.

My parents pondered the alternatives. They could send me—over my grandmother's undoubted resistance—to the Christian Brothers school. Its reputation was bad aside from the brothers' savage recourse to the pandybat. Besides, it would be of little help in the overall strategic plan of my education, which was to get me into Oxford.

Though only recently disengaged from the Communist Party and still—as always—of stout radical beliefs, my father held true to his class origins in pondering the contours of his plan. The route march to Oxford or Cambridge was well established: at the age of eight the raw recruits would go to preparatory—or prep—schools and there obtain the rudiments of an education sufficient to get them, at the age of fourteen, into a "public" (that is, private) school such as Eton, Harrow, Winchester, Westminster and so forth.

The alacrity with which parents of the recruits dispatched them from home at the age of eight has often been noted with bemused concern by foreigners. From that year forward the child would be at home for only four months in the year. Of course many parents are far happier to see the back of a son than they might care to admit and boarding school was as good an excuse as any. Besides, these schools allowed the recruits to the system to cluster with members of their own class rather than go to a local school where contact with the lower orders might be inevitable: in sum, these prep and public schools were—and are—the training camps in the long guerrilla war of British social relations.

The form was to put down your child for a prep school

as soon as he entered the world. (Girls were less of a problem and might never, at least in those days, be put down for anything at all.) My parents and I had spent a portion of 1941, the year of my birth, sitting in St. John's Wood underground station as the German bombs and rockets rained down overhead. My father was on the Nazi blacklist and in the event of an invasion they certainly would have shot him if his plan to escape by boat to Ireland had failed. The British authorities, scarcely less hostile to Communists than to the Nazis—and in many cases more so—were vacillating on how to deal with Reds. At first they reckoned it best to draft them, send them to the front and hope that the first Panzers they met would do their duty. But then, amid the stunning exhibitions of British military incompetence, it was feared that the Reds would foment discontent and even mutiny. In accord with this dogleg in government policy my father first got a set of peremptory call-up papers and then, almost at once, a countermanding set of instructions. Later a German V-2 rocket landed on our house and reduced it to rubble. Perhaps understandably my father had not got around to the business of putting me down for a prep school. One way or another it did not seem, in the early 1940s, that there would necessarily be prep schools to go to.

But of course the prep schools survived and the "public" schools survived and the British class system survived. For that matter, many of those who had engineered the destruction of our house in Acacia Road survived too. My brother Andrew found one in Washington, D.C., in the late 1970s. He was called Dieter Schwebs. He had been one of the designers of the V-2 and had gone to work for the U.S. after the war. By the time Andrew met him, Schwebs was in the General Accounting Office, rootling out fraud and waste in the Defense Department. Andrew told him about our house and Schwebs was full of concern: "Oh my heffens, nobody hurt I hope?"

I was nine, already one year late for prep school. It was July 1950 and the start of the school year was menacingly close. No suitable place willing to accept me had been found. Old friends to whom my father had not spoken in years were pressed into action and that filiation of patronage and mutual back-scratching called "the old boy net" was shaken into action. One midsummer day my father dismounted from the bicycle he used to go into the town of Youghal to dispatch articles, make telephone calls and have pleasant conversations in one of Youghal's quiet, dark bars. "Well, we've got you into Heatherdown. It's supposed to be one of the most exclusive and expensive prep schools in England. In a couple of weeks we'll take the boat train to London, and then go to Ascot and have a look at the school. If it seems alright we'll get the uniforms and so forth and you'll start there in mid-September."

The inspection trip was pretty bad. There were no boys about, naturally, but the headmaster described the amenities with a relentless glee which was unnerving. He tried to show my father the cricket pitch, of which he was plainly very proud. My father, who had no views on cricket pitches, tried to offset his lack of interest or knowledge by asking to inspect the kitchens and dormitories. The headmaster, confronted with this aberrant scale of priorities, began to form what became an increasingly dubious opinion of our family's values. There followed an expensive trip to Gorringes, school outfitters, and I was fitted out in the black and red colors that were Heatherdown's motif.

On a grim September morning I stood on the platform at Waterloo Station. Prep schools were clustered thickly around Ascot, perhaps drawn by the magnet of Eton in nearby Windsor, and there was a rainbow of other school uniforms, of Earlywood, Scaitcliffe, Ludgrove and Lambrook. I kept my eyes alert for the red ties and caps of Heatherdown and soon saw these colors adorning a small boy who was sobbing quietly. His equally stricken mother made a lunge to cover his tear-stained face with kisses but fought her off. Excessive displays of emotion by one's parents were a matter for great dread. In fact any display of originality or character by them, apart from a humdrum sort of parentness or hitting a six at the father's cricket match, was thought to be bad form. The train whistle sounded, my mother began some final gesture of valediction which seemed ominously tinged with sentiment. I scuttled into the same compartment as the sobbing child, the door slammed and we chugged into the home counties.

Daisy called. They had started filming and, "Daddy, we've found your photograph." Every boy leaving Heatherdown had his photograph taken. It was then framed and put up in the corridor outside the classrooms. There were all the boys who had ever been to the school, right back to Hely-Hutchinson, who had his photograph taken in 1914, which meant that he may just have escaped being killed on the Western Front by 1918. About a thousand boys had gone through Heatherdown since his time. In any given year about fifty-five noisy little creatures inhabited the place, along with masters, matron, maids and gardeners.

Daisy reported that my photograph was on the top row, near the music room. I could see in my mind's eye where it was. Next to me there was probably Miller-Mundy and next to him maybe Piggott-Brown or Legge-Bourke. Legge-Bourke's father was a Conservative member of Parliament who once flipped a coin at Prime Minister Attlee during question time, shouting "Next record please." By the time I reached Heatherdown the first postwar Labour government was slipping from power and no one at Heatherdown was particularly upset about this. Parents of boys at Heatherdown were very conservative; masters were very conservative and the boys were very conservative too. Word got around that my father was a Red. This was not quite as bad as being identified as Irish, even though I had no brogue. Six years after a war in which De Valera had kept Ireland neutral, feeling still ran high. In argument the ladder of escalation was soon well known to me: "Cocky's Irish, Cocky's a dirty pig. . . . Cocky helped Hitler in the war. . . ." and so on.

The Attlee government had just survived the election of 1950 but when another election loomed in 1951 excitement ran high. There were endless jocular references to groundnuts—the well-intentioned but ill-fated scheme of the Labour government to cultivate peanuts in west Africa, thus providing employment for the locals and nutrition for British schoolchildren. Cost overruns and mismanagement brought the scheme low and the word "groundnuts" could be guaranteed to arouse derision at any Conservative gathering between the years 1949 and 1964.

The night of the 1951 election a large electoral map of the United Kingdom was placed on an easel in the doorway of our dormitory. As the results came in over the radio a master called Hall would color the relevant constituency blue in the event of a Conservative victory and an unpleasant puce if Labour won. Legge-Bourke was in our dormitory and we naturally rooted for his father Harry, who carried the Isle of Ely by about six thousand votes. When we awoke in the morning an extensive portion of the map was colored blue—some of this being because Conservatives tended to win the large rural constituencies. A rout of Labour and of socialism was proclaimed. Actually Labour won the popular vote by about a quarter of a million, but gerrymandering saw the Conservatives win a clear majority of twenty-six seats over Labour. Thus began thirteen years of Tory rule which lasted clear through the rest of my education and ended only in 1964, just after I had left Oxford. More people, nearly fourteen million, voted for Labour in 1951 than for any British political party before or since, though this was not at all the sense of the situation one got at Heatherdown.

The headmaster was very pleased. At that time the entirely groundless fear that the Labour Party would somehow attack private education was still very great. At each Labour Party conference the rhetorical thunder against it outstripped even the tremendous bellowing against "tied cottages," the feudal system whereby farm workers dwelt in their cottages only at the pleasure of their employers and, at the end of a lifetime of ill-paid labor, were evicted to the local almshouse to make way for younger muscles.

Jokes about the Labour Party were a staple among boys and masters. I was a supporter of the Labour Party— partly because I had the reputation of being Red hellspawn to maintain and partly because it seemed sensible to oppose anything favored by most of the people at the school. But I felt—amid my support—the disappointment of a fan who knows that his team is making a bit of an ass of itself and that improvement is unlikely in the near future. The innate conservatism of British schoolboys in private institutions was always impressive. At my next school, sometime in the late fifties, there was a "mock election." My friend Freddy Fitzpayne ran as the Communist and got one vote. I ran as the Labour candidate and got one vote. The Scottish Nationalist got eighty-three and the Conservative ninety-five.

Fitzpayne and I represented that school in debates. Each team had its own topic to which it spoke throughout the debating tournament, no matter what the other team was talking about. Fitzpayne and I used to speak to the motion, Great Britain Must Leave NATO Now. When I sat down after proposing the motion, our opponent would rise and, depending on what school we happened to be debating, would reel off a speech about the monarchy, Scottish independence or, in the case of one debate with Dollar Academy, a spirited defense of some controversial form of pig breeding. Fitzpayne and I got as far as the semifinals with our seditious topic before losing to some polished orators from Edinburgh Academy. We were photographed in the local Blairgowrie paper toasting each other with large pints of beer and narrowly escaped being expelled.

The ground squelched wetly underfoot as I walked across Central Park, brooding about groundnuts, Heatherdown and the autumn reek of Berkshire bonfires. The idea of a quick return flight to yesterday, courtesy of trans-Atlantic standby, was growing on me. If the premise of the voyage was commonplace in one respect—to see how exactly the child had become father to the man—there would be the unusual twist of being there as father of the child.

Three days later I was standing on Waterloo platform, just as I had with my mother over thirty years before. Daisy had been nervous of the idea and I knew well her familiar fear: I would somehow make a fool of myself, embarrass her in front of her friends and the entire production crew of *Secrets*. She reminded me of the Poppy Day Affair, a tale I occasionally told to show what I had had to cope with when I had been a boy worried, just like her, about the embarrassment parents can cause. Even now the memory causes me to sweat and stamp about a bit.

Back in the early 1950s Armistice Day—or Poppy Day—was taken a great deal more seriously than it is now. At precisely 11 A.M. there would be two minutes' silence in memory of those killed in the two Great Wars. The service in the little mock Tudor chapel at Heatherdown had an extra piquancy because the headmaster would bring in a small radio, just to make sure that we all fell silent at exactly 11 A.M. We didn't associate God with radios, machines that contradicted the high-toned nineteenth-century flavor of our Anglican observances, in which diction was so etherialized that very often it was hard to tell whether we were praying for peace or for good weather on the sports day coming up next week.

As we gathered in the chapel upstairs waiting for the Greenwich Mean Time pips, parents who had traveled to Heatherdown to take their children out for the afternoon would assemble downstairs in the headmaster's study. Since my parents lived in Ireland they rarely appeared. Other boys would occasionally invite me out for tea in Maidenhead, or to their homes if they lived relatively close by. These were the very early days of television and often the parents' idea of an uplifting yet amusing afternoon was to assemble in front of the TV on which the BBC would run a dignified Sunday afternoon quiz show called "Twenty Questions." The contestants were the usual British salad for such enterprises, containing a couple of academics, someone known to be waggish, and a socialite in relatively decent moral standing. At the beginning of each round a voice, audible to all but the participants, would give the answer. It was a deep voice, tranquil with the power of absolute knowledge, and it would intone, "The answer is *porridge*; the answer is *porridge*." I always thought the voice of God would sound like that; unruffled and awful as He asked me why I did not believe in Him unreservedly.

On Armistice Day in 1953 my father, in London on business, traveled down to Heatherdown to take me out. He arrived downstairs just as we heard the GMT signal on the radio and fell silent. Obliged to remember and revere the fallen in war, I would think of my Uncle Teeny who had died of malaria in Italy in 1944. I had never known him but I would do my best to imagine him fighting bravely; then, after about thirty seconds, I would just concentrate on dead British soldiers generally and say thank you. Along my pew, past Walduck who was fat and who claimed his family name was Valdrake and had come over with William and Mary, I could see out of the corner of my eye MacLean, whose father had been killed in the war. Each year, about fifty-five seconds after eleven, MacLean would start crying. I think he felt he had to. There were about six boys whose fathers had died in the war and usually they all cried, chins tucked in and shoulders shaking a little. Though "blubbing" was normally despised, it was regarded as fine for MacLean and the others to cry on this particular occasion.

A few minutes later the service was over and I went downstairs to meet my father. He lost no time in hurrying me into an ancient taxi waiting outside and we rattled off to Great Fosters, a ghastly mock-Tudor establishment not far off, where we would while away the rest of the day. Even before we got into the taxi my father seemed to have a furtive, slightly hangdog air. Other parents seemed to be glaring at him. I surmised with a sinking heart that he had somehow attracted unwelcome attention—not perhaps as bad as the times he would barrack the actors in London theaters ("Perfectly sound tradition; Elizabethans did it all the time") but still alarming.

In the taxi he confessed all. He had arrived at about ten to eleven and had joined the other parents in the headmaster's study. "The conversation was a bit stilted and after a bit I thought I would try to jolly things along by telling them a couple of funny stories." My father was a very good storyteller, throwing himself into the anecdotes, which were often long. He used florid motions of his hands to accentuate important turns in the narrative. "After a bit," he continued, "I noticed that the other people didn't seem to be following my story with any enthusiasm. When I got to the punch line they were all looking down and no one laughed at all."

"Oh Daddy, you *didn't*!"

"I'm afraid so." So he had told jokes all the way through

the two-minute silence—a silence no other parent would break even in order to ask him to shut up, and meanwhile MacLean and the others were weeping upstairs. Most of the parents knew by now that Cockburn's father, Claud, was some sort of a Red and here were their darkest fears confirmed, with the scoundrel polluting the memory of the dead with his foul banter.

The train ambled along and the conductor cried, "Next stop Ascot!" The station looked relatively unchanged. On the far side of the main London road was Ascot race course. Ascot race week loomed large on the school calendar. Fathers, magnificently arrayed in morning coats and top hats, mothers with amazing summer confections on their heads, would arrive to take children for picnics of cold salmon and strawberries in the enclosure. All morning long on the Saturday of the big weekend we could see those great summer hats of the women as they drove in open cars to the race course a couple of miles up the road.

But now it was October, the track was bare and the enclosure empty. My taxi driver said that he had heard that Heatherdown was to be sold for real-estate development once the film crew had gone. The driveway, fringed with fateful rhododendrons, looked much the same and at last I entered the front door. Heatherdown had actually been built as a school just before the First World War, unlike many of the prep schools round about which were simply converted Victorian country houses with maids' rooms converted into diminutive dormitories. All such schools were divided into the boys' zone of activity—classrooms, dormitories and the like—and the headmaster's private quarters. The room of concern to us was the headmaster's study, thickly carpeted, fragrant with tobacco and terror. It was here that we were summoned for interrogation and punishment. In exact evocation of Freud's essay on *Haemlichkeit*—"homeliness" with a sinister and uncanny core— the study was both the closest echo of distant home and a parent's love but also the Colosseum for the unleashed superego. My own father never beat me. The closest he ever got to it was saying once that had any other father endured such injury (I had let down the tires of his bicycle to stop him from going into town one evening), this other father would have thrashed his son savagely. But here, hundreds of miles from the security of my own father's study, was this ersatz study, inhabited by the father-substitute who did indeed—on a few occasions—beat me with a clothes brush, once for repeatedly trying to conceal from Matron the fact that I had again wet my bed.

It was here too that the headmaster—a bouncy, bantam cock of a man called Charles Warner—interrogated me fiercely about the reason for my father's lateness in paying the hefty school bills. I knew the reason: not enough money. But this seemed a humiliating confession and I blubbed copiously as Warner plowed on remorselessly about the need for financial promptness. At least he didn't beat me for that, unlike Mr. Squeers in *Nicholas Nickleby*: "'I have had disappointments to contend against,' said Squeers, looking very grim, 'Bolder's father was two pound ten short. Where is Bolder?' 'Here he is, please Sir,' rejoined twenty officious voices. Boys are very like men to be sure. 'Come here, Bolder,' said Squeers. An unhealthy-looking boy, with warts all over his hands, stepped from his place to the master's desk, and raised his eyes imploringly to Squeers's face; his own quite white from the rapid beating of his heart. . . ."

When I read accounts of the early explorers surrounded by natives who "seemed friendly" but who suddenly "attacked without warning," I know just how those natives felt and I sympathize with them. To this day I have only to hear the words "X wants to see you in his office" to be thrown into the state of hatred and fear with which I used to approach Warner's study, knock on his door and hear that falsely jocose voice cry, "Come in." Sometimes as I entered to my doom his wife, Patsy, used to scuttle out, giving me a cheery Hello, though she and I both knew the somber nature of the occasion.

This fear and hatred has colored my relationship with authority, both privately and officially vested, and I count it as one of the major consequences of my education, just as my father's Micawberish struggle, pursued with heroic tenacity to virtually the very moment he died—he dictated to my mother a column for the *Irish Times* almost with his last breath—to keep clear of financial disaster greatly conditioned my attitude to credit.

Early in life in Ireland I learned to appreciate the color of the envelopes containing the day's mail. White envelopes were good. Brown ones weren't and my father would leave them up on the mantelpiece unopened. Over the months they would gradually get demoted from this high station to his study and then to the bottom drawer of a desk in his study. We would all laugh heartily over the form letter to creditors my father threatened to send: "Dear Sir, I am in receipt of your fourth communication regarding my outstanding account. Let me explain how I pay my bills. I throw them all into a large basket. Each year I stir the basket with a stick, take out four bills and pay them. One more letter from you and you're out of the game."

The whole school seemed silent as I walked towards Warner's study. Presumably they were filming elsewhere. I pushed open the door of his study. It was bare. Two film electricians were sitting on milk crates, drinking out of beer bottles. They said that the company was having lunch in the canteen out back.

I wandered upstairs and found myself facing the door of the school chapel. It used to have a thick curtain in front of it, as if to separate spiritual affairs from the coarse business of an English prep school. The curtain was gone and the door was ajar. Here I had begun my career as a choirboy, nicely done up in a sort of long red tunic and white surplice. I had a reedy alto. As the years progressed I rose to become a bass in the choir in Glenalmond—my public school. Thus, from the age of nine to the age of eighteen, my schoolmates and I had about thirty minutes of prayer each morning and each night—about three hundred hours of public worship a year. On Sundays, at Glenalmond, we had at least an hour each of matins and evensong. During these prayer-choked years I acquired an extensive knowledge of Scripture, of the Book of Common Prayer and of *Hymns Ancient and Modern*. It is one of the reasons I favor compulsory prayer at schools. A childish soul not inoculated with compulsory prayer is a soul open to any religious infection. At the end of my com-

pulsory religious observances I was a thoroughgoing
atheist, with a sufficient knowledge of Scripture to combat
the faithful.

There was a hymnal still in one of the pews and I leafed
through it. "As pants the hart for cooling steam / When
heated in the chase . . ." This had always been popular,
owing to the fervor with which one could hit the D in
"cooo-ling." "Eternal Father strong to save . . ." wasn't bad
either, with its mournful call to the Almighty: "Oh hear
us when we cry to thee / For those in peril on the sea."
But the big hit each term was undoubtedly "Onward,
Christian Soldiers," with Sir Arthur Sullivan's pugnacious
tune. "At the sound of triumph," we sang vaingloriously,
"Satan's host doth flee; / On then, Christian so-o-oldiers,
/ On to victoreee!" The general religious line at Heatherdown was that Victory was more or less assured for one,
unless very serious blunders let Satan squeeze in under
the door. We did not spend much time worrying about
damnation, except after a serious bout of cursing God's
name on a dare to see what would happen. I had once got
a tummy ache after cursing God and believed in Him for
at least a week. I went on leafing through the hymnal.
Here was a particularly chipper one, "All things bright
and beautiful," with its reassuring verse—omitted from
most American hymnals, as I later discovered:

> The rich man in his castle,
> The poor man at his gate,
> God made them high and lowly,
> He ordered their estate.

The class system was never far away. My father said
that his own radical beliefs had come as much from the
words of the Magnificat as from the works of Marx and
Lenin. You could see why. Even when chanted dolefully
as a canticle the words carried a serious charge:

> He hath scattered the proud in the imagination
>   of their hearts;
> He hath put down the mighty from their seat
> And hath exalted the humble and meek;
> He hath filled the hungry with good things
> And the rich he hath sent empty away.

At Heatherdown Christ was depicted as a limp-wristed pre-Raphaelite with tepid social democratic convictions, urging a better world but shunning any robust means to achieve it. Habituated to this version of Christ, I was startled at Glenalmond when the Bishop of Dundee, preaching for an hour one Sunday evening, reported on his own personal conversations with Christ from which it had emerged that He had powerful revolutionary views. "He meant what He said," the Bishop roared. "The furrrst sh-aall be last, and the last sha-all be furrst!" I was all for this in principle, though the town boys—who presumably would go to the front of the line while I dropped back—frightened me greatly.

I went downstairs and found Daisy and the others in the canteen, which had once been the carpentry shop. I had half-expected coarse film hands, rabid with cocaine and intent on debauching the girls temporarily at their mercy. To the contrary, they seemed a proper and restrained lot. To make up for lost school time a teacher had been imported and she would barely allow Daisy to talk to me before hurrying her away to her books. Daisy quickly steered me back to the main school building, along a corridor, and then pointed up. There I was in my farewell school photograph, looking rather like Daisy and exactly the same age as she was now. My eye wandered along the row: Piggott-Brown, who later founded a fashionable clothes store called Browns in South Moulton St.; Walduck, Cordy-Simpson, Miller-Mundy, Lycett-Green. I gazed along the corridor and saw another, slightly less familiar face; that of Sebastian Yorke, Daisy's mother's first husband, who had gone to Heatherdown some five years before me.

Daisy was full of gossip about the school. It had closed very suddenly. Boys going home for the summer holidays had fully expected to return. Mr. Edwards, who had taken over from Warner, had suddenly decided to sell up. A rescue bid mounted by another master and parents had only just failed. Now local real-estate interests were about to take over and had already announced the school's closure. Heatherdown would cease to exist—unless perhaps as a private nursing home. The photographs—the institutional record, as it were—would be thrown on the garbage heap.

It was the work of a moment to take my own photograph down, along with Sebastian's and one of the art dealer and historian Ian Dunlop, of whom I had no memory at Heatherdown but who was a friend of mine in New York. "Daisy to makeup," a voice shouted and she hurried away. I wandered along the corridor. A cupboard door was ajar and I peered in. The books were large and dusty and after a moment I realized with a shock that I was looking at the collective sporting memory of Heatherdown across half a century: the detailed record of every game of cricket played by Heatherdown's First Eleven between 1952 and 1978. The records of soccer and rugby went back to 1935.

I pulled out *The Unrivalled Cricket Scoring Book* covering the years 1952 to 1956. A note on the cover said that Heatherdown had played 52, won 22, lost 11 and drawn 19. I opened it and stared down at two pages detailing a game played between Heatherdown and Ludgrove on June 26, 1954. Ludgrove had won easily, by eight wickets. I remembered the game vividly. Ludgrove had a very fast bowler. Here he was in the book—Jefferson. He was vast and hurled the cricket ball down the pitch with horrifying speed. Our champions went out to bat and trailed back almost at once, out for 0, a "duck." Then our captain, Watson. Out for a duck too. I was last man in, and walked out slowly. There was a thunder of Jefferson's feet, a hard object swooped like a swallow down the pitch, hit my bat and spun away. "Run," screamed Lawson-Smith from the other end and I scampered to the other wicket and safety. Lawson-Smith was out next ball. Here it all was in the book, Cockburn 1 not out; Heatherdown all out for nineteen. "Lost by 8 wickets," Warner's notation across the page said gloomily.

The Queen's second son, Andrew, had gone to Heatherdown in the early 1970s and I turned to the score book covering 1971 to 1974 to see how he had done. The prince, flanked in the First Eleven by such revered names in British financial history as Hambro and Kleinwort, seems to have had his best game against Scaitcliffe on May 19,

1973, when he had bowled and got three wickets at a cost of fourteen runs. But in a needle game against Ludgrove on June 7 of the same year he was bowled by Agar for a duck and Ludgrove won by four runs. I dare say the memory haunts him to this day, and—should he ever assume the throne—will no doubt affect his overall performance. I found his brother, Prince Edward, battling for Heatherdown four years later. He doesn't seem to have done much better.

I turned to the book filled with soccer and rugby scores. Warner had started filling in the exercise book in 1935. His writing did not change in over thirty years. His last entry was for 1965 at which point he must have dropped dead, because another, more childish hand starts with the Michaelmas term of that year. I was good at rugby football, being left-footed and thus having an inbuilt advantage if I played in the position known as "hooker." Here was our great season—the Lent term of 1954—when we lost only one game. Because I had this aptitude for being a hooker in the "scrum" I could be regarded as "good at games," which was a great help at school. At my next school it meant that every other week we got in a bus and went off to Edinburgh or Aberdeen to play. At the age of eighteen I stopped playing rugby, stopped hunting at home in Ireland and never took any exercise ever again. It is as though, having had cold baths and gone for early morning runs for nearly ten years, one has paid in advance the physical rent check for the next thirty years.

D aisy came back from makeup in the school uniform called for in the script. It slightly reminded me of the uniform worn by the girls at Heathfield, a well-known prep school for girls right next door. My aunt had gone there in the early part of the century and almost the only other fact I knew about it was that David Niven had been expelled from Heatherdown—or said he had—for climbing over the Heathfield wall to steal a cabbage out of its garden. It seemed an odd piece of flora for a person who relished the reputation of a lady's man to pride himself on having stolen. I suppose he thought that no one would believe him if he had claimed to have stolen a rose. Heatherdown had absolutely no contact with Heathfield all those years I was there. Our school was very definitely in the non-coed tradition, holding to the view that juxtaposition of the sexes would lead instantly to debauch. Aside from the Heathfield peril, women were successfully kept at bay. Heatherdown was not as purely masculine as Mount Athos. There were Patsy Warner and Matron, a steely creature who maintained an insensate interest in our bodily functions but who—perhaps for reasons of what Herbert Marcuse later called hyperrepressive desublimation (rare was the week in which she did not seize my private parts in a chill grip as part of some diagnostic test)—did not inflame our imaginations. There were the older sisters who came and were ogled on Visitors' Day, and that was about it.

Daisy reported that Gavin Miller had agreed that I could watch a scene being shot and that although my presence might make her feel awkward she did not really mind. I followed her up to the old school library, where the technicians were setting up the next scene.

I had read the script of *Secrets*. It was about bonding rituals among teenage girls, and a great many scenes consisted of Daisy and a couple of her schoolmates parodying Masonic rituals. The scene in preparation was simple enough. It involved the same girls making moderate nuisances of themselves during a Latin class. I waited, eyeing the film crew. As always with movies, the setup went on interminably, and my attention wandered to the shelves of the library. The books seemed to be mostly the same as in my day: G. A. Henty, W. E. Johns, Baroness Orczy, W. W. Jacobs, Sapper, Jules Verne, John Buchan, P. G. Wodehouse, and for more sophisticated tastes, Nevil Shute and A. J. Cronin.

So far as politics goes these authors were all stoutly counterrevolutionary, whether it was some lad in Henty trying to thwart the Indian Mutiny, a Buchan hero heading off a black nationalist upsurge in *Prester John* or Bulldog Drummond and his "Black Gang" murdering Bolsheviks. Drummond could break a chap's neck like a twig and laugh while doing it. He dropped Henry Lakington into an acid bath, telling him as he did so that "the retribution is just." No author in our library had much time for the French Revolution or for Napoleon. Henty did not care for them and neither did C. S. Forester. The Scarlet Pimpernel devoted his entire professional life—if "professional" could be linked to so quintessential an amateur as Sir Percy, who yawned a lot and laughed down from under lazy eyelids—to the outwitting of the Committee of Public Safety and the stalwart revolutionary M. Chauvelin. And then there was Dickens too, with *The Tale of Two Cities* and the great sacrifice of Sidney Carton. In my case this ideological saturation bombing did not have much effect. One did a form of double-entry political bookkeeping—hoping for the victory of Sir Percy, Hornblower, Hannay or whoever, while simultaneously approving the deeds of St. Just, Danton, or Napoleon.

And of course the library permitted us to seek in literary guise the woman we were denied in bodily form. In Henty and Verne, women barely existed. Orczy tried harder. Sir Percy Blakeney concealed beneath his foppish nonchalance the tenderest emotions towards the Lady Marguerite and would, after she had swept away, lower his lips to the stone balustrade and stair where her hand and foot had rested but a moment before. In Sapper and Buchan women had literary utility as good little troopers—like Matron, only younger. The moment of greatest sexual tension in Buchan is when Hannay realizes from the effeminate nature of furniture that Von Stumm is homosexual ("I was reminded of certain practices not unknown in the German General Staff") and, in a panic bordering on hysteria, knocks him down.

Nevil Shute and H. E. Bates, powerfully represented in the school library, permitted certain intimacies. There was a strong scene in the latter's *The Purple Plain* in which the hero nearly persuades the Burmese girl Anna to bathe naked with him. In the end after many sufferings he gets into bed with her, with the imprimatur of Mrs. McNab. I wandered along the shelves and found the book—no doubt the same one I fingered excitedly thirty years before. Here it was: "Go in and lie down and sleep with her. Nothing will be said in this house about that sort of sleep together." *What* sort of sleep? I spent a lot of time puzzling about this. Couples in those sorts of books used to embrace, then there would be some tactful punctuation and then, "Hours later they awoke." I used to think sex and sleep were indivisible, just as everyone at my next school thought that one's virginity would expire just as soon as one contrived to be alone with a French girl. Words would be unnecessary, given the torrid and impulsive morals of these women, though just to be on the safe side we would complacently rehearse the words *Voulez-vous coucher avec moi.* It was curious, in the late sixties, to meet French adolescents rushing eagerly the other way, certain that Swinging London would be the answer to their problems.

It's hard to know where these illusions about French morals started. There was the French kiss and the French letter. Brothels were legal over there too. In Ireland there were no legal brothels, no legal French letters and the rules of censorship prevailing at that time did not permit French kissing in films. The great heads on the screen of Horgan's cinema would approach with lips puckered and then suddenly spring apart, lips relaxing after raptures excised by the scissors of the Catholic hierarchy. It was all very frustrating and I would retire to the adventures of my great hero, the shy, brilliant, and—to women—irresistibly attractive Horatio Hornblower. Who could forget the long-delayed embrace with Lady Barbara Leighton in *Beat to Quarters* or the spasm of passion with the Vicomtesse Marie de Graçay in *Flying Colors?* There were three copies of this book still on the Heatherdown shelves and soon I found the well-worn page: "It was madness to yield to the torrent of impulses let loose, but madness was somehow sweet. They were inside the room now, and the door was closed. There was sweet, healthy, satisfying flesh in his arms. There were no doubts, no uncertainties; no mystic speculation. Now blind instinct could take charge, all the bodily urges of months of celibacy. Her lips were ripe and rich and ready, the breasts which he crushed against him were hillocks of sweetness. . . . Just as another man might have given way to drink . . . so Hornblower numbed his own brain with lust and passion." C. S. Forester wasn't much given to this sort of thing, but he knew how to lay it on when he had to.

Sex was mostly literary at Heatherdown. Homosexuality, at least in my cohort, was unknown. My own psychosexual development was erratic. I liked to dress up in the holidays and would occasionally come down to dinner in long dress and carefully applied makeup. Years later David McEwen described to me the scene in some grim Scottish fortress when the son and heir of the house, then in his twenties, swept into dinner in long dress and white gloves. The aged butler muttered apologetically into the ear of the stricken father, "It's no' what I laid oot for him, my lorrrd."

Whatever unease my parents may have felt at such appearances would have, had they known of it, been balanced by the news of my engagement to Adrienne Hamilton. At the age of ten I proposed and was accepted in the course of a stay with Adrienne at Blarney Castle, owned at the time by her mother. Next term at Heatherdown Adrienne's cousin Henry Combe made a laughing stock out of me by publicizing the fact that I was "in love" with Adrienne. This was thought to be very ridiculous. Our engagement was canceled. I never forgave her for the betrayal and the experience no doubt has powerfully colored my relations with women ever since. When next I met her, thirty years later in New York, she laughed prettily when I reminded her of her treachery. No matter. They laughed lightly at the Count of Monte Cristo too, when he reminded them of a long-forgotten fellow called Dantès.

I put down the Hornblower. By now the technicians had set up the scene. My daughter was sitting more or less exactly in the position that I was long ago when Warner had announced that all boys in the school—some fifty-five—were doing well, except for one. This one was slacking. "Cockburn," Warner was a great finger-crooker, and his finger now crooked horribly. "Come here, boy." He had a habit of getting one by the short hairs right behind the ear and pulling up sharply. "Some of us aren't working hard enough, are we?" Jerk. "No, Sir." "Some of us are going to work harder, aren't we?" Another savage jerk. "Yes, Sir." A final jerk and Cockburn, blubbing with pain and humiliation, stumbled back to his place.

Gavin Millar kindly gave me a script. "Miss Johnson" is teaching a Latin class and the girls are not behaving. Millar cries "Action" and the girls, Daisy included, start making furtive animal noises. Amid their snickers Miss Johnson tries doggedly to explain the structure and im-

[255]

portance of the Latin grammatical construction known as the ablative absolute. Finally, peering irritably at one fractious girl, she says with heavy sarcasm, "Louise having been blessed with such talent, we don't have to bother to teach her," and goes on to outline the benefits of a classical education. "Ablative absolutes could be the key to your whole future. Think about it, Louise." Louise tries to look thoughtful and Millar says, "Cut."

Could it be that my classical education, commenced at Heatherdown, is at last going to be of some immediate, practical utility?

I raised my hand and saw, out of the corner of my eye, Daisy freeze with horror and embarrassment. It was clear to her that I was about to make a public ass of myself and, by extension, of her too.

"Gavin," I said quietly, "I don't suppose it matters, but your scriptwriter doesn't know Latin." I saw a tough-looking young woman bridle at this and realized that Noella Smith, scriptwriter, was in the room. I pressed on. "The clause 'Louise having been blessed with such talent' is really in apposition to 'her,' which in turn is the object of 'teach'—all of which makes it a participial accusative construction, not an ablative absolute. You could make it better by omitting the final 'her,' which would sequester the Louise clause as an ablative absolute."

Millar recognized superior fire power and "Miss Johnson" was instructed to drop the final "her." She kept forgetting and the scene was reshot five times. Millar pointed out the substantial sum my quibble had cost them. Daisy, having concluded that I had not made a major fool out of myself or her, hastened away to makeup and wardrobe, and the room emptied. Still pondering ablative absolutes, I looked along the library shelves till I found *Latin Course for Schools, Part One*, by L. A. Wilding, first published in 1949.

"The study of a foreign language," wrote Mr. Wilding in his introduction, "is an exciting matter; it is like a key that will open many doors. . . . By a knowledge of Latin we are introduced to a great people, the Romans. The Romans led the world as men of action; they built good roads, made good laws, and organised what was in their time almost world-wide government and citizenship. At their best, too, they set the highest examples of honour, loyalty and self-sacrifice."

I leafed through the book. Exercise 65: " 'By means of justice and kindness Agricola wins over the natives of Britain.' Translate." This must be Tacitus. Tacitus, married to General Gnaeus Julius Agricola's daughter, wrote a toadying biography of his father-in-law. Wilding's textbook was strewn with what I could now see was heavy propaganda for the benefits of imperial conquest, whether Roman or British. Exercise 171: "Render into Latin, 'It is just,' they say, 'to surrender our city to the Romans: such men know how to keep faith even in war. They have conquered us, not by force, but by justice, and we and the Roman people will hand down a good example to the human race.' " Exercise 65: "Render into Latin: 'By means of justice and kindness Agricola wins over the natives of Britain. He then hastens beyond Chester towards Scotland. He rouses his troops to battle and to victory. At first Agricola wastes the land, then he displays to the natives his moderation.' "

It is summer in 1952 and Mr. Toppin had us penned in, even though the bell has gone for morning break. We are in Latin class and Mr. Toppin is trying to give us a sense of occasion. "This is the speech of Calgacus to his troops before the battle at Graupian Hill in A.D. 84. Calgacus is the name Tacitus gives the Scottish general. *'Hodie pro patria adhuc libera . . .'* Cockburn? 'Today . . .' " "Today you will fight for a country still free against the Romans. . . ." "Good. *'Patriam vestram in dextis vestris portatis'?*" "You carry your country in your right hand. . . ."

Wilding left it in no doubt, in his simplified and polite version of Tacitus, that the Roman victory at Mons Graupius was a good thing. Ten thousand Scots fell that day, the blood of kerns flowing in the heather near Inverness, not so far from where I was born. The Romans slaughtered till their arms were tired. Night, as Tacitus put it, was jubilant with triumph and plunder. The Scots, scattering amid the grief of men and women, abandoned their homes and set them on fire. The day after, bleak and wet, disclosed more fully the lineaments of triumph: silence everywhere, lonely hills, houses smoldering to heaven.

Resolute to favor Roman imperialism over British na-

tionalism—Viking imperialism was a different matter—
Wilding suppressed the eloquence of Calgacus's appeal
to his troops, as conceived by Tacitus. Back in London
the next day I looked it up in the Loeb translation: "Here
at the world's end, on its last inch of liberty, we have lived
unmolested to this day. . . ." Calgacus gestures down
the hill to where the Romans—in actual fact Provençal
French, Spaniards and Italians—stand with their German
auxiliaries: "Harriers of the world, now that earth fails
their all-devastating hands—they probe even the sea: if
their enemy have wealth, they have greed; if he be poor,
they are ambitious; East nor West has glutted them; alone
of mankind they behold with the same passion of con-
cupiscence waste and want alike. To plunder, butcher,
steal, these things they misname empire: they make a
desolation and they call it peace."

Ubi solitudinem faciunt, pacem appellant. They make
a desolation and they call it peace. The phrase has echoed
down the ages as the tersest condemnation of Rome. Nothing of this in Wilding.

Those were the days in the early 1950s when the British
Empire was falling rapidly apart. On Sundays boys at
Heatherdown had to write a weekly letter home ("Dear
Mummy and Daddy, I am very well. How are you . . .")
and many of the envelopes at our school were addressed
to army posts in Kenya, Malaya, Aden, Cyprus and other
outposts of shriveling empire. At school I would hear grim
tales of the Kenyan Mau Mau and then go home to hear
my father consider such events in a very different way.

Both my father and I, forty years apart, studied classics.
A significant portion of this study was spent considering
the birth and practice of democracy in Athens in the fifth
century B.C. It seemed to be the consensus of our teachers
that between fifth-century Athens, the senate under the
Roman Republic and nineteenth- and twentieth-century
Westminster, nothing much of interest by way of political
experiment had occurred, and that the virtues and glories
of ancient Greece and modern Britain were essentially
the same.

There was a problem, of course. One of the first words
to be found in Wilding was "*servus*," meaning "slave." In
our Greek primer the word "*doulos*" soon obtruded itself.

Our schoolmasters could not conceal from us that Athenian "democracy" was practiced on the backs of hundreds and thousands of these *servi* or *douloi*. The fact of slavery was acknowledged, but with that acknowledgment the matter was closed. Thus the statement "Athenian democracy was a great and noble achievement" was accompanied by the footnote, "Athenian democracy was based on slavery." But the footnote remained a footnote and two people being given a ruling-class education in Britain at either end of the first half of the twentieth century were taught that democratic achievement and slavery were not mutually contradictory. This sort of instruction was helpful if one was to continue to run the British Empire with a clear conscience. (Twentieth-century British classics teachers were not the only people to remain somewhat silent on the matter of slavery in the ancient world. The great classical historian G.E.M. de Ste. Croix has written that he knows "of no general, outright condemnation of slavery inspired by a Christian outlook before the petition of the Mennonites in Germantown in Pennsylvania in 1668."

I left the library and walked down to the old dining room, now changed by the set designers into a school laboratory. Daisy was hurrying through, on her way to another bout of tuition. At her London day school she had decided against Latin and in favor of German, despite some dutiful lectures from me on the merits, even if only from the vantage point of etymological comprehension, of a classical grounding. This was, for the second time in my life, my last day at school, though devoid of that immense spiritual and physical rapture connected to "ends of term" back in the fifties. In those days I would go up to London on the school train and there be met by my father who would take me off to a treat, usually lunch at some restaurant such as Rules, Simpsons, or Chez Victor. Once we went out with Gilbert Harding, a noted radio "personality" of the day. This "personality" was of the choleric Englishman, perpetually raging against poor service and so forth. We were never able to get through lunch because Harding, in order to keep this income-yielding "personality" at full stretch, would burst forth after about ten minutes with curses at management and waiters and we would have to leave. Then, later in the day, my father and I would board the boat train at Paddington in the company of about four thousand other Irish passengers. It was so crowded that once my father could not even get his hand into his upper pocket to get out a whiskey bottle and had to ask the man his other side to help him.

In these more sophisticated times Daisy and I discussed our Christmas rendezvous in New York after her term was over. I had hoped to persuade the set photographer to take a picture of her standing in front of the same rhododendron bush as I, when I had my farewell photograph taken. But by now the novelty of the old Heatherdown-boy-with-daughter-in-film was wearing off. I remembered how revisiting fathers, trying to find the initials they had carved in their school desks, had seemed vaguely ridiculous to us and decided not to outlast my welcome. The taxi took me off down the drive past the empty swimming pool, and I had carefully on my knee my old portrait, saved by my daughter from the wrecker's ball.

LOST PROPERTY

Ben Sonnenberg

> *. . . God attributes to place*
> *No sanctitie, if none be thither brought.*
> —*Paradise Lost,* Book XI

I

"THE POLISH RIDER"

I have always had a weakness for *The Top Drawer* "By One Who Was Born in It," meals in Ivy Compton-Burnett are merely familiar to me, and in my worst recurring dream I am cut at a party by Henry James. All this is because of where I grew up, 19 Gramercy Park, which *The New Yorker* not long ago called, "Unquestionably, the greatest house remaining in private hands in New York."

A big house, it never was big enough: anyway never for me. "*Here's* where I live," I told schoolmates, taking them to the Frick. I wanted armed guards, as at the Frick. Not only to body forth riches and fear as neat museum guards seem to do. But also because their courtesy made me almost an heir. At home, by contrast, I was a kid at the mercy of angry help. A better-known liar, Ford Madox Ford, used this same technique. You know how French policemen salute on being approached in public. Ford was looking after the young son of friends visiting Paris one day. "Wait here on the corner while I go ask that policeman a question," Ford said. Returning, Ford said to the very small boy, "Did you see? He saluted me. Yes; and why? Because I'm a Papal Count."

Stories like these tend to make me glad, their theme being dissatisfaction with the (as it were) too ostensible truth. My own bears on an experience, general in the 1960s, where home turns out not to substantiate a historical revolt. Then, oh, for a Winter Palace! Oh, for an Escorial! It seems to be, in the touching words of Walter

Benjamin, "already announcing the flight into sabotage and anarchy that later makes it so difficult for the intellectual to see things clearly" if he grows up where money is "ruinously at the center of all."

That was as well the way being shown by Rembrandt's "Polish Rider" (allegedly Rembrandt's son): both in its gorgeous explicit self, as overarmed and ready for flight, as stupid but with the promise of reason in savage action; and no less in its domestication to the wall of a rich museum, once a private home, like the Frick.

THE TOWN HOUSE

Looked at from the street, my house was not much: large, but just to the standard of wealthy pre-Civil War New York, more "Murray Hill" than "Washington Square," and too sheerly ample for good design. Except for being a corner building (at 20th Street and Irving Place), it belonged to that bland type of mansion, plentiful in New York, which always is being converted from misuse or dilapidation into monuments to individualism understood as earning-a-fortune.

Inside, however, it stubbornly was of a class of singular dwellings. Typically rural, these often are dandyish as well. Baudelaire saw with the dandy himself that the need to be odd, at whatever the cost, is finally a heroic shape taken in their decadence by leisure and inherited wealth. "*Le dernier éclat d'héroïsme dans les décadences*," Baudelaire wrote. So it may be with houses, in other twilights, too. See Horace Walpole's Strawberry Hill. Nineteen Gramercy Park was quaint, self-conscious, a "mad" expense. But its finally heroic shape was due to its being in town: that is what made it conspicuous and expressive as an excess. A similar effort in Greenwich, Connecticut would have had different results.

Room after comfortable, colorful room: various, orderly, studied, profuse; devoted to what Henry James defined "the mysteries of ministration to rare pieces"; all brought together, and made to cohere: through force of furnishing, so to speak: in a sumptuous, costly, luxurious style known once as Capuan. It made a unique impression. Not, as with Frick and the subtle Duveen, of a wedding of riches to expert taste, but of something much more peculiar. In "Louis-Philippe, or the Interior," Benjamin says: "For the private individual the private environment represents the universe. In it he gathers remote places and the past. His drawing room is a box in the world theater." And the verb that follows will nail the point. My home gripped the imagination as wholly a fiction, a play, a dream: formal and yet almost overcharged with personal emblems and feelings.

COLLECTORS' CHILDREN

My parents conspired well in the house. They lived there for forty-eight years. My father had a compulsion to buy, my mother to decorate. Together they made a fetish of antique furniture. At first they collected like children, to renew the world. Later, with money, acquiring things was very far from naive. The justifications! the reasons! Good business was one. Well might it have been. Still, like all of the genus Collectors' Child, while I was jealous principally of my parents' unstinted passion, I hated worse their profession of a practical purpose. And why? Their passion suggested only that I was subordinate to Sheraton, second to George the Second, and not so much fun as a cheerful chintz: which a seven-year-old would of course resent but could nevertheless comprehend. But their tacit profession that all was not in fact what it so clearly seemed: that to me was trumped up! arrant make-believe! typical of adults!

OVER TWENTY-FIVE ROOMS,
MORE THAN THIRTEEN IN STAFF

The atmosphere was officious. After using one of the bathrooms (perhaps that described by the *New York Times* as "the finest . . . in a house of remarkable bathrooms"), Tennessee Williams was heard to say, "It looked so shabby when I took it out, I couldn't go."

Let me add further that somewhere in Freud there is a convincing progression from pissing to pyromania, that in *The Spoils of Poynton* burning down is the only possible end.

Then the house was ruled more with reference to the wishes and expectations of its large, exceedingly specialized staff than with thought (as *I* thought) of my own childish good. I had status, the servants had power. We had fights and they always won. *Real* English butlers and *real* Irish maids, they afflicted me with the moral zeal of the disciplined but disenfranchised, avid to show where I failed. With what literal force I later read, *And I have seen the eternal Footman hold my coat, and snicker.* I acted toward them vengefully, in turn, consoling myself by reflecting upon their replaceability. That was the ultimate fact, was it not? A wretched result has been that I still think status of more worth than power.

And yet how replaceable were they? The English butlers, one formerly with HRH the Duke of Windsor, another with Myron T. Herrick, our ambassador to France: a butler who, moreover, on May 21, 1927, loaned Lindbergh a pair of pajamas? The servants were truly needed. It showed in the numerous valuable plates they presented at even family meals, ceremonially, not to be eaten from; in the deference of silence to which they appeared, and which to me from an early age made a paradox of the then common ideal of unobtrusive service; and in their great importance as topics of conversation.

They were needed besides as mirrors, implicated thereby in the buying of very vast numbers of shoes and clothes which it also was their job to care for. This will account for the strong link I make between home life and the contexts of restaurant and retail store, where service, appearance, consumption, excess are comparably important.

HEARTBREAK HOUSE

All was phantasmagoric. To me at least, the house stood for taste and culture in an era of mass fright: quite as if these were enough armament, together with making money. For it to succeed, it had to exclude. And with exceptional force. Decoration was in, but poetry and music had no place. Talk of people was in, but not of ideas; of Democratic electioneering, but not of politics. Biographies, table talk, memoirs, "characters" crowded the shelves; portraits and "conversations" were everywhere on the walls.

It was more a venue for parties than ever an actual home. Like the Dedlock mansion in *Bleak House*, "Fairyland to visit, but a desert to live in." If a home, however, then Heartbreak House, so far as Shaw's play does indeed represent "leisured, cultured Europe" before the First World War. Only, alas, by the time I was nine, *two* world wars had occurred, and my mother and father had lived through both.

JOHANNA KIBBE

Another disturbance met with a stranger equivocation. I had a German governess during the Second World War. She was openly pro-German after the Allied bombing of Metz in her home region of Moselle. In fact she went off her head. She started telling me what I could do when the Nazis took over New York. "Just don't mention you're Jewish."

I was Jewish? I knew and I didn't know. It wasn't exactly a secret. My parents spoke Yiddish fluently; my grandparents lived on the Lower East Side; Bernard Baruch, Albert Einstein, Leslie Howard made us proud.

Yet to look at the walls with their portraits of Millicent, Duchess of Sutherland, of Lady Ottoline Morrell, at the Queen Anne this and the Charles the First that, at the bust of Pope and the braces that had once belonged to Disraeli—surely I wasn't Jewish? Or if I were, then so what? To ask, as it were of the Duchess or of my father's still more ducal "man," was to invite the answer, *You are as Jewish as you want to be.* That was the answer I got.

Little wonder that then it was left to one in a lunacy of sorrow to bring the effect of my question well and truly home.

SARDANAPALUS

Robert Hughes remarked, in *Time* magazine, that 19 Gramercy Park was "not comparable to the great mansions of Fifth Avenue at their height of extravagance . . . but [was] an astonishing survivor, a solid, heavy and opulent fossil." It did not express the power, wealth, and pride of a "new" social class but instead was a genuflection toward, and a parody of, making money.

More obviously, it was meant not to last. Suggest to my father that it be preserved, like the John Soane House in London or the Merchant's House on East 4th Street downtown, and he'd only jeer: Sardanapalus about to set his own pyre alight.

> So much for monuments that have forgotten
> Their very record!

I am not unsympathetic. I appreciate both his arrogant trepidation and the less esoteric plea that all, in the end, be seen, somehow, as for something more than his uses alone: recondite, forceful, and rich though these were.

STAND BACK!

Going there never was easy for me. Its too-thick carpets impeded my stride. Lately it was especially hard. The little displacements occasioned by so many expert inspections; the not subtle tags, on the tables and chairs, of the movers and auctioneers: unmistakable signs that all, that all, once transfigured through being collected, was being relaxed to its merchandise state: these were types of reversal: black magic.

Still, insolent though the house was to me, *My rage is gone*, as Aufidius says. Only how well it stood for what I am not.

A PRINCE IS VEXED

My father was an impressive man in the mode of the late nineteenth century: a "new" man to the dons and peers he loved to entertain, an "aristocrat" to the company heads he was hired by. His snobbism was the same as Morel's in *Le Temps retrouvé*, Proust having observed "with the infallibility of one himself susceptible," in Theodor Adorno's words, "that Anglomania and the cult of stylized living are found less among aristocrats than among those aspiring to rise." It led to peculiar locutions ("My man will show you out") as well as to the fairyland air of 19 Gramercy Park.

Walter Benjamin, brought up in town like me in a house with many servants, wrote in "A Berlin Chronicle" that "the economic basis on which the finances of my parents rested was surrounded, long past my childhood and adolescence, by deepest secrecy." This may be the rule in rich parvenu homes, whether Jewish or not. It certainly was in mine. Secrecy lay at the very core of my father's power at home. In addition, mystification was a genuine part of his work. He also justified earning by incantatory allusions to a fabulous boyhood (it seemed so to me) with actual deprivations; to growing up "an immigrant boy," as he liked to exult, "in a tenement-house on the Lower East Side" where the plumbing was out in the hall.

On the other hand, justification itself was called for by no one but him. He pointed thereby to a pre-bourgeois past that, to quote Adorno again, "survives in the shame felt at being paid for personal services and favors." The pre-bourgeois world, involving pogroms with dreams of consoling wealth, though frankly a legend, was used nonetheless to explain why he'd had to earn money in amounts as large as "they" would allow for as long as "they" would allow it. It was located for us in Brest-Litovsk, where my father was born in 1901, a city that was historically now Russian, now Polish, now neither, now both.

The shame had a meaning besides. His business was public relations. Our house was a blush for this fact. Not only in looking established, while public relations was deemed "fly-by-night," as he himself often remarked. But in being so brazenly stagy. This argued no real difference between the public and private. Indeed, when my father was showing off, there *was* nowhere private at home. What things had cost was a part of his spiel as he took strangers through the house. No one corner was different from the rest of the house in taste. The "style of the whole" was in cupboards and drawers as well as in every room.

Also staginess made an embarrassment of the truthful and ideal. I reacted the more against sound common sense. All was a shibboleth. "You'll have to earn your

[*267*]

own living some day." What sort of fool did he think I was? In this respect, I'm inclined to believe, the house was no less a frustration to him than a riddle to me.

"S'IL FAUT PARLER DES FEMMES . . ."

Patronage formed a very large part of my parents' lives. They struggled to strike the exact right note in nothing else so much. "You know how to handle servants," an accolade of theirs, resounded in my love of hotels, restaurants, and cafés. I later mistook affection for a kind of retail debt because stores and restaurants were so like home in their consecration to service. Judging from Restoration plays, as well as from George Meredith's *The Ordeal of Richard Feverel,* not to speak of Shelley and Baudelaire, I had the old inclination of sons of the upper-middle class to forge my habits of spending together with my erotic life into a compulsion upon too rigid or distant parents. A number of meanings of "folly" and "dissipation" are here.

My own mad habits began with clothes. I thrilled to my first handmade suit more than to my first real love affair. Both occurred at about the same age. At the next-to-last fitting I felt such content, I had to make an excuse. Like many at this precise juncture, I said to the tailor, "I've just had lunch." To which he replied, "We hope you will again, sir." The right note! And struck by a tailor kneeling to fix my cuffs! How it chimed with the insolent deference that I was used to at home!

My first love affair, though a clash, naturally, was nonetheless keyed to the house, showing how (in the harsh but moving phrase of one of the Frankfurt School) in a "conceptual hierarchy which relentlessly demands responsibility on *its* terms, only irresponsibility can call that hierarchy by its right name." I got into an actual physical fight with a butler who'd been instructed not to let me go out; I stole expensive objets d'art to give to my girlfriend (a woman with two children, like Sophie de Rênal); and I ensnared my parents by going to stores *en client sérieux* where I couldn't have paid the bills.

Yet how very detached I felt, in love as in the house: neither a stranger nor quite at home: misshapen by a peculiar burden of spirit, I think. I kept things from being surprising by that same sort of pride which at seventeen makes Julien Sorel pretend he is "accustomed to the subjugation of women." *Orgueil bizarre*: not propitious in love. I also tried to impersonate Stendhal at forty-six, the age he began *Le Rouge et le Noir,* by acting as if fully conscious of the qualities I was spoiling. Another odd thing: I was retrospective as more became an old man, like the narrator of *"Le Plus bel amour de Don Juan,"* in *Les Diaboliques* by Barbey d'Aurevilly, who laments that because of his pretty face he had never had as a very young man the profits of his timidity. In other words, I esteemed regrets. This precipitate nonsense is typical of the Collectors' Child, who wishes to pose as not wanting what in fact he wants most in the world.

Musset, in a striking paragraph in *La Confession d'un enfant du siècle,* compares a particular state of mind at almost the same stage of life to a room of the 1820s where vast eclecticism prevails; where all purposes, periods, nations, and tastes are assembled pell-mell; which Musset says feels like the end of the world. So much jumbled up, in a fashion both unprecedented and costly, *"en sorte que nous ne vivons que de débris, comme si la fin du monde était proche."* I think this akin to that special burden of spirit of mine: feeling you always have to appraise, to appraise and to be not unworthy also of *being* appraised.

MY PUNIC WARS

I went to two kinds of boarding school. One kind taught Robert Frost and took a position on Alger Hiss and on Ezra Pound and the Bollingen Prize. They were among the first places I heard, "We don't care how much money your family has." An out-and-out lie, I was sure. Only money had made them make room for me. Only sloth made me stint my revenge.

The other schools taught Tacitus. They were more to my taste. Like men's clubs they amplified talk of good: a good game, a good fit, a good book, a good lay. The prospect of pleasure they offered was like a view from the window at home. They travestied English public school life, like Captain Hook of whom Barrie writes: "Good form! However much he may have degenerated, he still knew that this is all that really matters." To provoke them I had but to trail my coat, showing the label of course.

There was a danger, however. They abetted sadisticness. They let us say "kike" and "jigaboo." They let us get beaten up. For being found in another boy's house. For wearing the wrong-colored tie. Apprised of these "punishments" in advance, the masters stayed out of the way. Once in Latin class, which our housemaster gave, after I'd been terrorized by older boys the night before, I quoted aloud from Horace in the ode about Regulus:

> *atqui sciebat quae sibi barbarus*
> *tortor pararet.*
> [And yet he knew what the barbarian torturer
> Had ready for him.]

To what effect, though? Did he so much as blink? Like all the others he couldn't be shamed by something he merely taught.

The trials of Oscar Wilde had come out in transcript the year before.

> Q. Do you drink champagne yourself?
> A. Yes; iced champagne is a favourite drink of mine—strongly against my doctor's orders.
> Q. Never mind your doctor's orders, sir.
> A. I never do.

Yet the trials were poor as a source of reproach. Not only because like most comic art, especially for the stage, they delighted too much in the very things they struck at and tried to reform. But also because no one I knew, at school anyhow, had read them. Nevertheless, I thought Wilde was me. Incorrigible, irresistible, foolhardy, funny and false. And I thought, yes, that is what a star is: someone important for his mistakes. And I thought, why not be a queer? No doubt at all, as Adorno declares in "The Truth about Hedda Gabler," "Retention of strangeness is the only antidote to estrangement."

I found the trials pornographic as well. First, in their setting lewdness with manners and often vivid expense, among other aspects of social class. Second, because they are mindful of taste as an urgent and complex question. And finally because it is frequently taste in furniture, furnishings, rooms. (Proust surely made this connection to have given his dead mother's furniture to the brothel he helped to set up.) Like everyone else I weep hot tears at Desdemona shrieking "*Ah! Emilia, Emilia, addio*" in Act IV of *Otello;* like not a few I am broken up when toward the end of *A Streetcar Named Desire* Blanche asks about the woman she hears is waiting in front of the house, who turns out to be the Matron, "I cannot imagine who this 'lady' could be! How is she dressed?" and Eunice replies, "Just—just a sort of a—plain-tailored outfit." But who besides me is affected by Wilde's last remark below? It occurs not long after his famous speech explaining "the Love that dare not speak its name" when Wilde was at almost his worst beset; it mentions his codefendant who procured for him.

Q. You saw nothing peculiar or suggestive in the arrangement of Taylor's rooms?
A. I cannot say that I did. They were Bohemian. That is all. I have seen stranger rooms.

5Y4, 7Y1

All our cars were outlandish-looking custom-built affairs, more stately comfortable carriage than streamlined automobile, nothing racy or aerodynamic like Ellery Queen's Duesenberg. They weren't machines, but sumptuous small interiors that moved, implying a not truly high regard for travel, let alone speed. "A Brewster body on a '39 Ford chassis." That sort of car. The chauffeur was always having to say; otherwise no one could know. "A '41 Packard town car," noticeable on the rainiest night outside of "21." Each of our cars had a pedigree, too. Somebody prominent had had it built. This or that "Mrs. Warren Wampum, a name as old as the Hudson." None was new with us.

We were driven on Sundays in one car to my grandmother's for lunch. My father's mother on Riverside Drive, up past the hulk of the *Normandie*, the Reichstag of the *rentier* class. And in another, a prewar Cadillac touring car, to summer houses resembling those of Walter Benjamin's youth: "outside from the point of view of the city; but from that of the summer, inside." Similarly, our summer car: convertible, but with four, not two, doors: never seemed really open, even with the top down.

We rented from people who'd never seen Jews up close before. My mother and father liked making this point. Their own kind could no longer rent as we could, bringing a full staff. Mannerly bankers with soft-spoken wives, good-looking dogs and Purdey guns, they had been ruined in the '29 crash. Ruined? They looked sounder than us. Their state of being before must have been unimaginably intact. We always left them our new croquet set (we brought a new one each May). Why this exactly, I never found out. But comic propitiation was soon my pass into adult life. At home, all that solemn permanence, tinged with absurdity more or less; away, an impermanence that also was equivocal, more or less. . . .

My conscious objectives were therefore not those usual at a later age when, to borrow a phrase of Rimbaud's in *Les Illuminations,* money first begins to seek use "in the perfection of vulgar generosities." Instead, at twenty or thereabouts, I consciously sought opportunities for a favorite sort of transgression. These were (in no special order) expatriation and retail debt, adultery and being a spy.

II

PANDAR'S ORCHARD

My father bought art and bought art and bought art. He and my mother appeared most at one placing this "amusing scrap" or shifting that "little piece."

Not only did art dealers minister to this otherwise troubled union, they had also always noticed me as at least an important object. I repaid the favor, trying to be as much like them as I could. I copied their accents, wore tweed caps and smoked *Le Khédive* cigarettes. Could such a life be mine? "And to think," I might say, in the late afternoons, over the drawings by Constantin Guys, the engravings by Félicien Rops, to some young woman bemused by my ritual delay, "there are men who'd show a young girl *this* . . . and *this*. . . ." Only twenty and already big with brokers, agents and props! (Or, twenty and still posing! Significant both of having grown up with ceremony and servants, and of a sadism that can be truly practiced only by liars.)

Choosing works of art to make girls has of course a number of meanings. One is that connoisseurship is an exemplary bourgeois fault. And so it naturally was with me, as also with Shakespeare's Troilus, whose "I am giddy" soliloquy is a typical false position of strength taken by privilege in its fight with even normal desire:

> . . . and I do fear besides
> That I shall lose distinction in my joys.

Art dealing had a high standing, unclouded as yet by the postwar swarm of customers' men and crooks: almost a learned profession; not quite a profession, in fact. Some had an added glamour. I mean the refugees. Refugees, but stamped nowhere by fear, sudden flight, conscience or peril or pain. They were defying Hitler by prospering in New York, by relishing America to a sometimes silly degree, and by always pledging allegiance to Toscanini and Thomas Mann. Their merest inclinations were now the feats of a strenuous politics. Riches here, fatality there. . . . Each was a Jew who understood art. Each was, as well, in his overseas home, under perpetual sentence of death, like Paul Henreid in *Casablanca*.

How pervasive the glamour of those who are like our parents but better at it! These Jews owned art but without the fuss of 19 Gramercy Park. They dealt, to be sure; only art dealing showed how little they were in thrall. The glamour spread to their daughters, their dogs, through their homes to their "little collections" of kitsch, to their lengthy meals. . . . To all but their clothes: Alice Schweitzer and Sulka and Knize. The women's hems always a fraction too long, the men's suit jackets too short. Still, in this New World city, where both sexes dressed with unflagging regard for Europe (especially then), even these tiny symbols of difference were powerful charms, seeming meant to evoke the historical Jew. Yes, and at no small expense.

Which appealed to me most? I never could decide. To be like them in their art-dealing work? To be like them as ideal victims of an ideal villainy? Or to be like them in their homes where property and pleasure were so indissolubly linked? Besides, they had glamour as cultured Jews who nevertheless were adept at imprecation and doom: most of all about music. If Sterba liked Schnabel while Mosse liked Kempff, then in the one's eyes the other was not only incurably stupid but unforgivably rude. And about *music!* The same with composers: on into the twentieth century, on back to before Buxtehude. I was certain no German or Austrian Jew could utter a word on the subject without thereby causing mortal offense to some other German or Austrian Jew.

Their absolutism was an effect of a then worldwide shriveling-up of judgment into a worship of "the barbarism of perfection." That, and the anguished dominion that émigrés and exiles seek in whatever city they stop. Still, for me, a Collectors' Child, for whom the wall was as much as the work, the donor as much as the artist, it translated from musical into general terms, becoming, first and foremost, a foil for the lax cupidity with which I appreciated painting (or watched it appreciate). And second, a very great comfort. For here were severe intellectual men (dogmatic and expert at least) to whom location, provenance and cash value were important. To please them, however demanding they were, I needed only to cultivate my own innate talents and tastes. By contrast, at home the formation of these led invariably to resentment and fights.

To be a Benjamin to them, what did I not do? I read German, studied lieder. . . . Their households were filled with women: I was gallant and flirted with them. Sisters-in-law and others like aunts, even *petites amies.* I wooed them by being mischievous, tender, and sincere. Not for the first time, I liked finding out that whereas with men I was usually tongue-tied and apathetic, with women I felt happy and free. This busied me so, I could scarcely have seen with what pain they perceived, men and women alike, living in a foreign land (New York City a foreign land!), the shrinking of propriety, by force of displacement, through no fault of theirs, into a sometimes convenient but mostly detested *vie de bohème*. I was also blind to why they were mad to be not Jewish but German.

One thing I did see, however. Art dealing wasn't for me. It offered sex, condescension, contempt (frequently all three at once), commercial excitement, and civilized calm; but its inventories and ledgers! details and dates and chores! . . . It was finally perhaps too much a case of "supplying a productive apparatus without changing it." Or being (in other than the fastidious words of Walter Benjamin) too much like hard work.

ADOPTED CHILDREN

Each household that I knew had at least one. Here Lizette and Ariane are talking to Mrs. Berner, a friend of Lizette's parents, during the intermission of a song concert at Hunter College.

> *Mrs. Berner:* They are being good to you, Ariane?
> *Ariane:* Like a mother and father to me.
> *Lizette:* To me too.

I sympathized with Lizette. My parents were always adopting young men: "gentlemen" of the penniless, weak, indecisive kind. These in my parents' view composed a significant part of any year at any Ivy League school, to none of which I was going. I consoled myself for the effortless way these youths seemed to harvest esteem by exalting the virtue of rudeness and exaggerating whatever it was that made them hate and fear me. For instance, I was brilliant. The trouble with this is well known: I was appealing for judgment from rivals I knew to have none.

Thus ambiguousness, and not brilliance, became my stock in trade. I brought it to bear in émigré homes where parents adopted me. It let me pretend I was loved because they (*Herr Doktor* and *Frau Doktor,* now plain "Sammy *und* Missus") discerned beneath my foppish mask of saturnine indifference a practically Russian profuseness of pure and noble feeling, as well as a Shelley-like loathing of property and wealth.

"YOUTH MEANS RETRIBUTION"

Ariane lived with the Rosenblooms. She shared their daughter's room. Hans Rosenbloom was a dealer in Old Master paintings and drawings. There was a Rembrandt drawing of a lion above Lizette's bed.

Rosenbloom had been a magistrate. His real love was music, though. He had left Berlin with his family in 1935. Like Adorno and Benjamin, he may have thought the Nazis would just disappear. Like them, he showed a measure of blindness and unhaste. First he settled in Holland. . . . He had served in the War, after all. The Great War. Anyway! how Jewish *was* he? One-eighth? Maybe not even that. After nineteen years in New York, Rosenbloom had the air nonetheless of not being a Jew but of somehow counting as one.

Another of Rosenbloom's airs he had not had in Berlin, I am sure. Self-made man. Wasn't that New York? And with it, the lures thrown incessantly to atonement, to expiation? Ariane rose to them. So did I. We teased his obsession with death. Well, not with death exactly. When he and his pals got together, the talk was all about funerals. How each would go off in some not large church: San Miniato, the Sainte Chapelle. . . . A *timor mortis,* already benign, made more soft by art. Mosse the psychoanalyst: "I want the Berlioz *Requiem* with Ernest Ansermet." Thielman, who'd married an Endicott and had "the wherewithal now" to collect: "Busch and the Mozart C-minor Mass." Arens the art restorer: "The Verdi, naturally." Then Rosenbloom would say: "Who with?" And Arens: "Toscanini." Then Rosenbloom would say: "Too late!" "Too late?" "Yes! I already got him! Ha! ha!" Everyone would laugh.

They would then look at me with a sort of chagrin. That made me feel important. Part Eros, part Nemesis, part Frog Prince: crystallizations of a before unconscious power, I thought. At other times I felt spellbound by my own duplicity. That's the faculty that made me apt for the art dealers' favorite pastime, the shaping of vignettes.

Yes, and over all the bewitchment of a faith in pre-
destination!

Why not? A function of being in love (Ariane and then
Lizette), that faith was fostered by furniture, too; by art-
works evoking the great and the dead, and by decorum
evocative of the great dead premodern world. It enabled
skills that from a child I knew very well how to prize:
cajoling women and outsmarting men, lying and domi-
neering through taste in clothes and art.

WHY I CLEARED OUT

Once my father lunched with a girlfriend of mine. At
The Colony. It was a flop. "She already *knows* you're
rich": that to me. "*You* know I'm rich," he told her. She
was a widow, so he may have thought being mundane
was all right.

They were seated at once. That was also a sign that
subterfuge wasn't the plan. Not about money. Not there,
anyhow: at the *"rendezvous de l'élite."*

My father moved in that nimble way common to short
public men. "Greetings!" His friends were everywhere.
Friends? His vast clientele.

Sitting down: "Nanette Nabob. *You* know who she
is. . . ." I used to love how he made those he knew
fabulous, even the famous.

One eye of his fixed you, the other eye roamed. His
talk was half confidential. However, the bombastic other
half, the roaming half, prevailed. It helped to annul the
distinction between lying and telling the truth.

Money talks: so I doubt if he needed to ask, "How
much do you actually want?" I also doubt whether he
came out and said, "I love my son. Do you?" Soon,
though, the air was heavy with terms. They quickened
too much or were still. By the time I arrived ("with the
coffee": that was our jaunty plan) she was looking angry,
frightened and sick. My God! was it just like a meal at
home? Didn't being out matter a bit?

He waved for and scribbled his name on the check.
He shoved back the table and left. "Now, children, I've
got to work." This last too palpable insult showed how
bitter and baffled he was. Yet again I'd conspired with

[*277*]

women to make him out to be crass! A bully, when all the while really he was a Talleyrand, a Disraeli!

"Angry?" he said to me later. "Bitter?" We were sitting in his library, not quite face to face. On his dressing gown, as in the lapel of every coat and jacket he owned, was his Legion of Honor ribbon (of which he liked saying the chic was in not accepting a higher grade). As a rule he was reading when he talked to me. "Not at all." I had time to stare. Facing Biography, I always made anagrams of the same titles. Emma Goldman: MADAM N. GOLEM. . . .

Then there it was: the last straw. In a month I was gone from the house. His last phrase to me was the voice of the place. "Not angry at all, *my dear boy*."

RADIOS

I was hired to work for the CIA by a Captain Dankbloom in Munich. 1956. That winter Hungarian refugees walked with me in the Englischer-garten. One afternoon I passed a shape, large, active and white, in the bushes. It made a funny noise. My mind was on Jenny, the wife of a friend. She lived across the Isar. Mostly we met at Jenny's house before her small son got home. However, on that day we were to meet in Schwabing at my pension.

"*Frau* Göhmann, a lady is coming for tea."

"Very well, *Herr;* I'll change the sheets."

A man in the park crossed my path. Casually. He crossed my path again. He held a lady's bag up against the short pinkish topcoat he wore. So I'd recognize him when I saw him again? How very soon that would be! At the Cuvilliés-theater, then at the Haus der Kunst; at the long delayed German opening of Chaplin's *The Great Dictator*. . . . Who was he? Who was he? And where did he sleep?

In that topcoat (known as a "British warm"), in ski clothes, in evening dress. . . . So when at last we were introduced ("Merle Dankbloom, Ben Sonnenberg"), at a party in Bogen-Hausen for refugee relief, I knew all about his wardrobe and he knew all about mine.

And that shape in the bushes taking a leak? "Oh, that!"

Manly laugh from an epicene throat. "My Voice of America girlfriend!"

Another true American voice, our host (Midwest academic) occupied a comfortable house belonging not to him. Like practically everyone there, he worked for one of the radios. VOA or RFE (Radio Free Europe); Radio Liberation (now Radio Liberty). That night he seemed to be saying, *For once we're acting well.*

For once and *at last.* For the radios had at least nursed the revolution. And then? . . . Many there took the blame on themselves. Truly, they blamed themselves. Therefore, how good to be giving aid, to be individuals; to counter the local atmosphere of savage frustration and guilt; to be free of such vengeful passions as their bosses had to exploit; not to be numb, to be humane; above all, to clothe those they couldn't have spared. . . . They gave voluptuously. Coming round to collect, our hostess would say (she herself employed by the front for a front, the Institut für Zeitgeschichte: or was it the front for the front of a front?), "It doesn't count till it hurts."

Each house had a "den." There, in spiffy shoes, Dankbloom made his pitch.

But first here was Jenny. Squeezing my hand, she led me back to the party. To where her husband was talking to a middleaged-looking couple. Meanwhile Jenny kept onto my hand. Her own was very cool. From her wanting to show she herself was cool, a cool hand, cool in the extremity; and from her clutching glasses with ice, palpable, also noisy and convenient, symbols of home. Holding onto my hand (her right hand, my left): too triumphant a sign to overlook, too tepid a one to provoke: Jenny introduced her friends. *Echt* München, the von Schons. Not minions of the US, she implied; like her husband and everyone else.

Back in the den Merle Dankbloom was gazing at his shoes. He looked all at once very sinister in his vanity of detail. He took out his notecase and showed me one one-dollar bill. Its serial number had something to do with how you knew who he was. Eighteen months, he said, and in return I'd get out of the draft. Really? So Captain Dankbloom declared. No having to undress with men, older and longer schlonged. Yes, but why me? Also I'd get a gun. Why me, though? Not that I asked. Too vain. Too vain, and the offer made sense: an infidel business to go with my incurably infidel life.

True, to hear Dankbloom was to indulge a puerile prospect of pleasure where others were fixed by my secret, where personal habits like lying were changed into professional skills. Beyond that, however, as being pronounced then and there, in a faithless epoch and in a dishonored place; as coming to me in a manner so manly and special and chic, Dankbloom's offer not only made sense. It was inevitable. In fact, it was everything I'd always known certain Jews could expect: in particular from the CIA, then beginning its degeneration from aristocratic plaything to everyday thing of use.

For in common with very many my age, not yet twenty-one, who read novels and went to the movies and grew up with money and art, I understood the CIA, for a time in the 1950s, as a shape of the Nineteenth Century, saying to youth in the words of Vautrin: *No principles, only events.*

CONTINENTAL ARMS

Dankbloom gave me a New York number. Wasn't I going home? Very soon; to show off. For example, at Christmastime in New York, me to my mother and father (very cruel, very serves-you-both-right): ". . . people I now know, related to the Fritz von Papens . . ."

Self-exiled son of a self-made man, I went home to draw blood.

I phoned the number from a phone in the St. Regis barbershop. I was given another number in Munich for when I got back. I walked over to Continental Arms, down the avenue from the St. Regis. I bought a "Chief's Special" revolver. The transaction was thrilling, muscular with equipment and craftsmanship. Its high point was in hearing I needed a custom-made holster. I went to a special gunsmith west of Broadway, in the Forties: Chick Something-or-other, said to be the best holster-man in town. Unfriendly and fat, as became someone met on a slumming visit like mine, he showed me a letter. It was from the Havana Chief of Police: about how when arresting a suspect they had overlooked a wee holster Chick Something-or-other had made, and two Havana policemen were killed, and the Chief of Police was writing to say, "¡*Caramba!* what a swell holster!"

I bought one, too; a small cartridge case; also a second holster that fit on my belt. Wanting Chick to smile (if not like me), I said, *very* man-to-man, "You realize most of my trousers are made only for suspenders?"

And fat, and with a holster of fantastic size over his ass: containing a long-barreled Colt of the kind called a Peacemaker, I believe: after a very long pause, Chick said (man-to-man, indeed!), "When you wear a gun, you dress for the gun."

MY BAVARIA

Egon von Schon was American on his mother's side. His father was half American; Harvard 1909. During the Second World War, Egon served in the American army. There he'd had just one assignment. Egon's father, Ernst (known as "Tui") von Schon, was infamous for his early support of the Nazi party. Then he became anti-Hitler in 1942. Arrested by the FBI, on a visit to the Warren Wampum, Seniors, in Bar Harbor, Maine, the summer before, Tui went from a federal prison to a comfortable sort of internment as an analyst for the US Army Air Force, living in Bethesda, outside Washington. "It seemed I could tell exactly what Herr Goebbels intended the Allies to think," Tui wrote in his long, immodest book, *My Own Struggle,* after the war. "According to General George C. Marshall, my instincts about propaganda were 'miraculous and uncanny.'"

Still more peculiar, Tui's son (by then a master sergeant) was assigned to be his jailor.

After the war Egon married and taught history at Columbia. His wife had gone to Smith. She was a magazine editor. Libby Sawyer, a plain intelligent girl who wasn't "exactly poor." They owned a house in Stockbridge; they lived on the Upper West Side. Yet all at once they pulled up stakes and settled in Germany. Libby worked for the family business: art book publishers. It was a fine old prosperous house, including a bookshop and art gallery, like the one in *"Gladius Dei,"* Thomas Mann's story of Munich.

One afternoon Egon visited me at the radio. On the very spot where the airfield had been: the porch, as it were, of the Munich Pact: Oberweisenfeld. It was my second winter, as cold as the one before. Now things were back to normal. Homes in the States had been found for most, if not all, of the refugees; my affair with Jenny had broken up; I owed lots of money, mostly for clothes; once again, I was set to get married.

Egon disliked me, and I disliked him. Still, he would talk, I would listen. People Egon's age were susceptible to exactly that kind of aggression; especially Germans craving a ceremony of judgment. I also liked it that while Egon's path was longer and stranger than mine, where they crossed it was with an eerie fit. On the one side, Egon's insistence upon heading the family business; whereas, in his father's Munich, in the 1920s and '30s, the von Schons had been the wellspring of social connections for Hitler, "old" money for the Nazis, and for once (as it seemed to all then) effective polite respect. On the other side, my stress upon beheading my family, so to speak; upon rectifying my father's career of "responsible" party politics.

Egon would talk of being a child, nine and ten and eleven years old, when he played in the Munich Brown House or the Berlin *Reichskanslei.* Hitler was good with children, Egon was that kind of child.

"Hitler could mimic machines."

"You don't say?"

We were standing in front of a console in one of the studios. They were transcribing a speech by President Eisenhower for transmission to Eastern Europe.

"Practically *any* machine."

"Is that so?"

They were dubbing real applause. Where was the sound effects record from? Egon wanted to know. Yes, the applause record: where was it from? They handed Egon the box. It read: "European Applause. *Reichspar-teitag.* Nürnberg, 1934."

EDWINA

Egon's mother was a high-toned managing matron of the Ethel Barrymore stamp. She answered to no one; her "people" were from Newport *and* somewhere else.

"Good evening, Edwina."

"Mrs. von Schon to you."

Edwina was one of just two women whom Hitler had wanted to marry. Cultivated enough, ladylike enough; beautiful and aristocratic. *Zu zehr kultiviert,* Hitler says of her in the *Table Talk.*

Old women for whom famous men once burned were fascinating to me; like those rare books of which true collectors feel, according to Benjamin in an endearing essay, merely to buy and possess them is to give dead authors new life. I had once struggled hard to befriend an exceedingly boring old woman of whom someone had whispered, "She used to be the mistress of Ferruccio Busoni."

Edwina had been all alone in the house on the night of the Munich *Putsch.* Hitler burst in and threw himself down in the drawingroom at her feet. The revolt had failed, Ludendorff was in jail—Where was her husband?

On business, downtown.

She saw Hitler's arm was broken, his clothing was dirty and torn, he said he was wanted by the police. It was November 9, 1923.

"He took out a big revolver and handed it to me."

Now Edwina came to the part she liked best, with its apt effect of needless-to-say. " '*Shoot me!*' he cried. '*I'm a failure!*' . . . And I didn't."

ENFANT PERDU

My job was mainly to help decide who of the many refugees should go where in America. I was also supposed to stay alert for possible AVO agents. Every two weeks I was paid in cash: twice in dollars and once in marks. At the end of six weeks I was fired, having let through to San Diego a zookeeper named Szabo, who, though he made no bones about working for the Hungarian secret police, declared to me that he was in fact a double agent reporting to the Committee for Cultural

Freedom. More seriously, Mrs. Szabo was a secret agent too, working for the Russians.

I left promptly for London. The puzzle to me at the time was not that our government had hired an incompetent like me. Nor even why I'd been paid in cash by the same US Army historian at whose house I had met the von Schons. But rather why Merle Dankbloom was with me on the plane.

LAST HOME HOLIDAY
A MEMOIR

Dan Jacobson

There was no such thing, it seemed, as the passage of time. The glittering iron roof of the house; the grape-vine's shadow on the back veranda; the weariness of late afternoons, when Namaqua doves called from the silver oak in the corner of the garden; flat streets lined with heat-shriveled trees and bounded on every horizon by blue-green dumps of treated soil from the diamond mines; above all, the sky unchanging in its slow, repeated changes, as storm clouds gathered in columns and toppling castles and lazy continents, and dissipated with no discharge of rain, until at last the stars came out—nothing had altered, what was there that could alter? The cracks in the polished, red-dyed cement of the veranda were like fissures in my brain; even the sag of a particular cushion on a chair, or the sound of a motor bike drilling through the stillness, was as much a recollection as a perception, a discovery not so much of something out there as of something that had always been within me. Every scent, every shadow and gleam or flare of light, every irregularity touched by hand or feet, was trancelike in its insistence on being what it always had been.

So time was absent; as if it had done away with itself. Yet there was nothing around me other than the depredations of time. Time lived through us or on us as a flame lives on the wood it consumes and chars; we were what it charred and turned to ash. Invisible flame, more powerful even than the sun! The dead, my mother first among them, were gone; sky, streets, and cushions bore no trace of them; the air was empty of them; the house was not inhabited by their ghosts. On pavements, outside the shops I visited in town, eyes encaged in wrinkles met mine in mutual recognition; schoolyard bullies, once-desired girls in gym slips, Africans who had worked for families no longer to be seen, scanned all that time had done to me, as I scanned their grey or bald heads, shriveled complexions, thicknesses and emaciations that could never have been predicted. We were all caught equally in one embrace, from which we could escape only by being delivered of everything we had known: body, mind, world.

My father shuffled down the passage to his bedroom. He was afflicted with palsy in his right arm, crippled by rheumatism, ravaged by the eighty-eight years of his life. He could no longer cut his own meat, he had difficulty in bringing his fork to his lips, his memory was erratic, his hearing thick. He slept badly, at irregular hours; it was a great effort for him to get out of an armchair. There were hours, on certain days, when he was talkative, malicious, self-deceiving, full of improbable plans for the future: killings he intended to make in real-estate deals; arguments he was going to have with the well-counted ranks of his enemies, living and dead; scores he had to settle with the Russians who threatened the well-being of the State of Israel or with his sons who hadn't done with their lives just what he had intended them to do. On these mornings he read *The Diamond Fields Advertiser*; he listened to the news on the radio, though he would immediately forget what he had heard; he would insist on being driven down to the business he still believed he ran, where he sat behind his empty desk for an hour or two before being driven home again. But there were also days when he would be unable to leave his bedroom, and could not tell morning from afternoon, and had difficulty in remembering which of his sons I was.

He still appears in my dreams in that form: his neck and arms shrunken; his ankles enlarged; heelless, torn slippers on his feet; the fringes of his underpants thrusting out beneath the single pair of flannel trousers he always wore, as often as not with a pajama jacket above; his mouth pursed forward and hanging to one side; his eyes alert and bewildered; someone about to be abandoned once again to the sprawling solitude of his five bedrooms, three living rooms, two dark, malodorous bathrooms, a long, high-ceilinged passage, a cement veranda back and front, a large garden reverting to so much hot sand, an orchard at the back, together with garage, shed, servants' quarters. Once all this had housed himself, his wife, his three sons, his daughter, at least two and sometimes three full-time servants. Now the rooms were for him and the one remaining servant alone. There were taps that did not run, electric lights that could not be switched on, an abandoned stove standing in a corner of the back veranda, an out-of-action refrigerator in the passage, parked alongside another which clattered and rumbled all night through, and which had not been defrosted for years, an entire bookcase full of steam-buckled books in one of the bathrooms. Empty, no-longer-worn suits—striped suits, summer suits, formal suits—hung in wardrobes above unused pairs of shoes; old letters and invoices lay in cardboard boxes, where they had lain for years, along with photographs and copies of *The South African Jewish Times* which had never been taken out of their wrappers.

I had come back to South Africa from London for three weeks: as much time as I could spare, or felt I could spare, from wife, children, work, the life I had made overseas. For twenty years I had been coming back at intervals to the house and the town in which I had grown up; occasionally my father had visited us in London; now he could travel no longer. It was December, midsummer. By day the heat and light outside were nothing less than grandiose; at night the dark stillness was stifling. I suspected (rightly, as things turned out) that this was the last such journey I would make. On some of the previous trips I had been accompanied by my family; but not on this occasion. Previously my father had spoken as though it were possible that either I or one of his other children, all of whom had left the town, would return to Kimberley, not for a holiday, but for good. This time, however, he did not speak of that hope; he expected nothing of us as far as that was concerned. We had let him down, finally. He was on his own.

Well, not quite on his own. Being so weak and so subject to confusion, he could not have managed alone for more than a day or two. Betty was still with him. She had worked for my parents for many years; then for my father alone even longer. She lived in the room across the backyard where she had always lived; a bell had been rigged up so that he could call her if he needed help at any time. Once or twice a week an African laborer came to do such work around the house as Betty herself could no longer do, or no longer wanted to do: polishing the floors, tidying

up what was left of the garden. For the period of my stay—
Betty had a free hand in such matters—she had also hired
a full-time if temporary assistant, an African girl, Rebecca
by name. Rebecca was many years younger than Betty;
she had a cast in her eye, which gave her a somewhat
wanton look, and a bold, straight-backed way of carrying
herself. To Betty she spoke in Xhosa; to me in Afrikaans;
of the two of us it was towards Betty that she adopted the
more respectful demeanor, on the whole.

Betty must have been in her mid-fifties at the time;
perhaps a little older. Her face was flat, smooth-browed,
pale brown in color; her eyes were faintly Oriental in
shape and tilt; on her head she wore a close-fitting cap
with an elasticized rim and a floral pattern printed on it,
though on formal occasions she would don a white,
starched affair, something like a nurse's. Her body was
broad and thick, though not nearly as much of either as it
had been when she had come to work for my parents a
couple of decades before. Her legs, which were darker in
color than her face, were swollen and scarred; on her feet,
invariably, was an ancient pair of sandals. She used her
hands, pale palms and fingers alike, in extensive gestures
when she spoke. Unlike most of the domestic servants who
had been in the house during my childhood, she preferred
to speak English to us, rather than Afrikaans. Her English
was often of a rather elevated kind. She never ran a
bath for my father, for example; she always "drew" it.
She was an expert at folding table napkins into the shape
of starched crowns; she was a practiced flower arranger
and silver polisher, as well as an excellent cook. These
genteel accomplishments were not her only skills. She
also served, in effect, as my father's nurse, for she helped
him to bathe and to dress, massaged his ankles when they
were especially painful, gave him her arm when he was
too weak to walk up and down the passage unaided. She
ordered meat and fish and groceries by telephone, and
bickered over fruit and vegetables with an Indian hawker
who brought a van round to the house. The household
accounts were paid from the business, since my father
could no longer make out a check: his hand shook too
much, and in any case he found figures of any kind
especially confusing.

Thus his physical and domestic well-being were wholly in Betty's hands. About this he felt no sense of shame, or even any special sense of obligation towards her, fond though he was of her. She was his servant. He paid her. She was black. She lived in a room across the backyard of the house. She called him "Master." So why should he feel anything she did for him to be a derogation of his dignity?

Have no fear, she got her own back on him. A ramshackle, lovingly vindictive version of the entire history of South Africa stood behind and within the relationship between the two of them. She was devoted to him; she would spend hours with him by day and night, talking to him or merely sitting by his bedside in order to calm him simply by her presence. She could also be a devious, drunken, hemp-smoking blackmailer, who knew just how much power she had over him, and who enjoyed using it. A favorite trick of hers was to frighten him reasonlessly: one day it might be with the announcement that "they" were coming to cut off the water; another that she had distinctly heard burglars and "*skollie*-boys" in the house next door. All the servants she hired for one temporary job or another, Rebecca not excluded, had their reputations thoroughly blackened before they were discharged. Though she could hardly get rid of them in quite the same way, she made many insidious suggestions to my father about my brothers and sister, and their children. Everything she said, he believed—for a while at least. The more he believed, the more she laid it on.

The relationship between the two of them was archaic, perhaps unimaginable elsewhere; one would have had to go to the literature of czarist Russia, to Gogol or Herzen or some of the tales of Tolstoy, to find parallels to its absurdity and intimacy, the depths of the affection and social distance it spanned, the mutual dependencies and assumptions of superiority, the strange combinations of slyness and candor, that marked every aspect of it. One night, quietly and almost casually, with an emphasis given to her words only by the sound of two fingers slapping against the open palm of the other, and a slightly laboring note in her voice, Betty said to me, "You mustn't worry. I will stay with the old master to the end. To the very end.

God's my witness I'll look after him until he needs me no
more." I believed her, and I was right to believe her. The
very next night, however, she was as doped and as drunk
as I was to see her during the whole three weeks of my
stay, Christmas and New Year aside. (Of those festivals,
more below.) She wandered about the house in a random
manner, exclaiming, "Precious!" whenever she saw me;
she put into the refrigerator the bottle of whiskey which
she had taken from the breakfast room sideboard, and to
which she had been helping herself, and put the day's
delivery of milk in the sideboard; she ceremoniously hung
a kitchen cloth over the back of one of the armchairs in
the sitting room, like an antimacassar; eventually I found
that she had passed out completely on my bed. Roused
with difficulty from there, she prepared the evening meal
by placing a can of salmon and a can opener in the very
middle of the dining table and then disappeared for something like twelve hours. When she returned it was in a
head-hanging, penitential fury of polishing, cooking, mas-
saging, ironing, the lot.

Whereupon my father decided to give her a severe talk-
ing-to. "You were drunk again last night," he told her, one
eye cocked at her over a pointing finger. "I can't understand it. You're a respectable woman. You lack for nothing
in this house. I never raise my voice to you. All the neighbors know who you are, and tell me how lucky I am that I
have you to look after me. So why do you disgrace yourself like this, in front of me and everyone else?" And much
more in the same vein. To all this Betty listened with
downcast, inflamed, hung-over eyes and sullen, slumped
shoulders. At the moment she evidently deemed to be the
appropriate one for a change of tactic, she began to snivel.
Then to cry more loudly. My father, too, was overcome.
His eye moistened. Also, a certain misgiving that he
might be overdoing it, and that Betty would repay him
by some even more provocative piece of misbehavior in
the future, began to affect him. So he concluded with a
few ingratiating words of commendation. In the end, the
insincere protestation that she would never do it again
came from him, not from her. Then he told her to go.

Betty obeyed without protest. Some time later she and
Rebecca were to be heard in animated conversation in the

kitchen. Later still, when I go into the kitchen, I find three
solemn white children, whom I have never seen before,
seated around the table. They are all girls; they all have
straight, flaxen hair coming down to their shoulders, and
smooth, tanned complexions; the oldest of them is about
ten years old. Betty is feeding them biscuits of her own
manufacture. It turns out that they are the children of a
house farther up the block, and that they often come to
pass the time of day with her and to eat her biscuits. The
oldest of them is wearing a white T-shirt on which, with
a felt-tip pen, she has painstakingly inked in the names
of several pop groups, a message declaring to the world.
"I'm my momma's big problem," and the emblem of the
nuclear disarmament movement. When I ask her if she
knows what the emblem means, she answers without hesitation, her mouth full of crumbs, "Ban the bomb!" (Or, as
her South African vowels would have it, "Ben the bawm!")
However, my intrusion has unsettled them all, and a few
minutes later I see the girls trooping across the backyard,
on their way out. In the hands of each one is a further
supply of biscuits; on their lips sweet cries of farewell, as
if they are about to go on a long journey. "Good-bye
Betty! Good-bye!" For her part, Betty stands on the back
stoep, the very model, in her apron and cap, of the kindly,
much-loved servant, provider of sweetmeats and folk
wisdom, and calls out to them a heartfelt, "Good-bye, my
darlings!"

Needless to say, Betty and the slant-staring, insinuating
Rebecca had a number of other visitors during my stay;
every now and again there would be a sociable coming
and going of people of both sexes and all ages across the
yard. These visitors were of course all black. Only once
did Betty actually ask me to meet one of them. It was in
the evening; the man was waiting for me, deferentially
enough, in the backyard. Though a thin moon was up, and
the electric light on the back veranda had been switched
on, all I could see of him was that he was not young, that
he was about my height, that his clothing was shabby,
that his shoulders had an obliging tilt to them. His features
I could not make out at all. Betty introduced me to him,
and told me his name; then, while we were shaking hands,
she added proudly, so that I might understand just why

she had wanted me to meet her distinguished guest, "He's a sergeant in the Special Branch." "A sergeant in the Special Branch?" I repeated in astonishment, my hand still in his. "Yes sah," the man answered with a quasi-military jerk of the head and a flash of teeth and eyeball, to indicate that he was indeed a member of the much-feared, ubiquitous, political police, the shock troops (as it were) of the government's apartheid polices. "You're a friend of Betty's?" "Good friend, sah." "Oh." We stood there. As far as I was concerned I felt there to be no threat from him. No doubt he had reported my presence in the town to his superiors; but so what? It had been in the local paper, anyway. I had no political purposes in making this visit. We exchanged remarks about the hot weather and the prospects for rain. Then I went inside the house and rejoined my father, who was sitting beside the radio in the living room. Supposedly he was listening to the news on the BBC Overseas Service. A great susurration, with a whine along its edges, was coming from the machine; in the depths of all this a voice was muttering incomprehensibly.

The voice on his defective radio was as much of a visitor as my father received during my stay. Even as a younger man he had never had all that many friends in the town; now, those he had had were dead or had moved away. Only one friend from my schooldays came to see me; I had been away for far too long to expect anything else. So I passed the time by serving as an audience for my father's random monologues, or in reading, or in carrying on with some of the work I had brought with me. There was nothing I could do down at the business, which, though it still employed two whites and about a dozen blacks, had become a mere pretense, an expensive delusion which was somehow necessary to my father's notion of himself. Occasionally I took the car, which nobody else used, and went to the swimming bath, or simply drove it about, among the withered streets of the town, immersed in a dreamlike world of glaring sunlight and heavy shadow which represented myself to myself more deeply than anything I had seen or felt since; and from which, at the same time, I felt myself to be utterly sundered. The streets were so flat, and were bordered by such small trees, and

such low corrugated iron roofs and fences, that everything I saw, even the mine dumps, appeared to be at no
more than forehead-level—insignificant, tinny, drab,
squat. Yet above there rose the naked immensity of the
sky. Every day the sun revealed it anew; every night the
moon labored unsuccessfully to reach its summit.

Sometimes my father would talk until quite late at
night; it was often from about nine in the evening onwards, in the living room, next to his radio, that he was at
his most lively. On the walls were the pictures that had
always been there; on the bookshelves were the books they
had always carried; on the white, old-fashioned colonial-
style, pressed-steel ceiling was a pattern of Grecian
wreaths and ribboned torches that seemed to look at me,
rather than be looked at by me. Many of my father's stories
I had, inevitably, heard from him before; most of them
were about his childhood in Latvia, which he had left, on
his own, at the age of fifteen. Listening to him I found
myself wondering to what extent it was the sense I had
always had of his having come from another world, and of
his having had to fight his way through this one, that had
determined my own migration, once I had come of age.
All differences allowed for, in settling in England and
making my life there, and thus "returning" to Europe, had
I not been imitating him and competing with him—the
two activities which are contained in the very concept of
emulation?

One story he told me during that holiday, however,
was new to me. It concerned an uncle of his, a man
who lived in the same village in Latvia, and who had had
the reputation of being something of an intellectual in
that narrow society: a freethinker, a newspaper reader,
a man who owned secular books in Russian and German.
This uncle got married when my father was about ten
years old. The wedding had been a big affair by local
standards. When the ceremony was over, the newlyweds
drove off in a sleigh along the snow-covered main road
out of the village. In the general excitement of the
occasion, a crowd of boys, my father among them, ran
alongside the sleigh; then, eager as he was, at every age, to
stand out among his fellows, and presuming no doubt on

the relationship between himself and his uncle, my father
went further; he jumped on the back of the sleigh, intend-
ing to ride on it for a hundred yards or so while the others
ran alongside.

Almost eighty years later, sitting in one of the front
rooms of our iron-roofed house in Kimberley, with the
French windows open to the warm stillness and darkness
outside, while moths and other furry or long-legged in-
sects ticked against the electric light, I could picture the
scene, or try to: the snow of the roadway scarred by tracks,
the untouched whiteness beyond, the smell of the horses
and the noises they made, the cries of the children, the
provincial or plebeian mirth of the occasion. And my
father, a boy of ten (could I picture him?)—small for his
age, like any other ill-nourished urchin, in threadbare
coat and a cap perhaps too large for him, jumping on the
sleigh, which must have given only slightly under the
weight of this extra passenger. My father called his uncle
by name, and the uncle, the newlywed, who was in charge
of the sleigh and had his bride at his side, turned and saw
the passenger he had acquired. Without a word, without
hesitation, he lashed out with the whip in his hand and
caught my father with it across the neck and cheek.

At this point in his telling of the story, his voice thick-
ened and he found it difficult to carry on. There were tears
in his eyes. He drew his hand across his neck, under the
ear, and down the side of the cheek, to show me where the
whip had left its mark. In the shock and pain of the blow
he had fallen off the sleigh and sprawled full-length in the
road. The other children laughed. Eighty years later, at
the other end of the world, with his left hand to his cheek
and his right hand shaking yet inert, inert yet shaking,
he earnestly asked me, as if I could give an answer to his
questions, as if such questions could be answered anywhere, "What sort of a man would do such a thing to a
little boy? To his own brother's child? And even if I hadn't
been family, if I'd been a little peasant boy, how could he
bring himself to do it? On his wedding day, in front of his
wife?"

The uncle was long dead in his grave in Eastern Europe;
my father shuffled down the passage to his bed. Another
day of the holiday was over. A few more to go and it

would be Christmas. It was to fall on a Monday that year; the following day would be Boxing Day; the shops were to close at Saturday noon. I consulted with Betty well in advance about what we would need for the long weekend. Armed with the shopping list we had jointly drawn up, I went to town and did the shopping on the Friday afternoon. By Kimberley standards the shops were full, even frantic. I bought everything Betty had instructed me to get: the fish we would have ("boiled, with milk") one night; the roast we would have on Christmas Day; the noodles for the macaroni cheese she was planning for another meal; the soup meat, the extra bread and vegetables. The open market in the middle of town was aswarm with Afrikaner farmers and their wives and their pickup trucks, Indian hawkers, bargaining townsfolk, copper-skinned, tattered, emaciated beggars of quite unfathomable racial origin, black urchins who would carry your bags. On granite slabs next to the reach-me-down Corinthian pillars of the old Town Hall, watermelons and *sponspeks* were piled high in green and scaly-gold pyramids; there were chickens in crates, piles of squashes and pumpkins, plateaus of green and purple grapes, openwork bags of green peas and of carrots as red and angular and jostlingly protuberant as lobsters. How was it that I had passed through this scene innumerable times during my youth and seen in it only the small-town drabness and confusion from which it was imperative for me to escape; that I had never once realized the market to be . . . *picturesque?*

Laden with sufficient goods to be certain that the four of us would not go hungry, and much impressed with the thoroughness of Betty's planning for the occasion, I returned to the house to find my father in a state of alarm. Where had I been? The place was empty. He had been abandoned. How could we have left him alone for hours on end? Thus I discovered that Betty, the planner and home economist, had disappeared. So had Rebecca. Goodbye. They did not return until late afternoon on Boxing Day. Heaven knows where they had caroused the festival away; they never told me. During those days my father and I had got by chiefly on eggs and tinned food and bread. I would have done some cooking—I had nothing else to do—but I simply could not figure out how the various parts of the ancient electric cooker could be got to work, and I was unable to find the places where Betty secreted such elementary things as flour, oil, and cooking salt. The system she operated, if there was one, was beyond me. She returned without any display of contrition or of anxiety about how we had fared in her absence; since we had not witnessed what she had been up to, she evidently felt she had nothing to feel guilty about. But she did prepare a particularly elaborate meal for us on the night of her return, and put out the best linen and plates, which were to reappear only on the night of my departure. This by way of recompense, presumably.

That night I tried to phone London—whether to allay or to exacerbate my own sense of dislocation and futility in the midst of all this, I do not know. What I do know was that the family in London for which I was directly responsible had by then become hardly more real to me than the vestiges of the family for which my father had been responsible and to which I had once belonged. In order to make my call, I had first to get through to the international operator in Cape Town. (This was before the days of international dialed calls.) The operator told me that he would call me back in due course; there was bound to be a delay at that time of year; he had five calls to England from Kimberley alone ahead of me in the queue. Five calls! I could hardly believe it. At that hour of the night? From a dusty nowhere of a place on the edge of the desert, like Kimberley? And there I had been, flattering myself with the thought that my life, my circumstances, my preoccupations, my dislocations, were something special, or improbable, or singular! In fact I was just another statistic.

A few more days went by and another holiday approached: New Year's Day. Again it fell on a long weekend. This time I was not to be fooled by Betty's elaborate preparations, or pretense at preparations. I did the shopping strictly with my own convenience in mind, on the assumption that she and her friend would disappear. But she fooled me once again. On the day before the holiday, Betty cooked and served a midday meal in the normal fashion. In the afternoon she and Rebecca entertained some of their friends in their rooms, in a quiet, conversational manner. The evening meal went off without incident, apart from some birdlike whooping from the backyard. The sound was loud enough to penetrate even my father's thick hearing. He looked up from his plate with a look that was simultaneously wary, tense, and drooping. It was as if his neck could not sustain what his eyes and face wanted to do. "What's going on out there?" he asked. I told him there was nothing to worry about. Betty washed up and went outside. My father and I spent the first part of the evening like all the others, in the sitting room. It was as hot an evening as every other; and, in our suburban street, as quiet. The sodium lamps outside had only themselves for company. The white-painted, wooden front gate at the end of the garden path hung slightly askew, as it always had. Then we went to bed, quite early.

My room was the one I had slept in as a child. I could hear furtive comings and goings taking place in the backyard, just a few yards away from my wide-open sash window, in its dilapidated wooden frame. For a long time I resisted the temptation to look out. Then there were sounds of grapplings, slaps, the back gate slamming. Loud laughter. Song. Exchanges in Xhosa or Sesuto, of which I could not understand a word. More bird cries and arguments. When I finally looked out, I heard suddenly, from every quarter of the moonlit, lamplit horizon, darkened only by the shapes of trees and houses, the hooting of car horns and distant voices. It was midnight. The New Year had begun. I went back to bed. Rebecca thrust her head through my window. The air was filled instantly with the smell of Cape sherry. She was wearing not much clothing; no more than a petticoat, as far as I could make out. "Heppy-heppy, Master!" she cried. "It's Heppy New Year!" Out of the darkness, prone on my bed, I solemnly wished her a happy New Year. Then I told her to make less noise. Her head withdrew. The smell of sherry lingered. Minutes later she was sitting directly under my window, on the veranda, sobbing industriously and resisting the drunken attempts of Betty and friends to move her away. She was crying, it seemed, because I had been "too cross" with her.

At that point I really did become cross. By about two in

the morning all was silent. Betty was back in her room.
The guests had departed. Rebecca, still wearing only her
petticoat, had wandered out of the back gate, headed in
no particular direction or towards no particular destination. I did not care. She returned some time during the
next afternoon. Betty was too hung over to do any work.
The cooking was in my hands once again. My father had
heard nothing of it all. He did not even know it was New
Year's Day, and complained bitterly because the daily
newspaper did not arrive as usual.

For my farewell dinner a week later Betty made a big
effort. My train to Johannesburg, from where I would
take the plane to London, was due at ten in the evening,
and a taxi had been ordered to come and pick me up well
in advance. For the first time during my stay, my father
and I ate not in the breakfast room at the back of the
house, but in state, so to speak, in the dining room, surrounded by the heavy mahogany furniture of late-Victor-
ian vintage which had been in the house when my parents
had purchased it forty years before. The table, the chairs,
the sideboards (one of them equipped with a mirror six
or eight feet wide) abounded in fluted legs and befoliated
capitals; they broke out in roses on every possible surface;
the wood was as gleaming and ruddy as something seen
by the light of a coal fire. Betty wore her smartest white
uniform, with a white cap on her head. Rebecca too had
dolled herself up for the occasion. Once again the best
napery, cutlery, and china had been put out. Four courses
came and went. The effect was overpoweringly funereal.

Yet the most emphatic and unexpected indication of
the specialness of the evening was still to come. Once we
had finished eating, Betty disappeared. Rebecca was left
to do the clearing and washing up. My father and I went
to the sitting room. About ten minutes later Betty reappeared. She had divested herself of her best garb as a
servant and had put on her best dress as a woman. It was a
floral print, rather gauzy in effect, with an elaborate,
frilled neck. She had also changed her cap. Now that she
was arrayed like a guest, she treated herself as one. She sat
in the room with us, which she had not done at any time
during my stay, and joined in our talk. Most of it was
about absent members of the family. Betty herself was

childless and—though she had had many male friends, some of whom had kept her company for years at a stretch —husbandless. Thus she had no family other than the one for which she had worked for the previous two decades and more. She knew everything about us and our children —birthdays, examination results, jobs, tastes in food. She spoke of all of us generously and affectionately; it would have been inconceivable for her to do otherwise on this occasion. My father listened, commented, got muddled up among his grandchildren, got bored, started fiddling with his radio and succeeded in producing sufficient noise from it to prevent the conversation continuing. So Betty and I sat together without exchanging any further reminiscences or speculations about the future.

The noise from the radio was not loud enough to prevent us hearing the sound of a car door slamming in the street outside, and footsteps coming up the garden path. It was time to go. The desolation of departure seemed to be limitless in scope and yet confined to a single, crowded, overtaxed place in my breast. There was also, as there so often is, a certain sense of relief to it. The thing had to be done. Then let it be done. Rebecca, as insouciant as a cat, and as curious, had come from the back of the house to lend a hand with the suitcases and to join in the leave-taking. Betty was in tears; my father almost so. He insisted on accompanying me to the gate. We exchanged only a few words. Once I and my bags had been installed in the taxi, I saw that he and Betty had already turned in the shadow and light of the path and were making their way back along it, towards the steps that led to the veranda and so to the open door of the house. He was leaning heavily on her arm; their progress could hardly have been slower. Then the car started. Every house we passed, at first, was as familiar to me as the camber of the road itself.

Strangely enough, it was not my father but Betty whom I was never to see again. She did indeed stay with him "to the end" as she had promised me she would: to her end. Nothing had been further from our thoughts, when she had used that phrase in conversation with me, than that things would turn out that way. Within about twelve months of my visit she died of a heart attack. At that point my father, finally, succumbed to the urgings of my oldest brother, and went to live in his house in Johannesburg. He survived Betty for little more than three years. Throughout that time, first month by month, then week by week, then day by day, he became more and more frail physically, and more and more clouded and distracted in mind.

KWI-KWI, KWA-KWA

A COUNTRY JOURNAL

Michael Train

He is sitting at the dining room table in his pyjamas. He's been there all morning having his breakfast and reading the newspaper which is right side up for once. He spills the porridge down the front of his pyjama top onto his lap. The rest goes onto the carpet. He doesn't smell very good. Every few minutes he asks, "What time is it?" He has been doing that for two years now. Whenever my mother goes by his chair he says, "I love you, dear." She goes by many times a day muttering to herself or exhorting the cats. The number of cats seems to grow every day. There are four or five indoor cats and at least twelve hanging around outside the kitchen door waiting to be fed.

He has been sitting in silence for the longest time. Suddenly he asks, "What's the baby's name?"

It is a dark day. Raining. My mother's mood is also dark. She is withdrawn and laughs mysteriously. I have to do Andrew's levée all by myself. I get him up from his hospital bed and change his pyjamas which are soaked with urine. I sponge him down, put him into his rubber underpants and lead him to the breakfast table. I am putting his wet sheets into the washing machine when the phone rings. My mother gets there first which is why I rarely get phone calls out here. "Michael has just been taken to the hospital," I hear her say.

Andrew's sister has come for a visit for the first time in more than a year. She is more haggard and etiolated than ever. With her fine pointed nose and chin she reminds me of the bust of Dante. The grey page-boy haircut (circa 1929) completes the effect. Andrew not only recognizes his sister but sheds a tear. Brother and sister sit together holding hands. I hope she doesn't mind his sticky fingers. Suddenly there is a loud fart.

"It's only a noise," I say reassuringly. By now I'm an expert of course.

"Oh good," she says but leaves soon after lunch.

In the afternoons the old folks repair to their beds. I busy myself in my study and make them tea at four o'clock when they wake up. I clear the tea things and wait for the evening news. After an early supper they retire again.

I walk past Andrew's armchair and hear him say, "I think . . . they're rather . . . secretive." He is looking closely at some turquoise beads which are on the side table next to him. He is looking at them at eye level the way a child would. I bend down and see them as he does, as tiny culverts—secretive and minatory.

Most of the time he enjoys tearing the subscription blanks from magazines.

I can already see that this journal is not going to be like the one I kept when I was sixteen. Then I ignored daily events and tried to impress myself by writing about the books I was reading and my "ideas." Reading the diary later, I was annoyed by the lack of detail. I never thought to note down who came to dinner, what was eaten and who said what.

With Andrew one is continually watching for signs of the increasing decrepitude that brings him nearer to death. The tension, the suspense is always there—anticipating the moment when he keels over and dies.

The other day I came back from the city and the first things I saw upon entering the house were his feet sticking out the bedroom door. I knew he was not dead. He had fallen and my mother couldn't lift him. He seemed comfortable on the floor wrapped in blankets, his head on a pillow.

"Would you like some lunch?" I said.

"Damn right I would," he said.

I found a human turd on the living room floor. It was as hard as a stone. Must have hurt the poor old man's insides.

If there is anything that makes my mother furious, it is having one of her delusions proved wrong. Her favorite one is that the furnace doesn't work. Today is a warm day and of course the furnace won't go on unless you turn the thermostat to nearly 90°. "It doesn't work," she insists. I turn the thermostat all the way up and, sure enough, the furnace starts up.
"What did you do to it?" she asks furiously.
"Nothing," I reply.
She is the picture of rage. "I suppose the next time the heat doesn't work I'll have to call you so that you can do nothing."

Several times I have arrived from the city to find that she has turned off the heat and the old things are shivering in a cold house. Sometimes she does this because she is convinced that the house will blow up. The last time she did that she bundled Andrew out to the garden (for some reason I was considered immune to explosions and I continued to sit and read in the living room). Occasionally I would look out and see them, a pair of crazed old white-haired things, he sitting bewildered in a garden chair, she sitting on the grass blinking and smoking.

On Christmas Eve I decided to make them a treat—a true *paella a la Valenciana* made with real *chorizo* and rice from Spain. It was tasty but soggy. I had trouble keeping my attention on the cooking because my mother turned off the main switch for the furnace as fast as I could turn it on again. Finally, I barred the way and she called me a "disobedient crap" and began to pummel me very hard. More unpleasant than that, she pulled my nose violently and tried to shove me down the cellar stairs.
Luckily there is a sort of wrestling mat at the foot of the stairs to prevent fatalities.

She went to the hairdresser and I had the rare experience of being in the house alone with the crumbling Andrew. Then I saw how hard these last years have been for her. If I were alone here, would I change his stinking rubber pants?

The peaceful life in the country. The pretty wood and the pretty river. Every view is a blessing. But I have no peace of mind. All this dying and nuttiness is bad for the nerves. I keep wondering what horror is next and I keep saying to myself that everything is all right.

Andrew's dull old eyes light up with joy when he sees me. I'm his friend. His only friend. All traces of the ornate gas-bag he once was have vanished. How could such a strong personality be effaced? How could such a dim infant be wearing his body? He has a certain sweetness now which he did not have before. And he rarely complains.

I passed his bedroom and I heard a tired old voice say, "This is no life."

I guess that a sure sign of growing older is that one can no longer sustain myths about oneself—as the great artist, as lover (despite all contrary evidence), as intellectual (despite a reluctance to read anything difficult) and so on. One sees oneself as a worm but a nice one. At this point one begins to like oneself, whereas before one despised oneself for failing to reach the unattainable.

Now, that's what a journal is *supposed* to sound like!

Andrew's way of letting off steam after a day's work was to call the President a chump, a fourflusher, a hallroom boy or a horse's ass. Franklin Delano Roosevelt was the crookedest man who ever held public office, a damn liar, a prize son-of-a-bitch, and so was Lyndon Johnson. In his late baroque period, Andrew terrorized the members of his club, The Brook, by calling Richard Nixon a motherfucker. Delighted by his own daring, he used to beam wickedly at his audience and say, "Now we're really cooking on gas!"

At that time the Brook club did not have Jewish members. I doubt it has any now. An elderly gentleman once told me, with the horror still fresh, that he was at the club one evening "when who should come up the stairs but Léon Blum. There was no one to greet him so *I had to*— Léon Blum!" Not only Jewish but a socialist!

At the Brook everyone dines at one long table and it is the custom for a senior member to preside. One evening I was Andrew's guest. The only other person present was a tall man with a guardsman's mustache who introduced himself as Jacob Rosenbaum, "an out-of-town member from the Pennsylvania Dutch country." We fell into an agreeable discussion of animal husbandry. After a while, a portly young man with thinning blond hair and discreetly glittering cufflinks came into the dining room and sat down beside Andrew, who introduced Jacob Rosenbaum. The young man listened to the cattle-talk politely and then broke in with the news that he had just come back from Paris.

"You'll never believe it, Andy," he said, "Paris is absolutely full up. You couldn't even get a room if your name was Jacob Rosenbaum." A silence ensued which Andrew broke by pointing to his right and saying, "Bobby, this *is* Jacob Rosenbaum." Bobby blinked and cried, "Why Andy, you old son-of-a-gun, you always were a kidder! Jacob Rosenbaum! Haw! haw! haw!" Another silence and Andrew leaned over and said gently, "I'm not pulling your leg, my dear sir, I distinctly remember having introduced you to our out-of-town member from the Pennsylvania Dutch country, Mr. Jacob Rosenbaum." Bobby stared fixedly across the room for a while, ate quickly, excused himself and left.

My mother, a naturalized citizen, asked Andrew to take down the dartboard portrait of Lyndon Johnson which he had hung in the cellar. She was made uneasy by these orgies of hate against the chief of state. And I was often mortified, when I brought friends home, to see the look of horrified glee on their faces as they discovered the variety of Andrew's prejudices. Attacking the President was good fun but when he went on to *sheenies, jewboys, kikes* and (his own invention) *kike-esses,* I began to squirm. He seemed to find the expression *baptized with a jackknife* extremely funny as he did *jig-a-boos, nigs, coons,* and *buck niggers.* He would tell you with a smirk that colored people possessed an unpleasant body odor which he had named *bouquet d'Afrique.* He also seemed to believe in the existence of "congenital homosexuals" (*pansies, fairies, flits*). These were identifiable (by whom? I always wondered) because their pubic hair grew in a straight line across the lower belly. In deference to my mother, Spaniards, Frenchmen and Mexicans were usually spared; but all upper-class Englishmen were stuffed shirts, Germans were blockheads who didn't know how to dress and Italians consumed unspeakable food (after years of marriage to my mother, Andrew still refused to eat salad or any green vegetable but spinach).

He was full of scorn for "the art world" and those he described as "artistical." Of the American painters of his generation only Hopper had his respect. The Modernists were incompetent—Cézanne didn't know how to draw; abstraction was a pretentious trick forced on the public by Jewish art snobs. And as for the musicians of the day: everyone knew that Leopold Stokowski was nothing but a vainglorious Cockney named Leo Stokes; Toscanini and Horowitz were always referred to as "the ninny and his son-in-law." No music worth listening to had been composed by anyone other than Beethoven and Brahms. Andrew loved to quote a lecture given by his old art teacher Joseph Pennell, the printmaker, consisting entirely of the following: "There was very little German art before Dürer and there has been none since."

Of course most of this was meant to be provocative, but I think he really believed it all. He was furious when one of my friends innocently asked him what a "sheeny" was. He refused to believe that she didn't know.

In his old age he told me that the love of his life was a Jewess who would not leave her husband. I wonder why I was so surprised. Should it have been my mother?

As she would say, "What do you know—co-co?"

I woke up this morning knowing by the sounds of the house that the cloud had lifted and that my mother would be something like her old self. She was at her place at the table having breakfast. She gave me a brisk and affectionate hello. "I've got to talk to you," she said. "I've been thinking. We can't go on like this. It's too hard on you. You shouldn't be tied down."

"You can't take care of Andrew all by yourself," I replied. "What's the alternative?"

The alternative is a nursing home. Something she will consider in theory but only in theory.

She hasn't gone out the door in weeks, but today she wants to go shopping. She gets down her favorite cookbooks and starts to plan a meal. "We must have people in for drinks," she says and I groan inside; I don't know how long her good mood will last. And there is always Andrew. An elderly couple came to call last week and Andrew got up, hobbled to the edge of the porch, pulled out his old dingdong and pissed out over the lawn. I don't think they will be back.

The people of the neighborhood are fond of her (and wary) not just out of loyalty to what she once was: on her good days she's feisty and funny. She makes them laugh.

Andrew's face has kept all its nobility, and his diction, when he's not garbling everything, is still superb. He often prefaces his remarks to me with a "Sir" in the manner of Samuel Johnson. The style remains after the content departs. The other day he said to me gravely and slowly: "You know, we've been saying several things ourselves and if you don't mind my saying so, we've forgotten the tune."

This morning, Andrew standing naked in the bathroom with his shrunken, sagging old body being worked over like a car in a minute car wash. My mother and I were washing him and dressing him and discussing him in the third person: "Turn him this way!" "He's not dry," and so on. The old boy flailed his skinny arms in the air and said in a loud indignant whisper, "I'm not dead yet!"

He feels the indignity keenly even though he doesn't say much about it. There is a popular idea that the senile don't react to things anymore, that they don't have feelings and emotions.

Several times I've heard people say, "I hope I don't get senile but if I do I won't know it, will I?"

He does.

I was scraping the shit off his skinny old leg and my mother was doing the other.

"God will reward you for this," she said.

"Like hell he will," I said.

This morning Andrew sat at the breakfast table eating a cake of soap. I rushed to take it away from him. His lips had swollen up enormously and looked like a vagina in a state of excitation. Little bubbles came out of his mouth. After some rinsing the swelling subsided and the alert was over. Last week he ate six bananas at a sitting.

I met a woman at a cocktail party in the East Sixties who said to me, "I used to know Andy when he was a young man. He was the most boring person I ever met." She'd had a few stiff drinks and was inclined to speak her mind. She came back several times to apologize in spite of my assuring her that I was not offended. I told her that to the contrary what she had told me was actually a sort of revelation. I had always attributed Andrew's repetitions to age—assuming as the young will (this was some years ago) that this is the fate in store for all who survive fifty.

As I look back I am astonished at how those of us who lived with him were able to bear the relentless tedium of his company. He could tell the same anecdote word for word, five times a day, every day of the week for years and years. I once knew them by heart and now find that I have carefully erased most of them from my memory. This is surely a pity for many of his stories achieved a great perfection of form after having been polished for so many seasons.

I always assumed that he was unaware of the paralyzing effect of his performances until one evening when he turned to me as we were going in to dinner at a friend's house and said with horrible relish, "Well, here goes— bore or be bored!"

There was no interrupting him: he would shout you down. And there was something relentless too about the grinding sound of his voice, and the dramatic pauses where you were supposed to ooh and aah until he slammed you with the punchline—invariably something crushingly witty which he had said to a prominent person. I not only learned to tune out but mastered the trick of tuning back in just in time to produce a laugh.

At his best he was a satirist with a true eye for significant detail. He had a marvelous set piece which consisted of a detailed description of the carriages lined up at the Yonkers railroad station waiting for the morning train down to Wall Street (circa 1910)—each equipage reflecting perfectly the standing of its owner.

His masterpiece was an account of his beginnings as an art student. His father had taken him out of boarding school to study painting at the National Academy of Design—a strange thing for a conventional man of business of that day to do. Seymour Harris, a Frenchified academician from Texas, had convinced him that Andrew's sketches revealed a potential talent comparable to that of the great Velásquez (at this point Andrew would screw up his lips in exaggerated fashion to pronounce the name to rhyme with Asquith). Harris, who wore a goatee and beret, did a portrait of Andrew's father which showed him to be a typical turn-of-the-century world-beater, a lean and sharklike Teddy Roosevelt. He was of a type caught by Clarence Day in *Life With Father*— totally self-assured, high-minded and determined. He knew what was good for everyone, especially his sons. He decreed that his eldest would go into the army, the next would join the family's Wall Street firm, the third would be an architect, and Andrew, he announced, would be a fashionable portrait painter. This hit the boy as a kind of doom for he was just getting used to the Hill School—the sort of school, he pointed out later, where the entire student body prayed to Almighty God for victory on the football field and where the headmaster gave mystifying lectures on the sinister effects of self-abuse.

And so Andrew found himself at the age of fifteen drawing from the antique at the Academy. Making charcoal drawings of plaster statuary is not a lot of fun (I know because I did it myself) and he looked forward to drawing directly from nature. But unknown to him, Andrew's schedule had been carefully arranged by his father so that he would never come face to face with the "undraped female." Inevitably, one afternoon he followed the other students into a studio where a model was posing, and when he got back to Yonkers that evening and displayed his day's work, there was a terrible commotion. Dr. Getty, the family GP, was summoned to examine the unhappy boy for possible permanent effects to his delicate sensibility.

At this point Andrew would pause. Becoming grave, he would say: "That summer, in August of 1911, my father dropped dead just as he was approaching the desk at Claridge's in London. He was fifty years old." Just how this connected with what had gone before, I was never quite sure, but it worked as drama.

Andrew's stories were *in toto* a true autobiography, and I became as familiar with the various chapters of his life as I was with my own (or so it seemed). I knew the names of his most distant cousins, of people he had met in Fairfax County, Virginia, in 1922, of some of the villagers of Walpole, New Hampshire, where he had lived for a while.

This knowledge more than made up for my own father's refusal to remember anything at all, but it was a cuckoo kind of knowledge—a borrowed attic in place of my own.

As Andrew's mind began to run down, the stories disappeared one by one. I now miss them and I try to bring them back to life. By and large, I can't. The winter be-

fore last I was there when he told his last story. It was
one I had never heard before.

"I was on a sketching trip down South," he said, "and
I went into a bar in Natchez where I met a damn good-
looking girl. The Chicago Symphony was coming to town
so I invited her to go with me. But the day of the concert,
my car broke down. We had to go in evening clothes on
the streetcar." He chuckled at that and went on. "Well, I
got the car fixed, and a few days later I remember she
was sitting in the back and she said, 'Come on and close
the door, honey, otherwise the rats will jump in.'"

Feeding cats has become my mother's principal occupation. She makes a vat of porridge which she enriches
with chopped meat and she doles it out to her petitioners
who are assembled outside the kitchen door. If they try
her patience she gives them a soft kick in the stomach.
She knows them all and if one is missing she asks about
him for a long time before he goes out of her memory.
So it was with La Tache, a fat spotted cat with a smudge
under his nose. (He was not named after the famous
vineyard in Burgundy.)

Not all the cats have names, but here is a list of those
who do:

The Monster

Varaná

Afghan

Chouchette

Mouchette

Nounette

B.D. Eyes

Mo

Fluffy San

New Jersey

"*New Jersey?* Why New Jersey?"

"Because he is a New Jersey cat," she says.

Having someone so old and fragile around creates a relentless suspense. Every day brings the same questions:

When is he going to die? Today?

Will he fall and break a hip?

[*311*]

Will he recognize me?
and then I ask myself:
Have I retired?
Will I ever do anything or go anywhere again?
What kind of life do I *want* to lead?
What can I do?

You can't get away from nature in the country. That's all you see out the windows. In spite of the row of field guides on my shelf, I still don't know birds or anything about wild grasses and the mysterious ecology of the undergrowth. When I walk in the woods I might as well be on Eighth Avenue. Eighth Avenue?—now that's *really* interesting.

Who would have guessed that Andy and my sprightly, vivacious, humorous mother would end up suffering so much? Who would recognize them in the pitiful creatures they are now?

My brother wept at the sight of them when he came up from Mexico City, where he lives with his family. The house was dirty and Andrew sat on the porch in filthy clothes. He was covered with flies. My brother sat next to him, but when he discovered that Andrew couldn't really talk, he never spoke to him again. All he did was drink Scotch all day long and say, "It smells like pig shit around here, pig shit!"
Afterwards he told me, "I looked into Andrew's eyes and I saw nothing, absolutely nothing."

When she comes to, she never stops talking. And like most old people, she is lost in remembrance. Paris before the Germans came. We always have the same conversation: the streets of the *quartier* have only to be named to invoke the past—rue Madame, rue Stanislas, rue Delambre, the vegetable market on the boulevard Raspail, the *baguettes* that our beloved Reine bought for us after school. My mother's memory of Paris before 1939 is intact. Mine is not. I know the cleaned up Paris of the

sixties and the vandalism of the seventies. I tell her of
the destruction of Les Halles. I tell her of the Tour Mont-
parnasse, which has sunk our *quartier* into the shadows.
None of this gets through until I tell her that they have
cut down the great chestnut trees in the place St. Sulpice.

"Why did they do that?" she asks.

"To build an underground parking garage."

Her eyes fill with tears.

I couldn't bear much of this if I didn't go into the city
frequently to see my friends. However, that doesn't always help.

One of my childhood friends has reappeared. He is a
wanderer, restlessly moving from Paris to San Francisco,
to Venice and New York and back again. Now he claims
to be on his way to Australia to settle down at last—but
he seems reluctant to move on. I visit him on the Upper
West Side where he is parking in the vacant apartment of
a friend. I usually find him brewing bitter herbal tea and
eating raw oriental vegetables. He is a millenarian socialist. With a worried frown he asks me if I think that
the Chinese, being a rational people, have switched to
brown rice. He seems genuinely saddened when I tell
him I am sure they have not. He worries about the way
I lead my life. He knew my mother in the old days and
was fond of her, but now (hearing my tales of turds and
madness) he exhorts me to leave, to let them rot so that I
can go off and lead my own life. At least, he says, I should
have them committed to an institution. It is no good to
tell him this would be contrary to my nature. He believes
that one's nature can and should be changed. I plead that
they are still human, that my mother passes whole weeks
when she is much as she once was, that to send them to a
psychiatric home for the aged would be like sending
them to a concentration camp. He is unmoved. My first
duty is to myself. I try to suggest that by caring for
them I am doing something for myself and that if to be
free means to be restless and depressed and lonely as he
is, I prefer my martyrdom (if that's what it is).

Afterwards, driving back to the country, I rehearse
all sorts of arguments that I can never get across because

he is such a relentless exhorter. It is also hard to explain why caring for them has stilled some terrible unrest deep inside me. Having always been emotionally dependent on them I don't mind having the roles reversed. It is I who sit at the head of the table now. The decline of Andrew has put down my rage. I have grown up a bit and I am not lonely.

I have discovered that one can buy *croissants* in New York that are just as good as the ones we used to have in Paris. They even make *petits pains au chocolat,* my favorite after school treat. I bring some back to my mother who takes one bite. "The chocolate is just as bad as it ever was," she says. She hasn't had one in forty years.

The word that recurs most often in my mother's conversation is "crap." When I displease her I am a crap, when a female displeases her she is a "crapesse." It is not an inappropriate word, since crap is what we have a lot of around here. Yesterday I came into the living room and declared that a cat had made caca in my bathtub.

My mother was furious. She said "How dare you use such a word in my presence?"

How I wish that they would die.

My mother reads popular fiction. She spent a lot of time on *Shōgun* and was pleased to find that her opinion of the Japanese was confirmed: "The Japanese are beasts!" For a while the cats were renamed Chouchette-San, Nounette-San, Monster-San, and so on (now only Fluffy-San retains his title). I don't know how seriously she takes *le péril jaune,* as she calls it, but I know her feelings against blacks go back a long way. When a black face appears on the TV screen she cries, "Shoot 'em!" Muhammad Ali and a reporter named Vic Miles are exempted. Muhammad Ali can do no wrong. When he appears she claps her hands in joy and says, "Isn't he beautiful!"

Not long ago she told me that the first time she had

ever seen a black person close-up was when we first
came to the U.S. for a visit in the thirties. We stayed at
the Croydon Hotel on Madison Avenue and 86th Street.
The buzzer sounded and when she saw the black maid
at the door, she was so frightened that she hid my
brother and me in a closet.

In 1940 we lived in an old-fashioned, rambling frame
house in Roslyn. I went to public school. With my Anglo-
French accent and my continental manners, I was an outsider. The other outsider of the class was a black boy
named Ernest and we became friends. Ernest and I
would dawdle together on the way home from school,
kicking, scuffing and doing whatever else schoolboys did
in that era. He was my first American friend.

One afternoon when I came home from school there
was a great to-do. It seemed that Ernest's parents, encouraged by our friendship, had paid a call on my parents. This was a catastrophe. For not only were they
black, they were domestic servants. My father described
himself as a liberal but in those days, it seems that that
didn't include hobnobbing with darkies let alone with
chauffeurs and cooks. I was made to feel that something
terrible had happened. I had to end my friendship with
Ernest at once. They could not make it clear to me *why*
it was so terrible; I just had to accept it.

The next scene haunted me all my life: After school
ended the next day I ran home to avoid Ernest, but I
paused at the top of a hill and looked back. He was waving and calling my name.

The next year we moved into the city. My brother and
I both fell in love with the maid who lived in the tiny
room behind the kitchen of our dark apartment on the
Upper East Side. Her name was Estie. She was nineteen
and black, the prettiest girl we had ever seen. To top it
all off she claimed to be the girlfriend of one of the Ink
Spots, the wonderful quartet who had a song on the Hit
Parade: "If I Didn't Care."

The other night I drank too much red wine and I got
weepy. I remembered the scene with Ernest and it
seemed to give me almost as much pain as it had then.

And I thought of Estie. I was foolish enough to tell all this to my mother.

"Estie was Ernest's sister," she told me, and seeing the shocked look on my face (why hadn't anyone ever told me?) she added bitterly, "You're just like your brother. You only like niggers."

When my mother is lost in her interior world there is no conversation at the dinner table. She blinks repeatedly and seems to be asleep while eating. Meanwhile old Andrew is daubing himself with food. Repeatedly he asks what time it is and doesn't listen to the reply. To amuse myself I play waiter. Andrew and my mother used to be the number one customers at the Brussels restaurant for years. Marcel was their waiter and Victor, the kindly dean of New York *sommeliers*, was a friend.

"*Bon soir Monsieur et Madame,*" I say, imitating Marcel at his most unctuous, "*Çe soir nous avons le Turbot, Le Carré d'agneau, Noisette de. . . .*"

"Oh, shut up!" says Andrew, but his dull old eyes light up when I whisk around and pour white wine into his glass. My mother is beginning to snore and teeters on the edge of her chair.

"Who wants ice cream?" I ask.

No reply from my mother, but Andrew cries happily, "I do!"

When she returns to earth for a few days she is full of talk, but since no one ever comes here there is nothing new to talk about. She is preoccupied with the subject of food. And her favorite speculation is about the origin of the potato. "What did people eat in Europe before the potato?" she never fails to ask. This leads to the Marco Polo question. Did he or did he not bring back macaroni from China? And of course it must have taken him a lifetime to come back from China. I suggest that it took him less than a year, but what I say makes little impression. "You think you know everything," she says witheringly, "but you know NOTHING." I once tried to point out that cats like to go out at night (she insisted on keeping them in) because they are nocturnal animals. She was full of scorn: "Where did you read that? In the encyclopedia?"

But as always, we go back to France "before the war." Not to Paris this time but to the other "farm," a country place not far from Fontainebleau. My father and mother had fixed up a peasant house and farmyard on the edge of a village named Le Fleuret. There she seems to have spent her happiest hours gardening with Ivan, our dear Russian caretaker, and learning how to cook.

"We grew our own vegetables," she says. "We had our own peaches, our own pears. American fruit has no taste. Once a week a truck came by with meat and fish but there never was any good meat around there, just tough old cows that the peasants had slaughtered. So we raised our own chickens and rabbits. We ate well at the farm."

Le Fleuret is a magic name which still stirs my sleeping memory. I remember the day we left it. I was eight and the Germans had crossed the Belgian border into France. We were in the car, my father and mother, my brother and I, all packed up and ready to go south to Bordeaux to catch the S.S. *Roosevelt* to America. I took a last look at the window of the *petit salon* where I sometimes sat on rainy days pressing my nose against the pane and watching the villagers trudging down the road behind their cows. "This is an important moment which I must not forget," I said to myself. I was right, for it marked the end of my early childhood. "I'll never see the farm again," I said to myself. I was wrong because ten years later, after the war, I came back for a visit on my summer vacation. I came back an American, a very young man on a motorscooter, wearing a leather jacket and a crash helmet. I arrived at the iron gates of the farmyard, led there unerringly by unconscious memory. I banged on the gates and a face appeared, the same face (though thinner and grayer) which had lived in my mind throughout the war years. I said who I was and took off my helmet.

"*Ce n'est pas possible*," said Ivan Nazaroff in his quiet Russian voice and then he swung back the gates—into sacred ground.

When Andrew and my mother started to spend most of the year in New Jersey, she revived her French country ways: rabbits appeared in hutches, she grew asparagus and raspberries, there were even pigs—to Andrew's disgust. The rabbits were made into plain *pâté de campagne,* the vegetables were preserved for winter and the pigs eventually disappeared to be replaced by sheep and finally by Andrew's pride, the herd of Charolais. The two of them set a good table. The house was a simple country frame house and the barn was full of hay. Simplicity was the way of the household, to the surprise of those who expected servants and a tennis court. The style was admired by many, particularly by some of my friends who thought that my mother "knew how to live."

Eric and Madeline had just married and were eager to find a style of their own. She had plenty of money and he knew what was good. Eric was a painter; he admired the width of the pinstripes on Andrew's Savile Row suit and he respected Andrew's achievement as an artist. But in the end it was my mother's laughing good sense that captivated them both and they were forever asking me what my mother would think. "What would she do in our place?"

Eventually they went to London for graduate study in style. They rented a "bijou" townhouse in Chelsea. Eric had his suits made by Hawes & Curtis (By Appointment to the Duke of Edinburgh) and Madeline waited for the electric van from Harrod's to bring strawberries and fresh cream. They were a handsome couple but they knew no one in London except a few threadbare artists in Charlotte Street.

That year my mother stepped off the edge. One summer afternoon she took Andrew by the hand and led him into the woods to see my brother's grave. Bewildered, he tried to tell her that my brother was very much alive, but she did not hear him. She only heard voices that told her that everyone on earth was starving, that everyone would die. She retired to her place on the living room couch, forgot the garden, the kitchen, the world.

These things happened almost twenty years ago.

And as for Eric and Madeline—they divorced. She went her way to Park Avenue and he went his to the Bowery, where he lived meagerly and made hard little pictures in the constructivist manner.

"Zum zum," says my mother. She starts sentences this way, as others do by saying "well" or "um." "Zum zum, do you think the Peruvians ate nothing but potatoes?" I have no opinion on this subject but brace myself for the introduction of macaroni into Italy.

Instead she says, "Of course Parmentier is responsible for introducing the French to the potato-ato."

I have nothing to add to that either.

"What did they eat in Europe before the potato-ato?"

"And the tomato-ato?" I reply, and curse myself for having said it. This business of repeating the last syllable of words is catching-atching.

She says nothing for quite a while and then breaks into her current refrain:

> Kwi-kwi
> Kwa-kwa
> *Voyez-vous ça!*

That's quite catching too and I find myself repeating it at odd times:

> Kwi-kwi
> Kwa-kwa
> *Voyez-vous ça!*

"But I thought you liked fish," I say to her. She looks at the grilled flounder on her plate as though I had served her a cow pie. "Do you mean to tell me that for all those years at the Brussels with Andrew you really didn't like the turbot or the shad roe or. . . ."

"Andrew liked it," she says. I now find out that the list of things that Andrew liked and she didn't grows all the time: fish, red meat, long railway journeys, cattle ranches, restaurants with elaborate service. . . . She never let on. She didn't like his etchings either.

When Ivan Nazaroff opened the gates I stepped in and looked at the cobbled yard, the ivy-covered farmhouse. Nothing had changed since we left. I looked up into the windows of the bedroom where my brother and I, maddened by forced naps, used to tear the wallpaper from the walls; I saw my father's study where he taught himself braille, having convinced himself that he was losing his sight. I heard the kitchen clock and fancied I could also hear the barking and chattering of the many animals we kept in those days—Firmain, the pet wild boar who grew to enormous size, the marmosets and the capuchin monkeys, the long silky-haired mindless Borzois; I heard the crowing cocks and groaning pigs; and floating above it all, the musical magical sound of the Russian tongue. It was my mother, of course, who rescued both wounded animals and down-and-out Russian nobility. There were plenty of the latter in Paris then. They drove taxis and pretended to be doormen, butlers, and cooks.

When we moved to this country, we lived on a smaller scale. We were reduced eventually to one servant, a rheumy old woman who cleaned our apartment on East 87th Street. But there, too, you could find a robin being fed with an eyedropper or a squirrel asleep in a shoebox in my mother's room. And of course there was always a Nadia or an Irina at teatime, speaking Russified French and holding a cigarette between thumb and forefinger. "You Americans," they would say to Andrew, "you do not understand the Soviets."

I don't think Andrew much cared for Mme. Kondratovitch and her beauteous daughter Olga, who lived with us for a time, or even for Mme. Popoff, the last of the émigrés. Mme. Kondra, as he called her, was a large, loud and contrary woman with a white powdered face and indigo eyeshadow. She believed in the authenticity of the *Protocols of the Elders of Zion,* as they all did, and pressed upon us poorly printed copies. Andrew, who was famous as a parlor anti-Semite and a baiter of "fellow travelers," now switched tactics, and became a scornful liberal. His aim was to provoke her into going away for good. Which she did, taking Olga with her. Olga was about seventeen: a classic ballerina with bewitching black eyes and perfect legs. Very fetching and very nasty. She treated me with that sort of contempt that Jean Simmons played so precisely as Estella in *Great Expectations*. She came into my room and looked at my bookshelf and asked me with a sneer: "Have you read all these books?"

Of course I hadn't and I was silly enough to be ashamed. I couldn't explain that if you like books you buy them to read and you buy them to have. But she had hit a nerve. I had some that were too much for me, hoping others would think I had read them: the latter volumes of *À la recherche*, *Progress and Poverty*, *The Golden Bowl*. . . .

I can still see the mean little smile on her pretty lips.

Mme. Popoff was a mousy old lady who sewed skillfully. She came out to the country and made my mother's dresses and cooked *côtelettes Russes* for us with canned peas. Her room, reached by a staircase that gave into the dining room, had that typically Russian smell of dill and stale cigarettes. Next to her bed was a snapshot of her father, an engineer of Kharkov, and a much-traveled photograph of an icon. She startled us one evening by coming down and announcing furiously that she was leaving, having distinctly heard one of us say: "Send the old monkey back to the zoo." Nothing my mother said could convince her that we weren't guilty, even when it was pointed out that we were speaking English, a language she did not understand.

My mother's arthritis is so painful that the doctor suggests (on the telephone) that I take her to the emergency room of the hospital to get relief and a prescription.

"What religion?" says the girl behind the typewriter.

"High church!" says my mother.

"High church what?"

"High church!" repeats my mother.

The girl waits and finally I say, "Oh, put down Episcopalian."

The machine rattles out the misinformation obediently.

Everything around here has deteriorated—standards of

dress, manners, everything: uncontrolled farting. When Andrew gets up from his chair he lets out a string of farts that sounds like Chinese New Year. My mother farts too, but being an irrepressible clown, she follows up with double-takes and winks and looks around in mock accusation at me and her bewildered husband. Having lived alone much of my life, I fart too, but usually after leaving the room. At a younger age, I would not have accepted the idea of my mother farting.

If I were married, I wouldn't be here.
If I had a job, I wouldn't be here.
If I had any sense, I wouldn't be here.

"We never see the great blue heron anymore," my mother says in the mournful tone she uses for a long list of vanished good things. "What a pity-ity."

"Why, I saw it just yesterday," I say. I thought it looked like a skinny old lady with an umbrella under her arm carefully stepping downstream. But maybe I see old ladies everywhere these days.

Next day: I see the bird again and find my observation exact.

The greatest event of Andrew's early childhood was when his father took him across the country by rail in a private car. The greatest event of his middle years was when he chanced to be made president of a railway for a while before it was merged with another. That meant that he could fulfill the dream of a lifetime—to ride with the engineer in the cab of a locomotive anytime he felt like it. He doodled locomotives while on the telephone, and one of his best etchings shows a freight train rolling along a bare Arizona landscape. I was looking at it the other day and it gave me an idea.

After rummaging around in a closet I find what I'm looking for—an old "high fidelity" demonstration record called *Rail Dynamics*. It was recorded on a rainy night in the fall of 1950 near the Peekskill station. I put it on for Andrew, who is sitting in his wing chair staring foolishly into the middle distance. The record is scratchy, but the sounds of screeching wheels and hissing steam are still amazingly real. Andrew doesn't react at first. Then, at the long sorrowful whistle of a passing train, he sits up and seems about to speak but doesn't. He is very attentive when, with a big blast of steam, the train slows down and when the engine huffs and chuffs its way out of the station, he holds up an index finger as if to say, *Hark!* I am pleased to get a reaction from him. I had no such luck with Brahms's second piano concerto which he used to love so much. "The most beautiful slow movement in the history of music," he never failed to say upon hearing this or any other slow movement by Brahms or Beethoven. Now he just looks cross and whispers loudly, "Oh, shut up!"

The result is that I rarely play music for them anymore and so my mother hardly ever dances. Her dancing is the quaintest thing I have ever seen. I put on a record and she whirls about the room with her arms out stiffly as though she was holding a baby. It is not a performance. She is as unselfconscious and absorbed as a four-year-old. Her favorite piece is *Petroushka,* which she saw in Paris done by Diaghilev's *Ballets Russes.* She shuts her eyes and tells me that she sees Lifar in the central role. After she sits down and catches her breath she says, "Of course Hitler shot Lifar from his box at the Opéra. Lifar was Nijinsky's son. You could tell because his feet were shaped like a bird's." She gets up and whirls around slowly a few more times: "I love to dance. It's good for me."

Andrew and my mother used to go dancing at El Morocco in the old days.

I joined them on their last train trip in Montana two summers ago. It turned out to be their last trip West too. Andrew had some cattle on a ranch near Miles City and we spent a few days around there staying at the Olive Hotel and taking our meals at the Met Café.

On the afternoon we were to leave, Andrew called from the hotel and learned that the *Northcoast Limited* was going to be late. We dawdled a bit before going to the railroad station and when we got there we saw a bunch

of people patiently sitting on their luggage. Not many
people took the train anymore. There was grass growing
between the tracks.

Andrew contained his impatience but I could see how
much he was looking forward to a "damned good dinner"
on the dining car. He loved to be served by black hands
in white sleeves on a white tablecloth glittering with
silverware.

We waited what seemed to be a very long while before
word came that the *Northcoast Limited* was three and a
half hours late. Silently we went back to the Met Café
on Main Street and ordered something to eat. All they
had was liver and onions. When the waitress brought the
drinks Andrew looked down into his bourbon-on-the-
rocks and said: "I'm too old to be insulted in this way."

When Andrew was old but still had his wits I asked
him, "What was I like when I was a boy?"
He thought for a while and said, "Sneaky."

Andrew is lying in his room and my mother is at her
place on the couch. She doesn't know that I am standing
in the front hall.
"We're both trapped here and you know it," I hear her
say. I know she's talking to *me*.

I have grown to like the quietness of a house where
old people live, but there is one sound that I will always
associate with Andrew's dying days. It is the song of the
mourning dove which the field guide renders as: "A hollow, mournful *coah—coo, coo, coo*."
"What a beautiful bird," my mother says. "Shoot 'em!"

The old man lived on for another year—the last few
months in a nursing home. After a while he spoke so
rarely you wondered if his brain worked at all. He was a
beautiful old man with a white beard and a sweet smile.
The nurses were fond of him and patted his head as they
went by his wheelchair. He seemed beyond unhappiness
or pain and yet, on one of the last visits my mother and I
paid before he died, he spoke. We were about to leave

when his voice came so faintly that I thought I had imagined it.

"I wish I could go with you."

Later on in the car my mother suddenly asked, "Did you hear what he said?"

I said yes.

The undertaker was a pleasant young man named Glenn. "Do you want to see him?" he asked. Discreet, he left me alone with the body. It wasn't Andrew. It was one of those painfully realistic polychrome carvings one finds in Spanish churches. A St. Peter perhaps, with glass eyes and real teeth.

I shed a tear nevertheless.

The ashes came in a small but heavy plastic bag. His death had pulled my mother down into one of her deepest depressions. Several days passed before she asked what had happened to them.

"The ashes are on the mantelpiece in the guest room," I said. "I think we ought to bury them. I'll get a shovel."

"Is that all that's left of him?" she asked when she saw the bag.

We buried him on the hill among the cedar trees. It was a lovely autumn afternoon.

A LATE DEBUT

E. M. FORSTER ON STAGE

Frank Hauser

Late in 1959 I was staying in Lahore, Pakistan, on my way back to direct another bout of plays at the Oxford Playhouse. I had just left a group of Playhouse actors touring the Indian subcontinent, and the parent company should have been preparing the stage version of *A Passage to India*. At it turned out, they weren't: I was asked to get back as early as possible. The play was due to open in six weeks and there was no cast, no design, and precious little money: only an "investment" (act of kindness) by Graham Greene, which would be forfeit if not used before April.

My host in Lahore was a young Pakistani actor, Zia Mohyeddin. He was born to play the Indian doctor Aziz and he knew it, which was just as well as the offer was twenty-five pounds a week (seven pounds for rehearsals) and pay your own air fare. From Lahore. After consultation with his wife, he agreed, and I went back to England to try to organize a production with four sets and twenty characters, many of them Indian, over one week, the week being Christmas week. And, of course, to talk to Mr. Forster.

Our initial meeting was at dinner in the National Liberal Club, an echoing marble parody of itself. Almost immediately Mr. Forster took charge. "You probably won't remember," I began modestly, "but we met once before."

"Actually it was twice before," he replied.

He was right, but the first time was a brief "How do you do" at some strange literary fete two years before. He was obviously a man with eyes at the back of his mind.

We went over Santha Rama Rau's dazzling adaptation in total agreement; then this eighty-two-year-old theater virgin looked benignly over his glasses and asked, "What would you like me to do for publicity?"

"Come to the first night," I said.

"I'm an old man, and it's a long way from Cambridge to Oxford, but if the weather isn't too bad . . ."

It wasn't. I'll skip the traumas of production: the race against time and money, the sets scrapped and redesigned, the endless technical rehearsal that leaked into the dress rehearsal that brought us dedicated and unready to the opening night. And Mr. Forster. And the full pride of the London press—*Times, Telegraph, Guardian,* the Sundays, the weeklies. Too exhausted to feel adequately frightened, I took Forster to dinner, then back to the theater. "Don't come to my office in the interval," I told him. "You'll be taken to the administrator's office. I'll be entertaining the critics." He sat in his seat and the performance began.

My instructions were disregarded. In the first interval he walked up and down the foyer with his friend J. R. Ackerley, saying to anyone who wanted to hear how splendid it all was: and the unwontedly fashionable first-night audience, Oxford dons, Oxford nobs, intellectual Oxford undergraduates, peered and gaped. In the second interval he put his head round the door of my office, blinked at the lions of the press and murmured, "Oh, I shouldn't be here." The lions mewed. He went round the room, firmly writing their reviews, while the toughest bunch of critics in five continents tried to hide their awe. For this was E. M. Forster, very much the king of his particular forest, someone we had all read when young and been changed by. First loves in literature and life are alike: there may be bigger and deeper thrills later on, but the first great writer you discover for yourself is the mythical one. *Howard's End, A Passage to India,* "Only connect . . ."—there they all were in that draughty dingy office, one stooping spry old buffer in a grey tweed suit, glasses glinting, the familiar rabbit-face miraculously piping words—"Quite right to finish with the trial scene," "How good that young Pakistani boy is," "Thank you, just a small one."

I took him back to his seat. "Would you like me to go up on stage afterwards?" he said.

"Yes."

"Yes, I thought you would, so I've prepared a few words."

The performance came to its astonishingly unharmed finish, and Mr. Forster appeared among the cast. "I shouldn't be here," he said for the second time that evening. "Miss Santha Rama Rau is the person to whom the credit is due. But in her absence I should like to thank various people. First, I should like to thank the actors, not only for being so good but for being so numerous. I am not fond of plays with one man and two women, or two men and one woman, or even two of each. I write for the variety of human experience, and I am glad to see it on the stage tonight. Next, I should like to thank those responsible for the production." (Offstage, I preened). "I particularly liked the setting for the mountain scene." (Ah, well). "Lastly, I should like to thank the audience. I have sat in the audience and been thanked from the stage. It has not caused me much emotion. Pretty habit, though."

And that was that: with the expert timing that marks your true professional, E. M. Forster had made his stage debut.

A month later he appeared again, at the Cambridge Arts Theatre, for what he called the play's "Deuxième." I saw him several times in his rooms at King's College. The London transfer had been arranged and Santha Rama Rau was due to arrive. Forster was affable, incurious; but I realized what a strain the Oxford opening must have been. This was a man under no illusion about his status, fiercely proud of his work, and open to the gravest of wounds had he been made to look foolish in public. The relief we both felt moved the talk along but did not make it especially warm. Only on the subject of a film sale was he heated. Later, Santha Rama Rau was to receive a slew of offers from film companies. One of them, Paramount, ignored her repeated "Mr. Forster has the film rights and he will not allow the work to be filmed," and spent two hours talking its offer up from $50,000 to $250,000 without any success.

A Passage to India opened in the West End to a distinguished audience which included Forster's old friend Mrs. Pandit, Nehru's sister and the Indian Ambassador to Great Britain. She was brought backstage by the author to congratulate the cast. "Why do you rake up these old stories?" she demanded. "We want people to know about the new India, not ancient history."

"I'd hope you would make an exception in this case," Forster offered.

Mrs. Pandit replied tartly, "No." The author closed his lips and said no more.

The London opening took place during Easter week and an early heat wave. The producers were worried. They muttered of cuts in royalties; but the sun went back in and the box office prospered. In November the takings fell again, and this time the muttering became a direct inquiry: would the Oxford Playhouse Company, and I as director, agree to cuts? I wrote to Forster saying that I personally was against this but would of course fall in with whatever he wanted. The reply came by return. No, he was not going to agree to cuts. "When a play is struggling to establish itself I can see that it may need help; but when it has run its natural course, I find no point in helping the producer to take it off more cheaply." To which there seemed no reply except "Will you be my agent?"

A year or so later I was again in Cambridge and went to call on Forster. He received me as always politely. We talked about the forthcoming New York production. He asked after various members of the cast, particularly Zia Mohyeddin, who he had insisted must play Aziz on Broadway. The beautiful set of rooms that King's had granted him seemed more like a cocoon than ever. When I left he saw me to the front gate. Once more he asked about Zia. The last thing he said was, "Give my regards to Hauser if you see him." I promised I would.

WORK-IN-PROGRESS
RITE OF SPRING

Djuna Barnes

Man cannot purge his body of its theme
As can the silkworm on a running thread
Spin a shroud to re-consider in.

FRINGECUPS

Sandra McPherson

Of a green so palely, recessively matched to the forest floor,
One asks if they will turn a color
For they could hardly fade more.
Around them, buttercups spread witheringly bright.

But there can be a deep pink sign of aging
On a cup's curled edge.
And when its style calves and the ovary splits,
One drop of cucumber-scented water sprinkles the fingernail.

Here I've found
The exhausted shrew, the kissy snail
In the green steam of a rainstorm.
But wildflowers do the mopping up.

Is it they who define the fringe?
Or the border made by the flooding, reddened creek
One cannot wade or swim across,
One's joy become impassable?

Not that there is anything beyond
This blurring, this infringement of full glory,
But one need, wonderer: you have friends
You are studying for degrees of bliss;

Monitor this—how first I became enamored
Of these fancy nothings, these teacups so small
Tempests can't get in.
It was while walking out of words and into the margin

As into the missed language of a foreign film,
Where all I understood was an edginess,
A century unrevisable now, a humor sometimes sexy
And ending in death

Like the occasional red lips of one strap of fringecups
In the midst of all the green ones.

By the time anyone might read this
It will be very much too late

For the fringecups' unconfident bells
And yet we will want to keep on
Hearing something. They looked
Like sound. They led us to believe they could ring.

Where did that strength of illusion come from?
The fringecup evanesced when the weather
Turned sunny. Its whole modesty now is gone.
No boasts are in its place.

MOORHEN

William Logan

To have
red mouth and green shanks
    like a sidewalk hooker
come up through the ranks
    of weeds does not disqualify
you from honorary membership
    in the upper class,
the community of spies,
    or any lowly clan
not put off by outer feathers that
    conceal the inward man.

Or hen in this case, unsexed
like Lady Macbeth or the Chairs;
    though no more rude than the next
species downstream
    you've never grown fat
like a capon on chocolate eclairs.
    The dictionary calls you
a *common* gallinule,
    an insult, I suppose.
Your family has elongated
    webless toes,

but all families have problems,
marital or genetic,
    in search of a mastering art
or a convenient aesthetic.
    Admiral, it's an admirable life
asleep on the water
    above crepuscular plants
and miniature pike
    that never need to be tended
and never go out on strike.
    You nose among the rank

[333]

roots, washed white and ghostly,
grasses weave on the bank,
      where bugs, I assume, have costly
apartments, and are always behind with the rent.
      And you, you're the rent collector,
dealing in first-born sons
      and daughters, grannies, long-lost cousins,
virtually everyone.
      How convenient to be a ridiculous
rapacious insectivore,
      much better than being dependent

      on a grocery store.
How convenient to maintain a demeanor:
      when chased or thwarted by fear
you sail between the weeds
      and disappear.
Did you descend from the moors,
      purple and lush with heather,
far away from the stores
      and with indifferent weather?
Better here in the lowlands
      full of *noblesse oblige*;

      where the rats own baby grands
Inland Revenue never lays siege.
      Reduced to one expression,
call it amused but grave,
      that achieves its own lesson
on the etiquette of where to behave,
      you plod with unwieldy grace
as if the ditch were a minefield
      and not a froth of lace.
I feel estranged
      that way too, sometimes—we all do, hen,

      but what's the use?
You'll wake tomorrow and the ditch
      will not have changed.

EMIGRÉ

W. S. Merwin

You will find it is
much as you imagined
in some respects
which no one can predict
you will be homesick
at times for something you can describe
and at times without being able to say
what you miss
just as you used to feel when you were at home

some will complain from the start
that you club together
with your own kind
but only those who have
done what you have done
conceived of it longed for it
lain awake waiting for it
and have come out with
no money no papers nothing
at your age
know what you have done
what you are talking about
and will find you a roof and employers

others will say from the start
that you avoid
those of your country
for a while
as your country becomes
a category in the new place
and nobody remembers the same things
in the same way

and you come to the problem
of what to remember after all
and of what is your real
language
where does it come from what does it
sound like
who speaks it

if you cling to the old usage
do you not cut yourself off
from the new speech
but if you rush to the new lips
do you not fade like a sound cut off
do you not dry up like a puddle
is the new tongue to be trusted

what of the relics of your childhood
should you bear in mind pieces
of dyed cotton and gnawed wood
lint of voices untranslatable stories
summer sunlight on dried paint
whose color continues to fade in the
growing brightness of the white afternoon
ferns on the shore of the transparent lake
or should you forget them
as you float between ageless languages
and call from one to the other who you are

THE PARTISAN

Nicholas Christopher

I was eating black olives in the sun
when the bullets whistled through my heart
and I heard children singing.
I glimpsed soldiers behind the rocks
watching me fall, but my last impression
was of my wife, whose hair had been the color
of the field flying away from under me.
Even as a student I had prepared myself
for that day, the hour I would be led
to a stained wall or rickety gallows,
blindfolded with set jaw and clenched fists;
I never imagined the possibility of
being ambushed over my lunch, years after
my last skirmish, temples greying and
old wounds blued into scars;
I had not even a delusion of my own martyrdom.
No followers, no weapon in my belt:
how they found me, why they were still pursuing,
and what price lay on my head, I'll never know.
I hadn't read a newspaper in years.
Nor spoken to a single soul.
I remembered the streets of the capital,
not as a maze of police and barricades,
but with nostalgia, with a boy's memory
of carnivals and parades, of my father
at the edge of a crowd smoking his white pipe.
In hiding, I devoured books of medicine and astronomy,
Pliny and Galen, Kepler and Galilei.
For a while, I considered going abroad.
Too late.
They buried me on the spot, in my boots and hat,
carpeting the grave with pine needles and stones,
blending it carefully into the texture of the hillside.
As if nothing had happened.
Rifling my pockets, closing my eyes,

they overlooked but one detail:
my mouth which never opened again,
which clamped shut with an olive pit under the tongue;
even now, I am waiting for the tree that will
one day burst forth, casting its shadow in my image—
plunging them into darkness.

ON READING A WRITER'S LETTERS

Mary Jo Salter

At last we have a picture of her life—
more colorful than honest, as her trade
led her to value more the thing that's made
than what it's made of. One must wonder if
even a scribbled postcard's a first draft,
knowing the curse that forced her to revise;
and once she coined a phrase, she spent it twice.
Her correspondents variously were left

with lines of a character nobody knew
wholly except for one, perhaps, whose talent
shows finally a self in overview:
she is this artifice, we'd say, if we
her readers, unacquainted but omniscient
narrators, were asked to tell her story.

TRANSLATING PROUST

Terence Kilmartin

There used to be a story that discerning Frenchmen preferred to read Marcel Proust in English on the grounds that the prose of À *la recherche du temps perdu* was deeply un-French and heavily influenced by English writers such as Ruskin. If at all true, the story could have come from some *salon* snob of the kind Proust ridicules in his novel. It stems from the 1930s when Proust was suffering an eclipse in France while enjoying a vogue in the English-speaking world amounting at times to a cult. He seemed to have become naturalized English, and C. K. Scott Moncrieff, who died in 1930, achieved a posthumous fame which few translators have ever known.

It was not till the early fifties that Proust was reclaimed by the French. His relative eclipse had been due, in the thirties and forties, to the pervasive influence of the surrealists, then of *la littérature engagée* and the existentialists. The success in 1951 of André Maurois's À *la recherche de Marcel Proust,* followed by the publication of Proust's own *Jean Santeuil* and *Contre Sainte-Beuve,* heralded a reversal of literary opinion, culminating in 1954 in the appearance of the magnificent Pléiade edition of À *la recherche du temps perdu*—definitive, purged of the manifold errors, confusions, misreadings and omissions that had disfigured the original edition. There was a boom in Proust studies in France, and it has continued from the heyday of the *nouveau roman,* through the structuralist revolution, to the present time.

Meanwhile, a recognition grew among English and American Proustians (those, at any rate, who knew À *la recherche* in the original as well as in translation) that Scott Moncrieff's version was not all that it should be. His publishers and his heirs were reluctant to allow his text to be tampered with. The final volume, *Le Temps retrouvé,* which he had not reached by the time he died—the work was completed by "Stephen Hudson" (Sydney Schiff) in Britain and Frederick A. Blossom in the United States—was re-translated by Andreas Mayor on the basis of the Pléiade edition; but it was only the impending expiry of the Scott Moncrieff copyright that persuaded the publishers to initiate a revision of the entire text.

I approached the task with some trepidation. On the one hand I was warned that my tinkering would be regarded as lèse-majesté if not sacrilege. On the other, I knew there were extremists who considered that nothing less than a complete re-translation could ever do proper justice to Proust. Not having studied the English version closely, I had a fairly open mind.

Was Scott Moncrieff as good as his supporters insisted, or as bad as his detractors maintained? The answer to both questions, I discovered, was no. As I worked my way through his text, I found myself alternating between delighted admiration of his elegant fluency and exasperation with his clumsy fallibility, his bowdlerising, archaising, prettifying.

Scott Moncrieff labored under two major disadvantages. In the first place, he had perforce to translate piecemeal what is, for all its enormous length, a single book. When *Swann* appeared in English in 1922 (the year of Proust's death), only half the novel had been published in France; *Le Temps retrouvé* was not published until 1927, by which time Scott Moncrieff was in the middle of *Sodom and Gomorrah*. The full meaning of *À la recherche*—in particular Proust's metaphysics of time and memory—only becomes clear in the final section, which illuminates what has gone before. The complexities of the opening pages of the novel are especially difficult to decipher without the hindsight provided by the later volumes. I myself noticed too late (after the new version had gone to press) that in the paragraph evoking the bedroom at Tansonville *la chambre où je me serai endormi* had become in English "the bedroom in which I shall presently fall asleep" (instead of "in which I must have fallen asleep"), thus giving the reader the impression that the narrator is writing at Tansonville instead of in Paris some years after the visit to Gilberte de Saint-Loup which itself does not occur until the final pages of *The Fugitive*. The French reader can take things on trust and wait for eventual enlightenment. The reader who has only a translation to rely on cannot know—though he may have an uneasy suspicion when he reads an incomprehensible passage—that the translator may have misconstrued it, thus making obscurity doubly obscure.

The very first sentence of the novel poses a problem for the translator. "*Longtemps je me suis couché de bonne heure. . . .*" The choice of the perfect tense, what in French is called the *passé composé*, the most familiar and immediate form of the past, seems deliberately ambiguous; it leaves the reader in a state of uncertainty as to the narrator's position in time. Roger Shattuck discusses the question at length in his *Proust's Binoculars* and suggests that Proust "may have wanted to keep this opening sentence free of any exact location in time and to begin in a temporal free zone." This is certainly the effect: but how to convey it in English? Scott Moncrieff's "For a long time I used to go to bed early" smoothly evades the issue; yet I could think of no alternative that would be consistent with the imperfect into which the narrating voice instantly slides: "*. . . mes yeux se fermaient si vite que je n'avais pas le temps de me dire: 'Je m'endors. . . .'*" Edmund Wilson, incidentally, compared that opening sentence to the opening chord of a vast symphony, and the musical analogy is an illuminating one—the change of tense corresponding to a modulation, which fails to materialize in the English version.

Scott Moncrieff's second handicap was the faultiness of the French texts. The root of the trouble lay in Proust's notorious working methods: his endless additions, revisions, insertions and transpositions. These must have driven his editors and printers to distraction; inevitably they often failed to decipher his almost illegible scrawls and to obey his directives. The 200-odd closely-printed

pages of notes and variants in the Pléiade illustrate the
extent of the resulting corruptions and confusions, which
in turn must account for some of the impenetrable obscurity of which Proust is often accused. Only *Swann*,
which Proust had had time to revise between its first
appearance in 1913 and its republication in 1919, was
reasonably free of errors; but even here, to take one
small example, an intrusive "s" in both French editions
caused Scott Moncrieff to refer to a "mirror with square
feet" instead of to "a rectangular cheval-glass."

Scott Moncrieff himself was aware of the problem,
as a note on the title page of *The Guermantes Way*
testifies; indeed in a preface to *The Captive* he promised, as soon as the English version of *Le Temps Retrouvé*
was completed, "a supplementary volume containing a
critical emendation of the French text as a whole."
Alas, it would have been a case of the blind leading the blind, for it has to be said (a third handicap)
that Scott Moncrieff's knowledge of French was far
from perfect. There is evidence of this throughout the
novel—signs of haziness and uncertainty that in a less
ingenious and resourceful translator would have been
crippling. Time and again he fails to recognize quite
ordinary set expressions. One finds him translating literally when English equivalents could and should have
been found. We have, for instance, the Duc de Guermantes telling Swann that he is "as strong as the Pont
Neuf" instead of "as sound as a bell." The Duke asks
elsewhere, "*Vous connaissez notre patelin?*," character-
istically choosing a familiar colloquial term for "village";
"You know our wheedler?," Scott Moncrieff mysteriously
makes him say. There is also someone "adopting a policy
of the least possible effort" when he is merely "taking the
line of least resistance"; people sleep like lead rather
than logs; things are constantly spreading like "spots of
oil" rather than "wildfire," and we frequently get "straw
fires" instead of "flashes in the pan" (*feux de paille*).

Like all translators from the French, Scott Moncrieff
was instinctively on his guard against *faux amis*: those
deceptive cognates that offer a different meaning in

French and English. At times, indeed, he seems to have bent over backwards (too far backwards) to avoid falling into these traps, and we get "chastise" for *punir* when "punish" is the *mot juste*. At other times his guard slips, and one finds him referring to "pretended" as opposed to "alleged" contingencies or describing someone as "laborious" instead of "industrious"; a *milieu interlope* becomes "interloping" rather than "shady," and more heinous still, perhaps, *actuel* ("present") is sometimes rendered as "actual."

More seriously, careless or ignorant misreadings can sometimes distort the meaning of a whole passage or even make Proust say the opposite of what he intends. For instance, in the passage where Swann interrogates Odette about her suspected lesbian experiences, and having extracted a half-confession from her, asks finally, *"Il y a combien de temps?"*—"How long ago?"—Scott Moncrieff, evidently confusing *temps* and *fois,* translates "How many times?," thus trivializing Swann's insane jealousy.

A second example, also from *Swann in Love,* concerns the crucial moment in the cab when Swann is about to kiss Odette for the first time. Here Scott Moncrieff's misconstruing of pronouns causes him to transfer to Odette what is in fact going on in Swann's mind (little, if anything, would have been going on in hers):

> Et ce fut Swann qui, avant qu'elle laissât tomber [son visage], comme malgré elle, sur ses lèvres, le retint un instant, à quelque distance, entre ses deux mains. Il avait voulu laisser à sa pensée le temps d'accourir, de reconnaître le rêve qu'elle avait si longtemps caressé et d'assister à sa réalisation, comme une parente qu'on appelle pour pendre sa part du succès d'un enfant qu'elle a beaucoup aimé.

Scott Moncrieff's version of the second sentence is as follows:

> He had intended to leave time for her mind to overtake her body's movements, to recognize the dream which she

had so long cherished and to assist at its realization, like a mother invited as a spectator when a prize is given to the child whom she has reared and loves.

An elementary trap: confused by those deceptive French pronouns, which must of course agree in gender with their nouns, he has taken the feminine *sa* as meaning *her* rather than *his* and the succeeding *elle* as referring to Odette, as in the previous sentence, rather than to the feminine noun, *pensée*. The absence of a neuter gender in French doesn't make things any easier. *Parente*, incidentally, is "relative" not "mother." So the sentence should read like this:

> He had wanted to leave time for his mind to catch up with him, to recognize the dream which it had so long cherished and to assist at its realization, like a relative invited as a spectator when a prize is given to a child of whom she has been especially fond.

In a third example (from *The Captive*), where Proust, describing Charlus's discomfiture at the Verdurins' musical *soirée*, speaks of ". . . this great nobleman (in whom superiority over commoners was no more essentially inherent than in this or that ancestor of his trembling before the revolutionary tribunal) . . ." standing there paralysed, tongue-tied, terror-stricken, Scott Moncrieff completely destroys the egalitarian point by making the Baron's superiority "no less essentially inherent."

The final example is another total *contresens*. Musing about his mother's attitude toward Albertine's living with him, the narrator remarks that, quite apart from the question of propriety, *je crois qu'Albertine eût insupporté maman* ("I doubt whether Mamma could have put up with Albertine"). The translator could be forgiven for not being familiar with this unusual locution, but the context should have told him that "I doubt whether Albertine could have put up with Mamma" could not possibly make sense.

[345]

When all this is said, however, it is extraordinary how successful Scott Moncrieff was in threading his way through the labyrinthine pages of À *la recherche du temps perdu*. Faced with those elaborate Proustian periods with their spiraling subordinate clauses, their parentheses and digressions, their wealth of metaphorical imagery: layer upon layer of similes derived from botany, physics, medicine, and biology, as well as from art and music—the translator might well feel tempted to unscramble and simplify, to split it all up into more manageable units. Scott Moncrieff—correctly, in my view—resisted the temptation and tried as a rule to stay as close as possible to the French text. Alas, in clinging as tenaciously as he did to the clause-structure of the original, he frequently put too great a strain on English syntax and produced some awkward, jarring, unnatural-sounding sentences, obscure and periphrastic in a way that the French is not.

E. M. Forster seems to have been aware of this when, in *Abinger Harvest*, he expressed reservations about Scott Moncrieff "because I was hoping to find Proust easier in English than in French, and do not." Forster went on to give him the benefit of the doubt: "All the difficulties of the original are here faithfully reproduced"—in other words, the fault was Proust's. Had he probed more deeply, though, Forster would have realized that the apparent fidelity of the translation was often a form of betrayal, that those difficulties were in fact aggravated by the translator's failure to make sufficient allowance for essential differences between the two languages. French possesses several structural devices not available in English that make it possible to write long and complicated sentences without sacrificing clarity—the existence of gender, for example, which facilitates reference to pronouns and antecedents, the ability to position adjectives either before or after the noun, the license to invert subject and verb, and a greater range of relative pronouns. Transposing these forms into English can create an effect of weirdness and impenetrability.

But whenever the shape of the English can legitimately be calqued on to the French, fidelity to the architectonics of the original has its rewards. Here is a characteristic example: a sentence of some four hundred words evoking the adolescent Marcel's emotions on hearing, one afternoon in the gardens of the Champs-Elysées, the name of the inaccessible, yearned-for Gilberte whom he had once glimpsed through the hawthorn-hedge at Combray:

Ce nom de Gilberte passa près de moi, evoquant d'autant plus l'existence de celle qu'il désignait qu'il ne la nommait pas seulement comme un absent dont on parle, mais l'interpellait; il passa ainsi près de moi, en action pour ainsi dire, avec une puissance qu'accroissait la courbe de son jet et l'approche de son but;—transportant à son bord, je le sentais, la connaissance, les notions qu'avait de celle à qui il etait addressé, non pas moi, mais l'amie qui l'appelait, tout ce que, tandis qu'elle le prononçait, elle revoyait ou, du moins, possédait en sa mémoire, de leur intimité quotidienne, des visites qu'elles se faisaient l'une chez l'autre, et tout cet inconnu encore plus inaccessible et plus douloureux pour moi d'être au contraire si familier et si maniable pour cette fille heureuse qui m'en frôlait sans que j'y puisse pénétrer et le jetait en plein air dans un cri;—laissant déjà flotter dans l'air l'émanation délicieuse qu'il avait fait se dégager, en les touchant avec précision, de quelques points invisibles de la vie de Mlle Swann, du soir qui allait venir, tel qu'il serait, après dîner, chez elle;—formant, passager céleste au milieu des enfants et des bonnes, un petit nuage d'une couleur précieuse, pareil à celui qui, bombé au-dessus d'un beau jardin du Poussin, reflète minutieusement, comme un nuage d'opéra plein de chevaux et de chars, quelque apparition de la vie des dieux;—jetant enfin, sur cette herbe pelée, à l'endroit où elle était un morceau à la fois de pelouse flétrie et un moment de l'après-midi de la blonde joueuse de volant (qui ne s'arrèta de le lancer et de le rattraper que quand une institutrice à plumet bleu l'eût appelée), une petite bande merveilleuse et couleur d'héliotrope, impalpable comme un reflet et superposée comme un tapis, sur lequel je ne pus me lasser de promener mes pas attardés, nostalgiques et profanateurs, tandis que Françoise me criait: "Allons, aboutonnez voir votre paletot et filons" et que je remarquais pour la première fois avec irritation qu'elle avait un langage vulgaire, et hélas! pas de plumet bleu à son chapeau.

No translation can hope to match the full resonance of this miraculous tour de force, but by obeying the structure of the original, something of its metaphorical richness, its complex rhythm and harmony, its syntactic onomatopoeia (those five main clauses governed by present participles, and extended by proliferating subordinate clauses and parentheses, imaging the rise and fall of Gilberte's shuttlecock) can be reproduced in English. Here is my revised version of Scott Moncrieff:

> That name 'Gilberte' passed close by me, evoking all the more powerfully the girl whom it labeled in that it did not merely refer to her, as one speaks of someone in his absence, but was directly addressed to her; it passed thus close to me, in action so to speak, with a force that increased with the curve of its trajectory and its approach to its target;—carrying in its wake, I could feel, the knowledge, the impressions concerning her to whom it was addressed that belonged not to me but to the friend who called it out—everything that, as she uttered the words, she recalled, or at least possessed in her memory, of their daily intimacy, of the visits they paid to each other, of that unknown existence which was all the more inaccessible, all the more painful to me for being, conversely, so familiar, so tractable to this happy girl who let it brush past me without my being able to penetrate it, who flung it on the air with a light-hearted cry;—wafting through the air the exquisite emanation which it had distilled, by touching them with precision, from certain invisible points in Mlle Swann's life, from the coming evening, just as it would be, after dinner, at her home;—forming, on its celestial passage through the midst of the children and their nurse-maids, a little cloud, delicately coloured, resembling one of those clouds that, billowing

over a Poussin landscape, reflect minutely, like a cloud in the opera teeming with chariots and horses, some apparition of the life of the gods;—casting, finally, on that ragged grass, at the spot where it was at one and the same time a patch of withered lawn and a moment in the afternoon of the fair-haired battledore player (who continued to launch and retrieve her shuttlecock until a governess with a blue feather in her hat had called her away), a marvellous little band of light, the color of heliotrope, impalpable as a reflection and superimposed like a carpet on which I could not help but drag my lingering, nostalgic and desecrating feet, while Françoise shouted: "Come on, button up your coat and let's clear off home!" and I remarked for the first time how common her speech was, and that she had, alas, no blue feather in her hat.

Another, briefer example (Proust is not always so interminably long-winded as he is often accused of being) will show, conversely, how failure to follow the syntactical logic of the French can weaken the impact. Proust is describing a sudden shower of rain:

Un petit coup au carreau, comme si quelque chose l'avait heurté, suivi d'une ample chute légère comme de grains de sable qu'on eût laissés tomber d'une fenêtre au-dessus, puis la chute s'étendant, se réglant, adoptant un rythme, devenant fluide, sonore, musicale, innombrable, universelle: c'était la pluie.

Scott Moncrieff, in this case losing his nerve, breaks the rhythm of the sentence halfway through:

A little tap at the window, as though some missile had struck it, followed by a plentiful, falling sound, as light, though, as if a shower of sand were being sprinkled from a window overhead; then the fall spread, took on an order, a rhythm, became liquid, loud, drumming, musical, unnumerable, universal. It was the rain.

In fact those present participles, succeeding one another with ever-increasing urgency to produce an effect of crescendo, can perfectly well be retained in English:

[349]

A little tap on the window-pane, followed by a plentiful light falling sound, as of grains of sand being sprinkled from a window overhead, gradually spreading, intensifying, acquiring a regular rhythm, becoming fluid, sonorous, musical, immeasurable, universal: it was the rain.

Despite his unfailing attentiveness to the original text, there is a significant difference in tone between Scott Moncrieff's English and Proust's French. He was twenty years younger than Proust, but his natural prose style was the product of an earlier generation, mannered, bellettristic, pseudo-poetic ("Heigh ho! Georgian prose," as Cyril Connolly said). In his hands, Proust's irony too often degenerates into whimsicality or facetiousness, his melancholy lyricism into sentimentality. His fancy inversions, his *I would fains* and *'twases* and *albeits* and *aughts,* are quite out of tune with the original; and he has a tendency to over-translate: Mme. Verdurin's "Atlanta-flights across the field of mirth" for *sur le terrain de l'amabilité,* "a mirrored firmament" for *le ciel reflété,* "beneath a spangled veil of buttercups" for *sous les boutons d'or.*

Not surprisingly, Scott Moncrieff is at his best in passages, especially of dialogue, where Proust gives free rein to his marvellous gifts as mimic and parodist: Legrandin's flowery preciosities, Bloch's mock-Homeric jargon, Brichot's donnish pedantry, Norpois's pompous diplomatic maunderings, Charlus's *vieille France* grandiloquence, cackling gossip and paranoid tirades. He is less successful with Françoise's old-world peasant idiom and the girlish patter of the *jeunes filles en fleurs.* But, as a review of the revised edition in the London weekly *Gay News* points out, he had a very exact ear for homosexual slang. The reviewer cites the passage describing how Charlus has caught the habit of homosexual chatter, where Scott Moncrieff adroitly translates *ce 'chichi' voulu* as "this deliberate camping"—perhaps the earliest appearance of this word in print, preceding the lexicographer Eric Partridge's tentative date of 1935 by six years.

Scott Moncrieff's strengths and weaknesses are neatly epitomized in the titles he chose for the novel as a whole and for the individual sections. They are stylish and ingenious, and at the same time slightly out of key. To Proust's English biographer, George Painter, the overall title, *Remembrance of Things Past,* is "exquisitely appropriate." Others have felt that it misses the whole point of the book. Proust himself, when told of it, said: *"Cela détruit le titre,"* and there is no doubt that the notion of "summoning up" the past contradicts the basic theme of the novel, which is a celebration of *involuntary* memory. Proust also complained about *Swann's Way,* but this was because he thought "way" could only mean "manner."

It is when one considers the possible alternatives that one warms to Scott Moncrieff's inventions (though not to all of them). Vladimir Nabokov offered his own literal versions of the titles instead of the "more or less fancy translations that Moncrieff inflicted upon Proust." *The Walk by Swann's Place* is certainly accurate, if somewhat inelegant; but can he seriously have expected his students to swallow *In the Shade of Blooming Young Girls?*

In his review of the "revised version" in *The New York Review of Books,* Roger Shattuck was mildly critical of my retention of Scott Moncrieff's *Within a Budding Grove,* pointing out that in Proust's *À l'ombre des jeunes filles en fleurs,* "it is incontrovertibly young girls that are budding—or blossoming" (or "blooming"). But he rebuked me very severely for failing to change the overall title—an omission which he seemed to regard as a sort of *trahison des clercs. Mea culpa:* I was indeed in favor of such a change, but allowed myself to be overruled by the publishers. I do not find it quite such a crucial issue as Shattuck and others do. Still, on balance I would have preferred to re-christen the novel *In Search of Lost Time,* even though the English phrase lacks the specific gravity of the French and misses the double meaning of *temps perdu:* time "wasted," as well as "lost." "The whole [book] is a treasure hunt where the

treasure is time and the hiding place the past" was
Nabokov's summary. There is more to it than that, of
course.

SPYING IN SPAIN AND ELSEWHERE

Claud Cockburn

Before he was revealed as a central figure—perhaps the mastermind—of the Burgess-Maclean-Philby spy scandal, the rapscallion Guy Burgess used sometimes to join me at a table in one of the bars of the House of Commons and, in the course of conversation, proclaim that he was an agent of the Soviet Government. This would come out in a drink—slurred roar, clearly audible to, for example, Ernest Bevin, Foreign Secretary, towering massively at the bar, as well as to any other politician or newspaperman in the place.

He would usually, somewhere in the talk, make another emphatic assertion. This was to the effect that he was the illegitimate son of the then Lady Rothschild. It was, he implied, a fact which accounted for his expert knowledge of international finance.

The claim about his illegitimacy was entirely false and quite a number of people who ought to have known better believed it. And his claim to be an agent of the KGB was true and no one believed it. It was a crude and entirely successful example of the double bluff. If anyone —and I suppose there were some such in British counter-intelligence—were to report a suspicion about Burgess's role, his superior was likely to reply with weary contempt, "I know, I know, he keeps saying so himself."

The ploy about Lady Rothschild appealed to people as a fairly titillating piece of gossip. It was useful to Burgess and he employed it for the same reason that his contemporary Brendan Bracken, Britain's Information Minister throughout the war and an immensely successful political and financial pirate, used to claim that he was the illegitimate son of Winston Churchill.

Reading the excitingly simplistic accounts of successive spy scandals in British publications, I find it useful to recall these facts about Burgess, which indicate in their own simple way how complex the detection of spies in our midst can be. We have had spy scares every few

[*353*]

years, and I have no doubt, are going to have more of them. In the same way, scares about terrorism—together with more or less fraudulent analyses of the supposed activities and motivations of terrorists—will certainly proliferate as the nervous system of the general public increasingly demands sedation in the face of horrifying phenomena.

The public nervous system may be soothed by false explanations. But unless people are encouraged to look rather more coolly and deeply into these same phenomena of espionage and terrorism, they will make no progress towards any genuine self-defense against either. At this point, it may be wise to remember that there are those whose hysteria on these subjects leads them to believe that any cool analysis amounts almost to a condonation. Such hysteria is of obvious help to spies and terrorists. Let us also note that nobody in any country can truly and totally evaluate the harm an enemy's spies may have done. The real experts in anti-espionage are a great deal more ready to admit this than the horrified public. Even the outstanding Russian dissident, Andrei Sakharov, "father" of their hydrogen bomb, is reported as saying that the secrets betrayed by Klaus Fuchs were of minimal importance in the development of the weapons in the Soviet Union.

A constant element among the facts and fiction about espionage is what we may call "Belief in the Spy as Superman." All intelligence agencies have a vested interest in convincing the world of their machinelike efficiency. Particularly in wartime, but at other times too, the notion of the spy successfully uprooting our secrets, like a pig uprooting truffles, is alarming in itself, and also because it fits and extends the idea which almost everybody has, that the enemy is not only wickeder but also cleverer than we are. Malcolm Muggeridge once told me how, while working for MI6 during the war, he became for a time profoundly depressed by what appeared to him the ineptitude and even clownish folly of some of our intelligence procedures. His gloom lifted when, after the Allied landings in Italy, his German opposite numbers scampered out of Naples without even burning their vital documents. To his relief he saw from them that the Germans had been proceeding with an ineptitude and folly at least equal to our own.

A frequent element in spy-alarm, notably in Britain and France, is the belief that spies belong to, and are protected by, a higher social and financial class than the common citizenry of the country on which they are spying. An awkward bit of this last element is that it often chances to be true, as is apparent to students of the relationships between certain members of the German and British nobility not only before the outbreak of World War II, but in the intrigues directed particularly against Churchill during the autumn and winter of 1939–1940.

The most insidious of the bases for fear of spies is subtler than the others, yet quite as dangerous. It is rarely formulated but runs roughly, and often subconsciously, like this: if some of our best educated citizens who have had every advantage our society can offer are nonetheless prepared to dedicate themselves to an ideology destructive to that society, may it not be just possible that there is something dangerously wrong with our own philosophy of life?

It is exactly this element that accounts for the extraordinary outburst of outraged surprise with which the British public greeted the exposure of Anthony Blunt as a KGB agent. As in the case of Philby and Maclean, here was a young man of good family who had enjoyed to the full the educational, cultural, and social advantages of a reasonably affluent student at one of Britain's two senior universities. He was as far from deprivation as anyone could get. There was no visible cause for him to turn against society. The thought that, despite all this, some extraordinary power of attraction in Communism's alien and hostile doctrines had seduced him was terrifying. To judge by the tone of many British commentators, it was as alarming as a discovery that a witch-doctor had been secretly at large, exercising black-magical powers over the citizenry.

Such thoughts paralyze the capacity to see and deal rationally with the problem. The true explanation is a great deal simpler. Blunt and the other young men concerned were at Cambridge during the Great Depression. About three million were unemployed, and at that time to be on the dole or in low-paid employment in Britain meant poverty that was often near the starvation line.

John Gunther, in his book *Inside Britain,* notes the astonishment of American visitors at the docility of the British working class under such conditions and the absence of revolutionary outbursts. In this desert of misery, Cambridge was an ostentatious oasis of civilized comfort. It is not at all surprising that Blunt and others should have, with some deep feelings of guilt, questioned the justification for such a state of affairs. On the contrary, it would have been surprising had any sensitive and informed young man coolly accepted his position as though by divine right. The Communists did not require secret recruiting sergeants; the economics of the time were doing the job quite well enough. By contrast, only a few years earlier at Oxford, when the economic situation was less spectacularly dire, the majority of the student population was almost entirely apolitical. If, as some recent publications have suggested, there were Soviet recruiters at the Oxford of that day, they should have been fired for incompetence. Politics was in the main a replay, more or less histrionic, of the Liberal-Conservative struggles of the years before the First World War, with Labour adding no more than flavoring to a familiar stew.

Some who delve needlessly deep into the motivations of international spies, and double and triple agents, have made much of the fact that many of what may be called "The Cambridge Group" of distinguished Soviet agents can be shown to have been homosexual or to have had homosexual connections. But let us note that at Oxford in the mid-twenties, homosexuality was as fashionable and obtrusive as Communism was not. From the London press, which liked to paint lurid pictures of goings-on at the university, you could have gathered that the undergraduates were about evenly divided between flaunting and artistically outré homosexuals and sturdy British "hearties" upholding the values for which the preceding generation had died in the war.

Such nonsense apart, it is certainly true that in the most flamboyant and "trend-setting" intellectual circles homosexuality was in some cases so nearly *de rigueur* that aspiring writers, artists, and above all actors, actually felt compelled to pretend to be homosexual. The slang word for it was "so." In reply to the greeting "How are you?" a common reply was: "So so, but not quite so so as sometimes." A friend of mine who had the most "normal" sexual tastes started a literary magazine which, it was immediately suggested, should have been called *Just So Stories*. When an undergraduate was actually sent down for homosexual practices, astounded observers held competitions to suggest what amazingly spectacular misbehavior he must have indulged in to merit this extraordinary action by the authorities.

Another odd fact is that at that time "womanizer" was a term of abuse. I knew a normally lusty American Rhodes Scholar who could hardly believe that even among those who vigorously deplored the existence of homosexuality, "womanizing" was worse than immoral; it was unspeakably vulgar. This must have had its historical roots in the long ages when Oxford was so successfully isolated by lack of transport from the outside world that prostitutes were the only women available during term time to all but the richest students who could afford gigs and other horse-drawn vehicles to get them at least as far as Reading. By my day the majority of heterosexual people were able to find ways and means of satisfaction, even in term-time, but always under the still somewhat inhibiting fear of being dubbed "womanizers."

It is a pity that so many who write of Oxford and Cambridge in the relevant years are so crassly ignorant of the prevailing atmosphere. They remind me of Mr. Vladimir, the Imperial Russian diplomat in Conrad's *The Secret Agent*, as he lectures the title character:

> And Mr. Vladimir developed his idea from on high, with scorn and condescension, displaying at the same

time an amount of ignorance as to the real aims, thoughts, and methods of the revolutionary world which filled the silent Mr. Verloc with inward consternation. He confounded causes with effects more than was excusable; the most distinguished propagandists with impulsive bomb throwers; assumed organization where in the nature of things it could not exist; spoke of the social revolutionary party one moment as of a perfectly disciplined army, where the word of chiefs was supreme, and at another as if it had been the loosest association of desperate brigands that ever camped in a mountain gorge.

We find a Mr. Vladimir at every corner today, spouting his confident but dangerously misleading lectures.

Still, in the areas of spying and terrorism, even the best are inclined to leave out from their sapient and (so far as they go) truthful analyses the factor of unpredictability. Or nonsense, if you prefer. Brooding on this situation, I constantly keep in mind my own experience in the field of espionage, or rather, counterespionage.

Early in the Spanish Civil War I was what, if one were inclined to pomposity, might be called a section leader of the counterespionage department of the Spanish Republican Government dealing with Anglo-Saxon personalities. My job was principally to vet applications by British and Americans for visas to enter Republican Spain.

It was, as I realized rather late, a "no win" situation for me. Either I allowed in some supposed friend of the Republic who turned out to be a secret enemy, in which case I could very well be shot as a saboteur. Or, over-cautiously avoiding this risk, I might exclude some character suspect to me who would later turn out to be a loyal friend of the Republic and a potentially powerful propagandist in its cause. Saboteur again.

It was under these circumstances that I had to consider the application for a visa for Basil Murray, son of Professor Gilbert Murray, whose family and connections were luminaries of the British liberal academic and political world. I was astonished, and more than a little suspicious, when Basil, in making his application, explained that having hitherto lived the life of a roustabout at Oxford and layabout in London, he had suddenly seen the light and wished to dedicate himself to the cause of the Republic. Specifically, he wanted to give radio talks from Valencia, where the government was now established.

Knowing and liking Basil, but still not quite convinced of the strength of his new resolutions, I discussed his application with the Foreign Minister, who thought that I was mad even to consider rejecting the son of so distinguished a figure in Britain who was as well the cousin of the British Foreign Secretary. (This last was untrue, a detail invented by Basil to help in obtaining his visa.)

Basil came to Valencia, and with much sweat and dedication produced several excellent broadcasts. Then he suddenly fell in love with a girl of whom one may say that had she had the words *I am a Nazi spy* printed on her hat, that could hardly have made her position clearer than it was. I reasoned with Basil, but found him besotted with love and convinced that, in some bigoted way, I was deliberately thinking ill of this splendid creature.

Just as my arguments ran finally into a blind alley, the girl herself suddenly quit the Republic for Berlin in the company of a high-ranking officer of the International Brigade who proved also to be an agent of the enemy. Although I was naturally careful not to belabor Basil with I-told-you-sos, he fell into a deep melancholy both at the loss of the loved one and the disclosure of her political vileness.

Soon after, wandering bitterly disconsolate along the quays of Valencia's harbor, he saw a tiny street menagerie of the kind that in those days was a common form of popular entertainment in Spain. The little group included an ape. And this ape, Basil said, was the first living creature that—since the defection of the Nazi agent—had looked at him with friendly sympathy. He bought the ape and took it with him to the Victoria Hotel, which was the hotel housing all visiting VIPs.

The next I knew, I received a call from the management of the Victoria, who said furiously that they had already strained themselves to the limit by putting up all the foreign visitors I had recommended, and that now, by God, my latest protégé was demanding a room for an ape. After I had pointed out that there were apes enough already living in the hotel, so that one more would hardly be noticed, it was agreed that Basil be moved to a room with a large bathroom, in which the ape might be accommodated.

This arrangement worked well enough for a matter of forty-eight hours. Then Basil, still disconsolate despite the friendly eyes of the ape, drank heavily and fell asleep naked on his bed in the fierce humid heat of a Valencia afternoon. He had locked the ape in the bathroom, but the ingenious and friendly animal became bored with this isolation and longed for the company of its new master. Somehow it picked the lock of the bathroom door and came into the bedroom looking for a game or frolic. Finding the new master disappointingly unresponsive, the ape made vigorous efforts to rouse him, biting him over and over again and finally in frustration biting through his jugular vein.

Apart from my personal regret at the loss of my old acquaintance, I was compelled to see that the situation would be politically damaging. One could surmise at once what a hostile British press would make of the news that a brilliant young Englishman of distinguished family had sought to work for the Red Republic, and had, within a very short time, been bitten to death by an ape. It was possible quickly to announce that Basil had died of pneumonia as a result of the treacherous Valencia climate.

It was also arranged that the British Government should send a light cruiser or frigate from its Mediterranean fleet for the purpose of carrying Basil back to Britain. A small cortege of suitable officials from the Republican Foreign Office accompanied the remains to the quayside. It was only when the remains were being moved to the cutter for transfer onto the frigate that a member of the cortege noticed that they had been joined by the ape. It sprang into the stern sheets of the cutter. Faithfully, it followed Basil up the companionway. It appeared on the spotless deck and there, in a gesture suitable for solemn occasions (learned, no doubt, from the owner of the menagerie), it raised its fist in the Red Front salute.

A British warrant officer—having doubtless been warned of the dangerous and even bestial character of the Reds and of the necessity for vigilance while the ship was in a Red harbor—reacted swiftly, drew a pistol and shot the ape dead. Its body fell overboard and disappeared into the Mediterranean. Basil, I believe, had a fine funeral in England, and the episode was closed.

But not really. For weeks afterwards I was pestered by the menagerie owner demanding compensation and heart-balm for his grief at the demise of the ape. He said that when he had sold it to Basil he had not at all envisaged the possibility that the creature would be brutally murdered by the forces of British imperialism, shooting down that helpless animal as ruthlessly as they had shot down innumerable people throughout their Empire.

In addition, the British diplomatic mission to Republican Spain immediately spread the story that we, the Republicans, meaning in this case me, had murdered Basil—poison in the wine, one of them said. Anarchists and others suspicious of the coalition government somehow spread a story that through the government's carelessness or connivance, a British agent had been introduced, and then killed when on the verge of damaging exposure. Enemies of the Murray family, and those disgusted that Basil should have worked for the Republic, spread in England the story that Basil had had improper relations with the ape. They even, I found later, substituted a bear.

As late as the 1950s a close and loving relative of Basil's was delighted to hear from me the true story, which confirmed the genuineness of Basil's determination to do something constructive with his life—however grotesque the actual outcome.

FOR GEORGE ORWELL

Christopher Hitchens

The reputation of George Orwell is secure among those who have never read him, high among those who have read only *1984* or *Animal Farm*, and pretty solid among those who have read his *Collected Essays, Journalism and Letters* for confirmation of their own opinions. The value of his work is debated only by his fellow socialists and anti-imperialists. And even they, by ridiculing or scorning his precepts, pay an unintended compliment to his influence. Orwell's standing approaches that "large, vague renown" which he bestowed on Thomas Carlyle in 1931.

"To have had a part in two revolutions is to have lived to some purpose," wrote Thomas Paine. To have been prescient about both Fascism and Stalinism is a possible equivalent, but it is not, in itself, proof that Orwell was a great writer or thinker. Only in the most primitive sense does scarcity define the value of a commodity; prescience is no exception. Orwell has been smothered with cloying approbation by those who would have despised or ignored him when he was alive, and pelted with smug afterthoughts by those who (often unwittingly or reluctantly) shared the same trenches as he did. The present climate threatens to stifle him in one way or the other.

"I knew," said Orwell in 1946 about his early youth, "that I had a facility with words and a power of facing unpleasant facts." Not the ability to face them, but "a power of facing." It's oddly well put. A commissar who realizes that his five-year plan is off target and that the people detest him or laugh at him may be said, in a base manner, to be confronting an unpleasant fact. So, for the matter of that, may a priest with "doubts." The reaction of such people to unpleasant facts is rarely self-critical: they do not have a "power of facing." Their confrontation with the fact takes the form of an evasion; the reaction to the unpleasant discovery is a redoubling of efforts to overcome the obvious. The "unpleasant facts" that Orwell faced were usually the ones that put his own position or preference to the test.

Virtues that Orwell never claimed, such as consistency, are denied to him by the textual sectarians, and patronizing compliments, such as the recurrent "quintessentially English," are fastened upon him by sycophants. In order to drag Orwell out from under this mound of dead dogs, as Carlyle said of his Cromwell, one may as well start with his sworn and stated antagonists:

(i) Orwell seldom wrote about foreigners, except sociologically, and then in a hit-or-miss fashion otherwise unusual to him; he very rarely mentions a foreign writer and has an excessive dislike of foreign words; although he condemns imperialism he dislikes its victims even more.

(ii) Orwell's writing life then was from the start an affirmation of unexamined bourgeois values.

(iii) Orwell prepared the orthodox political beliefs of a generation.

(iv) By viewing the struggle as one between only a few people over the heads of an apathetic mass, Orwell created the conditions for defeat and despair.

(v) Politics was something he observed, albeit as an honest partisan, from the comforts of bookselling, marriage, friendship with other writers (not by any means with the radicals used as material for *The Road to Wigan Pier* and *Homage to Catalonia*, then dropped), dealing with publishers and literary agents.

(vi) As far as he considered such matters at all, I think he felt that not to be a product of English history was a sort of moral lapse.

(vii) What Orwell said when he wrote for the Ukrainian readers of *Animal Farm* about his alleged commitment to socialism in 1930 is plainly an untruth, made the more reprehensible not only because Stansky and Abrahams show that he had no notion of socialism until much later, but also because we catch him unaware in 1935 "that Hitler intended to carry out the programme of *Mein Kampf*."

[*363*]

(viii) Is it fantastic to see in Orwell's *1984* the reflection
of a feeling that a world in which the pre-1914
British way of life had totally passed away must
necessarily be a dehumanized world? And is it altogether wrong to see the inhabitants of *Animal
Farm* as having points in common, not merely with
Soviet Russians, but also Kipling's lesser breeds
generally, as well as with Flory's Burmese who,
once the relative decencies of the Raj are gone,
must inevitably fall under the obscene domination
of their own kind?

(ix) It would be dangerous to blind ourselves to the
fact that in the West millions of people may be inclined, in their anguish and fear, to flee from their
own responsibility for mankind's destiny and to
vent their anger and despair on the giant Bogy-
cum-Scapegoat which Orwell's *1984* has done so
much to place before their eyes.

All extracts and quotations are, by their very essence,
"taken out of context" (what else is an extract or a quotation?). But I do not think that the authors cited above will
find themselves or the tendency of their arguments mis-
represented. They are, in order, Conor Cruise O'Brien in
the *New Statesman* of May 1961, Edward Said in the *New
Statesman* of January 1980, Raymond Williams in his *Orwell* of 1971, Williams again, Said again, O'Brien again,
Said again, O'Brien once more, and, finally, Isaac Deutscher in his 1955 essay "The Mysticism of Cruelty."

It can be seen at once that Orwell is one of those authors
who is damned whatever he does. O'Brien, in his rhetorical question (viii), does not ask "Is it reasonable?" (to
which the answer would be dubious) or "Is it interesting?"
(to which the answer might be yes). He asks, "Is it fantastic?" to which the answer is "Certainly." One is forced
to ask of O'Brien, is he as sure of himself as he seems?

Edward Said prefers the non sequitur. Suppose that Orwell's life *had* been one of "comfort," and suppose that we
do agree that the less comfortable bits (like the English
industrial North and the Catalan front) had been self-
inflicted. Suppose that we forget that he did keep up with

friends like Jack Common and his former POUM comrades of the Spanish Civil War until the end of his life.
We are still supposed to distrust him for his cosy relationship with agents and publishers. It is notorious, and must
be known to Professor Said, that *Animal Farm* was published only after strenuous battles with T. S. Eliot at
Fabers, who thought it was inopportune, with Jonathan
Cape, who thought it unpropitious, and with numerous
American houses, one of which (Dial Press) wrote to Orwell that it was "impossible to sell animal stories in the
U.S.A." The story of his quarrel with the *New Statesman*,
which refused to print his dispatches from Barcelona,
though conceding their veracity, is or ought to be well
known by Said. One is compelled to ask if there is not
some other animus at work. The same suspicion arises
when one contemplates O'Brien's liverish remarks in extract (i). What is he *thinking* about when he says that Orwell was scornful of foreign writers and even of foreigners
tout court? If we discount Orwell's unbroken hostility to
British imperialism, a hostility that he kept up at awkward
times such as 1940–45, and if we overlook his seminal
essay "Not Counting Niggers," which rebuked those who
talked of new world orders while ignoring the coolies, and
if we agree to minimize the extent to which racism was a
commonplace even among the educated in Orwell's time,
we are still left with some evidence. There are the essays
in defense of James Joyce, Salvador Dali, Henry Miller,
and (admittedly more grudging) the piece on Ezra Pound.
There's also a very well-crafted article on Joseph Conrad,
who was not in vogue at the time. Orwell actually made
rather a point of importing and introducing "exotic" authors into his milieus and into the insular and British
magazines for which he wrote. His "dislike of foreign
words" was a distaste for the very *English* habit of using
tags as a show of learning.

What can one say of Raymond Williams? His little book
on Orwell is a minor disgrace. It is a warren of contradic-
tions, not all of which can be mitigated by the plea of
sloppiness and haste. He writes that *1984* lacks "a sub-

[*365*]

stantial society and correspondingly substantial persons."
That's poor enough. But elsewhere he denounces the book
for "projecting a world that is all too recognizable." What
he means, and this at any rate he makes explicit, is that Orwell depicts a brute version of *socialism* as the setting for
his nightmare, and thus lets down the "progressive" side.
Well, imagine how much courage would have been required, in 1949, to base an anti-Utopian fiction on Nazism.
Such a book might have compelled or commanded near-
universal and quite consoling assent. But it would scarcely
have outlasted one printing, and would not have called
upon the "power of facing unpleasant facts." In 1949, socialism was thought, and (mark this) not just by its ad-
herents, to be the wave of the future. In that year, thinkers
like Williams were more at ease with that interpretation
than they are now. Some of them for good reasons and
some of them for bad ones; but any novel designed to make
people think had to be, to that extent, *contra mundum*.

Orwell went to the trouble, in insisting that his book was
"NOT intended as an attack on Socialism," to capitalize the
word not. This isn't good enough for his leftist invigilators
(or, come to think of it, for his conservative usurpers). The
first group evinces a certain unction. Said: "True, he had
courage and humanity." O'Brien: "To insist upon the limi-
tations of Orwell's thought is only to establish the limits
within which we admire him." Williams: "We are never
likely to reach a time when we can do without his frank-
ness, his energy, his willingness to join in." This patronizing stuff betrays a sense of unease. It is an obligatory clearing of the throat before getting down to the real business
of blaming Orwell for the Cold War. There is not much
doubt that this is, in fact, what they hold against him. The
difficulty here is that they object to the same thing about
1984 that Orwell did—which is to say, they are upset by
its reception. *Life* magazine said of the book that it would
expose "British Laborites" for reveling in austerity, "just
as the more fervent New Dealers in the United States often
seemed to have the secret hope that the depression mentality of the 1930s, source of their power and excuse for

their experiments, would never end." If you want a picture of the future, imagine (to vary Orwell's famous scene) FDR stamping on a human face—forever. This crassness was and is very widespread, and Orwell issued what he termed a *démenti* against it. But one has to marvel at the way in which certain intellectuals will still deliberately muddy cause and effect. It is the clear implication of all four of his senior socialist critics that an author is in some real sense *responsible* for misinterpretations or vulgarizations of his own work. Where this principle would leave Edward Said or Raymond Williams is a matter, perhaps luckily for them, only of conjecture. But notice that when Isaac Deutscher said of *1984*, "It has only increased and intensified the waves of panic and hate that run through the world and obfuscate innocent minds," he was not so much observing such a process as, if it truly existed, contributing to it. There's something self-destructive as well as self-fulfilling in helping to create an atmosphere which you deplore—what better confirmation could there be of the antisocialist character of a book than that it be subjected to panicky denunciations by socialists? Orwell's careful disclaimer, then, was a small voice drowned in a chorus of apparently opposed but actually collusive propagandists. In a way, that was the pattern of his life.

The question *cui bono* is commonly asked with the intention of oversimplifying. Some reviewers of *Darkness at Noon* noted that Koestler put the Stalinist rationale so persuasively, in the mouth of the interrogator, as to make it convincing. Suppose, what is not unthinkable, that the book had the effect of attracting converts to Communism? Would that make Koestler "objectively" an agent of Soviet propaganda? The proposition dissolves in hilarity (though O'Brien, curiously enough, takes this aspect of the book very seriously). Similarly, in January 1980 Said writes that Orwell turned "to an ideology of the middle-brow 'our way of life' variety, which in the U.S. at least has been dressed up as 'neo-conservatism.' " Exactly three years later, Norman Podhoretz steps forward ("If Orwell Were Alive To-

day," *Harper's*, January 1983) to take Said up on it and
to claim Orwell as a posthumous founder of the Committee
for the Free World.

These mutually agreeing images of the man are a serious nuisance and an obstacle to proper appreciation. Orwell stands now where he never wanted or expected to be
—almost above reproach. What, or which, are the qualities
that we treasure? It might be easiest to begin by admitting
what Orwell was not. For one thing, as already stated, he
was certainly not consistent. His writings between 1936
and 1940, in particular, show an extraordinary volatility.
He veered now towards straight anti-Nazism, now towards anarchism, then pacifism, varieties of *gauchiste* allegiance, and finally (with palpable relief) a decision to
support the war effort. Many of his least well-guarded
statements come from this period—he never actually proposed cooperation with antiwar fascists, and he never
quite said that the British Empire was on all fours with
the Third Reich (two allegations that have been made
against him). But he did flirt with a kind of nihilism because of his fear that another world war would (a) be
worse than any compromise, and (b) be directed by the
people who were most responsible for its outbreak. He was
not entirely wrong about either of these (especially (b)),
but his friends tended to wince at the letters they were
getting.

That specific period of mercurial polemic can be read
as a version of larger and more interesting inconsistencies.
Orwell was a convinced internationalist but an emotional
patriot. He was a convinced democrat and egalitarian, but
he often reverted or resorted to snobbery (especially of the
intellectual type). He thought that the United States was
an arsenal and ally of democracy, but he suspected its
global intentions ("advancing behind a smoke-screen of
novelists"), despised its mass cultural output, and never
showed the slightest curiosity about it or desire to visit it.
He was a materialist and a secularist—particularly hostile
to the Roman Catholic heresy—but had a great reverence

for tradition and for liturgy. He defended the heterodox and the persecuted, making a special effort for the least popular cases, but was prone to spasms of intolerance. One way of describing him, as well as of valuing him, would be to say that he was a man at war. There was a continual battle between his convictions, which were acquired through experience, and his emotions and temperament, which were those of his background and of his difficult personality. Large works on the famous Orwell-Blair distinction, most of them verbose and speculative, have been written to "explain" this simple point.

Orwell was conscious, at least some of the time, of the paradoxes in his style. He was, if anything, overfond of saying to people that they must *choose*. He chivvied and ridiculed the lovers of the middle ground and was often prey to a kind of absolutism, especially before and during the Second World War. When it was over, in 1945, he wrote in *Through a Glass, Rosily*:

> Whenever A and B are in opposition to each other, anyone who attacks or criticises A is accused of aiding and abetting B.

He added:

> It is a tempting manoeuvre, and I have used it myself more than once, but it is dishonest.

Here, however belatedly, is a recognition and a self-criticism. He may have sensed that the shaft about "aiding and abetting," so often used against himself and his fellow POUM dissidents in Spain, did not properly belong in his quiver. He might at times have relished using this moral blackmail against his old antagonists. At times, as he himself wrote of Swift, he may have been "one of those people who are driven into a sort of perverse Toryism by the follies of the progressive party of the moment." But, when he took an unfair advantage or employed a demagogic style, he knew that he was doing it. Here, I think, is part of the answer to those who blame him for getting a good press from the Philistines. Here, also, is part of the secret of his double reputation.

The occasional but still very salient element of nastiness and ill temper in Orwell's personality and in his prose is something that gives pain to his more peaceable admirers, such as Irving Howe. Orwell's asides about the "nancy poets" and his sniggers at the giggling, sandal-wearing Quakers are somehow at odds with the interminably reiterated image of his gentleness and decency. But perhaps if he had been all that gentle and humane he would not have had the spiteful, necessary energy to go for the hypocrites and trimmers of his day. Certain it is, though, that there are many critics alive and preaching who love him only for his faults.

Most conspicuous among these is Norman Podhoretz. Many conservative exegetes read Orwell as an anti-intellectual, concerned to defend the plain man against mischievous theory. This interpretation of him will never stale as long as there are people who believe simultaneously that (1) "The people" are wiser and more trustworthy than the egg-heads and (2) that it takes a really courageous intellectual to summon the nerve to point this out. Such intellectuals generally find themselves elsewhere, or downright opposed, when anything resembling a revolt or movement of real people actually takes place. This mentality defines the modern neo-conservatives—the Tories, as Orwell would have called them. In the personification, accurate as well as convenient, of the editor of *Commentary*, they have coated Orwell in sickly and ingratiating matter just as the other lot have heaped him with dead dogs. For example:

(i) The iron relationship Burke saw between revolution and the militarization of a country, each a side of the same coin, is highlighted by Orwell's treatment of Oceania's wars.

(ii) [Orwell] was a forerunner of neo-conservatism in

having been one of the first in a long line of originally left-wing intellectuals who have come to discover more saving political and moral wisdom in the instincts and mores of "ordinary people" than in the ideas and attitudes of the intelligentsia.

(iii) Michels saw what was coming in this respect at the beginning of the century, in the Socialist parties of Europe: in their ever-greater centralization of power and singlemindedness of dreams of use of this power. James Burnham made this fact central in his prescient and largely unappreciated *Managerial Revolution.*

This salad of misrepresentations has neither the venom nor the variety of its *marxisant* counterpart. But it is hardly less opportunistic or inventive. The first and last quotations come from Robert Nisbet, in his essay "*1984* and the Conservative Imagination" (published in *1984 Revisited,* edited by Irving Howe). The middle one is from Norman Podhoretz in the *Harper's* article already mentioned.

Podhoretz presents the least difficulty here. His essay claims Orwell for reaction, and relishes his attacks on homosexuals and dilettantes. It quotes, with particular savor, his review of Cyril Connolly's *The Rock Pool,* where Orwell allows himself to abuse those "so called artists who spend on sodomy what they have gained by sponging." It cites, as if it were to be taken literally, Orwell's remark that, "If someone drops a bomb on your mother, go and drop two bombs on his mother." (I should like to read Podhoretz's review of *A Modest Proposal.* It would probably be rich in keen, vicarious approval.) It consciously excerpts and garbles Orwell's piece on the need for European socialist unity in order to give the impression that he was an early supporter of American "peace through strength." For example, as I noted in a letter to *Harper's* (February 1983), on the question of America versus Russia, Podhoretz quotes Orwell as follows:

It will not do to give the usual quibbling answer, "I refuse to choose." . . . We are no longer strong enough to

[*371*]

stand alone and . . . we shall be obliged, in the long run, to subordinate our policy to that of one Great Power or another.

What Orwell had written, in his famous 1947 essay "In Defence of Comrade Zilliacus," was this:

> It will not do to give the usual quibbling answer, "I refuse to choose." In the end the choice may be forced upon us. We are no longer strong enough to stand alone, and if we fail to bring a West European union into being we shall be obliged, in the long run, to subordinate our policy to that of one Great Power or another.

In the same year he wrote that:

> In the end, the European peoples may have to accept American domination as a way of avoiding domination by Russia, but they ought to realise, while there is yet time, that there are other possibilities.

It seemed to Orwell that:

> Therefore a Socialist United States of Europe seems to me the only worthwhile political objective today.

I said earlier that all quotation is necessarily selective and out of context. But there is a sort of tradition that, when length or density of quotation obliges one to omit a few words, the resulting " . . ." should not deprive the reader of anything essential or germane. Podhoretz seems to me, by his inept ellipses, to have broken this compact with his readers in both letter and spirit. All in the name of Orwellian values . . .

Robert Nisbet is more scrupulous but no more useful. The idea of a genealogy connecting Orwell to Edmund Burke has at least the merit of originality. It also exploits the "large, vague" idea that Orwell is a part of some assumed English tradition. Only by his inspired attribution

to Burnham does Nisbet show himself to be altogether de-
luded. He does not know, or at any rate does not show
that he knows, that Orwell was intrigued by Burnham and
wrote a long pamphlet on his work. The pamphlet (*James
Burnham and the Managerial Revolution*, published by
the Socialist Book Centre, London, in 1946) finds Burnham guilty of power worship and distortion, and of a
poorly masked admiration of the very "totalitarian" ten-
dencies that he purports to abhor. Since I believe that it
is this polemic which, more than any other, marks off
Orwell for all time from his reactionary admirers, I'll go
on about it a bit.

Most of Orwell's most famous stands were taken on once
controversial issues that have been decided long since—the
Spanish Civil War, the Moscow Trials, mass unemploy-
ment. Only in his contest with Burnham does Orwell really
engage, before his death, with the modern questions that
still preoccupy us. (The antagonists were well matched.
Burnham liked to combat prevailing orthodoxy, had a piti-
less attitude to intellectual compromise, and was an ex-
Marxist with a good working knowledge of socialist
thought. In fact, when many of our present neo-conservatives praise Orwell, it is really Burnham they have in
mind.)

Like the Russophobes of the 1980s, Burnham assumed
that totalitarianism was more efficient, more determined,
and more self-confident than the weakly and self-indulgent
form of society known as democracy. He wrote contemptu-
ously of idealism, humanitarianism, and other hypocrisies,
which he equated with appeasement and saw as a means
of duping the masses. I cannot summarize his opinions better than Orwell did, but I'll "select" one quotation which
gives the flavor both of Burnham's book and of Orwell's
objection to it:

> Although he reiterates that he is merely setting forth the
> facts and not stating his own preferences, it is clear that
> Burnham is fascinated by the spectacle of power, and
> that his sympathies were with Germany as long as Ger-
> many appeared to be winning the war.

This was not because of any special fellow-feeling for Nazism on Burnham's part, but was the result of his conviction that countries like Britain were incurably "decadent." Orwell, who had flirted with this view himself at some points in the immediate prewar period, wrote of Burnham's line, "It is clear that in his mind the idea of 'greatness' is inextricably mixed up with the idea of cruelty and dishonesty."

Burnham borrowed lavishly from Michels and Pareto with his stress on the circulation of elites. (Neither Orwell nor Nisbet, incidentally, mentions the involvement of those two sapients with the later cleansing power of fascism.) In essence, the mentality in both cases contains the same contradiction. The "managerial" dictatorship will be leaner and meaner than flabby, sluggish democracy. But only an open society can allow real recruitment from the lower ranks, even of former dissenters. Burnham saw, eventually, that there was something self-defeating in the hierarchy and obedience of the fascist state. But this did not prevent him from grafting precisely the same attributes onto the Stalinist system, and warning of yet another decline of the West in the face of it. Present-day analogues of this mentality would be tedious to enumerate. Or, as Orwell commented:

> It is, therefore, not surprising that Burnham's world-view should often be noticeably close to that of the American imperialists on the one side, or to that of the isolationists on the other. It is a "tough" or "realistic" world-view which fits in with the American form of wish-thinking.

It's interesting, and perhaps important, to notice here that Orwell's critique of Burnham contains the seeds of his *1984*. A few citations should make this clear. In replying to Burnham's opinion that it is only the winning side that can define justice and morals, he writes:

> This implies that literally anything can become right or wrong if the dominant class of the moment so wills it.

[*374*]

Elsewhere he remarks:

> Jack London in *The Iron Heel* (1909) foretold some of
> the essential features of Fascism, and such books as Wells's
> *The Sleeper Awakes* (1900), Zamyatin's *We* (1923) and
> Aldous Huxley's *Brave New World* (1930), all described
> imaginary worlds in which the special political problems
> of capitalism had been solved without bringing liberty,
> equality or true happiness any nearer.

It was also, probably, in reaction to *The Managerial Revolution* that Orwell developed his idea of the trinity of Oceania, Eastasia, and Eurasia. Summarizing Burnham, he says, "The future map of the world, with its three great super-states is, in any case, already settled in its main outlines." He went on to scoff at Burnham's idea that the three would be Japan, Germany and the United States, because he did not share Burnham's view that the Soviet Union would be defeated any more than he shared his later view that it was invincible. Nonetheless, a thought seems to have been planted. Most appreciations of *1984* understate, if they do not ignore, the way in which permanent superpower conflict is made the necessary condition for the coercion and repression within. The Cold War, with its ancillaries such as the "military industrial complex" and the "permanent war economy" are, in all essentials, *Orwellian* concepts. And Orwell's own repudiation of Burnham prefigures this. It also affords some harmless amusement to the student of Professor Nisbet, who regards militarization as a function only of revolution, and who pleads Burnham with apparent innocence as a part of the Orwell tradition.

The most frightening moment in *Darkness at Noon* comes not when Rubashov is interrogated or when he hears of the torture of others, but when he ponders the possibility that "Number One" may after all be right. The worst moment in *1984* is not the cage of rats or the slash of the rubber truncheon but the moment when Winston decides that he loves Big Brother.

The essence of Orwell's work is a sustained criticism of servility. It is not *what* you think, but *how* you think that matters. What he noticed about the Moscow Trials, for instance (and long before there was any hard evidence), was the appalling self-abnegation of the "defendants." What he hated about the English class system was the fawning and the acquiescence that it produced among its victims. (The contemptible boy who felt that he deserved to be caned in "Such, Such Were the Joys" is the earliest symptomatic example.) What he disliked in intellectuals —not about intellectuals—was their willingness or readiness to find excuses for power. What he disliked most in prose was euphemism. It is decades now since Czeslaw Milosz wrote *The Captive Mind*, but one sentence there is especially apropos. Describing the Eastern European intelligentsia, Milosz remarked, "Even those who know Orwell only by hearsay are amazed that a writer who has never lived in Russia should have so keen a perception into its life." In some sense, Orwell *knew* what the actual texture of dictatorial collectivism would be. He knew because of a variety of things he had already seen—the toadying of the English boarding school, the smell of the police court, the betrayal of the Spanish Republic, the whining and cadging of the underclass, the impotent sullenness of colonized natives, the lure and horror of war fever, and the special scent given off by the apologist. Others may have had the same experiences, but in our time it was Orwell who knew how to codify his impressions into something resembling a system. He is quoted to the point of annihilation as having said that "good prose is like a window pane," but it might be fairer to say that his own writing resembles a mirror. Anybody looking into it and failing to find some reflected portion of the modern age, or some special personal inhibition about seeing it, is myopic. Many are the Calibans who detest the reflection, and many are the Babbitts who like what they see.

Take Orwell's remark, in the concluding sentence of "The Prevention of Literature":

At present we know only that the imagination, like certain wild animals, will not breed in captivity.

That is a looking glass, not a window pane. As a transparency, it fails: the imagination has been known to breed in captivity, and no doubt modern zoo keepers will coax even the rarest surviving creatures into doing the same. Nonetheless, there is both truth and beauty in the remark. The desecration of literature in Russia—one of its ancestral homes—is an instance. The emigration of genius from central Europe after 1933 is another. In his pessimistic mood, culminating in *1984*, Orwell seems to have believed in the almost literal truth of his aphorism. But, in his earlier essay on the literary dictatorship of Zhdanov, he was able to see a more hopeful side. A totalitarian society cannot *produce* any imaginative work; it can only *cause* it. Some achievements are quite simply beyond the tyrant, but remain, still, within the reach of the individual.

Would Orwell have remained a socialist? It may not be the decisive question, but it is an interesting one. He certainly anticipated most of the sickening disillusionments that have, in the last generation, led socialists to dilute or abandon their faith. To this extent, he was proof against the disillusionments rather than evidence for them. He hated inequality, exploitation, racism, and the bullying of small nations, and he was an early opponent of nuclear weapons and the hardly less menacing idea of nuclear blackmail or "deterrence." He saw how an external threat could be used to police or to intimidate dissent, even in a democracy. The spokesmen for our renovated capitalism, then, can barely claim that their pet system has developed to a point beyond the reach of his pen. Stalinism and its imitators have not striven to prove him wrong either. Cambodia makes his scathing remarks on Auden's "necessary murder" look pallid, while in China and North Korea the cult of Big Brother has far outpaced satire.

There exists a third school of Orwell that argues, more or less, that he would have remained as he was. Bernard

Crick, his thorough if uninspiring biographer, is a leading member of it. Irving Howe, the keeper of the keys (it would be hard to call him keeper of the flame) of moderate social democracy, is another. Lionel Trilling, who wrote the best review of *1984* on its publication, also saw in Orwell a confirming, undogmatic, sturdy, and (always that word) "decent" liberal. This opinion is unexceptionable, and those who hold it do not have to resort, as their rivals do, to distortion or caricature. The trouble is simply that they geld Orwell: make him into the sort of chap who should be taught to schoolchildren as a bland and bloodless good example. Stephen Spender evokes this fustian curriculum by his fatuous likening of *1984* to *Erewhon.* Howe rather complacently adds that we will end up with collectivism one way or another—the only question is whether it will be founded "on willing co-operation or on the machine gun." At least he borrows Orwell fairly and accurately here—the trouble is that we are left with an image of Fabian resignation and the prospect of good works.

Orwell detested the machine gun, but he wasn't an enthusiast for "willing co-operation" either. As much as he loathed the will to power, he hated and feared the urge to obey. For Orwell, as for Winstanley, Defoe, Cobbett, and Zola, it is the *lack* of power that corrupts. He is both a founder and member of a modern rebel tradition that, in political writing, comprises Victor Serge and Dwight Macdonald, Albert Camus and Milan Kundera.

REVOLUTIONARY REQUIREMENTS, ETC.

Dorothy Gallagher

"**D**uring my lifetime I have seen just about everything," said Vittorio Vidali on the occasion of his eightieth birthday. It was not merely an old man's boast. With equal truth he might also have said that he had done just about everything too.

Though he traveled widely, Vidali was not generally known outside Italy. A few radicals in the United States remember him as Enea Sormenti; in Russia some Bolsheviks who escaped the purges know him as Carlos; veterans of the Spanish Civil War speak of Carlos Contreras.

Vidali died in 1983, the same age as the century. He was not a tall man, but he was powerfully built, forceful in character, swift to action, intelligent and a riveting speaker. Had he been without politics he would have been an adventurer. As it was, he was an ideologue: by his own depiction a Stalinist. Last year one of the many volumes of memoirs that Vidali poured out during the last decade or so of his life was translated into English. It is his *Diary of the Twentieth Congress of the Communist Party of the Soviet Union* (Lawrence Hill & Co.; translated from Italian by Nell Amter Cattonar and A. M. Elliot), a personal document of that momentous event by a revolutionary to whom Stalin was the embodiment of revolution.

In his long life he had indeed seen just about everything. When Mussolini came to power in 1922, Vidali was attending Bocconi University in Milan, a student of accounting. He was already a communist and he fled Italy. He wandered Europe for a while; at the German frontier he was arrested and sent to prison. He was in Algeria when he learned that the Italian consulate was looking for him; with the help of some sailors he stowed away on the *Martha Washington*, which docked in New York on August 22, 1923.

Vidali lived in the United States for four years, using the name Enea Sormenti. Quite soon after his arrival he became Secretary of the Italian branch of the Communist Party in New York and editor of its newspaper, *Il Lavoratore*. Fascism was the overriding concern of Italian-Americans in the early 1920s. Vidali was active in the Anti-Fascist Alliance of North America, which began as a coalition of socialists, communists, anarchists and labor unions. By 1926 this precarious unity shattered as the labor delegates withdrew, charging the communists with setting up fictitious branches in order to increase their voting strength. Vidali-Sormenti was AFANA's new Secretary.

The Department of Immigration caught up with Vidali in 1926 and ordered his deportation. Vidali called on numerous defenders: Clarence Darrow and the American Civil Liberties Union appealed on his behalf, as did Carlo Tresca, the anarchist, Vidali's comrade in AFANA, who wrote that "The cause of Enea Sormenti . . . is the cause of liberty of all people." Appeals availed to the extent that Vidali was not returned to Italy, where prison or possibly death awaited him; he was allowed to leave the country voluntarily, which he did in July 1927. He chose Soviet Russia for his destination.

Vidali arrived in Moscow when the Russian party was already a battleground between Stalin and Trotsky. Two months later he left in a state of exultation. From Riga, he wrote to a friend in America. He spoke of his love for Russia and for its heroic people, of his belief in revolutionary Russia's "emancipating function for the international proletariat." He had had, he admitted, some brief disillusionments during his first days in Russia but these were soon stilled by his realization that they were "due to the petit bourgeois atmosphere that still had not disappeared from my soul. . . . One leaves Russia more happy to fight. . . . One must become an iron revolutionary with a creative mind. . . ." He advised his friend that "a Marxist has got to be a cold rationalizer. A Leninist must aim straight to his own goal. . . . In political life you need strength of will. . . ."

Vidali was hardly alone in being stirred by revolutionary Russia, but his was a nature attracted to absolutes. He "attended the program of one of the best academies" in

Moscow: "Many go [to Russia] and understand. And those that do not understand return home to fight against her. I have understood," he wrote.

As a revolutionary he went to Mexico where he met, among others, Diego Rivera, David Alfaro Siqueiros and the photographer Tina Modotti. In 1930 Vidali was recalled to Moscow; Modotti soon followed.

In 1931 when the Spanish monarchy fell Vidali was sent to Spain. He was there again in 1934, when the iron miners briefly took control of the province of Asturias, and in 1936 when the military rose against the Popular Front government. Now, as Carlos Contreras, Vidali was a prime organizer and the political commissar of that most impressive of Communist-led regiments, the Fifth Regiment.

Vidali wrote much about his years in Spain. Not unnaturally he gave himself a hero's role and there is no doubt that he was a physically courageous and powerfully persuasive leader. Those journalists who went to Spain identifying the Soviet Union with the interests of Spanish socialism admired Carlos greatly. Claud Cockburn described him as a "husky bull-necked man who combined almost superhuman driving power with an unbreakable gaiety. . . ." Anna Louise Strong quoted him on the formation of the "Steel" Company: "We decided to create a special [military] company which should give an example of discipline. . . . For this company we established special slogans designed to create an iron unity: 'Never leave a comrade wounded or dead in the hands of the enemy. . . .' 'If my comrade advances or retreats without orders I have the right to shoot him. . . .' "

By 1937 Vidali was known in Spain to be an enforcer of discipline, which meant, given the nature of Stalin's concerns, that he was involved in battles not only against Franco's troops and the Italian fascist army but also against those leftists in disagreement with Russian aims in Spain. The Spanish anarchists, the POUMists, all denounced as "Fifth Columnists" and "uncontrollables" by the communists, were, in the words of La Pasionaria, to be exterminated "like beasts of prey."

For Vidali's actual role, there appears to be only anecdotal evidence. Ernest Hemingway told the journalist

Herbert Matthews that the skin between the thumb and index finger of Vidali's right hand was badly burned due to the frequency with which Vidali had fired his pistol in the communist campaign against deserters and fifth columnists. Matthews later wrote about the massacre of hundreds of prisoners, perhaps a thousand, in Madrid's Model Prison: "I believe myself that the orders came from Comintern agents in Madrid because I know for a fact that the sinister Vittorio Vidali spent the night in the prison briefly interrogating prisoners brought before him and, when he decided, as he almost always did, that they were fifth columnists, he would shoot them in the back of the head with his revolver."

Enrique Castro, with Vidali a leader of the Fifth Regiment, later said that Contreras had personally executed Andres Nin, Political Secretary of the POUM. Men who had fought in Spain—Julian Gorkin of the POUM and Gustav Regler, the German communist writer, among them—believed for the rest of their lives that Vidali had a direct role in the murders of leftist dissidents.

In early February 1938, Catalonia fell to Franco's troops. As the population fled ahead of the approaching army, Tina Modotti, who had been in Spain since 1934, sat alone at an outdoor café. According to Modotti's biographer, Mildred Constantine, an old friend from Mexico, Fernando Gamboa, passed by and asked what she was doing. She was waiting for Carlos to come through with the Fifth Regiment, Modotti said. Gamboa walked on, later recalling, "It was more or less about six in the evening, the sun was shining but gave no warmth . . . the winter sun, the peasants escaping from the mountains, the army retreating and the image of Tina, sitting alone . . . sitting alone and waiting . . ."

On his eightieth birthday, forty years later, Vidali recalled only communist glory in Spain. Hundreds of fascist planes had bombed the International Brigade positions at the battle of the Ebro: "We had already begun to say, 'It's all finished. They are all dead. There isn't one soldier left to fight. We have no reserves. This area is lost to us.' Everyone appeared to be buried in the mud. But suddenly we saw—living bodies arise from that mud as if from nowhere. Men covered with mud and blood . . . And those men formed a company and marched once more against the enemy. . . . Look, those are the communists; when you think they are dead they turn out to be more alive than ever!"

Vidali was wounded in Madrid when the city fell in November 1938; five months later he and Modotti managed to get out of Spain and find their way to asylum in Mexico, where Modotti died in 1942.

In Mexico Vidali was officially attached to the communist newspaper *El Popular*; less officially he was a member of the staff of Constantine Oumansky, NKVD chief for North and Latin America. After the Nazi-Soviet pact was signed in August 1939, the United States Office of Naval Intelligence reported that Vidali was a principal contact between Mexican communists and German agents; and in May 1940, when the first attack was made on Leon Trotsky's life—for which David Alfaro Siquieros was arrested—Vidali's name was openly mentioned as an organizer of the attempt. No action was taken by the Mexican police, but the story of his involvement was repeated often—by Jesús Hernandez, once Minister of Education in the Popular Front Government, by Julian Gorkin and by General Valentine Gonzales, *El Campesino*.

I first became aware of Vidali's existence while working on a life of the anarchist Carlo Tresca. The lives of the two men—both Italian-born, both revolutionaries— had been entangled at certain points, so for a time I followed Vidali's career as closely as I did Tresca's. By the mid-thirties the assassinations of anarchists in Spain and the Moscow trials had caused Tresca to break his relations with the communists and become their insistent opponent. In 1942 he turned specifically on Vidali. In his newspaper, the *Martello*, Tresca identified "Commander Carlos" as the head of "a band of assassins [who] work in Mexico for Stalin . . ." Tresca's concern at that moment was that a communist takeover was being planned in Mexico of the antifascist organizations which would have a voice in the postwar reconstruction of Italy. In Mexico, the communist-led Garibaldi Alliance responded by asking the Italian-language communist newspaper in New York to publish a defense of Vidali, who had been basely slandered by "Carlo Tresca and other Trotskyites using methods typical of agents of Mussolini, Hitler and Franco." Tresca was murdered in January 1943, after telling several friends that Vidali was in New York. He had said: "Where he is, I smell murder." Many people accused Vidali of having a hand in the murder, though my research has convinced me that Tresca's death had its origins in another quarter.

Vidali returned to Trieste in 1947. After the break between Tito and Stalin, Radio Belgrade reported rumors that Vidali was planning Tito's assassination. An American journalist interviewed Vidali in 1950 and was told by him, "The Yugoslav people will handle [Tito], not Vidali." In answer to other questions concerning Trotsky and Tresca he said: "Wherever I happen to be they always say I'm organizing agents to kill some anti-Soviet personality. . . . I don't believe in killing opponents of the Soviet Union through my own actions. Tresca always had a wild imagination."

Vidali served as a communist deputy from Trieste beginning in 1958, and later as a Senator until 1968. Until his health began to fail he often made speeches throughout Italy condemning the terrorism of the Red Brigades. As an old man he was an indefatigable teller of stories about his life; he took on the persona of a fierce yet lovable old revolutionary. When the time came to mark his eightieth birthday, children embraced him, a young girl presented him with a bouquet of flowers. And when he spoke, it was with some concern for his place in history. "During my lifetime I have seen just about everything. I was thinking about all that in these last few days: this is the fortieth anniversary of the assassination of Leon Trotsky. And after forty years, the international press continues to peddle the story of my participation in that murder. They have created a legend which only now, through my books, I am trying to put an end to: the questions of the murders of Tresca, of Nin, of Trotsky. And I will have to continue to write because, as you know— slander, slander—they will continue to slander, and some of it will be effective . . . sixty-three years of political activity constitute an enormous volume, and my life is an open book. . . . Naturally this book is badly written in some parts, incomprehensible in others, full of errors, erasures, notes. . . . In these sixty-three years I believe I have always done my duty. . . . I was a [Stalinist] for thirty or forty years. . . . I must still struggle against the remnants of Stalinism in myself. . . ."

That is the bare outline of Vidali's life, and it brings me to his *Diary*, written from notes made contemporaneously with the Twentieth Congress and first published in Italy in 1974.

Vidali arrived in Moscow in February 1956 with some foreboding. Neither he nor the other foreign delegates to the Congress would hear Khrushchev's secret speech denouncing Stalin, but Vidali knew that something was in the air. He read the signs accurately—no portraits of Stalin at the meeting hall, speeches that referred to a "certain person" who had fostered the "cult of the individual." Hard as it was for him to believe, it seemed that the master purger was about to undergo a purge himself. Vidali records the meetings he attended, the movies and plays he saw. But the essence of his *Diary* is in his conversations with old comrades and his own musings on earlier days; his recollections only miss being admissions that what he was hearing was not exactly news to him.

Of course his old comrades had aged a great deal. Yelena Stasova, once Lenin's secretary, later accused of Trotskyism by Stalin, tells him that tens of thousands have suffered execution, prison and exile under Stalin's reign. Of their friends, Stasova says, many are dead; the few still alive are "human wrecks" from the suffering they endured. Further, she says, the assassination of Kirov in 1934, which Stalin had used to justify the purges, had been arranged by Stalin in the first place. Vidali finds it difficult to sleep that night. He was "speechless," he writes, "horrified . . . all of this is fantastic, atrocious."

The next day he met with another old Russian friend whom he had known in Spain, and he asked about the Russian officers they had known there: Pavlov, Goriev, Berzin. Dead, almost all of them dead, he is told—though he could not have been in ignorance. "Shot as traitors for having plotted against the Soviet state." Stalin devastated the army, the old Russian says, even though he knew that Germany would attack Russia.

The atmosphere in Moscow has certainly changed since the old days, Vidali reflects. In those days he and his comrades spent the evenings in talk, singing and drinking until they "went to bed filled to the brim with sentiments of international solidarity." He is referring to the 1930s here, but it is difficult for the reader to reconcile that happy recollection with Vidali's memory that in 1934, having come under suspicion by Yagoda, deputy head of the secret police, he himself barely escaped Russia alive.

He goes on musing, naming the dead to himself: Willi Muenzenberg, expelled as a Trotskyite, found dead in 1940; Bela Kun, Tukhachevsky, Rosengoltz, Rykov, Bukharin, all designated as "monsters" by Stalin; Mayakovsky, whom he met in 1930, shortly before the poet's suicide. Old comrades from International Red Aid: "I could still see their faces: Shevlova, Lawrence, Eveline . . . many, many others; all of them had been arrested and condemned, some to death, others . . . in prison or concentration camp."

As the Congress goes on, Vidali grows morbid with his thoughts. He counts the days until he can leave Moscow, though, oddly, he wonders why he is "fed up and depressed" when he knows that, after all, the socialist system is going forward. True, Stalin intensified the repression. But, "Was it really necessary to resort to death?" he wonders. "Couldn't they have acted as had been done in Lenin's day? Discuss." Could it be that Arthur Koestler was telling the truth in *Darkness at Noon*?

Vidali rallies. Who *is* this Khrushchev, anyway? "Who knew him until recently? . . . In fact it was Stalin who discovered [him] and guided him with a fatherly hand." Marx was right. Doubt everything. "And begin by doubting the present critics of Stalin and their actions." Who knows that Stalin would not be rehabilitated some day, just as those he condemned are now being rehabilitated?

Before leaving Moscow to go back home to Trieste, Vidali met again with his old comrade Stasova. He complained to her that not enough guidance was being given to the foreign delegates who, after all, would be required to explain matters when they got home: "We could explain everything with . . . dialectics," he pointed out; "we could justify many things by speaking about history, about revolutionary requirements, about the struggle of the new against the old, etc."

Vidali regained his equilibrium; dialectics, history, revolutionary requirements, "etc.," enabled him to explain away what he had been told in Moscow. To his constituents in Trieste he said that it was necessary to draw a balance sheet on Stalin who, while he undoubtedly committed errors, even crimes, had also led the Soviet Union in triumph through the sieges of history.

Vidali's equilibrium is echoed by Robert G. Colodny, formerly of the Fifteenth International Brigade, who has written the introduction to Vidali's memoir: "That Red Star which in your youth just appeared on the horizon now moves toward its meridian. And in years to come, Carlos, when your grandchildren are as weighted with the years as you are, they will be able to say, there was a man who spoke; there was a man who pioneered the way."

Etc.

THE CULTURE GULCH OF THE Times

John L. Hess

Publish or perish.

It's a competitive world.

The very survival of your educational institution may depend on your skillful use of modern marketing and advertising techniques to help fill classrooms this fall.

One marketing tool that's targeted to exactly the people you must reach . . .

The New York Times
1984 Summer Survey of Education
Sunday, August 19
(Advertising closes Friday, July 27)

Your advertising, published in this special section, delivers 4,000,000 New York Times readers nationwide — men and women who know the value of education. And who can afford today's spiraling costs, too.

The New York Times, 1984.

It is hard to exaggerate the influence on our culture of *The New York Times*. The above advertisement may have succeeded; that special section probably did not deliver anywhere near four million readers, affluent or not, and the survival of colleges may not have hinged on their buying space in it. But it's not so farfetched. An ad in the *Times* every day is a costly necessity for New York theaters, its best-seller list controls displays and sales in bookstores around the country and, professionally speaking, its notices are matters of life and death for serious workers in all the arts.

Many grumble about the *Times*, but few care to do so on the record. One established journalist told me about this project: "It's a piece I could not write. I have a book coming out." That he should fear reprisal would surprise no one familiar with the recent behavior of *Times* Execu-

[388]

tive Editor A. M. Rosenthal, summarized in a tabloid's headline: "Abe Doesn't Take Prisoners." Even praise herein of worthy survivors at the *Times* might cause them harm. So in the article that follows I withhold some anecdotes as traceable to them and grant most sources anonymity. I can only vouch for my accuracy and my biases as one who worked for the *Times* from 1954 to 1978 in a variety of posts, often rewarding, whose only ground for complaint is a conviction that the paper has not lived up to its best traditions.   J. L. H.

•

When Paul Valéry was asked who was the greatest nineteenth-century French poet, he replied, "Victor Hugo, *hélas.*" The question which is our greatest newspaper must also be answered: *"The New York Times,* alas."

So wrote Dwight Macdonald in *Esquire* in 1963 in a brilliant dissection of the cultural coverage of the *Times* and particularly its *Book Review,* which he showed to be stupid, boring, badly written and relentlessly middlebrow. It was a paper whose editorials had expressed nervousness about Picasso and Joyce, whose Sunday tyrant, Lester Markel, was "a perfect genius of Philistinism," whose daily reviewers could call Faulkner overrated and Herman Wouk "a far finer novelist than his numerous detractors admit" and whose drama critic could be described as "conducting his education in public."

Conceding that the turgid news columns of the *Times* did offer a considerable supply of facts for the patient researcher, Macdonald thundered: "But a critical judgment is not a fact and the way in which it is expressed is inseparable from it, indeed *is* it. Here the intellectual mediocrity that has always characterized the *Times* becomes a clear and present danger."

Momentarily, he relented. "The *Times* isn't much of a help in arts and letters," he wrote, "but neither does it exploit them in the slick, smart, knowing manner that is now common among our more lavishly produced weeklies and monthlies," offering a choice of "rustic honesty against sophisticated duplicity."

Then he turned gloomy again: " 'You know, it is getting better,' people have been saying to me for some thirty-five years now. 'Look at that piece by X last week; not bad at all, really. And now Y and Z are writing for it.' " Macdonald said he had shared that illusion, especially when he and other *"Partisan Review* types" were asked to write for the *Book Review,* and again when Harvey Breit was editing it. But these were interludes. "No," he concluded, "it isn't getting better. It may have gotten worse."

He compared the Christmas issue of 1912, which had pieces by G. K. Chesterton, Bernard Shaw, Walter Lippmann, Ludwig Lewisohn and Louis Untermeyer, with the Christmas issue of 1962, in which "the agreeable [Edward] Weeks was the closest approach to a name."

Plus ça change . . . In the more than two decades since Macdonald's jeremiad, a dramatic transformation has swept that sector of the *Times* which its toilers call Culture Gulch. And in that time, many have said, "But you must admit it has gotten better." Like Macdonald, I reply with a symbol spanning half a century: In the mid-1920s, the *Times* subsidized Admiral Byrd's expedition to the South Pole; in the mid-1970s, it subsidized an expedition to photograph the Loch Ness monster. No, the *Times* did not get better. It got worse.

A myth has arisen that the great changes of the 1970s— the vast expansion of what broadly may be called cultural reporting in a Section C of the daily paper and its consolidation with a jazzed-up *Sunday Magazine, Arts and Leisure* section and *Book Review* under Executive Editor A. M. Rosenthal—were the result of financial necessity. Tom Wicker, who had been elbowed aside by Rosenthal in a struggle for power, has generously said of the transformation, "In many ways, it saved the institution." Yet myth it is.

When Dwight Macdonald was writing, the *Times* was already dominant in the richest metropolitan market in the world. The other standard-size New York dailies were dying. The tabloids were and are irrelevant—indeed, when the *Daily News* was on the verge of extinction a couple of years ago, an editor of the *Times* declared that he hoped it would survive because the *Times did not want its readers.* He meant of course that its *advertisers* did not want those readers; that an editor would see it the same way illuminates the direction in which the *Times* has traveled.

A newspaper that holds a monopoly in its area is a machine for printing money. The *Times* was such a machine in the 1960s. In fact, it did not make much money. This was in part because its publishers were not good businessmen; they built a thirty million dollar plant and tore it down, they sent incompetents to manage new editions in Los Angeles and Paris which failed, and they foolishly incurred long and futile strikes. A more creditable reason, however, is that they were not particularly interested in making money. They were dedicated to putting out a great newspaper whatever it cost.

That has to explain why the *Times* survived. The *Herald Tribune* was far livelier, better written and better edited. The composer Virgil Thomson, who was one of its music critics, explained recently that its publisher, Ogden Reid, loved fine writing, whereas the *Times* "is deeply suspicious of intellectual distinction." It was also suspicious of color and personality. ("We had a great human-interest story going there," a rewrite man growled one night, "but the desk caught it just in time.") It is related with condescension that founder Adolph Ochs long resisted the introduction of a crossword puzzle on the ground that the *Times* was not an entertainment sheet. Yet surely it was his stuffy dedication to "All the news that's fit to print" that saved the *Times*. In a world in turmoil, middle-class readers found its endless gray columns a reassuringly unchanging supply of facts. And the advertisers followed, perforce.

Even Macdonald half accepted the notion that the *Times* had to pretty up. While mocking the choice of illustrations in the *Book Review*, he said wistfully, "Only people interested in books would plow through a picture-less review section." Yet consider the *Wall Street Journal*. At the close of World War Two, with ten times the circulation of the *Journal*, the *Times* was the nation's dominant business newspaper. It also was investing in facsimile transmission with the aim of becoming the first national daily. But its business reporting and editing were atrocious and its technology faulty. With first-class journalism

[*391*]

and competent technology, the *Journal* overtook and sur-passed the *Times*—without ever compromising its tomb-stone makeup.

So, contrary to myth, the *Times* did not have to take the primrose path. With a monopoly on its market, it could have kept its gray makeup and its dedication to straight news, and tried to improve its writing. Again, contrary to myth, the decision to do otherwise was not Rosenthal's but Arthur Ochs (Punch) Sulzberger's.

Young Punch had a reputation as a lightweight. On his father's retirement as a publisher in 1961, he was passed over in favor of a brother-in-law, Orvil Dryfoos, but on Dryfoos's untimely death two years later, the family de-cided that Punch could not be slighted again. Punch set out to prove that he had the stuff to be a captain of in-dustry, and he did. He made the Times Company one of the Fortune 500, a communications empire. But at the start, its absurdly low per-share earnings gave it few bargaining chips for the merger game. He needed to remedy that.

His model seems to have been money machines like the *Miami Herald*, the *Los Angeles Times* and the *Washing-ton Post*, fat with all manner of sections stuffed with lucra-tive advertising. But the *Times* presses could only print ninety-six pages. Punch took the momentous decision to adapt them, at considerable cost, to print up to one hun-dred twenty-eight. He also set up task forces that would, in the current management fad, brainstorm in motel re-treats to plan the *New New York Times*. The group that pondered the future content of the paper was headed by his new managing editor, A. M. Rosenthal. It was called the Product Committee.

One of the first signals to the staff of the change to come was hearing editors refer to our paper as "the product." Another sign was the appearance on the managing edi-tor's desk of *Women's Wear Daily* and *New York* maga-zine. *Women's Wear* was offering a new service to the fashion trade: bitchy gossip and advice on what the Beau-tiful People were doing. It told garment makers and visit-ing buyers which discos, resorts, shows, performers, res-taurants and even foods and drinks were *in* or *out* this season. Clay Felker of the defunct *Herald-Tribune* took these services, a dash of New Journalism and a pinch of investigative reporting and created *New York* magazine, a sensationally successful vade mecum for what was then called the "upwardly mobile" and now would be called the Yuppies. Eyeing the demographics, the chairman of the *Times* Product Committee was frankly admiring. When, years later, Stephanie Harrington of *New York* asked Rosenthal if he hadn't been influenced by Felker, he replied: "You bet your sweet life!"

R osenthal and his team, the most intellectual of whom was a former Broadway reporter named Arthur Gelb, never mastered the glitzy flair of Felker (nor did Felker's successors at *New York*, alas), but as ever the *Times* made up in quantity what it lacked in quality. The first vehicle of its Felkerization was the daily Section C, and particularly its *Living/Style*, *Home* and *Weekend* editions. When in 1976 Rosenthal took control of the Sunday department as well, with its *Magazine*, *Book Review* and *Arts and Leisure* section, he became the most powerful figure in cultural journalism.

Looking at the results a year later, Earl Shorris commented in *Harper's*: "Two themes carry through all of the new or revised sections: gossip, which is a service to the mean-spirited, and acquisitiveness, which is a service to the envious." But the *Washington Journalism Review* was more admiring:

> With [the new sections] Abe Rosenthal made that dull, diligent gray lady fashionable. You can take her to a dinner party now, and instead of just going on about the finance minister of Iraq, she discusses food, clothes and decoration—gourmet food, the most elegant clothes, the most tasteful decoration. Under Rosenthal the *Times* learned its way around the Hamptons, around Soho. The paper now goes to auctions and cabarets. It has a marvelous recipe for Pintade au Vin Rouge. "For some people Craig Claiborne is now the most important writer in the paper," says [James] Reston, uncritically.

Food, clothing and décor as cultural news—why not? That the review of an expensive restaurant should receive more space and editorial concern than that of a new symphony may be only a quibble. The joke on the Yuppie readers, including the *Washington Journalism Review*, was that the elegance and taste were spurious and at times meretricious.

Claiborne, for example, enlisted as his partner the executive chef of Howard Johnson's, and they did not disdain to plug Howard Johnson's canned beef gravy. The Claiborne style was women's page twitter: ". . . quite swallowable" . . . "wonderfully versatile, if not to say sublime" . . . "the vegetables with which we dipped were eminently serviceable" . . . "since we are enthusiastic in depth for the cooking of China, Mexico, India and so on, we find fresh coriander absolutely essential to our peace of mind" . . . "An untrimmed sandwich is in my eyes vulgar, crude and uncouth." The theme, the essential ingredient of "elegance" at the *Times* today, is money—the infamous Page 1 $4,000 dinner for two, the homey meal for eight at $900, a full-page *Magazine* spread on what to do with leftover caviar (one recipe calling for a full pound).

The Claiborne style is much admired in Culture Gulch. A recent *Home* section featured the décor of a nouveau milliardaire's private jet, including sculpture by Rodin, Brancusi, Moore and Giacometti—the last in the plane's toilet. It said he wouldn't fly without a supply of his favorite hors d'oeuvres: Doritos with peanut butter and jelly. The high life, *quoi*. Helpful service pieces for the newly affluent are headlined "Life With a Live-In Servant" or "Putting the Pool Under Glass: A Benefit Is Year-Round Use." These people need help. They are informed about the entry of custom bathroom plumbing into living spaces, about the chic tenement look, and about a beach house that mingles "seriousness and whimsy, dignity and playfulness" and "while deferential to the sea, manages not to roll over and play dead beside it." A sample lead: "Have you ever wondered how television stars on the way up live?" Another feature, about a decorator setting up a party at the Metropolitan Museum of Art, opens: "How dare he rival the masters, this blue-eyed son of Greek parents, this Christos Giftos, mounted on a ladder, his face buried in blossoms?" How dare he, indeed?

Serious problems were not excluded from the new

New York Times. A *Magazine* piece headed "THE
SQUEEZE ON THE MIDDLE CLASS" described the
effect of inflation on a young, childless suburban couple
earning only $60,000 a year in 1980 dollars. But it ex-
punged the lower classes—those unlikely to shop at
Bloomingdale's. Space for city news was cut hard and,
worse, limited to zones of affluence. When I asked at a
staff meeting in 1976 why we had a correspondent in
exurban Suffolk County but none in the Bronx, Rosenthal's second-in-command, Seymour Topping, replied:
"We have more readers in Suffolk." This seemed to me a
non sequitur; the *Times* then had four correspondents in
Africa. The Bronx was burning, a big story, but Bloomingdale's was not interested, so neither was the *Times*. Soon
afterward, it sent a second reporter to Suffolk and a dozen
more to nearer suburbs, but none to the Bronx. Not long
ago a dispatch from Mount Vernon, which borders on the
Bronx, identified it as "this suburb of Manhattan," and a
dispatch from Grenada helpfully described it as the size
of Martha's Vineyard—which is also, it did not say, the
size of Queens. . . .

Rosenthal was pleased to repeat something that Harrison Salisbury, his gentle and unsuccessful rival for the
top news job, had told him: "Well, Abe, you're gonna be
the first managing editor of the *New York Times* who will
have to worry about money." Salisbury, however, was
worrying about the news-gathering budget; Rosenthal
was the first managing editor to worry about the bottom
line, profits, and to consider advertising and demographics
in shaping news strategy. He said Clay Felker "was the
best originator of service material I've ever seen. He used
to drive me out of my mind!" Under Rosenthal's direction,
service material drew a flood of ads. Profits soared, and
Times stock was split three for one.

Oddly, Rosenthal's team never mastered a new kind
of service material, consumer reporting, which was
being taken up by the best media around the country. A
series of reporters were assigned by the *Times* to the consumer beat, but crashed on the editors' insistence on im-
partiality. An early casualty, Frances Cerra, has written in
Quill: "The *Times*, probably more than any other news-

paper, has enshrined the goal of objectivity to the point where it has become a muzzle upon its reporting staff." She eventually quit after a piece of hers was killed that accurately foresaw the economic disaster of a nuclear power project on Long Island and she was ordered off the topic as biased. A preferred successor wrote an editorial in 1980 headed, "So It's a Carcinogen, But How Bad?" A nice headline in 1984: "Science Meeting Hears 2 Sides of Toxic Waste." *That's* balance.

Objectivity was only one of the traditional values of the *Times* that Rosenthal pledged to preserve while adding revenue and readers. He told Stephanie Harrington that he hoped the *Magazine* would thenceforth "have the highest intellectual content in the world." This was apparently an allusion to the dullness and predictability for which it had been celebrated. An old joke had it that Lester Markel made Barbara Ward rewrite an article seven times, and published all seven drafts. But Markel's *Magazine* was serious. Under Rosenthal, it would run a hard-breathing cover story on the "real" Cary Grant—his ineffable charm, his trips on LSD, his lifelong *fear of girls!* The piece was one of several reprinted in *US*, an inferior imitation of *People* magazine launched by the Times Company. (As noted, the *Times* never did manage a flair for vulgarity; *US* lost money until it was sold to a more efficient entrepreneur.) An *US* editor, looking back at the Grant story, said, "It was just right for *US*—not quite up to *New York* magazine."

But it was quite up to the Sunday *Times Magazine* under Edward Klein, a Rosenthal recruit from *Newsweek* who abruptly replaced the serious-minded Lewis Bergman. "Under Lewis," an editor said, "words and ideas mattered. Under Ed, the thing is not to get Abe mad." Friends of Rosenthal and Gelb, such as Beverly Sills, Mike Nichols and Joseph Heller, and conservative public figures such as Henry Kissinger, Jeane Kirkpatrick, Edward Koch and Pat Moynihan were assured of admiring coverage, while Bella Abzug, for instance, in her race with Moynihan, would be denigrated in pictures and prose. Two of the most notorious covers of the Rosenthal-Klein era were those on the party-giving fashion designers, the Oscar de la Rentas, headed "Living Well Is Still the Best

Revenge," and on Jerzy Kosinski, of which more later.

"The emphasis now," the anonymous editor said, "is on how the *Magazine* looks. We'll print the most appalling shit if the art is good. You get a good picture for the cover, then you rush out a piece you might have thrown away. That's how 'Cambodia' happened—they committed the cover." The reference was to an absurd piece about a hike into rebel-held Cambodia. When Alexander Cockburn revealed in the *Village Voice* that paragraphs had been lifted from a novel by André Malraux, the *Times* ignored it until four weeks later the *Washington Post* exposed the whole piece as a hoax. Thereupon the *Times* performed a shocked autopsy of the affair, void of any self-criticism. Similarly, when Sophy Burnham advised Klein she had been plagiarized by Stephen Birmingham in a *Magazine* article, she had to threaten a lawsuit to get a grudging acknowledgment of the coincidences. And when Section C splashed the discovery of Egyptian hieroglyphics that confirmed the Biblical parting of the Red Sea, the exposure of the hoax in learned journals was never fully explained in the *Times*. As the anonymous *Magazine* editor put it: "I often reassure new writers: 'Don't worry, our standards are very low now.'"

Klein has been quoted as defining the standards thus: "If Abe likes it, I love it." William Honan, who directs Section C and *Arts and Leisure* under the title Culture Editor, has said much the same. And their loyalty is requited. For at least five years, the *Times* has been swept by wistful rumors that Klein was about to be fired for his latest gaffe. As this is written, the firing has not yet occurred. The consensus on the paper is that Rosenthal will not expose an error of judgment by sacking an appointee under fire; an office humorist suggests that Klein, aware of this, kept his place by committing a new horror whenever the memory of the last one had begun to fade.

A kinder explanation is that Rosenthal, a sentimental man, values loyalty above all other virtues. Only this can account for his appointment as editor of the *Book Review* of Mitchell Levitas, whose abrupt removal as metropolitan editor a while before had set off a champagne celebration by the city staff, and who had been credited with recommending the Cambodia piece to Klein. A writer said of the appointment, "It shows what Rosenthal thinks of books."

One of the *Review* editors said that Levitas had "an active, positive malice toward literary persons," that he "had no idea how to assemble a stable of good reviewers," that he was "trotting down to the Third Floor all the time" for approval and instructions, and that he was often overruled, which meant yanking a major piece near deadline. "I felt as though I was working on *Pravda*," the editor said. It was a sad echo of a comment by R. P. Blackmur in the *Kenyon Review* back in 1959: "It was not money that was needed by the managing editor . . . ; it was such a change of psychology as would permit him to appoint a strong and independent editor of the *Book Review* and then to abide by that editor's decisions."

That was almost the situation during John Leonard's editorship in 1971–75. Leonard recalls that he occasionally got flak from Dan Schwartz, the Sunday editor, as when he dedicated most of an issue to Neil Sheehan's passionate essay on Vietnam books. He thinks he was close to being fired for it, but raves in national media calmed Schwartz's nerves. There was no prior restraint, however, until Rosenthal took over the Sunday sections.

Leonard had meanwhile returned by choice to writing for the daily. He was probably the most brilliant and distinctive writer on the paper, and developed a wide following. But he also met growing editorial control. Early on, a piece of his about censorship in the Philippines was killed by James Greenfield, a Rosenthal factotum. Leonard revised it and slipped it to the *Book Review*. It is Leonard's view that nobody could get away with that now.

Under the new standards, politics and personal friendships and dislikes became decisive. Leonard reviews of a Lou Cannon book on Reagan and of Judith Exner's scandalous one on John F. Kennedy were killed, and his praise of a Nat Hentoff work was watered down, he says, "into a book report." Rosenthal told him his praise of I. F. Stone was excessive, and Honan, the Culture Editor, said of another review, "You can't call somebody a Marxist—it's libelous!" Gelb asked him one day what he was going to say about a Joseph Heller novel; when he expressed surprise at the question, Gelb explained that he was running a cover piece on Heller in the *Magazine*. Heller was a friend of Gelb and Rosenthal. So was Betty Friedan. When Leonard panned Friedan's revisionist book *The Second Stage*, Gelb protested, "This belongs on the editorial page!" Leonard was cut from two reviews a week to one. He finally quit.

D wight Macdonald was probably wrong to wish that the *Book Review* might become something like the *New York Review of Books*, whose birth he announced in his article. The *Times*, like its readers, has to be middle-brow, and its reviews should try to cover the news about books. But there is no excuse for its coverage to be boring, dimwitted and petty. As it often is.

The makeup has changed, but basically the *Book Review* is pretty much as Macdonald found it. He grumbled about the crass commercialism of the best-seller list and said the editors, who were rather ashamed of it too, planned to cut it from fifteen books to ten—cutting off the dog's tail an inch at a time, so to speak. Instead, they have computerized it and now list sixty-five best-sellers. (It's still controversial. One author has sued because his book sold 100,000 copies but never made the list; another, Stephen King, chortles that his *Pet Sematary* made the list before it reached the bookstores. But no matter.)

Macdonald quoted George Kennan as saying, "The letters are dull because they reject 'controversial' ones." More precisely, the rule still is that the *Book Review* prints no letter that reflects on the judgment of the editors. In 1978, after long protest, it published letters by Ellen Willis and Susan Sherman responding to an attack on a feminist novel—but it deleted their objection to the assignment of the book to an antifeminist ideologue and their charge of general hostility to feminist writing. (The editor twisted the knife by inserting the abjured titles "Mrs." and "Miss" in their letters.) In 1984, the *Review* published a cover piece on Ed Koch's *Mayor* by Gay Talese, Rosenthal's friend, biographer and admirer. ("In my lifetime," Talese had told *New York* magazine, "I don't know anybody who has the talent Rosenthal has as an administrator, writer and editor.") It was the only favorable review of that nasty book I have seen. It was, in fact, a rave, closing with this

[399]

comment on Koch's presidential dreams: "Why not, someday, the Jewish comic Mayor from New York—the man
who stood up to the unions, who restored fiscal sanity to
the budget, and who is the first white man in New York to
talk back to a black? Why not indeed?" Differing opinions,
including mine, were not published.

Selden Rodman told Macdonald his experience with
the *Review*: "When poetry started getting academic and
dull and I said so . . . I was no longer given poetry. Ditto
with art books—as soon as it was clear I was attacking the
Establishment (the MOMA, abstract expressionism, the
Greenberg-Hess axis) I no longer got art books." People
in all the arts still complain that Culture Gulch serves
mainly the big institutions and scants what is truly new.
An apparent exception was the pricey New York "avant-
garde," centered in a few uptown galleries and patronized
by such as Nelson Rockefeller. The critic John Canaday
didn't care for it; another critic was engaged to reassure
the art crowd and ultimately to replace him.

Two personal anecdotes: From Paris once, I tipped
New York that trustees of the Museum of Modern Art
were negotiating to buy the fabled Gertrude Stein collection and divvy it up among themselves and the museum.
Gelb replied that to print the story might cause the French
government to queer the deal. (I chided him that that
was none of our concern, to no avail.) Back in New York
in 1973, when Canaday blew the whistle on secret sales
of art by the Metropolitan Museum, I was assigned to
check his story; I found abuses even worse than he had
charged. It was a great series, which ran for months with
Gelb's support but then met increasing shortage of space
and complaints by Hilton Kramer and others in the trade.
I had to threaten to resign to get my last piece in the
paper. The gamy underside of the art biz has been largely
ignored by the *Times* ever since. First I and then Canaday
were persuaded to review restaurants.* Eventually we
both left.

---

* The editors did not consider the assignment a demotion. On the
contrary, it was accompanied by a pay increase and a substantial
expense account. Incidentally, the system of rating restaurants by
stars was extended to colleges in a *Times* guidebook that judged
campuses for ambiance among other qualities—not including food,
however.

Virgil Thomson jokes that the *Book Review* must alternate editors, because he finds about one issue in four interesting. Macdonald long ago noted that the *Review* lifted its sights during the brief reign of Harvey Breit, and always when it used British guest reviewers. "Even the *Times* can't get Englishmen to write badly," he said. Just so, the prose of Culture Gulch has lately been enhanced by such imports as the art critic John Russell, the drama critic Benedict Nightingale and the bookman John Gross. But Nightingale soon left.

At the time Macdonald was writing, it was almost unheard of for anybody to quit the *Times*. In the Rosenthal era, the departure of the best and the brightest has been endemic, and a customary salute to the parting by colleagues is a heartfelt "Congratulations!" One reason antedates Rosenthal but persisted: the inane editing. Renata Adler, who reviewed movies in 1968, has written: "The idea at the *Times* is that reviews are not edited at all, but the reality was a continual leaning on sentences, cracking rhythms, removing or explaining jokes, questioning or crazily amplifying metaphors and allusions." She cited a movie's reference to one Jean-Sol Partre, which an editor "helpfully explained in a parenthesis to be 'a pun on the name Jean-Paul Sartre.'" Everybody who writes for the *Times* has a thousand scars like that. A typical case in the paper before me as I write (August 30, 1984): "Mr. Gemayel, who neither drank nor smoked, married his wife, Genevieve, in 1934." The reporter whose name appeared on that article certainly did not commit that sentence. A piece of mine from Paris that referred to the Boul' Mich' came out reading Boulevard Michigan. An article of mine with the phrase "at a time when the stock market was going down" came out "at a time when, according to officials, the stock market was going down." This last is a remarkable example of the *Times*'s "objectivity" gone insane.

The conflict between writers seeking to express their individual talents and an army of copy editors dedicated to reducing them to gray homogeneity goes 'way back on the *Times*, but it turned bloody under Rosenthal. The upheaval of 1968 was a watershed. Then metropolitan edi-

tor, Rosenthal accompanied police officials to a disturbance at Columbia University and was horrified; he wrote
what young reporters considered to be a less than objective report. Later Anthony Lukas, one of the brightest,
publicly lamented that the *Washington Post* had been
able to cover the trial of the Chicago Seven "in a way that
has been almost impossible for those of us operating under
tighter restrictions." Lukas then chose freedom. In *New
York* magazine, Edwin Diamond reported that the reviews of John Leonard, Christopher Lehmann-Haupt and
Vincent Canby were meeting editorial objections, that an
interview of Jean Genet by Israel Shenker had been
killed (Genet deplored the repression of the Black Pan-
thers) and that a review by Clive Barnes of a play about
the Rosenbergs had been censored. This last led to the
gathering of a group of *Times* writers who obtained a
meeting with Rosenthal and underwent a stormy lecture.
"The Cabal," as it was called in an allusion to Rosenthal's
paranoia, soon subsided.

Diamond surmised that Rosenthal was feeling the heat
from Vice President Spiro Agnew, who (with William
Safire as his ghost) was denouncing the *Times* as the most
nattering of the nabobs of negativism, the most élitist of
the organs of Eastern liberalism. This underestimates Rosenthal's nerve, and his Archie Bunker standards. He found
Judith Exner's revelations about Kennedy's sexual con-
duct unfit to print even if true, and he paid Agnew an
unusual tribute that has not, I believe, been previously reported. When Agnew pleaded no contest to charges involving his taking of bribes, the *Times* Style Book had for
some years dictated that a convicted felon was not entitled to the dignity of a "Mr." Rosenthal could not so
denigrate a man who had been only the proverbial heart-
beat away from the Presidency of the United States. He
amended the Style Book on the spot. Since then, bowing
to the hobgoblin of consistency, the *Times* has Mistered
rapists, murderers, child-molesters and bribe-takers alike.

A "Cabal" of sorts reappeared in April 1978. It was a
case of history repeating itself, the second time as a
farce. The unlikely subject was *Dancin'*, a costly musical
mounted by the Shuberts and Columbia Pictures. It had
received considerable advance publicity in the *Times*, as

big-ticket shows do. Arthur Gelb, Rosenthal's minister in charge of all the cultural sections, ordered Richard Eder, the drama critic, to leave the choreography aside for separate, qualified treatment by the dance critic, Anna Kisselgoff. Eder recalls returning from the opening to find Gelb waiting for him. What did he think of the show? Eder looked surprised and Gelb said that he was thinking of running his review on the front page. (See Leonard above.) Eder said he had found some things good and some things bad; his review ran inside. It opened: "With appealing audacity, the proclamation is made right at the start that this is to be 'an almost plotless musical.' But it is like the frosting declaring its independence from the cake." It reported that there were "a few marvelous numbers, and a good many weak ones," but concluded that the show was "a gaudy mask covering nothing: a deification of emptiness." The next day, Eder heard nothing directly from management, but that office bearer of bad news, John Corry, told him, "Boy, are they mad." Their discomfiture was no doubt deepened by the Sunday report of Walter Kerr, which was headlined: "Dancin' Needs More Than Dancin'."

Times readers never did get an expert opinion on the dancin'. Kisselgoff's critical review was killed. It was this that sparked the second "Cabal"—that is, a letter signed by most of the *Times*'s critics, expressing a concern about editorial interference and requesting a meeting with Rosenthal. Instead, he called them in one by one and accused them of insolence and disloyalty, with intent to defame him by a leak to *New York* magazine. The story did not leak, and that was all there was to the second Cabal. Looking back on it, John Leonard says that what he now resents most was Rosenthal's and Gelb's assurance to him that Eder's job was safe and that he could write whatever he chose. "They lied to me," he said.

Eder recalls a series of complaints from Rosenthal and Gelb over the year following *Dancin'*.

"Abe told me I had an insufficent sense of the fun of the theater, I was too judgmental," he said recently. "I replied that there wasn't much fun to be had just then. When there was, I was happy to report it. I thought I was rendering a service in holding up a mirror. The reason it hurt is that I did love the theater. You have to be angry. . . . I said in a speech about then that the theater reviewer of the *Times* has to be ready to be fired, that the only way to do the job well is to be willing to lose it."

What appears to have been the last straw was the musical of *I Remember Mama*, starring Liv Ullman. It was another big and much publicized show, which Eder described as "not a marriage but a divorce of talents" and "a tedious failure." Still, the show sold lots of tickets, and the *Daily News*'s gossip columnist Liz Smith sneered that Eder could not pick a winner. Rosenthal called him in and offered him a demotion to second-string critic. He declined that and accepted an assignment to Paris instead, but resigned not long afterward and took his critical talents to the *Los Angeles Times*.

Many colleagues and competitors regard Eder as one of the most brilliant and thoughtful critics to have served the *Times* and the theater. The consensus is that, though there *was* pressure from the industry to oust him, what moved Rosenthal and Gelb in the end was their inability to control him and so to influence the theater, to reward people and shows that they liked. Gelb, himself a former Broadway news reporter, had once told Eder he loved the tension of opening nights when the *Times* critic dashed up the aisle and everybody else waited for his verdict, to know whether the curtain would rise again. This power (over serious plays if not fluff) has troubled many theater lovers including *Times* critics. Rosenthal and Gelb love it.

A veteran critic described the post-Eder situation this way: "When a show comes in produced by a bunch of investors from New Orleans and it stinks, the *Times* justifiably kills it. But when the networks and Broadway blow five million on a show and it stinks, the *Times* ties itself into knots to avoid saying so."

Along with others, this critic admired the knot-tying craftsmanship of Eder's successor, Frank Rich. He cited Rich's review of *Cats*, a dreadful British musical imported by the Shuberts in late 1982. Rich's lead said accurately that it would be around a long time—not because it was brilliant or affecting or "has an idea in its head," nor because of all the publicity, but because it "transports the audience into a complete fantasy world." "Whatever the other failings and excesses, even banalities, of 'Cats,' it believes in purely theatrical magic, and on that faith it unquestionably delivers." Beginning in the seventh paragraph, the show "curls up and takes a catnap" and we learn that the choreography "does not add to quality" and just about everything else stinks, but the review closes on "a theater overflowing with wondrous spectacle—and that's an enchanting place to be." The ads write themselves: " 'Theatrical Magic'—*Times*" or " 'Wondrous Spectacle'—Frank Rich."

"It's sad," the veteran critic said. "New Yorkers are wise to it, but out-of-towners see those ads and say, 'The *Times* likes it, let's go.' "

Knot-tying is a common practice at the *Times*. Many reporters play the official puff straight but tuck in a few unpleasant facts well down in the story. Combining praise and blame covers both flanks. One recent restaurant reviewer developed a sort of oxymoronic criticism: One place was "glowing and plush, if undistinguished," another was "undistinguished" but "bright and felicitous," a third "colorful and refreshing but head-splittingly noisy," a fourth "pleasant, comfortable and unprepossessing." In a fifth, the beef was "fine if served rare but dull if overcooked," while in a sixth it was the pasta that was fine "provided it is not undercooked or overcooked."

The most embarrassing episode in recent *Times* history began early in 1982 with one of those fan pieces that afflict the Sunday *Magazine*. This one was by Barbara Gelb, a frequent contributor who is also the wife of the *Times*'s minister of culture. It was about Jerzy Kosinski, the novelist and café-society character whose portrait in polo costume, bare to the waist, graced the cover. The piece said he'd learned to ride in a Polish orphanage, and recounted similarly improbable adventures in his escapes from Nazi and Soviet occupation, culminating in his emergence as a literary genius and the husband of an American heiress. Calvin Trillin has written that it was fortunate that Kosinski didn't tell Mrs. Gelb he was the long lost Princess Anastasia. Staff members now say Mrs. Gelb was quite aware of Kosinski's reputation as a fabulist and of the fact that he hired editors to vet his prose but decided it would be unkind to say so. A reason cited by others is a passage quoting a sick friend whom Kosinski had visited: "I've never experienced such solicitude from another man." The friend was not identified. He was Abe Rosenthal.

Three days after the Gelb piece appeared, Christopher Lehmann-Haupt reviewed Kosinski's eighth novel in the *Times* and observed, "The author's long affair with the English language is not going well." Nothing the author had done since his first, autobiographical novel, *The Painted Bird*, seemed to the critic to have any value.

The *Magazine* blurb was fading in memory when the *Village Voice*, four months later, ran a piece headed "Jerzy Kosinski's Tainted Words." In it Geoffrey Stokes and Eliot Fremont-Smith, a former *Times* critic, revealed that Kosinski's editorial help was more extensive than had been known, and hinted that it was not certain that he had actually written *The Painted Bird*.

Now, the *Times* has long regarded the *Voice* as unworthy of mention in its columns (a rule that was once laid down to me by Gelb). Not this time. Michiko Kakutani, a young reporter on the book beat, was assigned to expose the slander. After several weeks of investigation that included an encounter with Kosinski, she asked to be excused. John Corry stepped in to fill the breach.

It was a turning point in his career. Until then, Corry had been a bright writer on small matters, chiefly involving the Beautiful People. Earl Shorris had written in *Harper's* (October 1977): "John Corry's column is the paradigm of the new [*Times*] sections. He idealizes the rich with overt bootlicking, teaching manners and morals to ordinary people as Gucci teaches shopgirls their place by closing during lunch hour."

Corry took over the new assignment with enthusiasm. In a phone call to the *Voice*, which it recorded, he said: "Do you think the *Times* wants to rehabilitate Jerzy Kosinski? Sure, so do I. I want to exonerate him. He was slandered." The rehabilitation took the form of a six-thousand-word polemic bannered in *Arts and Leisure* on November 7, 1982: "A Case History: 17 years of Ideological Attack on a Cultural Target." Its thrust was that the *Voice* smear was only the latest in a long campaign mounted by the KGB.

The salvo shocked *Times* staffers and readers alike. The *Times* had a long tradition of professed objectivity. Rosenthal himself reminded the staff of that whenever a liberal bias seemed to him to have slipped past the desk, and Gelb, as noted, had told Leonard that his feminist opinion belonged on the editorial page, not in a book review. Another *Times* rule had been to regard outside criticism as beneath notice. Now, when Charles Kaiser wrote in *Newsweek* that the Kosinski blast had been "a spectacular example of overkill," columnist William Safire described Kaiser as a disgruntled former *Times*man, and Rosenthal told the Moonies' *Washington Times*, "I was happy to see him go." To many staffers, among them the most eminent, it seemed that an era of personal favoritism and spite had taken over a paper once dedicated to telling the news "without fear or favor."

John F. Baker of *Publishers Weekly* drew further implications. While saluting the *Times* as "the premier book review resource in the country" and its criticism as "generally intelligent," he wrote:

> But at a time when the *Times* seems to be growing increasingly conservative in tone—as indicated by such straws in the wind as its concentration on terrorism as a Communist monopoly and its highly equivocal attitude toward the nuclear freeze movement—publishers who specialize in books critical of the social and political status quo are beginning to worry.
>
> On several recent occasions we have heard complaints from such publishers that their books were either not reviewed at all or were relegated to a lower status than seemed appropriate (and in order to make clear that this is not a case of special pleading, it should be noted that other major book review sections gave the books in question the kind of space the publishers felt they deserved). We are not suggesting that anyone at the *Times* is deliberately ignoring or relegating to lesser review status books that advocate controversial or unpopular ideas; that may not even be necessary. When a certain kind of climate of opinion has been created, it tends to be self-perpetuating, in the sense that people working within that

climate learn to read signals and to second-guess themselves. In most ways that count, the *Times* remains a great
newspaper. But it would be a sad day for its readers, and
for the publishers who publish for its readers, if the kinds
of attitudes embodied in the Kosinski story were to become more firmly rooted.

The sad day was already there. An example prior to the
Corry piece was another splash in *Arts and Leisure*, by
Flora Lewis. It was about the forthcoming Costa-Gavras
movie *Missing*, a dramatization of a book about the murder of an American during the Chilean coup of 1973. Like
most critics, Vincent Canby would find the picture grip-
ping; Lewis saw it as a slander of the U. S. Embassy. Her
own bias is at least consistent. Thirty years ago, she wrote
a still memorable paean in the *Magazine* to the pistol-
packing U. S. ambassador who overthrew the last democratic government of Guatemala; in a 1984 dispatch she
referred to "the overthrow of Chile's pro-Soviet Government of Salvador Allende"—who was, of course, a democratic socialist. But in the old *New York Times*, reporters
with sympathies toward the Right might be offset by such
distinguished, if disparate, luminaries as Harrison Salisbury, David Halberstam, Homer Bigart and Herbert Matthews. Under Rosenthal, the foreign staff has been steadily
purged of liberals and loaded with Right-thinking ideo-
logues.

Culture Gulch was not neglected. Following his Kosinski exploit, the gossip Corry was promoted to TV critic
in charge of serious material and the able John O'Connor
was restricted to entertainment. Objectivity took on new
meaning. Corry denounced a balanced documentary on
the Alger Hiss case on the ground that, since the courts
had found Hiss guilty, any evenhanded treatment must be
ipso facto biased. On an Oxford Union debate between
Caspar Weinberger and E. P. Thompson, the peace acti-
vist, he wrote: "Mr. Weinberger makes a good case rather
poorly. Mr. Thompson, by contrast, takes a bankrupt case
and makes it rather well." Corry complained that *The
Day After*, ABC's drama on nuclear war, "engenders a
feeling of hopelessness" and "conditioned us to accept
disarmament, or at least, to call for a nuclear freeze." He

dissented from the notion that Walter Cronkite was a fair reporter, recalling that the fellow had said in 1968 that the only "rational" solution in Vietnam was to negotiate. "He virtually declared peace!" Corry exclaimed.

In the same column, Corry said: "A high point of this season's political coverage was David Brinkley's comment that 'a machine, an honest machine, is still the best way to run a city.' This viewer treasures the moment, not only because he agreed with Mr. Brinkley, but also because of Mr. Brinkley's style."

In this, Corry was agreeing not only with Brinkley but also with his superiors. In 1976, when I was trying to expose how thievery and waste had contributed to the near bankruptcy of New York, the editor in charge of city politics chided me, "Corruption is the lubricant of democracy." The next year, Stephanie Harrington commented in *New York* magazine (July 18, 1977): "The profiles of public officials served up by the paper would lead a visiting Tibetan to suppose that the city's political machinery runs on holy water." (Headline on a piece about Edward Koch, running for re-election in 1981: "Tough, Yet Benign Mayor.")

To be sure, this policy goes a long way back. Robert Caro's *The Power Broker: Robert Moses and the Downfall of New York* (Knopf, 1974) is a terrible indictment of the *Times*. Moses was the czar of New York from 1934 to 1968 and very nearly destroyed its physical fiber. During that time, when Moses was not writing for the *Times* he was being praised in it. "The *New York Times* fell down on its knees before him and stayed there year after year after year," Caro wrote. "The *Times* and other papers printed Moses's handouts as if they were gospel, fawned on him in thousands of editorials, brushed aside citizens with evidence and even proof of wrongdoing and put down those few on their staffs who itched to investigate what he really was doing."

This is not a digression. Surely nothing so profoundly affects our culture as architecture, zoning and transportation. When Moses was ravaging the city according to the dictates of pelf and modernism, Lewis Mumford was hurling imprecations from the *New Yorker* and Jane Jacobs fought him to a standstill in one corner of Manhattan, but their effect was marginal. "Unfortunately," Mumford said, "there is a huge vested interest in raising hell with nature, and there is very little money—in fact, none at all—in letting well enough alone." And besides, Moses and his bulldozers had the support of the mighty *Times*.

Moses is long gone, but nothing has changed. Zoning policy and development have in fact grown worse; hideous high-rises spread across a shrinking sky. It is an ill bird that fouls its own nest, yet the *Times* enthusiastically supports billion-dollar projects that will strangle its own neighborhood. In one of those demented exchanges of air space so popular with developers, the once handsome and rococo and now modern-uglified Times Tower is to be razed. One proposal is to put an 80-foot Big Apple in its place. The *Times* architectural critic, Paul Goldberger, gave it the treatment that Frank Rich would give a *Cats*:

> The Venturi plan is shocking, difficult to accept at first—and brilliant. Like the best sculpture of Claes Oldenburg, the apple has meaning as a symbol and as an abstraction, and the genius of this work lies in its ability to manipulate proportion and the element of surprise in such a way as to make us think of the apple as a monumental object, not as a common piece of fruit.

Goldberger is normally wary in his judgments, but he did boldly allow *Newsweek* to quote him as saying of Arthur Gelb, "He is one of those extraordinary forces, like Harold Ross must have been at the *New Yorker*." (Ross was of course the man who hired Lewis Mumford.) A colleague told Goldberger, "That's a Pulitzer quote," and sure enough the *Times* nominated him for, and he obtained, a 1984 Pulitzer Prize for criticism. The *Times* reported later that the Pulitzer Board had overruled its jury in granting the award for a novel. It did not report what was thought newsworthy elsewhere, that the board had also overruled its juries in ten of the twelve journalism categories, including the award to Goldberger.

In a kindly memoir of the *Times*, *Without Fear or Favor*, Harrison Salisbury offers a glimpse of Rosenthal, looking across the city room and asking, "Why do people hate me so?" Salisbury abandons the question right there, but the foregoing may offer some answers. We might also now, after twenty-two years, reconsider Macdonald's question: Which is our greatest newspaper? Well, surely the *Times* was not greater than the *Washington Post* in the year after Watergate; the *Times*'s reporting day by day is not distinctly better, and its judgment in news play is generally worse. (Stories like Reagan's joke about bombing Russia tend to get buried in the *Times* until other media demonstrate their importance.) The *Wall Street Journal* is more competent in its field, and perhaps overall. And a number of newspapers cover their own communities better than does the *Times*.

But Macdonald's question begged a larger one: Is our culture today capable of producing a great daily newspaper? The talent exists, surely. We also no doubt have many citizens of an intellectual stature comparable to that of the delegates to the Continental Congress—but we don't send the likes of them to Congress today, much less to the White House. A billionaire with vision might create a great newspaper some day. Pending that, here in our cultural capital, we are stuck with *The New York Times*. Alas.

DISHONORING *PARTISAN REVIEW*

Murray Kempton

I t was, as any schoolboy knows, Oscar Wilde who observed that every great man has his disciples, and that
it is usually Judas who writes the biography.

The Truants (Anchor Press/Doubleday) is William
Barrett's recollection of life at *Partisan Review* in the
1940s, and it is not without echoes of the testament
Judas might have written if he had allowed himself the
time for repose and reflection. Barrett does not mean to
be a Judas, to be sure. But then we are entitled to doubt
that Judas did, either, since his fee, while more than
enough to buy the rope, could otherwise barely cover
his passage and dinner on the road back to Nazareth.
Economic interpretations of a man's infirmities are only
too often caricatures. The Judas complex, while seldom
attractive, ought not to be thought rooted in dishonor.
It arises instead from the particular character disorder
that impels its victim to over-enthusiasm in the first
place and excessive recoil in the last. And Barrett's case
is more typical of an ailment that conduces less frequently to betrayal of one's friends than to a kind of
treason to one's younger self. Selling a friend to the
police for a pittance is only the most extreme of those
expressions of self-distaste that we can more sensibly
think mistaken than call indecent.

One of the pities about Judas's rush to degradation is
that it disqualified him for historical witness. The cross
was inevitable anyway: a Jesus scuttling from a SWAT
team is an unimaginable Christ. If Judas had simply carried his disillusionment to some private place and there
set it down as a reminiscence, we might know what we
can otherwise only suspect: that Jesus was over-suscepti-
ble to invitations to the tables of the rich; that the Holy
Mother exhibited pretensions to aristocracy inappropriate to a carpenter's wife; that James had a writing block,
Peter a spiteful tongue and John hallucinations. All that
would, of course, omit most of what is worth knowing

about the Holy Family and its apostles, but would have been a useful balance.

However, if *The Truants* provides the same sort of limited enlightenment that Judas's autobiography might have, there is all too little left to balance it against. Jesus has a living temple, but *Partisan Review* molders in a crypt to which fewer and fewer pilgrims repair.

The Truants has, at this writing, passed into its third printing. But then we live—and will die, I suppose—in a society whose educated inhabitants mark their arrival at entire cultivation by the moment when they are relieved from having to pay attention to the tale and are free to concentrate on gossip about the teller. The life of Delmore Schwartz, of all Barrett's *personae* his closest friend, is a parable of this intellectual disgrace. For everyone who cares to read the poems Schwartz wrote when he possessed his angels, there seem to be a thousand who delight to read about the years when his devils possessed him.

Philip Rahv and William Phillips were *PR*'s editors when Barrett worked there, and I can thank *The Truants* for jogging my elbow enough to send me back to Rahv's own work to rediscover that he was a very great critic indeed: not better than, say, Edmund Wilson, but different. Still, to read Rahv again makes it seem even less fortunate that the marketplace where the literate shop has too many customers who, given the chance to learn about Chekhov and Dostoevsky from Philip Rahv, prefer instead to learn about Philip Rahv from William Barrett.

Fortunately, there still survive all those issues of *Partisan Review* from the period of Barrett's lost commitment, and, the test of the fruit being finally in its taste, any urge to reproach him for lack of full justice almost gives way under the shock of how much more dimly they shine under scrutiny than they had in the memory. To go over them is to begin to understand that Barrett came to *PR* in an hour of crisis that was not confronted, but only drifted through in irrelevant quarrel until it arrived at the decline that we can best describe as one of those imitations of life not much different from its extinction.

I do not suppose that anyone who was not ruled by it in those days can properly appreciate the weight of *Partisan Review*'s authority in the three years before the European war began. *PR* broke upon us in 1937 just when the Moscow trials and the Spanish Civil War had cost the American Communist Party pretty much all the credit it had ever had with any element of its country's intellectuals except the coarsest.

The myth that sympathy with Stalinism continued, until the end of the 1930s, to hold any real sway over the more consequential exemplars of the American culture has endured so persistently that Barrett, who ought certainly to know better, treats it as fact. The reality is that, by any standard of quality, the American Communist Party and the amorphous horde it counted as its fellow travelers had only too few exhibits worth boasting about by 1935.

In philosophy, John Dewey was then his country's most eminent figure, and Sidney Hook and Ernest Nagel its most promising: all three adhered to the non-Communist left and the likes of Edward Berry Burgham could not plausibly be compared to them. Radical non-Stalinist criticism was represented by Edmund Wilson and Lionel Trilling, while the Communists could only serve forth Granville Hicks. As to the novel, we can concede Dreiser to the Communists only if we overlook the vagaries that made him a most erratic comrade. After that there is only Howard Fast, who would make the skinniest of lions in the path of James T. Farrell and John Dos Passos whose *U.S.A.* was permeated almost as much with distaste for the Communist Party as with protest against the American social system. The master workmen had defected by the middle 1930s, and only the journeymen remained. By 1937, even the less inert apprentices were straining against indenture.

It was upon minds already clearing and ready to look things in their face that *Partisan Review* fell like some grand illumination. Its first issue's lead article was André Gide's "Return from the USSR," the diary of a pilgrimage that had begun in thrall and ended in disenchantment. Here, instead of grumbling from some malcontent

Trotskyite, was the testimony of a *grand maître*, the voice of a Europe that spoke from somewhere before—and would endure well after—Hitler and Stalin. We had been lifted above and would be carried beyond the topical to the traditional; we had been introduced to the authentic Europe and had no further use for the carica-ture offered by the Comintern. Until then we had thought that to leave the party would be to go naked into a chill world; but now we knew that the true elect, the true elite, resided not here but out there. We had been shown the weapon of snobbery.

The term of *PR*'s rule did not last much beyond the next three years. These were bounded on one side by Gide's *envoi* to his illusions and on the other by the pub-lication of "Burnt Norton" and "East Coker," the first two of Eliot's *Four Quartets*. Then there was the war, and when it ended there was, at *PR* as in so many other quarters, the challenge of reconstruction. There had been casualties in this population as in so many others, and no one ought to have been better equipped to recog-nize their loss than Rahv, who had always felt a particu-lar, poignant identity with Chekhov in the letter where—as Rahv said—he "explains why plebeian writers must buy at the price of their youth what the writers of the gentry have been endowed with by nature."

The prewar *Partisan Review* had been especially en-riched by the commingling of writers like Rahv—whose origins we can without condescension call plebeian—with others like Dwight Macdonald, F. W. Dupee and George L. K. Morris, who, although they would have been em-barrassed to be called genteel, had all been undergradu-ates at universities that offered meager encouragement in those days to applicants from the public schools. The comradeship of Rahv with Macdonald, and of Green-berg with Morris had been as much a blessing for them as for the rest of us, since it was a juncture of two polarities of provinciality. Their true achievement may not have been so much to make their country less insular as to make one another less so.

Then the war divided them. Macdonald went off to establish *politics*, a freer-floating outlet for his anarcho-pacifist spirit. He took with him a great part of *PR*'s élan, and the deficit was never quite repaired. An ineffaceable cast of the dour would always remain after his departure. The note of peevishness that bespeaks the loss of community crept in, asserting a claim to a long-term lease.

The end of the war all too briefly lifted the spirits of *PR*'s editors with the prospect that Europe's old currents would rise again to sweep them out of the shallows. "What new writers or new movements in the arts and philosophy awaited our discovery?" Barrett asked himself then; and Rahv and Phillips seem to have enlisted him as an associate editor because he appeared so uniquely suited to provide them with the fulfillment of their hopes for a renewal of the inspiration they had drawn from prewar Europe. He was fresh from duty on an OSS team that had been assigned to locate Italian anti-Fascists of particular distinction and to bring them to safety behind the allied lines. "I had just come from Europe, I read the languages, and perhaps I could help out in this area."

Barrett applied himself earnestly and brought the good news of Existentialism. But Europe had little more than that to offer; and oddly enough *PR*, whose editors had expected so much from a renascent European culture, was almost the first magazine in America to announce the disappointment of those hopes in Arthur Koestler's letters from London and Nicola Chiaramonte's from Rome that reported only stagnation and rot everywhere around them. And given the actual condition of things, no man of sense needed long to decide that, if what was new in Europe was only Sartre, the new Europe wasn't much worth bothering about.

Europe itself may already have reached the same conclusion. The dankness of Barrett's memory is freshened only when he recalls the escape to the plastic arts that brought him close to the abstract expressionists. He makes Willem de Kooning seem not just livelier personally but more stimulating intellectually than any of his colleagues at *Partisan Review*. Thus:

Once the painter Marca-Relli came [to the Cedar Tavern] with an Italian visitor in tow. The Italian was from Venice, and had insisted on being taken to the bar for the express purpose of meeting de Kooning. After the introduction was made I pointed out the historical significance of the occasion to de Kooning: Venice had once been the center where the pilgrims from Northern Europe had come to learn about painting; now the scene had shifted, and a Venetian had come to New York to meet him. De Kooning blinked for a moment, trying to take in the full sweep of the idea, and then his face lit up with a grin: "Gee."

The great westward tide was running: "the significant innovations in culture henceforth might just as well come from America as from Europe."

Barrett's associates had, then, been looking the wrong way: toward a Europe so bored with its own desperate inanition that it was itself looking mainly to America. *PR*'s old resource had been exhausted for a while, and its editors were cut off from the new because they thought themselves isolated so far out on its rim that they often felt that, as "Delmore said, New York itself was not an American city—it was 'the last outpost of Europe' on those shores"—one of those utterances about as far from the true condition of affairs as we are apt to get once we start imagining that we are what we are not.

PR, then, had been left behind by a shift in fashion— the most acute of crises for a public organ, whether its editor be Henry Luce or Philip Rahv—and you might think that this clutch of circumstance would have brought its editors to some useful quarrel about what was to be done. Instead, only one dispute reached heights consequential enough to inspire Schwartz to refer to it thereafter as "the great confrontation." And this was it. His fellow editors had borne Rahv off to lunch and there assaulted him with three complaints. Their major grievance: "Rahv had talked too freely against the other three behind their backs, and particularly to the wrong people—publishers and editors who might thus be dissuaded from allotting certain favors, or heads of foundations who were in a position to dispose of certain grants."

Grants from the heirs of Henry Ford. Advances from the avatars of William Jovanovich. Are we to take seriously persons for whom such things are all that can arouse the heart's outcry? (That, of course, is the message of *Making It*, the earliest of the comic masterpieces that Norman Podhoretz issues every six months or so in the disguise of autobiography; but this is hardly the moment in the history of the American polity to propose that Podhoretz could ever have been right about anything.)

Well, yes, we are to take them seriously. They were all—or anyway had all been—much better than they sounded. They had simply gone astray and arrived at the despair that is usually the explanation, and almost the excuse, for all sorts of frivolities.

Barrett was still green, though, when Rahv felt that the time had come to face up to Soviet aggression. "'Those goddamn liberals,' he fumed, 'they'll end by giving away the whole of Western Europe to Stalin.'"

"'The magazine should have an editorial on the subject,' [Barrett] suggested one day." There was immediate agreement. But who could write it? Barrett thought of the apostate Macdonald, who would have been "ready at a moment like this—if his heart were in it—to bat out a sparkling polemic." ("Bat out" and "sparkling" are curious criteria for a call to the hot gates.) But Macdonald was not to be had; Rahv himself was unavailable because he was preoccupied with preparing his essays for publication; Phillips was still beating against his writer's block, and Schwartz was between divorces. There was nobody to hurl into the breach except Barrett, the rawest of them all.

He has printed the result as an appendix to *The Truants*. Allowing for its hyperbole, it can be read as a sound enough analysis of contemporary issues at least by those ready to imagine a *Nation* and a *New Republic* capable of giving away whole continents to anybody.

But what is more to the point is that here are four men certain of the weight of their collective voice in the very future of civilization, and one of them is too busy with a publisher's deadline, another is for the moment at a loss to think of anything to say about anything, and the third is off with a new love. All agree that here is a task of cosmic importance, yet three-quarters of them are too taken up with variations of domestic distraction to be available for duty. There is no explaining this sort of thing except as the frivolity of despair.

Perhaps Rahv had come to that recognition awhile before. Of all of them, he was best qualified to identify the station where the train had finally stopped, although I don't believe he ever did, explicitly. But one of his essays goes off on a byway that leads only to an unnecessary attempt to absolve *PR* for having published Leslie Fiedler's "Come Back to the Raft, Huck Honey," to the scandal of Twain scholars. Rahv says that he had at first regarded Fiedler's performance as a *jeu d'esprit*, only later to discover that its author took it seriously.

Now, it hardly appears plausible that an editor who cared much any longer would, first, entirely misread a contributor's intent and, second, publish as though it were a solemn pronouncement what he took to be a joke. The critic would never lose his reverence for literature, but the editor had gone most untypically far in the direction of contempt.

But then, on the ladder of functions, the critic has the higher rung: his only concern is to draw us to reflection, while the editor has to keep us talking about his product. That may be why most memoirs of magazines in decline run so morosely to occasions where spite had expelled most vestiges of humor. In that business, when people have stopped talking about you, there is nothing left to do except talk about them and one another with increasing rancor and diminishing wit.

After a while, Barrett's remembrance of life at *PR* becomes almost indistinguishable from other men's chronicles of the last days of the *Saturday Evening Post*. Yet PR was—or at least had been—a good deal more than that. And those of us who are rightly saddened by its withering away ought not to let Barrett's version linger too long in our minds, because if we did we might be glad *Partisan*

Review is gone. It will always be fashionable to point out that the heart we give away in youth is generally wasted on an illusion. Like so many fashions, this one happens to be more often wrong than right.

NOTES ON SELLING OUT

Dwight Macdonald

I'VE sold but not, with one large exception, out. That is, I've made my living by my typewriter, but I've written in my own style on subjects of my own choice. The exception was my seven years as a hack in the stables of *Fortune*. Excuses swarm: I was young, the articles weren't signed, it was Hard Times, I needed the money to support my mother and myself. By 1936 I'd learned all I could from Lucean journalism and had become profoundly bored with its dynamic simplifications. I was tempted, morally, to keep on selling out— $10,000 a year wasn't hay fifty years ago—but it had become neurologically impossible: I kept falling asleep in the very act of prostitution.

In Henry James's story "The Next Time," a brilliant novelist can't buy shoes for his children because each new work is greeted by critical acclaim and near-zero sales, while a romantic lady hack is distressed because her novels are always panned in the serious reviews and always sell enormously. Both attempt to change their spots: the man writes down, trying for a cheap, popular potboiler, and the lady writes up, trying for something that will impress the critics. Both fail: his potboiler is widely acclaimed and widely unsold, her serious effort is panned by the critics but sets a new sales record.

Or compare Edgar Allan Poe and Erle Stanley Gardner; the former invented the detective story in one of his many attempts to sell out (which always resulted in high art and low sales); the latter, the most prolific and best-selling exploiter of the genre Poe invented, couldn't sell out either—because he was, like Zane Grey, perfectly sincere and perfectly modest about his output. Both thought of themselves (correctly) as entrepreneurs, not as artists: they manufactured and sold to the public the merchandise it wanted and didn't worry about the art it didn't want.

In the old days a magazine called *Liberty* used to run every week a one-page one-thousand-word short story for which it paid one thousand dollars. My late friend Delmore Schwartz needed one thousand dollars very badly then, as always. He had written some highly praised stories—"In Dreams Begin Responsibilities" was one. So he tried, twice, to sell out and write a piece of junk that *Liberty* would crown with a thousand-dollar check; both times he failed. Moral: You have to be sincere to Sell Out; it's like making money—if your heart's not in it, the customer, or editor, sees through the imposture.

Finally, the writer Arthur Roth once gave me some Advice to the Young: "If you're going to sell out, do it early. You'll find the market goes down steadily with age."